MW01658230

Alice E. Tolle
and
Chenault Kelly
October 7, 1992

THE EMMALINE LETTERS

by

JAMES Y. KELLY

compiled and edited by
Emma Chenault Kelly
and
Alice Elizabeth Tolle

DORRANCE & COMPANY, INCORPORATED
828 LANCASTER AVENUE • BRYN MAWR, PENNSYLVANIA 19010
Publishers Since 1920

Copyright © 1981 by Emma Chenault Kelly and Alice Elizabeth Tolle
All Rights Reserved
ISBN 0-8059-2787-5
Library of Congress Catalog No. 81-65042
Printed in the United States of America

Dedicated
to
The Memory
of
Our Mother
Alice Chenault Kelly

Contents

Foreword

The Emmaline Letters were written by my father James Y. Kelly to his daughter during the twenty years she was not living at home. "Emmaline" was his special name for her. Dad wrote the first letter when she left for college in 1925 and kept on writing to her until she came back to stay in 1945. Once every week—sometimes oftener—the letters went out to her as my father sought to encourage her and create for her our lives at home.

They were not, however, usual run-of-the-mill "letters from home." Roosevelt and the Depression, isolationism and World War II, Lindbergh, the Government, farming, religion, and education—all these were subjects for his pen. The tales of family "doings" and small-town life, however, were continuing threads from which emerged characters, descriptive passages, and story.

About my father: James Yateman Kelly III was born and reared in Georgetown, Kentucky—one of seven children. After graduation from Georgetown College, he "read the law" under the guidance of his father, Judge James Y. Kelly II, in Georgetown. It was my father's plan that he would then enter politics as a Republican and not as a Democrat. I should interject here about my mother's Aunt Nannie—mentioned in *The Letters.* Aunt Nannie was wont to categorize a person according to his politics: one was either a "*staunch* Democrat" or a "*rank* Republican." It is therefore understandable that when Judge Kelly—a truly staunch Democrat—learned of the planned defection, he is said to have advised: "Son, if you are determined to become a Republican, you would be wise to go up North where the Republicans are."

That is the story. Whether true or not, the younger Kelly did go North, to Springfield, Illinois. The choice of Springfield as the place to settle had been in part determined by the fact that Grandma Kelly of Georgetown had herself been born near Springfield, where a few "kinfolk" still lived, and that she still owned land in Sangamon County. Son James Y could—and of course would—look after it for her. Once in Springfield, the young J.Y.—as he came in time to be called—studied for and passed the Illinois State Bar examinations, and in 1902, began his practice of law. A year later he married our mother, a Miss Alice Elizabeth Chenault of Mt. Sterling, Kentucky and brought his bride to Springfield where, in due time, my sister and I were born and where we always expected to live.

But twelve years later, Mr. Kelly was offered the position of legal assistant to the honorable Franklin K. Dunn, a judge on the Illinois Supreme Court Bench. It would mean J.Y.'s giving up private practice and moving from the prestigious state capital to Charleston, Illinois, where Judge Dunn lived and maintained his office. Our father and mother, after seeing the small town, were attracted to it. Built on hills and near a river, it reminded them of Kentucky and home. There was a quaintness about it, a friendliness too, and there was the Normal School with its Model School offering superior educational advantages. So, J.Y. accepted the offer and in the summer of 1915, and on a very hot day, moved us all to Charleston.

The college town did indeed prove to have educational advantages. The Normal School President, Livingston C. Lord, was an exceptional man and staffed his school with exceptional teachers for the Model School and the two-year college. By the time we were ready for high school, a four-year high school had been added and when it came time for college, the four-year degree in education was being offered, so that we did not have to leave home, even for a bachelor's degree.

In 1925, however, it was decided that my sister, Emma Chenault, after two years of college in Charleston, should enter the University of Kentucky at Lexington to earn a degree in Fine Arts. Emmaline, though away from home, would be looked after if need be by various aunts, uncles, grandparents, and cousins—all of whom lived in or close to Lexington. At the time this decision was arrived at by our parents, Emma C. and I had been spending our summer vacation in Mt. Sterling, Kentucky with our mother's relatives and in Georgetown with our father's. Word came by letter that Emma was to stay on down there and register at the State University: I was to come home and finish my education in Charleston at Eastern. And so, she did—and so, I did.

Thus it was that my father began writing to "Emmaline." He once referred to her "itchy foot," as well he should have, for in the following twenty years she was to travel to far places and try many different things. There were fourteen years teaching—first in Cicero, Illinois, and later in Madison, New Jersey. There was living in different quarters sometimes in private homes, for a while at the Three Arts Club in Chicago and at the International House in New York, eventually in apartments. There were art courses taken and a Master's Degree squeezed in at Columbia University: there were ventures for a time into the worlds of advertising, writing, and publishing; finally, there was service in the WAC's during World War II which took her to Fort Oglethorpe and Bainbridge in Georgia and to Tyndall in Florida. Somehow and at some time, during those peregrinations, she managed a trip to Europe with a friend, Alice Rost, and a cruise to Nassau with our parents.

But always and faithfully the letters went out to Emmaline. There would be intervals, when time would elapse without his writing at all—Easter, Christmas, or summers when she would be home.

The wonder is that my father wrote at all considering the tedium and amount of work demanded in his position. Every case appealed to the Supreme Court in Illinois for a decision would come to Judge Dunn's office for study. My father's duties consisted of writing an opinion for each case after studying the laws pertaining thereto in his law library. Long hours of research and thought might ensue before an opinion could be formulated, written out in his small, cramped penmanship on pages and pages of the lined yellow legal tablets, and then handed to the Judge's secretary for typing. No matter: there was still the letter to "Emmaline"—and perhaps enough time in the day left. . . .

My sister saved most of those letters—in shoe boxes—more than three hundred of them! For they were good, and she thought: *"Someday, somehow* I may publish these." Two years ago when I for the first time read them, I too recognized their special quality, and so for the past year we have worked together in the process of compiling, typing, and editing. Now, and at last—more than thirty-five years after their writing—we offer you *The Emmaline Letters*.

—Alice Elizabeth Tolle

Acknowledgment

For their unwavering support in the preparation of these letters for publication, Ramona and Richard Wise of Eastern Illinois University, Charleston, have the editors' deep appreciation.

1925

August 27, 1925

Dear Emmaline:

Your mother came in yesterday afternoon on time, hot and dusty but in good shape, and I was more than glad when I got a glimpse of her sport dress as the train slowed up and passed me.

The proposition that you attend Kentucky State College is the only one that has had much appeal for me. The more I investigated other schools the colder feet I got. I like the location and no doubt it has a good corps of instructors. Also, you are "in" better in central Kentucky than anywhere else. I wonder if your Aunt Helen,* the next time you are out there, would run up to Lexington with you, look the situation over, find out when school opens, and what your chance to get in. If you can get in you may register, if registration is open, and draw a check on me for such amount as may be necessary for the registration. You will probably have to pay the $50.00 but maybe not. Also learn what your musical instruction will cost you. I think you should push that now, especially if you get credit for your work in that line. But you will have to be the judge. Aunt Helen will advise you.

I think if you have the opportunity to become a member of a good sorority and live in its house you will do better than otherwise. They have housekeepers and chaperones I think, but at that you are old enough and well-trained enough to know your duty to yourself and do it without swerving.

As far as the expense is concerned we will meet it so far as we can as it arises out of our income and not consider borrowing yet. I enclose two checks—one to sign for registration fee and the other to get money to come home on. Your mother thinks, if school does not open till September 28, you had better come home with Alice E. and then go back in time for school. But I leave that somewhat to you. I do not think you should wear your welcome out and think your mother is right.

Lots of love,
Affectionately,
Dad

September 25, 1925

Dear Emmaline:

We have all enjoyed your letter of Wednesday very much. Your course seems well arranged and rather heavy. It also looks interesting and I suspect

*Helen Kelly Shropshire—sister of J.Y. Kelly.

you will enjoy it. You should get some pleasure out of botany. I skipped that in college with the approval of the teacher and have felt the effect ever since. You would be surprised to know how often in a lifetime one wishes to be able to recognize the different plant families. Useless information in a way, but nevertheless the personal satisfaction of knowing would have been well worthwhile. I do not know of Funkhouser, of course, except as you have told me of him. Am glad that you get the chance to study under him. Life is a study of people in many of its larger phases, and a study of outstanding characters like Mr. Lord, Judge Dunn, and some people you have known already is a real part of a liberal education.

Get a slicker if you need one, unless you want me to send you one of the raincoats that your mother bought several years ago. Be sure it is good enough to shed the rain. Buy yourself a powder puff at the ten-cent store. I am mailing you a parcel containing some beads, a ribbon and handkerchief.

Miss Case thinks it would be a mistake for you to appear too anxious to make a particular sorority and that you should distribute the favor of your acceptances among several, first, second, third, etc. choices, and I too think this wise, as otherwise, first choice might not choose to invite you and the others might refrain from inviting you as a useless gesture.

. . . You seem to be camping out almost. This situation will be relieved soon, I hope. In the meanwhile, the trunk would seem to be the best place for most of your clothes. I do not see how they would fail to suffer from hanging around promiscuously. How soon do they expect to have Boyd Hall ready for use? It's nice of your cousin Paul to be taking so much interest in you. You are worth it, of course, and equally of course it is entirely unnecessary to remind you to be appreciative, for you are always so for favors or courtesies.

Use your judgment as to visits to Georgetown—go when you can without interfering with your work or schedule. As the president said in his address, a copy of which you sent us, your success will be a great deal dependent upon your systematizing your work, laying out and following a schedule for your out-of-class studies, recreation, etc. and then following it consistently. System is very much lacking among our family and I would be pleased if you would develop a habit in this regard. An orderly habit of life will conserve your resources and energy not only in school but all through life, no matter where its lines may be laid.

You should be able to get a good deal from the preachers of Lexington. You know Transylvania University is there, a college for the Christian Church, and Lexington has always been the center of activities of our church. Perhaps for that reason the church is strong there, and preachers there in the two big churches are usually big men. I think the two preachers there now represent two lines of thought—the fundamentalist and progressive. I think, but am not sure, that the Broadway Church is fundamentalist and the other church (on Short Street, I believe) has as its preacher one of the biggest of the progressives. Your Cousin Paul can tell you or you yourself can attend the two churches alternately and get the two different viewpoints. This discussion, as you know, is a big issue in religion and religion is one of the biggest things in life as you will realize as you grow older.

You are no doubt considering that this letter contains enough of sage reflections and are wondering why I don't tell you something of the things at home. Well, I leave that for your mother and Alice E. They seem to want to write all the time and that leaves nothing for me to say. I will, however, tell you a few things in outline following the plan perhaps of Wells' *Outline of History.*

Billy Hite broke an arm. Mother and I ate supper away from home last night. The night before were at a bridge party. Alice Elizabeth had a caller last night. The weather has been cool. I had pancakes for breakfast and ate alone on the back porch where the thermometer registered 50 degrees.

Lots of love,
Affectionately,
Dad

October 3, 1925

Dear Emmaline:

Your special got in this morning before I came to the office and I wired you our congratulations when I came down. Your letter was a good piece of literary work for it put the situation vividly before us and showed us exactly the difficulties that surrounded you. At the outset we want you to know that we approve without reservation your course. Furthermore, you showed that in your character, which we felt sure you had, that will bring you through all the difficulties of life—the grit to stand up to your judgment under the most trying conditions. That's one thing, by the way, that I have lacked somewhat and most of my troubles have been caused by my lack of that very desirable thing you have showed that you have. Money cannot buy it and it is very valuable.

I, of course, know nothing about sororities except what I have learned in the last few weeks. But it is clear some have only a local advantage. Others have a general value available through life. The personnel of the local and the national, etc., also enter into the matter. To us at home it seems that if you cannot get in the best, you would be better advantaged to remain outside. Your character, training, education all entitle you to the best. Moreover, it is not sure that you will not be in the best before Christmas. As Miss Case told you, the first chance does not close the matter. But you know all these things better than I.

. . . Keep a stiff upper lip, Old Kid. Violin, scholarship, wit, charm will work wonders in the sorority world as elsewhere. I have been so much interrupted in writing this letter that it is more or less sketchy and disconnected but it will do, I reckon. At any rate I want to mail it now.

Lots of love,
Affectionately,
Dad

October 9, 1925

We had your mighty fine letter of the 6th, I believe it was and have all got a big kick out of it—"all" meaning we three, Miss Case, Mrs. Miller, Mr. Hardin, and Aunt Lillian* who came in yesterday. You have got your bearings fine, and the course you have outlined for yourself will bring you everything you want which is worthwhile. You remind me somewhat of the rabbit that I shot on the place near Springfield where we lived a couple of years. The snow was on the ground and I wanted to hunt. As I had no shotgun I took the pistol and out in the garden Mr. Rabbit was sleeping all huddled down in the snow. Now you know it is mere chance if I hit the mark with a pistol. So I got as close as I dared and aimed at Mr. Rabbit's head. I pulled the trigger, the gun roared and Mr. Rabbit straightened out and gave a few feeble kicks and seemed to be thoroughly and conclusively a dead rabbit. I picked him up by the hind legs and gave a long swing and quick jerk to snap his head off but my fingers were cold and slipped, and Mr. Rabbit hit the ground but lit on his feet and lit a runnin'. And so you, dazed by the new surroundings and the smother of rush, were jerked into consciousness by the snap of bid day, lit on your feet and lit a runnin'.

I am curious to know your estimate of the relative value of instruction there compared with Eastern's. You know, as a rule Southern education, taken as a whole, is not, here at least, considered of equal value as Northern education. I have always thought that the impression is false in some respect—that it arose out of the fact that educational facilities for the Negroes are not very good, there is considerable illiteracy among them. As a matter of fact, the higher educational institutions of the South compare very well with like institutions elsewhere. . . .

No one was up when I left home this morning. We are running the furnace as it is pretty raw. I fear a frost will come soon and ruin our flowers. We have had flowers for all purposes since March 28 and I would like the

*Lillian Kelly Bohon, J.Y. Kelly's sister.

dahlias to get a chance to bloom for a week or two. Their time is just starting, but we will hardly get through this spell without a frost when the sky clears up.

With a great deal of love from all of us.

Lots of love,
Affectionately,
Dad

October 12, 1925

I am sending you a cake of soap and two paperweights. The soap your mother bought somewhere. What its peculiar purpose or use is I do not know, but the directions accompany it and you may inform yourself from the directions. I suppose it cures anything from a headache to sore eyes. The paperweights are my own idea. One is for you and one for your roommate—but not to throw at one another. Nothing more substantial than pillows or the barbed word should be thrown. The barbed word is a bit dangerous also, for it has somewhat the tendency to return tipped with venom. So you had better confine yourself to feather pillows in choosing weapons.

I will tell you where we got the paperweights. Do you remember a trip which we took in the red car of a man named Harryman? I think you will at least remember the man. And I think Aunt Nannie and Mother Chenault were along. It was a pretty drive through a section of the country for which Mr. Harryman and his daughter had some sort of fanciful name which I have forgotten. It touched the river at two points—the first at a wooded place along the hill at the bottom of which the road ran; the second where was the swinging bridge. Well yesterday after church the clan assembled at our house—the Millers with their picnic baskets and car, and we with our picnic basket, Mr. Hardin and his Marmon car. The baskets had in them coffee, homemade buns, pickles, mustard, celery, hamburger meat, onions, and pumpkin pie. It was almost spitting rain so we decided to go to the Country Club to cook our dinner, but as we came out the door it was no longer spitting rain and the clouds seemed high and not threatening. So Mrs. Miller, Aunt Lillian, Miss Case, and Mother got in the Marmon and Mr. Miller, Byron, Alice E., Miss Voight, and I got in the Miller Ford and were told to lead the way. We went straight out 6th as far as we could go on that street, turned east on Lincoln street, down by Wrightsville, up the hills and down the hills and across the bridge and down to the first place where the road touched the river. There we disembarked and after some discussion as to the place to build the fire, finally built it among the trees—for the wind was tolerably raw and the sand at the river's edge was too exposed. Mother cooked the coffee and Mrs. Miller the hamburgers. We all cried over the smoke, and Mother and Mrs. Miller got a fine color from hanging over the fire and then, when all things were ready, we ate and ate until there was nothing more to eat. Then someone looked around and saw the pies. Mother tried to divide them equally. Mr. Miller, Byron, and I being around, each picked the biggest piece for himself and soon there were no more pies.

We went to the river's edge and skipped flat rocks across for quite awhile and wandered around. Then, in the cars again, we started on to the swinging bridge. The floor was all out of the bridge but several men were coming across it very slowly and carefully—the last carrying a little yellow dog in his arms. It was interesting to watch the dog—how his eyes sparkled as he sat up and watched everything and how careful he was not to move as the man picked his way over the river and the bridge swayed beneath—oh so far above the water. Then we went on and, just at the place where we stopped on our other trip and got out and the river was so pretty, there was a parked car and other cars were coming up—four in all—all new and glittering, and in them were beautiful Indians—or maybe they were a wandering tribe of gypsies—all girls they were—but when we came up to them we could penetrate the disguises and found that they were all Charleston girls. I think the Kiwanis Club in their costume and warpaint. We did not stop and I suppose they were out at the river for dinner perhaps.

The Ford was leading as we went along and after awhile the Marmon honked us to a halt and we received orders from the authorities to lead on to the Lincoln tomb where we wandered around awhile through the old cemetery there and then back to town. As it was not yet 5 o'clock, Mrs. Miller and Mother held a council of war and we were then ordered to Mattoon where we all met in the confectioner's shop and had something to drink; then back home and to bed about 7:30. It was quite a pleasant trip.

Mr. Hardin is planning to take us to Champaign sometime this week to dinner there in honor of Aunt Lillian and the Millers and the Craigs—the Millers being in part the hosts—and after dinner the picture show and home by midnight perhaps. There are also a couple of dances at the Country Club on in the next week and a card party at Mrs. Tate's. All through this time the special meetings at the Christian Church will be going on and we do not much relish the idea of being recorded by the paper as attending dances and card parties while the meetings are being held, but I do not know any solution—do you?

I note you are playing cards for a dinner or something. I sometimes am matched up at golf for a dinner, but never voluntarily match myself up. Of course there are times when good sportsmanship requires a matching for some such stake as a dinner, and I never shirk. But it is extremely essential as I look at life not to let it develop into gambling. I can't gamble even if I wanted to, for I cannot afford to lose any money—nor do I think it right. You, of course, if gambling is ever presented to you, will decline. You will be more highly considered by declining. It was once offered in our own home—Red Dog—when the chow mein crowd first met there. We declined and were thanked by the Taylors and others then members for doing so and breaking up the gambling. As you know the chow mein bunch still meets and has mighty fine meetings but there is never any suggestion of gambling.

Well I must close as it's time to go to work this Monday morning. The paperweights I picked up from the river's edge where we had dinner.

October 26, 1925

Mother had your card today and of course we were glad to know you were well when it was written, which I presume was Saturday. We had the preacher, his wife, and his mother-in-law for dinner yesterday. The pièce-de-résistance was a leg of lamb. It was surely fine—also the best rolls Mother ever made—browned potatoes, etc. winding up with pumpkin pie. I'll bet it was better dinner than you had at Boyd Hall. At any rate, all seemed to enjoy it and the preacher and singer ate rolls one after another, a roll at a time but for a long, long time. They sure did love the rolls. After dinner we had some music—your violin was much missed. Then when the preachers left we called on three homes, finally winding up at the Millers in time for Sunday night sandwiches.

The meetings at the Church are drawing big crowds and a good many accessions to the Church—several coming every meeting. Mr. Hayes is in fact working up a great deal of enthusiasm, sticking close to the New Testament, giving full credit to miracles, etc. and demonstrating that in truth the people are more moved by the story of the Testament than by all the learning of the scientists. It causes me to wonder whether the few or the many are right. When I see the big majority on one side and myself on the other I wonder whether my brain is so good and great as I would wish to consider it.

Your mother is recovering from her excess of work and social endeavor and is today making a new dress for Alice Elizabeth—blue wool with a gold collar. It will be very fine and she was in great need of it. Mother also needs a dress but whether she will make one or not I don't know.

Aunt Virginia* will get here tomorrow for a four-day's visit. During that time will be a masque ball at the Country Club, perhaps a chow mein supper

*Virginia Chenault Corbin of Indianapolis, sister-in-law.

and a trip to the Lincoln Theatre. What else is in the offing I have not yet been informed. However, I will be charmed when life quiets down and I will be able to recover some of my lost sleep, and restore my shattered nerves to the extent of permitting me to do my work satisfactorily to myself; and that, I am not able to do now.

I suppose there will soon be coming in your score card for the first term. As usual I suppose too that you have flunked, and as usual I reckon you will get a good grade. However, I will be interested to see the reports as soon as you can conveniently submit them to us.

Alice E. is still going to glee club practice twice a week. She brings home with her a youngster whose name is Cannon. She has had what is termed a weekend engagement with this big gun; that is, he took her to the picture show, I believe, Saturday night and to church last night. Young Robinson—I think that's the name, at any rate the man who sings, a teacher at the high school—called one evening last week, and so it goes. I suppose she too will fail in her school work, and I suppose too her grade cards will give the lie to my forebodings.

We are anxiously awaiting your next book of your life and acts as a junior at Kentucky University, or maybe I should have said the next chapter of the book of your life there. It is a continued story which maintains the interest of your readers exceedingly well and as in the case of all good continued stories, we can hardly wait for the next installment.

There isn't much news here. I heard your mother say you will be home for Christmas. I wonder how she knows. I was in doubt, thinking that you would perhaps spend Christmas holidays circulating around through central Kentucky. You seem to have no trouble getting to Georgetown or Mt. Sterling or anywhere you want to go.

I have no picture of me which your mother will consent to send you to hang up on your wall in the most prominent position. I have one which *I* think is all right. It was taken in Bloomington some years ago and the curl stands up beautifully from the center of the desert area which is sometimes denominated "a bald spot"—the place where the hair has quit growing—and your mother says it won't do. What do *you* say? I think'st will do as well as another. Well, it's time to go home and I must close.

November 3, 1925

We had the typewritten effusion from Harrodsburg enclosed with the Sunday evening production in yellow and black, and the song set to music. Alice E. says that you have too many fractional notes to the note, or something of that kind. I don't know just what the trouble is but guess she will work it out. You know sometime in the dim and distant past you wrote that you were trying out for the orchestra and asked our prayers. Well what happened? You worked us all up to a high pitch of expectancy and then casually went off and left us. After it was over and you perhaps made it, did the matter then seem of very little importance? It furnishes us a chance to philosophize, does it not? Isn't it so, that a human being after reaching a goal that he has set must put the goal behind him and go on higher—else he becomes a failure? Even the best golfer must expect to do better sometime—otherwise the game would become stale. But enough of philosophy.

The Church meetings are still in progress. The preacher, Mr. Hayes, draws big crowds and many are joining. It is remarkable, as Alice E. says. She doesn't quite understand how it is done and why it can be done. No more do I, and yet I know enough about life and people to understand in part. Mother has been working in the yard, raking, putting out bulbs, etc. Alice E. is also busy with school, music, Cannon and Robinson. . . .

November 10, 1925

We have heard from you right along and have enjoyed your letters very much. In fact I suppose we are more homesick to see you than you are to see us. You mustn't allow any homesickness—nostalgia, I think is the word—to bother you in your work. We are getting along all right and it will not be very long till December 23. You will be astonished how quickly the last two weeks or so will pass. I do not believe you mentioned whether the 23rd is the last day of school or the first of the vacation. We of course hope it's the first of the vacation, for if so, you would get home at 5:30 that afternoon.

You mention frequently the difficulty you have in spending money carefully and spending time in study lavishly. If you have told me in your letters of each check that you have drawn, I am of the impression that you are doing very well indeed in the conservation of money. It was not to be expected that you could get along without spending a little money foolishly, and if I know of all the checks, you haven't spent much foolishly. I would not want you to seem to be too much of a cheapskate or too miserly, yet I do not want you to try to buy any popularity by spending. The latter course is more foolish than the first, for a popularity depending upon spending is gone with the end of the spending.

You will of course have to so order your time as to permit the necessary amount of study. Really, as you know, if the scholarship in school life fails, all else also goes by the board. I do not doubt that you understand that very well, nor do I doubt that somehow or other you will find the time to do your work and do it well. As a matter of fact, if you could bring yourself to the task of working for a scholarship or for one or two of the honorary societies, you will discover that that alone will make the whole school life decidedly more worthwhile in every way—socially and otherwise.

By the way, if "stayed" is one of the parts of "stay"—and it is—I see that you cannot get it through your pen that "payed" is not one of the parts of "pay"—and it is not. "Staid" means steady or sober in character; therefore, the past of stay must be "stayed."

There isn't any news. The game season opened this morning and hundreds of nimrods are out to kill the beautiful birds. The sound of guns has already been heard here in the office. The meetings at the Church have closed with more than 100 added to the Church roll. Homecoming was a success though the rain fell in sheets all day. The football game was played (not plaid) in mud and water. When a man fell, water and mud splashed 20 feet or more. I saw the last half of the game. E. I. lost 13 to nothing. I think Kentucky lost to Alabama, did she not, by a horrible score.

I am working now steadily and will be all through the winter. That's one of the pleasures and necessities of life. Work is really the salvation of the soul. Your mother has your red dress about ready. She went to Mattoon yesterday to get the buttons.

November 12, 1925

I notice that no letters to you have passed through my hands in the last few days, and, therefore, I will write a short note to inform you of the state of the weather and the condition of your family. I have no words at my command to adequately describe the weather this morning—will merely say that the rain began to fall steadily sometime during the night, and it is still falling steadily. I am writing this as I sit at my desk by the window, but am writing by artificial light and it's considerably after 8 o'clock in the morning. The wind is in the east also and is good for neither man nor beast.

I wrote you that your new dress was about completed. It remains in *status quo*, as your mother has been a bit sick and unable to give it, or the housekeeping for that matter, any of her time. She remained in bed yesterday. I think she will get up this morning, though I took her breakfast to her before I left home. Nothing is seriously wrong with her and I think she will be herself again very soon, and much profited by the enforced rest. . . .

We enjoyed your last letter very much. I thought you would get a kick out of the church there in Lexington and that's one of the experiences I wanted you to have. You see why now. I see no reason why you should not make the suggestion, at least, that your violin be used by you in church. It may be that the musical director wants something of that kind. You cannot know his ideas until you have tried it out. Cousin Paul might make the suggestion, or, for that matter you could very well do it yourself. I know you can add to the beauty of the services. Furthermore, I would like you to do it. Try it out . . . .

November 19, 1925

I haven't noticed any letters leaving here in the last day or two and the thought just struck me that perhaps you would be interested to know that Mother is improving in good shape. She is not now confined to her bed all day but spends her time in her room yet, working on a hook rug, reading, etc. I think by the end of the week she will be around the house—up and down stairs. Alice E. is well, though the extra work of cooking and dish-washing keeps her stepping to get her other work out of the way as well. Her practicing has suffered some.

By the way, we have not heard from you for more than a week, but if there had been any news we would have got it by now, so we are not particularly worried, though we do enjoy your letters and of course are inclined to be disappoined a bit when too long a time comes in between. We are today having one of the very beautiful days that this fall has presented. It is not cold but bright and cheerful—the kind of day that makes indoor work seem rather a bore and tempts one so engaged to envy him who is not confined by four walls and a roof. The ground however is wet, and if one should spend the day out in the open he would have to protect his feet well or pay for his pleasure by contracting a cold probably. The last two mornings the weather has been such that I could get out long before daybreak and work in the yard. If I can get three more such mornings I will have the yard all set and ready for winter.

This morning I heard the strains of Edward's* violin as I worked and of course thought of you and became rather homesick to see you and hear you making chords and dischords on your instrument, but I suppose you are grinding down the walls of the basement of Pat Hall every day, smoothing them off with the tones which you produce, in a way sandpapering them with music, and so when you do come back I—even I—will be able to note your progress. There isn't any news. Mother is missing a good many parties. The Parkers are having a dance tomorrow night and Mother flatters herself that she will go. Knowing her as you and I do, don't you think it an even break that she will go? I do. Let us hear from you when you can.

*Edward Thomas—son of the Thomases who lived next door.

November 27, 1925

I think it was Monday that I ordered a duck for Thanksgiving Day dinner. On Tuesday, Charley Miller, the Preacher, the dog and I went "a-hunting," and after a long and busy day devoted to that sport, I returned with 5 quails and a rabbit. (I shot the rabbit "sitting" while the dog was not looking and got him in my bag. The dog never learned that I had been so unsportsmanlike as to bother with a rabbit.) So on Wednesday I told Pinnell to sell his old (or young) duck to someone else, which he did.

Alice E. cooked the 5 birds for Wednesday night and we each ate one. Then Alice E. ate part of another one. She left orders not to be called, but she heard me messing around the kitchen and after I got down in the yard working, she came down and ate all the quail that was left. Then she came out on the porch and directed me to put the rabbit out in the cold as it wouldn't be cooked till Friday. She didn't want to eat meat too many times in one day. She had the very same expression on her face that a cat has that has just eaten a mouse. So for dinner we had turnips, beans and apple pie. Think of it will you—that for a Thanksgiving dinner! However, at supper time we all went over to the Millers' and had chow mein there and it sure was fine. Mother was along, so you see that she is improving. She was tired when she got home but the visit did her no harm. It was the first time she had been out of the house since she got sick. I served her breakfast to her in bed this morning, oatmeal, cakes, coffee, and she enjoyed it, or at least said so.

Well, it's only about four weeks before you get home. That's not long, is it? We will be very glad. I charged $70 to my bank account for your board which you said you would pay soon. So that's taken care of. I believe there were a few checks you didn't write about (small amounts). At least I didn't get them on my book. You really ought to let me know about every check. Otherwise I will never have my record straight or know where "I am at" with the bank. My bank account is not so plethoric that I can permit myself to be unfamiliar with its condition—I really have to know whether it is reasonably husky or getting low. It has to be fed from time to time and I should know when it needs feeding.

So you are going into politics. That's a bad game in a way. Yet I can see nothing wrong with your plan. In Kentucky the authorities are all Democrats, as everywhere south of Mason and Dixon line. Your cousin Henry is a Democrat. If a pull is needed, I think he has one. A pull is probably needed. He probably would not care to know my politics. At any rate it is not wise or essential that he know. You are you and I am I. If anyone exerts a pull to get the place for you, *you will owe him nothing* except courtesy and respect. I do not know what treatment state employees are accorded in Kentucky but suppose that there, as is usual everywhere, upright conduct and merit make the social standing. In every new place, standing must be earned. If anything else is expected, then the place is not worth having and you could resign and come home. So, as I said, I can see nothing wrong with your idea, except that our own personal pleasure would be better served by having you at home for the two months.

I have not heard from the University as to your grades and am about to conclude that you may be getting by, surprising as that might be considered by one who had no knowledge of your capabilities. There isn't much news here. Alice E. spent the night at the Millers' after the chow mein supper and I haven't seen her this morning. Byron was in Springfield for the night with his grandparents. They drive home today. Charleston lost their game to Millikin yesterday, 21 to 3. A good many went from here. Alice E. wanted to go but we finally concluded she should stay here and get some rest as she had been "boning" for ten days for her examinations and also doing most of the cooking and all the dishwashing.

December 3, 1925

I am instructed to mail the enclosed letter written by Alice E. very hurriedly and at the suggestion of her mother this noon. You needn't answer it by next mail as she suggests. The first chance I get will see what prospect there is along the lines you suggest. I imagine not much.

I have read both your letters—the one to Mother, the other to me, and am tempted to make a suggestion or two that may give you an idea as to how to meet the young teacher you spoke of whose name I do not now remember. We will start with the adage that any fool can ask a question that a wise man can't answer.

To his question whether you would care to change your parents, the answer is obvious. Of course no one is perfect. The question whether you would prefer to have been a child of some prominent man is rather unfair. It is a condition that cannot be brought about. But unfair as it is, the orderly progress of evolution demands that the child excel the parent. A child of Lincoln, for instance, would be unable to do so. His position is impossible for more is expected of him than he can attain.

The question, "What is a kiss fifty years later?" I don't quite see what he is driving at. Being a young man, of course, he is more enamored by his knowledge than an older man would be. An older man knows that he does not know it all—that he has been and may again be mistaken. Your character sketch of him suggests to me that he belongs to the very ancient school of Epicureans, rather than the school to which our wider experience and broader knowledge should demand that we conform in our thinking. The old—original—Greek, Epicurus, taught the philosophy that pleasure is the *summum bonum*, the highest good, but was wise enough to also teach that honor and uprightness of character were essential to the production of the highest pleasure. His teachings were afterwards modified in popular thought to mean that the best way to govern one's life was to pursue pleasure regardless of character and the virtues, etc. The modern philosophy is tending to become again Epicurean not in its original but in its perverted sense.

On the other hand the Christian philosophy—one of service and of growth or evolution of character of individuals and masses. Your studies in evolution inform you of the laws of growth. You have already seen illustrated in yourself the growth of character, the growth of mind and body but not alone the growth of mind and body. They are important, very, but would you say that they are as important as the growth of ideas, the growth of character? It is important; for, as you learn from evolution, one has the ability to transmit something of his character to his children—as intimated in the Bible—for seven generations. It may be longer. There are already in America records of families that have produced literally scores of criminals and abnormal-minded. Your professor would probably admit he would enjoy more being the ancestor of a high-minded normal boy than of a feeble-minded or one with a criminal instinct. . . .

You have been sufficiently trained so that you can think out both philosophies for yourself. You are able to eat all meats of information. I wonder if your teacher realizes that perhaps many in his class may receive from him the ideas that will ruin their ultimate happiness here—that many have not the strength to digest the diet that he is providing. The young idea should be taught how to shoot, but woe to that man who teaches it to shoot wrong. A little learning is dangerous to the unqualified mind—the unbalanced mind. But enough of this. You will be able to meet him on his own ground as soon as you get your thoughts coordinated.

1926

January 19, 1926

I have noticed that letters have gone from home to you pretty regularly and so there was nothing for me to write about and my letters have been "non sent." There is, however, no letter to mail this morning and as I want to thank you for the maple sugar, now is a very good time to tell you I appreciate it very much and am enjoying it thoroughly, not offering it to family or visitors. If any of the family wants a taste, she must ask for it and I shall not talk about it to outsiders until it is all gone. So you see it is lasting very well. It is good and tastes and looks like the real thing, and I eat it on the theory that it is unadulterated maple sugar. That idea makes it all the better.

There isn't any news that I can tell that has not been told. Alice E. and Wendell went to choir or glee club practice last night and got back from the picture show at 11 o'clock. She had much work she just had to do last night but passed it up for the picture show. One thing we all lack something of is the determination to follow up our good intentions by carrying them through. Too easily we turn aside for the flowers along the roadside. Turning aside is very well at times but not as a habit.

There has been a better thinking-out of the plans for next summer than when you were here. First, though, I will tell you that Alice E. heard from Springfield. It is a rule of the office that grading papers shall not be entrusted to one who has had no teaching experience, and that eliminates both of you. They offered clerical work for a week or ten days in July, but of course that did not fit in the picture. The ambition that your Mother and I have for the next two years is that you finish at Lexington next year and Alice E. finish here. The year after that we hope that it will be possible for Alice E. to attend a conservatory of music in the East, perhaps at Boston. If an unexpected stroke of luck should happen, it would result in your both having that privilege. We feel sure that we can manage the next year in Lexington (barring changes which cannot be foreseen). We are not so sure of the following year at the conservatory, but that is what we will work to get.

If Alice E. does go to the conservatory, its value to her from a musical stand point will come from the thoroughness of her groundwork. She has never had a chance to put in three or four hours day after day that are essential if she is to actually get the foundation that she will need at the conservatory. We want her to, and she wants also, to take next summer for this work here at home, actually doing musical work of an exacting type several hours a day under Mrs. Thomas. If she does get to a conservatory this is essential—will be invaluable. Therefore unless some change comes or some places are offered to you and her that are simply too good to let slip by, she will work on her music here at home. As for yourself, we will want you at home, and we rather think you will wish to be at home between the school years. By June you will find that it may be harder than you anticipate to put in the summer somewhere else. Of course if the boat rocks between now and then you may have to get a place to work to help out on your final year in Lexington, but we hope not, and we think the four of us here could perhaps have the first summer of our lives together—and at the ages of you and Alice E. it may be the last full summer together—golfing, music, cooking and dishwashing and what not, all that go to make up home life at 820 South 6th in the Chenault-Kelly family in Charleston. So don't worry too much about unemployment next summer. It may be necessary and if so we will do what is necessary, but if it is not necessary we will snatch at the joys of life as we pass by—at the flowers along the road of life.

Your exams will come out all right, if you set yourself to prepare for them. You have the ability; all you need is to use it. That sometimes is a difficult thing to do with the many distractions, but the ultimate aim of college life is to acquire what is known as an education—theoretically, an education. And the theoretical education is almost essential to future advancement—a theoretical education that is beyond the average—and that means a degree. The successful negotiation of exams is a prerequisite to a degree and therefore you will pass them.

I have had a number of interruptions in writing this letter and the time has so passed that I will have to bring it to a close. Your mother is doing just fine and is picking up flesh—not flabby but hard, and by summer she will be able to beat you at golf any day—rain or shine. With a great deal of love. We are pulling for you in your exams.

January 21, 1926

I see no letter addressed to you this morning, so will write a line or two to let you know we are all well and your mother continues to make a very apparent improvement. Mr. Miller leaves for Florida tomorrow, and today they and we eat the noon meal with Mr. and Mrs. Mike Miller, and a chow mein supper with the E. H. Taylors. That's quite a bit for your mother to take on in one day, but I guess she will get by without hurt. Last night Carbondale's team was here to give the Teacher's College a drubbing but couldn't do so. It was close, till the end of the first half, but after that the Carbondale team was eating out of our hand. At the close, but one—Foreman—of our team was playing; the four others were subs. Alice E. could not spare the time to go but I found I couldn't miss it. You remember last year's game with Carbondale was a tight game. Eastern Ilinois has been whipped once this year—by an Indiana team. It was a good game and I believe the Indiana team was the better though the game was in doubt most of the time. It was the most exciting game I have seen and at one time the gym roof was lifted—feet almost—when Charleston put in one of her subs and he rang up four baskets in quick succession and tied the score.

Mother has had Miss McMorris fix or change a couple of dresses and I will mail them to you, probably tomorrow. She and Alice E. are very much pleased with the result and if they are pleased, so am I. We are thinking about your exams, and pulling for a pass with a good grade. Of course the whole program depends on success in studies and of course we want success there, as do you. We haven't much doubt about it where you are concerned. Nevertheless, will be glad when the returns are in. I have to leave the telling of news to Mother and Alice E. as I find I do not keep very well posted, but I rather imagine they keep you well informed.

January 25, 1926

No letter seems to have originated at home for mailing to you this morning and so I will write a line or two to let you know that we are "waggin" along in a very good shape so far as I know. I qualify that statement because Alice E. went to Mattoon to visit on the 2 o'clock interurban Saturday afternoon and got back, via auto, between 10 and 11 last night after we had gone to bed. She was not up when I left home this morning and so I say, as far as I know. Your mother was also still sleeping when I left. It was past 8 o'clock and I had not heard Irene* stirring and perhaps she was due to be late at school this morning. She also was away from home Saturday evening until about 10 o'clock last night and so your mother and I had the house to ourselves all day yesterday, except that Mrs. Miller called just as we were eating a very light evening meal and ate with us and stayed till about 9 o'clock.

Today your exams start. We are not a great deal concerned about your passing since your letter to me. Also, like the course that you have outlined for the next term. It seems to be pretty heavy, but if a good start is made, the success of the entire term is almost assured. If one gets behind at the start, the entire road remains rough and difficult as a usual thing. While the exams are on we will not expect much news from you, but in your days of leisure you may write us a book unless you are traveling around among the folks too much.

Alice E. has a new black suit of which she is exceedingly proud. She wore it to Mattoon and sure looked stunning. I think its base was a suit which Aunt Lillian left or sent to her. At any rate it's a peach. I hardly think you

*Irene Fields—highschool teacher and temporary roomer.

will be able to cop it for the festivities of the new term as she was tolerably short of clothes.

Helen Etnire and Halleen Crowder were in an auto wreck at Harrison and 6th Saturday afternoon in which their Ford Coupe (Crowder car) was turned over a time or two, and they were badly jarred, Helen Etnire being made unconscious for a time, but they came out without serious injury.

I don't know of any other news I believe. We are having the usual run of January weather—for the most part, disagreeable. Am glad you are dropping Knight. That was the logical thing to do. As he grows older, if he is worthwhile, he will get a saner view of life, and it was not necessary or advisable that you be embarrassed by another term under him. Remember me to Bebe. With a great deal of love and hoping you knock 'em cold at the exams,

Affectionately, Dad

P.S. Did you get the two dresses?

February 6, 1926

The days are getting materially longer and spring grows closer and closer. It hasn't been very cold here lately and this morning the sun is shining brightly and there is a south wind that has more than a suggestion of spring in it. Nevertheless, the weather has not been very good for the general health, because it has been fickle and damp and raw, just such weather as leads to colds and flu. By the way, it has been some days since we heard from you and of course are wondering if you have been well. Suppose, though, that the activities of the new term have consumed your time. The mail has not come in this (Saturday) morning yet and there may be word from you coming today. The last news of your doings came from Mother Chenault, which told something of your visit in Mt. Sterling.

We are well. Alice E. has invited Miss Hurst of Mattoon to be her weekend guest beginning this afternoon but does not yet know whether or not she will be here. Your mother and I went to a church play last night, "The Clod-hopper" it was. This was the second performance, the first having been given a week earlier. It was given at the Chamber of Commerce Hall which was packed on both occasions beyond the point of safety, more than 600 being crowded in each time. Really, it was a first-class performance. Mrs. Hayes took the part of the clod-hopper and was excellent in the part—the star of the show. In fact, all carried their parts well and the general opinion is that it was way beyond the usual amateur performance. The orchestra was a brass band affair of women in bright costumes. All instruments were capable of producing but one sound, the mouthpiece being replaced by a small instrument which produced something of a humming sound. Mrs. Trimble, whom you may remember as being very fat and rather short, had the snare drum and stood out in front of the rest. She did very well with the drum and was a good sport and so got most of the applause that was given the band.

There isn't any particular news that I know of. Alice E. has taken a date a time or two with a young man other than Cannon. He called last night but I have forgotten his name. Don't think Cannon likes it very well. I have received no notice of any failure on your exams, and so am about to conclude that you made the grade in everything, including Knight's darkest English.

Remember me to Bebe.

February 17, 1926

We are very much pleased that you are a Tri Delt pledge and share with you in your happiness over it. No doubt the unsettled period was very trying and your nerves are horribly shattered, but that will wear itself out.

I am doubting whether it is quite honest to even try to leave Boyd Hall at present. The rule you spoke of is founded on reason. Boyd, as I understand it has niggardly support from the state and its charges are the lowest amount possible to get by on. Its arrangements for income must be made from semester to semester; without your $140 it will be just that much short of what might properly have been counted on. So the rule is almost a necessary one and I do not see how they can afford to violate it. This from the point of view of the hall management.

Then from your own point of view. It is undoubtedly better for yourself to have the wider field for development that you have at the Hall. At the frat house it is unquestionable that your "circle" will be more limited. It will probably be more difficult for you to prepare your studies there, at least for the period of your novitiate, so you see my judgment is decidedly against leaving the Hall at present. Another thing you must consider with relation to any changes is the expense, and this I know nothing about . . .

You have not told us how your exams came out. There were four still unaccounted for—four grades—when last you thought about or were interested in them. We are anxious, at least I am anxious, to know the result. Your letters contain a misspelled word now and then. One that frequently occurs is "payed," incorrect for "paid" which is correct. The word correctly spelled is painful enough. Spelled incorrectly, it is maddening.

Religious discussions are very seldom of any value whatever. Each one engaged is usually "set." If a discussion "unsets" one, he is left up in the air, so to speak, having exchanged that which satisfied him for nothing. My position is that one of the necessary characteristics of God is truth. Therefore, God cannot fear truth. When truth is *fully* known, it will be found not to destroy God but to confirm belief in Him.

So far man does not *fully* know the truth. It is impossible for my mind to conceive that the universe came into being without an order or direction from a Creator. The latest searches of man tend to indicate that all creation is the product of natural laws, the working of a force applied by unchangeable laws. Laws are orders. Who gave these orders that are called natural laws? Who directed that force should so operate as to assume the form of matter out of dust of which life should spring—all according to law? I cannot conceive that it just "growed" so, like Topsy. Can you?

All this is, I will concede, unsettling so far as many previously accepted ideas are concerned. Of course one of the most interesting questions to all men is "What or Who is God?" No one has answered satisfactorily.

My idea, subject to change as knowledge develops, is that the god of any generation is the sum total of all the highest ideals and aspirations of the generation. The god of any individual is the sum total of all the highest ideals and aspirations of the individual. Search yourself for ideals and you find your idea of God. Honesty, morality, love, charity, mercy, power, wisdom, music, art, science, etc., etc. This for the present satisfies me, for it is still consistent with what little I actually know.

Practical religion with me concerns solely this life—to so live and conduct myself as not to violate very many of my ideals.

As yet I cannot know what death leads to and am not concerned about that. I do know that I can produce a hell for myself and my family and associates here if I go very far from my ideals of life. This satisfies me for the present as I have said, but there are millions of people whom it does not satisfy. Therefore I avoid religious discussion, for if I should win one to my idea I would simply have dissatisfied him. I reckon you have had a very good lesson in this respect and my homily was not needed.

As you know I am extremely interested in your getting good grades and taking part in as many of the honorable activities of the students as possible. This is the chief aim of college life. Your music is as important as any other study.

February 27, 1926

When I went home last night I found Mother almost standing on her head over the two birthday letters from you. Of course we are tickled plum pink that you are making Phi Beta Phi. Now another honorary society or two and your next year in Ky. U. should be very happy and satisfactory.

The most important thing, it seems to me, to write about this morning is "International Law." Of course you won't drop it and equally of course you will get the hang of it soon. I judge from your letters that you are afflicted with an inferiority complex with reference to this subject. There is no justification for such a feeling. It comes from the fact that the field is absolutely new to and unexplored by you. If you will forget your complex you will find the new scenery in the field is not dangerous or hard to get over or around. There are paths all through it which are not so hard to travel. The thing to do now is to "go through it" with the belief that you can understand it, and you will find that it will be even as you believe. The outline I sent you will not be in many respects applicable to cases of international law—but from it you can pick out the things that are applicable. How did the case originate? What is involved—law or fact? The facts, the law applicable? Those things ought to cover any case, under "the law applicable," from the previous cases of the same or similar kind. *Now forget your fear,* and you will make good at it. The new subject is strange, and only because it is new and strange does it seem so difficult.

Don't forget to let us know when your orchestra is to broadcast. Also find out before then and let us know what wave length the broadcasting station will use so that we may pick it up more easily, if we can do so at all.

March 4, 1926

I suspect I better write you a line or two though I am tolerably busy with income tax reports added on to my usual load. I wrote to the Registrar of Ky. Univ. a few days ago telling him that I had not received your grades and suggesting that he send them to me, or to you at Boyd Hall. I have not received them. If you have done so, will you send them on to me when you are through with them? Am very sorry that they were not high enough for the thing you had in mind. Yet if you make good ones this semester you may make your goal early next year. Furthermore, if your grades in your major study are not good it will be more difficult to land a good job when you have finished.

I hope too that you master "International Law." You are under the chief of the school in that and apparently he has noticed you. What impression he gets of you may have something to do with getting a good place when you graduate. Then in law I hope particularly you excel and develop a legal mind, as it were. Otherwise, it may appear that your dad must have no legal mind or you would have inherited it. So be sure and be very busy on this as the days come and go, and on your English as well. On the side do as much society as you can without ruining your health, but get your work. This I know is not necessary to say to you, but dads must lecture.

I have your short letter yesterday and enjoyed your long one at noon today along with a very fine cherry pie that your mother had made. The two, the letter and the pie, were in the same class—both A 1. When you write to me again let me know the probable cost of induction into the two frats, so that I may be prepared. Your mother and sister are well. Spring vacation between terms, today, and Alice E. is expecting to do some resting, and perhaps some other things. I think a young man by name of Cannon or Gun or something of that kind takes supper with us tonight. You should be here to wait on table or in some way help entertain him. Your mother goes to a missionary meeting tonight and I fear I will go too. We went to a picture show last night—a wild thing called "The Spook of the Opera" or some such title. It was spooky and different from the ordinary show.

March 12, 1926

March still continues to do her stuff. This morning a mantle of white covered all outdoors. The snow was sticky and clung to the trees and made every twig a thing of beauty. It got a little colder during the day and snowed some more but the sun came out late this afternoon and bothered me here at my desk. I will be very glad when March begins to behave like a lady and leaves off being a rowdy. All of which has nothing to do with international law except as climate affects the disposition of individuals or peoples.

I send you back the list of subjects. Any one would make an interesting topic for study. My information about international law is not very broad nor very accurate. Yet is much more broad than accurate. For instance, I know something of every topic that is suggested. I have seen them all discussed more or less, I should say in the past twelve months, somewhere, but where? The chances are that the discussions were in the *Literary Digest*, for that is the only general magazine I read with regularity. I haven't much doubt that you could take the last 52 issues of the *Digest* and get considerable information about almost any of the subjects, except perhaps the 2nd and 4th, 5th, and 6th. I am under the impression that I have seen a discussion of the 3rd in a law magazine lately but am unable to find it, and by the way, the 3rd suggests itself to me as perhaps the most interesting because there is in it the question of the right of foreign nations to maintain a court within China before which cases involving nationals of the foreign nation are tried.

There is, I believe, some precedent for the maintenance of such courts but in what countries the precedents were established I do not know, except that

England has maintained them in India. Personally I doubt whether they can be justified but it's a very interesting study. The status of women in international law is interesting, too. In fact, any one of the topics is interesting. Are you expected to get your material from current publications? Is there a library available? If you will choose your subject I will see what material I can dig up, though my sources of information are limited. Mother says we have a lot of old *Digests*. The *Congressional Record* should furnish an inexhaustible supply of information on most any of the subjects, but I do not know whether the *Record* is indexed. . . .

We are well. It's now about 6 p.m. and I have worked at my desk since 7 this morning with an hour off for lunch, and am ready to quit. Am and have been pretty busy and so my letters have been shorter, but will do better when I begin to get the load lightened.

March 18, 1926

I am enclosing a letter from your cousin Paul which I think will be pleasing to you. At least it was to us, very much so. The reason is evident.

This is the first real spring day. Otherwise, every day of March but one has been horrid. March has always had a bad reputation, false and fickle, and this year the Vixen has almost surpassed her reputation. But her time is growing short and perhaps she has done her worst. At least that is my hope.

Your mother and Alice E. are well. We have been to a couple of dinners and card games lately, and yesterday I felt the effects of loss of sleep . . . but am in good shape this morning and expect to get a satisfactory day's work done. The time till June is not very long now—two months and a half will bring you home and we are glad the time is slipping away. It goes rather fast for me at least, for neither the days nor the weeks are long enough to get the work cleared off my desk as I plan.

There isn't any particular news. I believe I will ask you to save and return Cousin Paul's letter to me as it is certainly appreciated here at home. Do you get the compliment? He thinks having you in his home is a good influence for the boys, and that's higher praise than most anything else that could have been said. With lots of love from all of us. Believe me, we are anxious for you to get back here, at least for the summer.

March 26, 1926

I am sending you the *Report of the American Bar Association*, Vol. 1 for 1925. At page 275 you will find an address on "American Policy and Chinese Affairs" by Frank B. Kellogg. At page 219 you find "The Codification of International Law" by George W. Wickersham. At page 200 "The Legal Aspects of Our Relations With Mexico" by Charles Beecher Warren, and at page 401 the report of the Committee on International Law, all very interesting. This is my permanent volume and bring it back with you. I haven't read it and won't have time to do so till August.

Yesterday was a big day at Normal in music. The St. Louis Symphony Orchestra gave two programs—afternoon and night. Alice E. attended both, your mother the afternoon program, and I didn't go at all. Elsa Koch sang at night and after the program Mrs. Craig and Mrs. Thomas entertained them all at Mrs. Craig's. Miss Geer, the Thomas girls and Alice E. were guests, and Alice E. had a great time, getting home about one-thirty this morning. We are all well and I just have time for this note.

Lots of love,
Affectionately,
Dad

P.S. I have older Bar Association Reports which I did not examine the other day with reference to international law. When I get time will do so.

April 6, 1926

You haven't had a lecture from me for some time and must, therefore, be more or less uneasy about the condition of my health. It is to relieve your mind that I am putting a period to my work at 5 o'clock to administer a measure of sage reflections.

We are well. Alice E. had a few days vacation which she used to very good advantage by postponing her only assigned school work until last night. I think you probably followed the same plan. It was too cold and wet to tempt housecleaning and so none of that was done. Not very much cooking was indulged in either. I still followed my time-tried and experienced-tested plan of getting my own breakfast as the safest way to assure my presence at the office at a reasonable hour.

Cannon went home, but on Saturday Byron, Catherine Shaffer and Alice E. lit out in a car and drove to Tower Hill where they picked up a larger car, and Cannon and his sister and another young man, and went on, taking dinner in Pana, going to a show in Decatur, back to Tower Hill for supper and home before midnight. Sunday your mother and I were guests of the Dr. Hites on a car ride in their new car. To Mattoon, Neoga, Sigel, Effingham, down the National Trail to Marshall, up the Dixie to Paris and then home—150 miles in all, getting in at 9 o'clock. Alice E. and Cannon were at church and think Alice E. read your mother a lecture about being out so long and making her uneasy and fearful of an automobile accident, etc.

We enjoyed your letter written from Mt. Sterling. I don't believe I congratulated you on your political success. It may be we will run you for office after you finish school. I think you have the making of a good politician in you. At any rate you may think it over. There is a certain fascination about the game; perhaps arising from its very uncertainty. I believe I wrote you of a plan we have in mind for you this summer, the first six weeks while Alice E. is in school. You know Mr. Jeffries is a veritable mine of golden character sketches and of facts suggestive of plots that have been lived. Charleston has been full of life, and he has preserved in his memory a world of information that you might be able to dig out and use to your advantage in writing. So we are planning that you interview him every day. If he is talkative you will get something worthwhile I am sure, to put down at night, enlarge upon, etc. It's very well worth trying, and I think he would be pleased. From him you can get a background of life that would take years of living otherwise to get.

On the China question. There is a volume just off the press, issued by the *Chicago Daily News* called *World Chancelleries*, consisting of interviews of the chief chancellors of the world. It is dedicated to the memory of Victor Freamont Lawson who was editor of the *Daily News* and who backed the interviews as a step toward international understanding. The last interview in the book is of Dr. Tang Shao-Yi and concurs with the Chinese point of view. If this is to be had there in Lexington it will be of value in the preparation of your paper. I cannot send the copy which I had the pleasure of reading. You might ask Dr. McVey if he has the book and if so will lend it to you.

By the way, the next chance you have to go to Georgetown I wish you would take your violin along and play some for Papa and Mamma. I know Papa would enjoy it, and I feel sure both Papa and Mamma will appreciate your showing them even slight attention. You cannot appreciate yet the loneliness of age, and how much very small courtesies count for. When you reach my age you will know more about it.

Now, child, dig into your work. History and International Law you should make to eat out of your hand. I really expect you to make history take the count this term, and of course you will do well enough in International Law. So far I haven't a complaint to register except that you have deeply surprised me and pained me in letting a little thing like history plant a puny "C" on your chin. That isn't like you, and I cannot get it through my head that it's even so. Seems to me you are due for a comeback on this. There isn't any real news. With lots of love from all of us.

Affectionately, Dad

P.S. Your mother voted and then went to a bridge party this afternoon.

April 22, 1926

Alice E. and I each had a letter from you a day or so ago which the three of us enjoyed very much, as in fact we enjoy all your letters. We of course know that there are many things to occupy your time and that you do not have a chance to write a book to us telling about all the events in which you have part, but the time for you to come home is not far off now and when you get here you may just talk and talk and talk. Personally I am deeply interested in your grades stacking high this term, and hope that you will make it your chief purpose in school life for the balance of the school year to see that they do come up.

There is nothing much new with us. We have had three or four pretty days and in them have got a good start on our yard and garden, have set out some vegetables and flowers. The early yellow flowers and the hyacinths are in full bloom and are very pretty. The pretty weather has made us think of the river and the fish that are supposed to be there, and in digging I have turned up some of the finest fishing worms that you ever saw—big, fat, industrious fellows who I think would work hard to land a fish for us. So the Millers and we have have been "sorter" whispering about next Sunday, hazily working over the idea that maybe next Sunday, if it's a pretty day, we will get some baskets and put some food in them for cooking, hunt up the old fishing poles and figure out a way to get some bait, and after church hike to the river; but it's raining this morning and the thing doesn't seem as attractive as it did yesterday and maybe we don't want to go anyway.

I cleaned the cellar some this morning while it rained and got myself very dirty. Mother has been expecting to start housecleaning any day but the weather has not been propitious and the furnace fire is still burning—the same old fire I started early last winter about the time you went to Kentucky. The house is very dusty as no attention to it has been given since the prospect of housecleaning loomed close. Judge Dunn should return to Charleston from Springfield today or tomorrow and the new work will be on.

My idea is that you may get character sketches from Mr. Jeffries, of the unusual, and perhaps the unusual are the usual. At the same time you will get incidents in the life of Mr. Jeffries and in the lives of the others that have much of dramatic value. Of Mr. Jeffries and incidents in his life short stories may be made, a character may be created that can be followed from month to month in some publication—something of the kind that Cobb has made of a judge there in Ky. somewhere, or another author has made of

"Scattergood," published in the *American* occasionally. The suggesting of material Mr. Jeffries has, and a good imagination will do the rest.

May 20, 1926

We received your letter telling us that you were actually getting your "China" paper ready for publication. I would be very much interested to read this and if it should be published or you get the paper returned to you, I want to read it. Your grandmother is with us as you know. You are not to let that interfere with your asking friends to visit you, for we will just have to go along with our plans. I suggested to Mother the other night that it might be a good idea for you to attend the first 6 weeks of summer school here as Alice E. has to do so, and if it should chance that you could not return to Ky. U. you would be in shape to go on here and graduate with Alice E. I don't know how your year's work in Ky. U. would fit in with E. I.'s schedule, do you? But I suppose you could graduate here in 1927 if the worst should come to the worst.

I don't know yet whether your mother will come to Kentucky with Mrs. Winter or not. She has weakened considerably on this plan since she learned that Aunt Lillian is not to be in Kentucky. Her absence would make the trip less to be desired.

Have been so busy that I have had very little time, or at least very little inclination to write anything but my work, and now that I am writing there is but little that I have to tell you about. We took a table out in the yard this noon and ate dinner there. It's a glorious day. The yard is pretty and the flowers have been fine. Irene bought herself a Ford run-a-bout for $75. It isn't worth anything. She drove to her home in Bloomington in it leaving here about 5 o'clock in the afternoon and getting to Bloomington before noon the next day. She finally gave up about 2 o'clock at night and someone towed her and her car to a house where she went to bed and had breakfast an hour or two later. Mother had her take the phonograph home with her, so that no longer disturbs us. We will be very glad when she leaves and you come. Cannon still shows up regularly.

You haven't made a suggestion as to how your work has been coming on for a long time now and so we suppose that you have been doing fine. No news is reputed to be good news, and in this respect we hope the reputation is deserved. Do you know yet about what day you will get home? I want to begin counting the days pretty soon. Well here's hoping it will be soon. Drop us a line between examinations as you find the chance, but don't make any effort to do much writing, for you can talk it out when you get here.

May 27, 1926

Just a line. Mrs. Winter and mother have renewed their plans to drive to Kentucky and I am writing to Aunt Helen and Uncle Tandy trying to arrange for them to spend two days each in Mt. Sterling and Georgetown. I really think now they will come down and it will be well for you to make your plans accordingly. If you think best your friend may be included in the plans.

The schedule is not at all arranged. They will probably leave here Wednesday the 2nd of June spending that night in Indianapolis and the next night Thursday in Lexington. They will probably want to take in Shakertown and the big dam. Whether Cousins Paul and Sally will want to have them for a meal or anything, I leave to you, even the suggestion to Cousins Paul and Sally that your mother and Laura are coming. Personally I am not crazy about your camping trip but you arrange that to suit yourself. If you go, just hang your clothes on a hickory limb but don't go near the water, for the Kentucky River is indeed treacherous and one can't treat it with the slightest disrespect and get by. It's not the Ambraw by a whole big river full. You have no fear of water and I am glad, but you must respect its power, its seeming kindness in a moment changes into treacherous, sullen, invincible power, and don't forget that for a moment at the Kentucky River.

I will start your mother with some but not much money. If she or Mrs. Winter runs out of money you will have to supply them by your very efficient method. Personally, I will be tickled pink when I get all my family back home again. Really I don't want to miss you during your last year of school, for after that I feel that I will only know you as a visitor, and that's not a very satisfactory feeling for your father. I have enjoyed Alice E. and her work so much this winter and I want to have the two of you for the last year perhaps. We are well.

October 11, 1926

Your interesting letter came in some time ago and in place of simply reporting your good wishes to the two Alices, I took the letter to them and they had the pleasure of reading it and so got the message at first hand. . . .

Think you are following a good plan with the organization. Success often consists of advocating an idea and talking about it till you become a bore. If the idea has merit, eventually your associates will give it effect in practice, as Christ put it, I think, not so much because of its merit but because of much importunity. Of course this isn't a quotation but you may look it up and you will find that, in substance, was his expression. We have just had an illustration in golf affairs. One of our members who is a long driver and a good player has wanted a longer golf course, so more than a year ago he began talking about it, talking to everyone who would listen and meeting with no encouragement, in fact finding everyone indifferent, yet he continued to talk and talk and talk. It seems now as if he will get what he wants, for we have a committee appointed and an expert has been consulted and several changes staked out on the course that look good and if made will give us a standard course about 3000 yards or a little better, where we now have only about 2400 yards. And what is more, most everyone seems to be of the opinion that the changes are desirable. So at first, if your efforts don't seem to be getting anywhere, be not discouraged, just rest content with the merit of your proposition as a fulcrum and your much importunities as a lever to eventually get results.

October 14, 1926

Your mother handed me the letter to mail and told me to add a line or two myself. So in obedience this is being written. You are a voter now as you know and will be entitled to vote at the election which comes in November. An application for an absent voter's ballot will be sent to you which you may fill out and return as directed. Later a ballot will be sent upon your application which you may vote and return as directed. Your application should state that your business is that of a "student."

When your ballot reaches you and you are preparing to vote it as directed by the instructions, you may be glad of the suggestion that for Senator neither Republican nor Democrat meets my approval in the least. Smith is the Republican candidate. He is the man who was head of the State Utilities Commission which had in charge important matters pertaining to the public utilities of the state and while he held that office became a candidate for the nomination of U.S. Senator. Between $150,000 and $200,000 was furnished by Samuel Insull to secure Smith's nomination. Insull is our biggest public utility man in the Middle West. For that reason I cannot vote for Smith.

The Democratic candidate is Brennan who is out on a wet platform and I cannot vote for him. Under the circumstances a Republican was nominated to run on an Independent ticket. His name is *Magill* and I shall put a cross in the square before his name. The second suggestion is that Albert Moore's father (Stanley Moore) is running for sheriff on the Democratic ticket. You may feel inclined to put a cross in the square in front of Moore's name.

When I vote a split ticket I usually disregard the circle at the head of the ticket—leave it blank and just put a cross in the square in front of each name for whom I wish to vote. When you have voted your way, destroy this letter and forget that I have ever suggested a split ticket especially as to Moore. As to the senatorial race I am out in the open against Smith but as to the sheriff's race I am not in the open.

About your room. I agree exactly with what your mother has said, and am more than anxious that her questions be answered. We both feel that you are thoroughly alive to the dangers and that it isn't necessary to say anything whatsoever or make any suggestions. Yet out of excess of caution perhaps, we are constrained to tell you what you well know.

In this connection I am reminded of the lawyer who had a case in the Supreme Court. It involved, among other things, a simple well-understood rule of law, a rule which even a beginner might be expected to know. Yet in making his argument to the Supreme Court, composed as it was of men who had reached the topmost level of professional honors, the lawyer went into a thorough discussion of the rule, its history, and application and reason. After a time one of the judges interrupted him asking if the Court might not be presumed to know the rule, for it was axiomatic. The lawyer answered that he didn't like to make the same mistake twice and he had made the mistake in the trial court of supposing that the trial judge knew the rule.

So here, while what your mother says is axiomatic, yet, in view of the trend of modern literature, a man may not entertain a woman in his apartment, nor may a woman, married or single, entertain a man in her apartment, without proper chaperonage, without properly giving rise to a reputation of immorality. This is axiomatic. Therefore, by taking an apartment you have foreclosed yourself from entertaining anywhere except at the frat house, for having an apartment it is probable that your landlady's parlor is not open to you. If her parlor is open to you, you will have to use *good* judgment to determine whether entertaining there might give rise to the report that you are entertaining in your apartment.

Mother wanted me to ask the further question. Has the Dean of Women been consulted and given her consent to your new arrangement? Her consent would, as you will understand, operate as a certificate as to the character of your landlady. We have no doubt that she is all right and your arrangement is all right, yet we wish to know these things.

Mother has just telephoned that we have received a box of candy from Lexington. There was no card, but of course it came from you and we thank you and appreciate your remembrance of October 14* as marking an event in our lives which was very important to us and to you.

October 21, 1926

Alice E. had your letter yesterday and as she no longer comes home to dinner your mother and I read it before she did. Your mother says we are

*Their wedding anniversary.

authorized to open all letters that come from you. I believe I wrote you, we are very much pleased with your room and board arrangements. Might have known that you would work it out in a very satisfactory way, but you know one of the impossibilities for mothers and fathers, whose natures are as ours, is to understand that their grown up children are competent to take care of themselves. Considering this impossibility, I know you will find an excuse for us.

We had a rain Tuesday and it was cloudy and raw yesterday, but last night the clouds cleared away and this morning the ground was white with frost. I doubt whether vegetation was killed, but don't know yet. Today is bright and clear, a brilliant fall day that tempts one to load a basket with bacon and eggs and coffee and bread and onions and all that is necessary and to get out in the open, there to remain until the shades of night begin to close in around the embers of the dying campfire. One should have his affairs so arranged that no such day as this could get by without one being able to respond to its call.

The usual number of automobile accidents are happening around here, some resulting in death, some in physical injuries and some merely in damage to the cars involved. The big Lincoln car in which, as you may recall, I rode to Shelbyville (35 miles in 45 minutes) was wrecked night before last down about Marshall. It turned over two or three times and seriously hurt the driver (Huesman), the same man who was driving it when I went to Shelbyville. The car was a fast one and Huesman was a fast driver. He will recover, it is thought. Can a fast driver be considered a good one?

Well, I must close, as there is work for me to do.

November 3, 1926

Somehow or another I do not seem to have made as many opportunities to write to you as I have wished. Really there should be no excuse for me and I am not offering it as an excuse that I have been busy. No matter how busy I may have been is no reason for having denied myself the pleasure of writing to you now and then, reading you a lecture perhaps, or giving you some advice that might or might not be very good under the circumstances in which you may find yourself. Now it's ten minutes to six in the evening and I am waiting for your mother to let me know what she wants for supper.

Well, I got so far with the letter when Alice E. came. Mrs. Winter was below in her car, and we made the round of the grocery stores to accumulate the essentials for a sausage-waffle supper for the three families—Millers, Winters, and Kellys. The waffles came on apace. There was almost a miscalculation in estimating the amount of batter that would be necessary to supply the needs of seven hungry sinners, but when the last meagre waffle was consumed everyone seemed to have had almost all he or she wanted. Then we sat and talked before a wood fire till 10:30.

Magill for whom we voted didn't run very well. Smith seems to have won easily. The wet and dry referendum went wet. All of the local Republicans won except that Moore was elected sheriff. So much for politics in which I know you are not very deeply interested. Someday, though, you may be President.

The incident you described in your recent letter that occurred the night you stayed at the frat house was interesting and interestingly told. You have really some rather heavy responsibilities but your ingenuity seems to be sufficient for the emergency and your sense of humor will carry you through without hurt to your nerves. You are remarkably gifted in getting the comic side of life, and that is a gift that is exceedingly well worth having. We are well, of course. Alice E. is deep in her practice teaching and seems to be showing some speed and ability; however, the experience is making her wonder if she has chosen her life occupation very wisely.

There isn't much news. Yesterday we mailed you some cookies which Mother made. Write when you can. How is your violin work? Are you in the orchestra? Are you finding any of your lessons difficult?

December 1, 1926

I had your letter yesterday stating that in just 24 days, 6 hours, 35 minutes and 40 seconds you would be home and it made me feel good, and when the two Alices read it they felt good too. But just see how time flies. You will be home Dec. 23, at 5:39 (I think) in the afternoon. This letter reaches you at 12:17 p.m. on Dec. 2. So that from the time this letter reaches you, just 21 days, 5 hours and 12 minutes will intervene before you get home. Now isn't that fine?

I do not know how far apart you and I are in philosophy—imagine not very far. When I left college I was a notable pessimist and all through life, in spite of the good that I have seen in men and women, and an occasional glimmer of good in myself, I have had an inclination to look too exclusively on the shadows, though I have trained myself to an ever-present consciousness that even when looking upon the shadows there is always a rift of sunshine if I will but shift my mental eyes just a little. I think that sometimes one is inclined, either by natural tendency, or as the result of some disheartening, disenchanting experience, to shut himself out of the ability to appreciate the good and attractive that do exist in almost every thing and every person. One therefore has to be on guard all the time else, by deprecating everything else one destroys one's own chance for contentment.

But enough of philosophy. We are well. Monday night the old crowd, the Hardins, Craigs, Millers, Winters, Barnfields, and Joe Reat (Mrs. Reat being in Florida) had a fine combination dinner at our house, after which cards, and after cards a discussion of the farmer and the country and the relation of the condition to the general spendthrift conditions that exist over the country and find particular expression in the attitude of us individuals. The discussion was animated and prolonged until midnight when Alice E. switched the lights on us and the crowd disintegrated, Mr. Hardin saying as he left, "I had an awful time," without knowing, until it was called to his attention, that he had omitted a very necessary word from the usual formula.

Margaret Coon and Alice E. are associated, as you probably know, in teaching a class in English and the term closes this week. So they were together Monday night and worked till midnight preparing for the close of the term. It was when they quit work that Alice E. switched the lights. . . .

There isn't much news. Life seems pretty full, but there is something in the philosophy which has as its motto: "It's better to wear out than to rust out." Am still busy. Hunted part of the day Thanksgiving and went to a football game in the afternoon. A good game in which E. I. was the victor. You must make a note of the things you are to tell us when you are at home—else they will be lost forever. All send lots of love, and all of us are sure hurrying Christmas along because we want you to come home so much.

December 5, 1926

Your mother and I have just waked up to the possibility of your being busted. I therefore enclose a few checks. If you need money between now and the time you get home just cash checks on me for such amounts as you need, letting me know when you do so.

Alice E. has been enjoying a respite from school work of which there was none to do Friday afternoon, Saturday and today. Nor will there be any to do tomorrow or any paper to get out, so that tomorrow, Monday, is free. You perhaps understand from your own experience what a relief this must have been to her as she has been literally burning the midnight electric light right along. She got one A and three B's, I believe. Last night Iole was with her and they had a couple of men from Mattoon come over, Tolle and another young fellow whose name I don't recall. He is redheaded and originally from Arkansas. Iole and Alice E. were just coming down to breakfast when I left home. They were wrapped in dressing gowns and ready for breakfast.

The Millers, Awtys, Greers, Harrymans and Kellys are giving a dance at the Chamber of Commerce the Monday after Christmas and are deep in their plans. Mrs. Harryman is expected to be the disturbing factor. It will be a dance for the young folks (with the parents who are giving it there to run it so far as the young folks permit). We are to eat dinner at the Millers today. This afternoon Miss Garabedian, accompanied by Mrs. Thomas, is to play on her violin at our house for the benefit of the Iknayans and a few others of us. Wish you could be with us and hear and watch her. They were playing when I went home last night and I enjoyed the music very much.

There is very little news. We are well. Your mother is buying Christmas presents. There are numerous gift shops around. Mrs. Giles runs one in her home, Miss Messer another, and Mrs. Hite and Miss Harding a third at the home of Mrs. Hite. The merchants don't like it very much but, of course, have to lump it. We have had no real cold weather so far, but the furnace burns considerable coal each day anyway, and so life goes. It's only 20 days till Christmas, only 18 days till you get home and that's the best part of Christmas this year. Your mother has engaged a turkey and will have a number to help eat it—the Millers, the Hardins. It may be that Aunt Lillian will be here. I think that she will if you urge her a little. She is to see you soon—this week, I think—as she will be around Georgetown and Lexington. Give Paul and his family our love.

1927

January 26, 1927

I enclose the story of the gavel. We are very well and Alice is plugging along at school trying to make up for lost time. The "Follies" was presented at Normal the other night. It was good. I enclose a program. Harold came over that night and took Alice E. He was also over Saturday night. I haven't seen a letter for you for some time but suppose Mother has one this morning as she has not phoned to find out if I have heard. The way of the pedestrian has been difficult, snow and ice—slick going. The ways of the automobile have been more difficult and exceedingly devious. The cars get in the ruts and won't climb out without a lot of effort, the ruts being deep and of ice. The Yellow Peril (street car) makes a straight but halting course up and down Sixth Street waiting for the automobiles and Fords to jump out of its way. Am exceedingly anxious to hear from your exams and suppose that time will relieve my anxiety. What news there might be to tell I suppose you get from the folks at home, as I mail letters for them now and then. Will write again when I have more time. Used all that I had to spare on the gavel letter.

February 6, 1927

We had your very interesting letter telling of the result of your examinations a couple of days ago and all of us enjoyed it a great deal. I have appeared to be derelict in my correspondence with you lately but it has not been because of actual neglect. I have merely been busy with other matters that occupied my time and thought almost to the exclusion of everything else, though at odd times I have wished for a chance to write you a long letter full of wise saws, etc. as I usually write to you. Even this morning, though it is Sunday and Sunday school time I have not the time to write much, as there is a matter of business and I will go to church.

Alice E. went to Mattoon last night to spend the night with Iole and I think the new scenes and surroundings will be good for her, as she has found her school work, including the making up for lost time, rather trying. She is however getting along all right and she or Mother will write you of her visit when they get the chance . . . .

We are with you in your feelings of dissatisfaction toward Farquahar. He, I know, must have been wrong, for you were interested and under that condition you do good work and we have not the slightest doubt that you did good work under him. So feeling, we do not think it was at all fair or just for him to cut your grades down just because he had the power and perhaps has been eating too much or doing something else to make a grouch out of him. That he cut so very many grades is pretty good evidence that there is something wrong with him. Nevertheless, as you have a heavy course under him for the remainder of the year, I suppose you will have to grin and bear it and continue to do good work so that he will not be able to flunk you however unfair he may feel like being toward his students. It's too bad but life is often that way. We haven't got to the point in the regulation of society that one always gets what is justly coming to him, and this failure will continue as long as the human element enters into it, and that will be always. Well, I must close. Mother will write you the news. We are well and send lots of love.

February 11, 1927

The family and I enjoyed your letter very much. I reckon it's true that we are not writing to you very frequently, either from the home or the office and I don't know that excuses would be of any value. Rather think that you know we all enjoy writing to you and enjoy still more hearing from you. We are anxiously waiting for your pen sketch that your letter promised. Glad to find that the president and his good wife have learned to know upon whom to call for wisdom or social assistance. Of course I as your father understand perfectly why they have reached the conclusion that is shown by their action. Your meeting must have been interesting and we imagine you were not as thoroughly squelched as you suggest.

Alice E. is enjoying her release from hard work. I believe she goes to a dance tonight at Mattoon Country Club, with a young man whose name is Tolle I believe. Your mother is visiting the dentist, Dr. Tym, pretty regularly and will find opportunity to visit him even at more times before he pronounces her finished. He keeps her mouth in bad condition, and at times eating is quite a task for her. The office work goes along slowly. I find it a real task to get down to work at all and realize that I need familiar association with a garden fork regularly for a few weeks to get myself in satisfactory condition for office work. Some time I will have to arrange for indoor exercise during the winter, I suppose. We have had some pretty weather. Today is bright and not very cold.

Every time I think of Farquahar going off at a tangent and spoiling your chance for a real high grade I get "sorter" mad. That sort of injustice you get more or less of all through life, but it's hardly necessary to begin to dispense it to kids in school. It's a plum nuisance that you have to go on with him and take a chance of his throwing another fit about June, but I suppose the best thing to do is just to do good work under him and trust to luck to put him in a good humor at the proper time.

February 24, 1927

Well, I haven't taken my pen in hand for quite some time now to write a line to you, nor have I much to tell this morning. So far as I am concerned life goes along pretty much in the even tenor of its usual way. With the usual time spent at home and the usual time spent in the office in the usual way. Last night Teachers College High, 2nd and 1st teams, played Charleston High, second and first teams, losing both games by narrow margins. Both games were start to finish; the high school gym was very crowded and very noisy as is usual on such occasions. I went down to see the game, had a good seat and was highly thrilled as the games went along. Alice E. has had another cold and couldn't go and Mother also found herself unable to leave the family.

Your mother has had Wes Titus cleaning the yard, doing the fall work that we didn't find time to do last fall. She has sowed a lot of grass which your Uncle Kirtley and Aunt Helen were good enough to send us, and now the place looks much more trim and neat than it has looked all winter. We are up with the work and ready to go ahead just as soon as the season opens officially. We have had some beautiful spring weather—so perfect that it is hard not to believe that spring cannot yet be with us in earnest.

This is the income tax return season and with some of that and my office cases on my mind I reckon I am a bit absentminded at times. Was counting the months till June this morning and find there are still three to go. I had thought the time was shorter, but not so. Sure will be glad when you get home with your sheepskin. I feel this is the best year for your development that you have had and am therefore much pleased. The Frat work cannot help but have given you a valuable experience of people and outlook on life. The value will be found if you have been able to yourself keep a sane and honest viewpoint. I have no doubt whatever that you have done so and am, therefore, greatly pleased. So many are not able to get the experience and themselves remain just and upright, and disaster begins where ideals leave off.

Your philosophy ought to be worthwhile and that reminds me of Dr. Terrell. I should remember him better, but in truth he is only a name to me. Am rather inclined to think that he did not teach in Georgetown until after I graduated which was in 1899. Then I left Georgetown soon after that, and I have a faint recollection of his name as that of one who became interested in the Kellys perhaps through his interest in your aunt Eliza. You need not let him know that my memory has proved so treacherous. However, I am sure you can and will make good with him or any other reasonable human being who is your teacher. However, I do not put that English teacher in that class. You will make a passing grade with him because your work will force him, reasonable or unreasonable, to accord you that much, but I don't expect anything better than passing.

Well, remember we enjoy the letters that you find time to write. Also, remember that we understand that your time is otherwise well occupied and if at anytime your letters should become scant in numbers, we appreciate that it is not caused at all by want of inclination to write but by the press of living the life of a senior and a fraternity president at the modern state university. Some life no doubt. With the exception of Alice E., we are well. I think she is about well. Her mother gets worried over her taking cold so easily, but her heart and lungs are in good condition and the doctor only advised real physical exercise, and that is, I think, what she needs.

March 28, 1927

I had your letter Saturday but just at that time was unable to answer it. As soon as Mr. Jeffries comes in I will get a suggestion as to the supposed fake wedding. In writing of these actual incidents it is advisable that the scene be laid in a fanciful town—that is, not under the actual name of town or person either, for the immediate descendants are alive.

Alice E. has been rather active since Byron came home. Saturday night she and Iole went to the Normal School party respectively with Harold and Byron. She and Iole spent the night at the Millers'. Alice E. came home during the morning and cooked dinner for Mother and me. (The dinner was fine, consisting of baked chicken with the trimmings), and Mrs. Miller had Byron and Iole, Dorothy and Turk, and Alice E. and Harold to dinner. After dinner they drove to Terre Haute in Mike Miller's car and had something to eat on the way back in Paris. They were rather late about getting in. Your mother and I spent the day at home before a grate or wood fire. Mrs. Wyeth came over about 5:30 and we later had a chicken sandwich lunch. Your mother, as you probably don't know, has had a severely sore throat—was in bed for four days with it, but is now about well and hungry most of the time. She woke up this morning just in time to get my first cup of coffee, egg and toast.

March has been more like March should be for the last few days. The nights have been frosty but not freezing and the development of foliage is being retarded. That was coming along too fast for a time. Mother has had a few jonquils to bloom and many more buds are ready to open upon the first invitation of the weatherman. I have cut the long grass at the back of the lot and the grass on the terrace, my lawnmower has been adjusted and sharpened and I am prepared to keep ahead of the growth of grass over all the lot. We have a wide expanse of grass to care for this year and it might be very attractive. You perhaps know that Kirtly and Helen sent us a lot of blue grass seed and your mother reseeded a lot of the yard. Whether it is still there and will sprout after awhile depends upon the unanswered question: Did the two heavy rain falls which we had wash it away? At any rate we have a fair stand of grass everywhere almost and should have an attractive lawn all summer whatever may have happened to the new seed. . . .

You should let me know how much more money you are to borrow to get you through and bring you home in plenty of time so that I can send the note to you, get it back here and the money on it, for you not to be embarrassed by lack of funds.

I will be interested to read your stories about the specific people. You must be sure to have an extra copy so that they cannot by any possibility be lost in the wastebasket of the teacher. Am sorry you are not interested in botany. The details of it would, I think, be a bit monotonous, but the fieldwork would be interesting. My misfortune with botany arose out of the fact that in the last school year I had a conflict of time between it and astronomy and the good, kind little man who taught botany couldn't see anyone suffer, and so he told me that he would sign my diploma anyway with only two hours to my credit. Alice E. is having a time to learn to distinguish trees. The elm tree seems to be the hardest for her to learn. She almost thinks that something is lacking in her makeup. I took her over our yard—we have as you know 15 different samples of trees there—and gave her one lesson. Don't know whether it was of any particular value to her or not.

In the good old days, Uncle Dick Stoddert, then a young blade, was the "life of the party," full of fun, playing jokes, etc. He was particularly attentive to an attractive young lady of the time and at a coming party his friends planned a back-acting practical joke on him. A mock wedding was arranged in which the young lady and Stoddert were to be the principals. Uncle Dick and she fell heartily into the arrangement. Their friends saw to it however, that it should be an air-tight wedding, procured a license, a preacher or justice of the peace and the wedding went off in fine shape, producing merriment for all. The next morning the friends industriously spread the report that the wedding was not mock but real. The principals, at first startled, investigated, learned the fact; the more they thought of it the better pleased they were, and so they fell into the matrimonial harness and pulled together for life. . . .

March 29, 1927

I enclose an interesting story of early Coles County history. When you have finished with this, *return* it *at once* to me for it belongs to Mr. Jeffries and he would not lose it for a good deal.

You will note that Dr. Van Meter is mentioned. The doctor had many good traits. There are also many stories concerning Usher F. Linder whose part in the story is a basis for English work in the South, but that will be up to you. You will note that Lincoln was on the wrong side. However, according to the story his heart must not have been in it, for his argument was considered weak. In reading this story you must remember that the slave question at the time was loaded—sudden death was liable to attend its discussion and the settlement of a particular case. There were here many slavery sympathizers but those of the contrary view were in the majority.

Mother is about well. The weather has been very nice for the last three days including this one.

April 16, 1927

I don't believe the sun has broken through the clouds for even a moment during the last week. Maybe my memory is at fault, but it surely seems that there was never such a thing as sunshine. It rained pretty much all last night—I don't mean sprinkled, but rained. I came down with the aid of an umbrella this morning while there was a letup—while only an ordinary garden variety of rain was falling, but for the last half hour there has been a continuation or resumption of the downpour. It has found the weak points in our office roof, and as I sit here writing to you the music from the dropping of water into buckets that I have placed around in strategic positions punctuates almost every letter that I write. Mr. Jeffries has Wes fix the roof of this building after every real rain, spreading buckets of paint here and there, but the job is never what one would call 100 percent successful. I suppose that if graded according to school terms the usual performance would call for a C or lower, perhaps C–.

Your special delivery letter made me still more anxious than I had been, if that were possible, to come down to Kentucky at the time of your graduation. That is a self-indulgence that I want very much to gratify, and I think that I shall, but I cannot yet make the absolute promise to myself. You of course do not fully appreciate the gratification of a parent at the successful completion of a course of education by his kid that results in a bachelor degree. Nor can you quite realize just how pleasing the mere formal ceremony of conferring the degree is. It's a thing that I don't want to miss, and you may be sure that I will not do so if it is possible to do otherwise. However, I cannot yet be entirely sure.

Your mother has been cleaning house this week. Washing woodwork, etc. This is a big job. Yesterday with the aid of Alice E., she got the bathroom and sewing room all cleaned. The bathroom shines like new as all the walls and ceiling have been washed. The paper has not been cleaned in the sewing room and of course it does not shine like the bathroom. The two front bed rooms have also been cleaned. Nothing has been done downstairs. Alice E. goes back to school tomorrow while your mother will continue digging at the job.

I went to Danville, Illinois, Thursday to the judicial convention called by the Republican party to nominate Republican candidates for circuit judges of the district. (Judge Marshall is one of the three circuit judges of this district which consists of Vermillion, Edgar, Clark, Cumberland and Coles Counties.) He was renominated at the convention Thursday. A few minutes before the convention convened he asked me to put his name before the convention and I did so. Mr. Jeffries, Fred Moore, Dr. Bisson and I went up in a Lincoln car driven by McArthur. Danville is close to 70 miles from here but there is a slab all the way. We had to drive slow getting into Danville, which is a city of about 50,000 people, our time for the last 8 miles being about 20 minutes, but from the courthouse here to the courthouse in Danville consumed just an hour and twenty-five minutes and our average speed was about 60 miles an hour. We came back in the same time. The highest point that I noticed the speedometer reach was 75 miles an hour on the long straight stretch between Paris and Kansas. I sure like to go fast in a good car with a good driver, on a good road.

As I glance out the window the water is still falling in torrents. I telephoned your mother and she told me it was running in a big stream through the back yard from the cistern corner of the house. Before I left home I turned the water from the house into the cistern and guess that it has run over. Your mother said she would send Alice E. out to turn it in the other direction. Hope it hasn't washed away any of our hard-won new grass.

There isn't any particular news to tell. Suppose Alice E. will tell you of her trip when she writes to you. Your convention is over, I guess, and you are probably relieved but tired. Now comes the final stretch. Get out of examinations if you can. That means to keep your work up-to-date.

May 11, 1927

Well, the May 10th cold snap is here. It is sure raw and disagreeable. The Millers came over for supper last night and I built a fire in the furnace which I replenished this morning. The house would be impossible without heat. After supper the Millers sat for a few minutes, but as we were all tired they went home in time for us to be in bed by 9 o'clock. It was a dandy supper—fried ham, asparagus, cottage cheese, slaw with oil dressing, strawberries and gingerbread.

I don't know where to address your mother, and this letter will be somewhat in answer to hers giving me instructions relative to the planting of the things she got in the mountains. She sure enjoyed her trip to the mountains and I am glad she is "knocking 'em cold."

The mountain plants got in here day before yesterday which was a very rainy day even for this rainy weather. When I got home the rain was falling fast, "and wusn't there a heap of it!" Nevertheless, the plants were apparently in need of a change. So I doffed my business raiment and donned overalls, a flannel shirt and an old coat, and went out into the rain and the mud and set the plants, doing the best I could under the circumstances, both in choice location and in getting roots well-encased in mud. I also became rather encased in mud in spots during the process, and thoroughly wet, but as it was not then cold at all, there were no bad results. I believe most of the plants will live. Your mother's letter of instructions came in the following morning, and I don't believe a change of any of the plants to another locations is required. . . .

Alice E. has been doing considerable society "stuff" lately, partly in Mattoon and partly in Charleston. Mattoon seems to be her destination frequently. I was at the golf club Sunday. The golf course is now a real course, taking much walking and many strokes. I was in unusually bad form, even for me, and used 75 strokes to get around. . . .

If you happen to see your wandering mother at any time soon, let her read this so that she may know that we are well and enjoying, all the time, the knowledge that she is having a good time, is near you, and that you both can be just kids together again. We are getting along just fine, are remembering that your birthday is getting very close now and are wishing you may have all the happiness which you deserve (and that is much) in the years that are to come to you.

By the way, don't forget to let me know again sometime when the diplomas are to be conferred. Somehow I lose the dates set for the future—don't carry them very well. When you write me next time I will put it down in a memorandum book, and try not to lose the book.

1928

December 7, 1928

I received your mighty nice letter yesterday and swallowed whole all the good things you were pleased to say with reference to your mother and me. Get this, however: we do know that you two do love us a lot and we are very grateful and appreciative. You may not have thought so because we spend so much of our time cautioning you about your conduct and giving you sage advice, some of which does not accord with your own ideas. I suppose, though, you have noticed that for some time now our cautionary remarks have dealt more with your physical safety and well-being than with your standards of honesty and uprightness. In fact the latter standards ceased to be of much importance as a topic for discussion with you and Alice E. a good while ago, for we realized that they had been fixed at a high place leaving nothing further to be said.

But as to your physical condition your ideas have not been so satisfactory. You have been too prone to tax your vitality beyond the danger point and to consider too lightly the danger that attends one in traveling about after dark. You have eaten too carelessly, worried over your work too much, and have shown that you did not fully appreciate the absolute necessity for a strong and healthy body if the mind is to be at its best and happiness is to be secured. I think in all these things you have snapped out of it and can now be depended on to care for yourself. Therefore, there is little need for further lectures.

I was unable to show your letter to the two Alices yesterday for I am temporarily a widower. Your mother got a letter from Elizabeth Pasfield* inviting the two to make a visit, and so they slipped into the Ford yesterday morning and were on their way. They should return some time Saturday. . . Last night I took your advice as to going to bed early and was there at 7:30. I stayed until 7 this morning, not sleeping all the time, but I did rest and feel the better for it this morning.

The *Tribune* has been announcing for two days the winners of the rhyme contest. The second and third prize winners have been announced and two thirds of all others. My name was in neither of the two lists. Really, I want the first prize or none. That's the one I went after and my rhymes were the best I could produce. If my name should appear in the bunch as winner of $5.00 or $10.00 I would be just as disappointed as if it did not appear at all. Yet I don't want you to think I will be disappointed, for I have had full realization that in a contest of wits with the number of others who admire their own wits that must have competed in this contest, it's almost beyond the bounds of possibility that I should win first prize. I was satisfied with the lines I sent in, for the most part, as no doubt every one who competed

*Sangamon County kinfolk.

was satisfied with his own. Yet my point of view may be altogether different from that of those who had to judge. The rest of the winners will be announced tomorrow. I have not let the matter bother me any and in fact enjoyed the competition. I had the pleasure of playing with it, which was in itself worthwhile.

By the way, the fact that people think you must have a tolerable set of parents—people who judge from you and know nothing of your parents—gives us the highest type of pleasure, for the people who form that impression have been looking for an explanation of the good things in your character and have concluded that you would not be explained entirely without reference to your parents. You can see me smile all over when a thing like that occurs.

Well, I must close as stacks of work wait for my attention.

December 13, 1928

I am enclosing a renewal note for the bank, the old one being due Dec. 15. The old one was for $300 and the new for $200. It must have cramped you a good deal to pay the $100 on this note with all the buying which you have had to do. Maybe after the New Year money will not find so many places to go and you will feel easier. Now remember this, *don't* do without food and don't let yourself be embarrassed for lack of money. That sort of embarrassment is very unpleasant, and if you need money I would rather furnish it than have you embarrassed for lack of it.

We are well. It's sure a rainy, bleak day. The rain is coming from the east and that's the very worst sort of rain. You had a long letter yesterday from Mother I think, and I suppose she told you all the news to that time. Mrs. Tolle and Mrs. Rogers and Helen* and a couple of other ladies were over last night, as were Harold and George. They brought a lamp, picture, three silver tablespoons, a clock, two dishes, and looked like Santa Claus when they came in. The green bedroom is rather overflowing. Well I haven't time to write as I had already spent about an hour and three quarters writing some letters at Mother's suggestion and the afternoon is getting by without my doing any work. I begin to fear that I will be a very poor workman for the rest of the month. Take care of yourself and be in fine fettle when you come home so that you can have your full part. That's right important.

---

*Alice E's "in-laws to be," bearing gifts for the impending wedding on Dec. 31, 1928.

1929

January 8, 1929

I am tired of working and am quitting now at 4:30 for the pleasure of gossiping with you for a little while. Time has been slipping by faster and faster and it is almost impossible to realize that already we are more than a week away from the excitement that ruled at home for most of the month of December and was all-absorbing for its last week.

I suppose you have followed the trip of Harold and Alice in letters from them but maybe not, as I don't know that they had your address. They made Terre Haute the first night and did some shopping there the next day. Wednesday I think they went to Vincennes and were there long enough to look over the historical aspects of that town—a thing you will remember we all expressed an intention of doing when we went through there last summer. They then drifted on to Louisville and were there eating at various places and taking in the shows until Monday or maybe until today. I think their next stop was to be Harrodsburg, and they are probably there tonight. We do not know just when they will be home but imagine their trip will be concluded by the 15th.

Warfield got into Mattoon at 2:30 and was met by George, Helen, and Edna, and they spent the rest of the night at Tolle's. Your mother and I drove over after Warfield* through the rain the next morning, and she started home at noon. We have not heard from her or from you and are hoping that you got safely home Friday night and she Saturday night. I still harp on the foolishness of a girl being out after dark, especially in Chicago, and I believe I have harped on it so long and to such good effect with you that only in a case of necessity will you take the chance alone. It's gambling with the stakes too high. Chance of disaster may be small, but when diaster comes it's pretty final. Warfield, I think, was perfectly satisfied with her trip. She wouldn't have missed it, but neither would she have given a nickel for its continuance.

And by the way, you and I both might very profitably follow—not too closely perhaps—Warfield's financial ideas. If we could just mix hers with ours and strike the average, I believe we would be just as happy and immeasurably better off for we would enjoy the feeling of satisfaction which must be the lot of one who doesn't squeeze a nickel too hard, but who yet realizes its material value, and so always keeps a few for the emergencies which seem always to be just around the corner. Let's try it out. Your mother and I promise ourselves a good try at it, and indeed it is "needs must" with us at least for the present. By the way, when you draw a check on me let me know as you used to do for I still have the same necessity for knowing that I used to have.

---

*Cousin from Kentucky and bridesmaid at Alice E.'s wedding.

There have been a good many people who have seen fit to comment on your beauty the night of the wedding. I have always thought you rather good-looking and am rather pleased to find so many who are of my opinion. It gives me some confidence in my own judgment. The *Lexington Herald* copied the *Courier's* account of the wedding adding some comments as a heading. Your mother was referred to as the "beautiful Alice Chenault." You and Baby* and I can have no controversy as to where you two got your good looks. That's one thing we can agree about, isn't it?

January 22, 1929

Alice E. called up while I was resting at home today and asked us to supper. Your mother promised we would come. There is some considerable threat of snow and that perhaps may materialize and keep us at home. I hope though that we get to go, for I have not yet seen the apartment. They have their new davenport and chair and we sent over the walnut drop-leaf table on which used to sit the radio. So they are probably pretty comfortably located by now, and I think Alice E. has been quite interested in her cooking. They came in Sunday night to see how we were and Alice E. was also over Saturday afternoon for a little while. . . .

In your last letter you spoke somewhat pessimistically of your work at Roosevelt school. I know that the state of mind must be temporary with you for you will succeed at it as well as it is possible with the material with which you have to work. To do a good job anywhere takes about all that one has to give and I think that your work is perhaps exceptional in its demands, but somehow, knowing a little of you, I haven't very much doubt but that you will do the job in shipshape.

It is now blowing great guns and raining cats and dogs, and it is very dark though the time is but 4:20. It may be we will be bluffed out of our proposed trip to the apartment in Mattoon. Neither of us is in first class shape and we would not like to be snowbound there. The weatherman predicted snow by night. It is still warm but may easily become cold. One never can tell.

Well, I must bring this wandering letter to a close. We didn't hear from you today and are always a bit uneasy when there is too long a time between your letters. Will you make a bargain with me? I like to write to you at least once a week, and I will agree to do so regularly if you will write home twice a week. We do feel that we should hear from you at least that often because you are there in the suburb of the great wicked city and all, all alone. A

*Alice Elizabeth.

goblin might get you or something and we not know it for a week. You know how parents imagine all sorts of things when they don't get a letter at the regular time.

Well the rain is about over and way off in the west is a golden rift in the clouds. Prospects for the Mattoon trip are decidedly better.

January 29, 1929

We had your letter with the enclosed pictures of you and Phyllis and enjoyed it so much, especially as it gave a very attractive estimate of your home surroundings. Alice and Harold were over last night and Alice announced that the picture of you was hers and she intended to take it to Mattoon with her. I told her gruffly to get her own pictures and keep her hands off ours. I also tried to keep an eye on her as she left, but it wouldn't surprise me if she got it. You know how kids are.

Your mother and I drove to Mattoon Sunday afternoon to call on them in their flat. We found them at Mrs. Rogers' where they had taken dinner and went from there to their flat—pardon me, their apartment—and talked awhile. Homer came in a few minutes before we left. They told us they had nothing in their larder for supper, and as it had snowed some while we were there and we wanted to get home before night and were "sorter" hungry, we came on home.

The Ford behaved beautifully on the slab and we came about 25 miles an hour, being a bit careful on account of the snow. As we turned off the slab onto Division street the car skidded a bit, and as we started down the hill there by the schoolhouse your mother and I both thought we had better go into second, which I did, and at the foot of the Hospital hill we decided to go into low. Well, we almost never got to the top; the wheels turned but didn't get anywhere and I was from one side of the street to the other, but eventually got two wheels into the gutter on the right side and crawled on up. I don't care for driving in the snow.

Yesterday was pretty, and your mother drove to Mattoon and got Alice early in the afternoon and we had a good supper of steak, french fries, peas, and carrots, salad and biscuits which was ready just as Harold showed up. After supper we played bridge and Alice E. and I tried to show your mother and Harold up but they showed us up good and plenty. . . .

Take care of yourself. Your picture shows you in good condition. Let us know occasionally of your successes and failures in your school work.

February 4, 1929

I have gathered from the newspapers during the past month that the vicinity of Chicago has been a cold place in which to live. It has been, as somebody put it, just one cold wave after another and I reckon you who live there have become immune to the cold down here in the south. January was also a real winter month. I believe I shoveled more coal into the furnace and carried out more ashes than I ever did in a single month before. The last few days the wind has been from the east which is said to be good for neither man nor beast, and though the temperature has not been much below 20 degrees it has been raw and disagreeable.

Alice E.'s curtain material came in Saturday morning and your mother drove over directly after noon to help make the curtains. The job turned out to be rather difficult and by night was a long way from being done. So we (I went over on the bus for supper) brought most of it back with us, and Alice E. comes over on the bus this morning to help the work along. Harold will come over for supper here. We had dinner yesterday (your mother and I) at the Eat restaurant. After dinner we read the newspaper and finally went for a drive. Had enough when we got to Ashmore and came on back, calling for half an hour at the Millers', where also were Dicky Winter and his two subjected parents. The Millers and Winters went to a musical program at 5:00 at the Presbyterian Church, and your mother and I went home where she read and I wrote an income tax report after which we had a dairy lunch and read awhile, then to bed early. It was a rather uneventful day.

Your mother and Alice E. talk of driving to Chicago to bring you back on the 21st. I suppose the weather will have something to do with the success of the plan. If the groundhog is right it will still be winter then. At least he had the opportunity to see his shadow here.

If Chicago were just about 100 miles closer it's a cinch that your mother and I would spend many a Sunday driving up to see you, but 400 miles in a day is just a bit too much for us to undertake. It is on a Sunday that we are most anxious to see you somehow, and you are most in our minds. When you finally settle down it would be mighty nice from our point of view if it could be within driving distance for a day—going and coming. So often we give the Sunday to that use. When it wouldn't be at all convenient to give more than a day.

There isn't any real news to tell. Take very good care of yourself because we want you to do so. It is not, I think, in your nature to give much care to yourself because of self-interest, but I believe you will be more inclined to do so because you wish others who are interested in you to be happy. Therefore I do not appeal to your self-interest but to your unselfish character. We enjoy your letters, first to know that you are well and happy, and second, to know such of the details of your life and work—whether entirely successful or not—as you care to give.

February 13, 1929

I haven't any particular news to tell, or advice to hand out. We are all well. Weather conditions justifying, the Alices will drive to Cicero next Wednesday, the 20th, picking you up at your *school building* where *you* will *wait* for them. If they are unable, after having started to get to your school building at a reasonable hour, they will wire you, but if they leave here at all they will leave in time to be there when school lets out.

The Alices drove to Champaign yesterday where Alice E. had her picture taken in wedding gown and veil. I think she is to get the proofs tomorrow. We may drive to Jacksonville Thursday. That also depends on the weather conditions. I want a rest from teaching the Women's Class (Mrs. Miller's) at Sunday school and I think they want a rest also. Then I would like to see the farm tenant also before March 1. Old Man Winter is a real hard old codger this year and there is no telling what his next trick will be. He has a bag full of tricks, it seems. Well I have been disturbed for a quarter of an hour, and a letter so interrupted usually becomes disconnected and unsatisfactory. If we go to Jacksonville will take the H. V. Tolles.

Your mother told me last night, Alice E. had a short letter from you yesterday I believe. Alice E. is writing her letters of appreciation of wedding gifts. This was too long delayed but better now than not at all. I am sorry but I have to close this letter, entirely unsatisfied with it. Remember us to Pat and Phyllis, and we send you our best love.

April 26, 1929

I take it that our end of the correspondence with you has been sadly neglected and so I am writing now that you may have word by Sunday that we are well and our negligence cannot be attributed to sickness by one and watchful waiting at the bedside by the other of us. We have had a lot of rain and it most seemed for two or three weeks that the wind was pegged in the east . . . and since the pleasant summer days of March we have had to keep a fire going practically all the time. For a while we work industriously carrying wood in to the fireplace and then, when we cannot stand the chill of the rest of the house, we put a fire in the furnace and fume about having to do so after most of the white woodwork has been washed and most of the house cleaned.

Your mother has been doing it all herself and is now getting along toward the finish. I offered to wash the kitchen ceiling. You know the kitchen ceiling and walls carried a heavy accumulation of greasy smoke, and everything in the kitchen, ceiling, walls, cupboards, stove, etc. had to be washed. Well, I got a special cleaning mixture and one night started in on the ceiling. In a couple of hours I had cleaned about a third of the ceiling—streaking it up somewhat—and had a crick in my neck that was unbearable. It made your mother ache just to watch me. And so I had to stop for that night and figured it would take me three hitches to clean the ceiling. The next day when I got home the ceiling and walls were all clean and even the streaks I had left had been taken out. Your mother had done it and didn't seem very tired and by the end of the next day, which was yesterday, the woodwork, stove, floor, cupboards—inside and out—had been cleaned. How she does it I don't know.

This morning when I looked out over the back lawn at 6 o'clock the sun was shining brightly and I believe the yard is at its prettiest in the early morning light; the grass and flowers and foliage have a wonderful charm at that time, the dew glistening in the sunlight. It's still pretty cold though I wore no overcoat to the office. The wind however is in the northwest and if it will only keep away from the east we should be content.

We have enjoyed your letters a great deal. Your mother says for you to wait other orders concerning the "pine tree" rug. We too are counting the weeks before you are to come home. Soon we will be counting the days and soon after that we'll be seeing you and worrying about your driving the car and in general enjoying you. . . . The house is about ready so you all can drive down anytime and find it and the yard attractive. We are expecting the Kruegers and you and Mrs. Mathews and Pat between now and vacation. Give us warning if you can, but if you can't, come on anyway.

P.S. Our offices have been thoroughly cleaned, new paper, new paint on the floor, the shades reversed, the curtains washed and my desk, since it was refinished, stands out—a beautiful piece of furniture.

April 30, 1929

I am sending this with the pin and with the hope that the pin my reach you in time for the use to which you wish to put it. We sure are planning big on the visit you and the Kruegers are to make on the 11th. We will pick you up in Champaign on the 10th, and early on the 11th the Kruegers will show up and we will have a great day.

Harryman and Eleanor were at the Country Club lake yesterday morning and had quite a bit of sport with the fish. They caught several good bass. The funny part was that they had no bait but worms. It's unusual for a bass to be tempted by a worm. We should have minnows for both bass and croppie and I don't know just how I am to get some minnows without getting my feet wet. Am getting a bit old to wade around as Charley and I used to do, but reckon I can do it once each spring without getting hurt, and if Herb will take one end of the seine we can get the minnows and you or Alice and Harold or all of you can play golf while Mr. Krueger and I feed the fishes. How does that sound?

They say the golf course is fine and they are using all but one or two of the permanent greens already. We have not tried it yet, for as is so often the case, there is something else to do when otherwise we might. Housecleaning is over and your mother is now painting the porch furniture. She is sure in good health and full of pep. The funny part is that the busier she is the more life and strength she has.

There isn't much news and I haven't very much time for writing today. We were at Normal College last night to a reading—an invitation affair held in the art room. Alice E. and Harold were also there. It was very good indeed and, as I prepared with a couple of cups of real coffee, I enjoyed it thoroughly. Sunday noon we had dinner with the Arthur Craigs. I taught her Sunday school class and she prepared the dinner.

September 21, 1929

I started to write you a letter a couple of days ago and after I had written a page and was beginning to draw the letter to a close, it dawned upon my memory that I had only that morning mailed you a letter from your mother who must have told all the items with which my letter was concerned. So I tore mine up regretfully and added another unit to the column of figures in Life's record book entitled "wasted effort" and eventually to be charged to profit and loss. Since then but little has occurred. Harold and Alice were over for supper night before last. The supper was built around calves liver and onions. As we are running a furnace fire and the house is mostly closed, faint reminders of the supper still linger around the house. . . .

Yesterday Mother's card club had their terminal dinner at the U. S. Grant in Mattoon and afterwards their business session to plan for big things for the coming winter. . . . The business session as reported was animated and more than touched and tinged by the personal characteristics of the participants. I think you would have much enjoyed the reports made fresh from the scene of the conflict. Apparently the matter of prizes caused most contention, closely seconded by conflicting views as to whether the meetings should each begin with a luncheon. Laura, not wanting either prizes or luncheons, thought best to withdraw. Her conclusion is still open for her reconsideration however, and the general opinion is that the prize question may again be reviewed.

Last night the Millers and the Kellys took their supper at the magnificent food emporium called the "The Eat Cafe." It was the 24th anniversary of the Miller wedding and after partaking of the viands served to us there, not with any particular enjoyment, except such as arose out of the human association, we went to the Digbys where, the crowd being supplemented by the Barnfields, we had two tables of bridge until 10:30. Then home and to bed. Such are the simple annals of the Kellys, so far as their social life is concerned, since your mother wrote to you. . . .

There isn't any other news. The Tolles are still industriously planning to build and I believe their plans have been submitted to contractors. Byron has gone to school and Normal is in full blast here. We are certainly glad you are so happily situated, both as to your work and home life, as your last letter indicated. A little extra weight is very becoming to you and the German cooked dishes seem to be the right diet for you. I, too, am still putting on a little weight—veree, veree slowly but still steadily and I am much pleased with my progress so far. My ultimate aim is to outweigh anyone of the Kelly quartette and thus my aim is high, but it may be possible to hit that mark. Well, write as often as time and convenience and inclination unite.

September 25, 1929

Elizabeth Pasfield called Monday night by phone and urged your mother to go with her to Kansas City for a visit there of ten days, to make the trip in Elizabeth's car from Springfield on Saturday the 28th. We took a day to decide and because of the fact that the trip will furnish a chance to see Barnett* and so find out how he is making it, we were much inclined to accept. Last night we called on the Tolles and they undertook to keep house for us while your mother is away, and so your mother is to go to Springfield Friday and from there to Kansas City on Saturday.

There isn't much other news . . . . The ground has been as nearly without moisture as I have ever seen it, as there has been not enough rain to settle the dust hardly at any time since you came home from Kentucky.

Your mother and Alice E. were out hunting furniture practically all of Monday, traveling at least 100 miles and returning with a picture frame and a chair, both old, for which they paid 25¢ each and having had a lunch of cheese and crackers along the roadside for which they paid 20¢. It is remarkable what the automobile tempts one to do. Well now, child, take good care of yourself and have a good time both in and out of school.

---

*Barnett Young, a Missourian—brother-in-law of J.Y.

October 4, 1929

. . . . Your mother is still away and we do not yet know when she will leave Kansas City. Barnett called on her a few days ago, and I have not heard from her since his call. . . . She was very thoughtful to let us know by special delivery mail of her safe arrival.

There is practically no news. Your visit home from my point of view was just about perfect, though of course your mother's absence was inopportune, yet we think she was enjoying life and I know we were. . . .

Alice E. and I were out in the woods about an hour a day or so ago. We marked several white oaks, and jack oak, some sassafras trees and some bittersweet vines which we may move later on, part for planting at home and part for Mattoon. It's considerably back from the road on a lane which would be no good in real wet weather, so weather conditions will settle the matter, I think. We got a pretty good bunch of bittersweet berries and the neighborhood looked fine for quail hunting, though we saw none.

There was a church dinner Wednesday night which Alice E. and I attended. We took along as our contribution two squash pies made by A. E. and some sandwiches and in return we got a good meal. . . . Alice E. went to the Teachers College from here to consult Miss McKinney about something, punctuation I think, of something she had written.

Well, take care of yourself and always let us know how to reach you whenever you make a change.

October 29, 1929

I have two reasons or excuses for writing you a note. One, that I had a mighty nice letter from you which I enjoyed much and would be delighted to answer at length if I had the time, and two, that I today sent you by prepaid express a box well-wrapped up and containing a fancy pillow and your rubbers and raincoat. We are managing to keep pretty busy, your mother trying to keep up the various activities at home and I trying to find the proper solution of lawsuits, and at night we are attending church. The meetings will finish next Sunday and I will be very glad. In such meetings I always feel that I am very intemperate to go every night. In fact to my way of thinking I think one can be intemperate in religion as well as other things. However, tomorrow night we are going to cut church and go the party at the Country Club. . . .

Last night about 11 o'clock, flocks of wild geese began to go over, talking to one another in goose language, keeping us awake and when we dropped off to sleep, waking us up or troubling our dreams. The last batch went over about 5:30 this morning, and it was then light enough for me to just make them out against the sky.

There isn't much news to tell you, nor much time to tell it in. . . . Hope you get here Armistice Day. We will see what the turkey thinks about it.

November 17, 1929

We had your letter yesterday and were glad to know that you got back to Chicago safely. We felt that you had, as neither the school authorities nor Mrs. Ray* had made any inquiries and the *Tribune* did not report that your train had been wrecked. I think your mother rather expected you to roll into Mattoon Friday night, but that seemed to me almost too good to be true, and it wasn't true.

There is not much news. The weeks seem to rush by, each one just about as full as the one before—full to overflowing—and yet when done nothing much has happened. Hardly enough to form the basis for an interesting letter. Many old-time teachers and alumni were back for homecoming. Your mother and I had some touch with homecoming events. . . . We went to the show at the School—three one-act plays really better than Mr. Giles used to put on, it seemed to me. The orchestra is good, too, under the leadership of Hassburg. Yesterday your mother went for Alice E. and the two went to Chapel and spent most of the morning at school. Many of the old teachers were on the platform, including Mr. Hankenson. Today Alice E. is coming over early on the bus (Harold has gone a-hunting) and tonight your mother is having a dinner in honor of the Colvins. Miss Ford and the Lantzes will be there. This concludes, I believe, my store of news. By the way, the three of us went to the ball game yesterday and saw E. I. trounce Carbondale to the tune of 9 to 6. It was really a good game and was attended by the largest crowd I have seen at the field. Well, I must close as it's time for Sunday school.

*Mrs. Ray of Oak Park, Illinois, where Emma C. was rooming.

1930

January 31, 1930

Your mother suggested that I ought to write to you once in a while, and as sometimes her suggestions have the force of commands, and as I have been promising myself the pleasure of writing the first time I could find space on my desk vacant of work, and as that condition has happened this morning, I take my pen in hand to let you know that we are well and hope you are the same.

We are now deeply concerned with the prophetic words which fall day after day from the lips of the weatherman. You know this has been a real winter, one of the kind that only happened when we were young, Maggie. The snow, deeply overlaid with soot from a thousand belching chimneys, seems to be with us permanently. There was a bit of melting yesterday and the packed ice in the streets left no chance for friction, yet your mother took the Ford out and after having a tooth filled and her whole stock of teeth cleaned, drove on over to Mattoon where she spent the day with that delightful sister of your delightful self, and came slipping in the back way just before the shadows of dusk changed into the shades of night.

During this cold winter I have almost sprained my coal shovel and there are enough ashes out by the garage to make my driveway perfect forever, so it seems. Therefore, we are concerned with the weatherman. Would there were some way for us to win his favor. If we could only have him to a dinner of duck and all its trimmings cooked by the best cook in the world, the best and prettiest, your mother. If we could do something like that perhaps he would take pity on us and order a dark and gloomy day, without a hint of sunshine in it, for Sunday, and then our winter troubles would be over, and Mr. Groundhog, not seeing his shadow as a frightful enemy after his long hibernation, at a time when he is weak and wobbly from lack of food, would find nothing to disturb him and as a result would stay out of his winter quarters and thus assure us that winter is over. At present we have nothing unpleasant to say about the weatherman. No matter if he has bombarded us with snowballs and pelted us with sleet, no matter if he has driven the thermometer down into the ground and chilled our aging blood. All will be promptly forgotten and completely forgiven if he will only have a heart and cause the sun to hide his face throughout the day on February 2.

There is no news. Of course, you and Alice will enjoy being with one another. Where will you go after your visit with her is over? I suppose you will keep your room at Mrs. Ray's. Alice E. has joined the church choir across the way from her. I imagine it would do you and Alice (Rost) good to join a church choir or some other church organization across the way from you, whatever might be the result to the choir. Think it over. We young people must live our own lives, to be sure, and churches are passé, yet our lives are what we make them and such as they are, they are our own. True education, as I have frequently orated, consists in a proper understanding and appreciation of values, and the application of such proper understanding and appreciation to our life as it is lived. Think that over, or in other words, put that in your pipe and smoke it, or, to be more explicit, chew on that awhile. It's a mouthful, isn't it? I can't laugh it off, can you?

Well, I have wandered on for the full limit of the time I have at my disposal and have said nothing in the way of news. You don't know, for instance, that we had a fine letter from your Aunt Virginia yesterday and she and hers are well; and that she hears that her mother is dead-bent on going to housekeeping though she is perfectly located as she is with a radio—all electric—and everything, and couldn't keep a house thirty minutes. I wonder if there's anything in that name "Chenault" that has a tendency to make one who bears it want to change from the thing he is doing to something else, from the shady spot along the bank of the river to another because it looks a better place for worms to do their bit.

Well, write us a letter, child. We enjoyed your visit home, and it seemed shorter than any visit you have made.

February 8, 1930

Here it is Saturday again and I am reminded that I have not given myself the pleasure of writing to you this week. It is true that there has been very little in my life that is worth writing about, and in fact, practically nothing that would be of interest to you except that we are and have been well, yet, though there is nothing to write to you about, I still like to do so. Your mother has been to Mattoon a couple of times, once in her own car and once with Laura. And Alice E. has been here once. She came over that time to get your mother to help dye some goods for her rug. And was good enough to stay all night and your mother drove her back to Mattoon the following day. She and Harold were also here last Saturday night for supper, and the Waffles and Hughes came in after supper and we had some bridge as it is played in Charleston among the highbrows.

The night Alice E. stayed with us, Wednesday I believe, your mother and I invited the Stovers to go to a picture show, "Chasing Rainbows." It was fairly good but left no permanent impressions. In fact, just at this moment, I do not recall what it was all about. "Hallelujah" left an impression, but one which I would prefer not to have made. I am not one of those who is at all anxious to hear of or see the brutal side of nature. Enough of that is forced upon one's attention anyhow, and I would rather keep in mind the ideal, so far as possible, than the unpleasant real. If one gazes too long on that which is horrid, may it not cease to be horrid? Therefore, I didn't like "Hallelujah."

Your mother's quilt is making remarkable progress. There are two reasons: first, your mother is very deeply interested and second, Miss Petran is equally interested and can hardly wait to get home from school to see what progress has been made. Miss Petran's interest is such that she has to be in on the planning of what is to come next, and between the two a quilt is being developed which is certainly a credit to the architects, and the pace is speedy. You'd be surprised. Am certainly glad you and Alice Rost can have a month's visit. Now be careful and don't either one of you spoil your friendship. Sometimes a beautiful friendship is spoiled by too close associations. You have read stories of men shut in together for weeks at a time who were ready to kill each other before the end. Well, I must close though there has nothing come to my mind to write about.

March 10, 1930

Your mother told me to write you something this morning and I don't know exactly what it was especially, so will tell you about all I know of recent happenings and maybe will thus inadvertently obey instructions. I left home about 7:45, having looked at the gas, oil and water in the car and brought it around front. Alice E. had gotten over in the 7:30 bus and your mother and aunt were washing up the breakfast dishes and Alice E. was drinking coffee and eating bacon and eggs. They were in the state of excitement that is usual with them when starting on a long journey. They expected to get going at 8 o'clock and I presume they did get started by 8:15 or 8:20.

The Ford has been entirely overhauled so far as engine is concerned and it's quicker than it ever was, quiet as a purring cat, and as we had it washed a day or two ago, looks trim and efficient. It seems, so far as appearance goes, to have stood up much better than most Fords and, believe-you-me, it's in fine mechanical condition. We wouldn't swap it, even for a new Ford, because we know its habits, etc. They might be in Indianapolis by noon, but the best car may go wrong and I reckon that might happen to our Ford. Your mother and Alice E. expect to be back Wednesday night.

I am enclosing the Eastern letter you asked for and also a copy each of the *Daily Jim* and the *Courier*, which give pretty well the truth as to the Bank matter. The *Daily Jim* is a bit overdrawn perhaps in some minor details. The failure took the town by surprise—really shocked the people. "Shock" is not too strong a word. It was touch and go for the last day or two, but those of us who knew the condition kept our mouths shut, though the rumor was out sometime Friday and the absorption was completed just in time to save the financial situation of the town. We paid your note a day or two before, so your paper didn't come up for consideration. There is considerable loss to the stockholders of the First, of course, but I had no stock there and have no personal loss. Depositors are to be paid by the National Trust. Well, I have been interrupted and my spare time has gone.

March 27, 1930

Yesterday the "Line" had some clear comments about the storm through which you are still slipping and stumbling. I wish you would sit down and write me your own account of it and see if you cannot produce something bright and clever. I have confidence that you can. Sometime when I get to it I am going to write about the sycamore tree and the river.

When your mother and I got the sycamore tree a week or so ago I think I found out why the tree can survive right at the bank of the river, year after year going safely through the freshets when the waters swirl around and tear at its roots, and I think there is material for a poem in the relation of tree and river. In the end of course the river always wins as year after year it claims the fallen trunks of such trees, but the sycamore often will come through until its great bole is hollow from base to branch from age and the ordinary chances of tree life ere the river loosens its roots enough in the dirt to topple it into itself—and the river goes on and on forever.

There isn't much news with us. We are snowbound here, but not so seriously as you. The Mattoon road is still unopened I believe. Your mother is anxious to get to Mattoon to help Alice E. with her curtains and one thing and another and if she can, will go over on the bus today. Yesterday she spent in giving your room its spring cleaning, and we went to a picture show last night which was fairly good. It was a Mexican scene, supposedly, in colors, and I believe the star actress was Bebe Daniels. As usual, I can't recall the name of the play.

I have been thinking some about the 18th Amendment. In my judgment, which I think is well-based, intoxicating liquor is the most dangerous thing to character with which we are wont to toy, though there are many things dangerous to character and happiness. As one goes through life one comes into contact with pretty much all that there is in life of good, bad and indifferent. One cannot hope, indeed one would not want to be cloistered and never come into contact with anything not worthy and beautiful. A character so formed would be the most insipid, I think, possible. Yet familiarity does produce indifference, both to good and wise. The old saw has it that familiarity breeds contempt. Intoxicating liquor has, as Solomon concluded, the sting of a serpent and the bite of an adder. The danger, or rather one danger, lies in its treachery. When one least expects it, who dallies with it, he has for the moment lost his reason and, being without reason, makes a false step that puts him out of the running for the rest of his life. Some people have in them the tendency to become subject to it—a slave to it—as it used to be put. That is not so very important, for that only leads to a rather unpleasant death. It's the deprivation of reason and the results which may follow which are more to be feared than anything else. I think, too, there is danger in one getting into his character so great a familiarity with evil that nothing in life remains worthwhile. I have a fool notion that happiness comes from oneself. One must find happiness if at all, in his own character, and character is made up of that which has become so familiar and common in his life as to become indeed a part of the individual.

In the *Literary Digest* poll I have hardly known how I would vote. A police regulation ought not to be in our Constitution. I was opposed to ever putting it there. Yet when I look back on the old saloon, I don't know whether it's right to draw back or not. The saloon was a legalized place which was used for the germination of crime of all sorts, and many of the best lives and minds were also ruined by too much drinking as well. We see practically none of the effects of bootlegging here and of course conditions here are far better than under the legal saloon. It may not be so in Chicago. In the old days saloons had their side doors and booths for women, or most of them did. Drinking by women is not entirely a new thing. It was old when I was young. Its results were more serious with women than with men as is also true now. But from the saloons were coming day after day the stream of wrecked lives. I can't believe conditions are as bad today as then. Yet the police measure ought not to be in our Constitution which is composed of fundamental principles of government. How should I vote?

Well, I don't know how I got started on this subject, but I have used my spare time and will have to close. We sure enjoyed your visit and the candy is fine and lasting beautifully. I had a cold and headache when you left and they continued for a couple of days and I have eaten only three or four pieces, but your mother has been eating a piece or two a day and finds that it's a great help to have it around in housecleaning time. Write when you can. You are too thin; watch your eating and sleep more for awhile.

March 31, 1930

This is not going to be a letter. Your mother intended to write you last night, but callers came and when they left it was bed time and we were tired as our day had been full. We went to Sunday school and church, ate lunch downtown, read the paper, got out the Ford and made some calls, drove to Mattoon and got home at 6 o'clock. Didn't see Alice E. Her home was not prepared for callers and her plan was to be away from home. We didn't stop to see. Sure enjoyed your letter about the big snow and your experiences. I thank you for the letter. It was well-done and I believe worth the effort to do it well. We thought so much of it that I sent it to my mother with directions to return it to me.

Your mother asked me to send you the enclosed newspaper clipping. We had the best supper I have ever eaten at the Church and I have had some good ones there. After the trial Mrs. M. Miller presented the book with remarks that ought not ever to be said of a man until he is safely dead and past the chance of making any fool mistakes. I was horribly embarrassed and at a loss for the proper words to express my appreciation. The trial was mostly impromptu and screamingly funny. As a witness I tried (an easy and natural job) to appear feebleminded but couldn't resist a chance which presented itself to insert a remark at an appropriate or inappropriate place, which about wrecked the crowd. Mrs. Arthur Craig, who was on the jury, has sore sides yet. The whole thing was funny, and I was not the only goat of the occasion. The funniest part to me was the line-up of lawyers. You will probably understand this reference.

There is no news. Your mother has been working the past three days including today making curtains for Alice E. She was the first to go in a passenger car over the Mattoon road Friday after the big snow, and it took her an hour and a half to do it. I won't describe, after your letter, the snow here. It was bad, of course, but after the returns from Chicago were all in, we concluded that the snow we had didn't amount to very much. It was a record, of course, but stacked alongside of your unique snow, was merely an incident of no particular importance.

We plan to go to Kentucky the morning of the 9th and return the evening of the 14th. Should you wish to reach us in the interim, you can get us, if plans work out, c/o Thomas G. Kelly, Second National Bank Building, Cincinnati, the morning of the 9th, as we expect to eat lunch with Cora and him. The 10th and 11th at Georgetown and the 12th and 13th at Mount Sterling, in c/o the relatives at either place. We expect to pick up your grandmother and possibly Virginia at 3360 Broadway, Indianapolis, the afternoon of the 14th.

We are well, and as this is the third of the letters which your mother planned to write yesterday, but did not, and which I have written this morning, my time is up and I will have to bring it to a close. Let us hear often and enjoy life as much as you can consistently with good school work, etc. Lots of love. Have you cooked up the next excursion? These excursions bring the brightest parts of the months to us.

April 7, 1930

I am sending you Saturday's *Courier* because Mother thought there were some items in it of interest to you. We were glad of your call Saturday night but sorry for your toothache and that you were "sort of" homesick. We get homesick for you too, and almost count the days between excursions. It would have been nice if you could have arranged to go with us, but suppose you cannot do it as it would mean two weeks loss of time which is a good deal to pay—more than we expect the whole trip to cost. We plan to take lunch Wednesday with Tom and Cora and supper that night in Georgetown. Then two days there and two in Mount Sterling, a night in Indianapolis and home Tuesday morning. Alice E. is also, as you are, torn between two fires. She and Harold are giving every minute of time to fixing up their house and begrudge all loss of time. Yet she wants to be a passenger with us. Don't know what the result will be. We plan to leave about 4 o'clock Wednesday morning as it's a long drive to Cincinnati for lunch.

There isn't any news. Lots of love. Hope you are not homesick this morning. When you are, we feel like just telling you to quit teaching and come on home for good, but wonder if that is really what you want.

April 24, 1930

I have been sitting by the back window and back radiator in Judge Dunn's office where I had heat both from the sun and the radiator. There has been no heat from any source in my office all morning, but as I sit down to write this note I feel heat coming from my radiator. A little thing to write about, but though the sun has been shining, the wind is in the northeast and the thermometer was at 40 this morning.

We are well. But Mrs. Dunn, as you probably know, died yesterday morning at 5:30—just passed away quietly in her sleep. Her death was not anticipated as a probability, just as a possibility, and so far as could be told she was suffering no ill effect from the broken leg except that she was still confined to her wheelchair. Her death, of course, disrupts our schedule. The funeral will be Friday at 2 o'clock. It would be very appropriate if you are so disposed for you to write a word of sympathy to Ruth. It's true that one is never prepared or ready for the death of one of his own people. It's a shock despite everything that can be done or said or anticipated.

Beyond this, there is really no news, and I will not attempt a letter this morning. I don't know when Virginia and her dog are to come, nor what arrangements can be made for a bed for the dog. Dogs should be kenneled out-of-doors, and only occasionally let in as visitors or callers for a moment, but we cannot have Virginia without the dog, and so the dog has an invitation and will be treated with tolerant courtesy. Lots of love. Again, your visit was all too short. After next year you will have to quit teaching and come home to nurse the old folks—perhaps.

May 1, 1930

I believe May 1 is May day and as I am down at the office close to 7 o'clock this morning and the day is beautiful even for a May day, am going to treat myself to the pleasure of writing you at least a note though there is nothing much of interest to tell you.

Your grandmother Chenault is still with us and I think is enjoying herself quite well, though at this time of the year, as you know, the yard absorbs us from 5 o'clock until dark, and at times I think she thinks it's a long time till supper, and maybe she gets lonesome too as it's rather difficult to get her out in the yard to watch us messing around.

Suppose your mother or I wrote you that we have made a small addition to the rock garden—a little extension which comes up toward the house with a view to giving that particular garden a little more pronounced appearance when seen from the house. We have procured some pansies and petunias in bloom and they have been planted in the flower garden—which seemed to bring it out at once and it almost appears as if it had been there for a long time. The iris is coming into bloom and the whole place is now beautiful. The Stovers and we are still planning to go over toward Indiana and try to get some beech trees. This time we plan to go Saturday afternoon as it seems impossible to go over on a Sunday. It either rains or something else prevents as we have discovered in the six weeks that the scheme has been on our minds.

Your mother was in Mattoon yesterday afternoon. Alice and Harold find their time absorbed by the yard and the furniture that has to be painted, etc. Both seem to have a strong and continuing interest in getting their place in fine shape both inside and out. Their grass seed has sprouted and is coming along fine. Their driveway must be fixed. Harold is making screens for the windows and of course, they will want to screen the back porch. The bedroom set is being painted and the dining chairs and table which need finishing just have to go till a more convenient season. I seem more anxious to see them finished than most anything else about their house, but other things are much more pressing for attention. Have now written about all I know.

Sorry you are not to get a chance to change schools next year. Two years is certainly enough where you are and no teacher ought to be expected to take more of that particular work. We are well. It seems quite awhile already since you were home and the next excursion seems a long way off. It sure is good though to have you home, even for a day or two, every month. You bring quite a bit of sunshine with you.

By the way, I cannot close without adding a bit of advice. A letter from me would not be complete without a touch of that sort of thing. You were thin when you were home. It's becoming to you, and you looked very charming, but a bit more flesh is a bit more becoming and makes you a bit more charming. So look to it that you get your nerves quieted and take on some flesh. A word to the wise is sufficient.

May 6, 1930

Big doings at the Kelly homestead. It has become a bathing resort for many of the feathered tribe. Two squirrels are disporting themselves in the trees, on the roof and, as Judge Cofer would say, "around and about," seeming anxious to play with me when I threaten death and destruction, not being able to understand that I actually want them to cease trespassing on our grounds. The place is spotted with brilliant colors of flowers massed in spots or blooming singly. The back porch was all cleaned and dressed yesterday and this beautiful morning was a perfect setting for the breakfast table.

Virginia came yesterday—with the dog. The dog is rather attractive in a way. Already she knows the place thoroughly, and I think she usually is warned to return and she seems quick to leave. When she needs exercise in the house she trots around the circle—kitchen, diningroom, livingroom, hall, library, back to the kitchen. What with her trip yesterday and the bit exploring expeditions over the grounds, she had a big day and was slow to wake this morning, as it is reported.

Your mother also is in big things. The Millers, including Mrs. Mike, were over to dinner Sunday. Mrs. Neal entertained for your grandmother yesterday afternoon, and Virginia was here in time to go also. This morning your mother has a bridge and follows it with a luncheon. There is some talk of going fishing and cooking supper on the river bank. Various other things are in the offing for the balance of the week, but I do not know exactly what they are. I think your grandmother will stand up under them beautifully.

Your mother and I had an interesting experience with the Stovers Saturday afternoon. We have wanted a beech tree for some time and for six Sundays had planned to go with the Stovers to get one. They thought they knew where we could find some young beech trees and they wanted one, as did Alice E. Mr. Stover wanted some samples of various kinds of woods also, for use in his classes. The owner of the place where the beech trees might be was the owner of a saw mill in Paris. So we drove to Paris in the Ford and waited an hour there while Stover hunted up a lot of short pieces of plank of various kind. When stacked in the rear of the Ford they filled it up about even with the back seat so that riding there was not too comfortable. Stover then got permission to take some beech trees if we could find them.

The tract of land is just south of "The Pines" about 5 miles west of Paris and we drove there and started into it through a little road that started in, and very soon we saw we would be bogged if we went on and so we spent quite a little time getting turned around. First thought we would have to back out but finally negotiated the turn. Mrs. Stover took off her fine stockings which she didn't want to ruin and put on a pair of old stockings and walking shoes. I had on old clothes. The tract is of 80 acres and is a virgin Illinois forest with untouched growth and underbrush. Nothing has been cut except dead trees. Some trees—oaks—are six feet or more across at the base.

We started in. I followed Mrs. Stover who went fast regardless of poison oak and possible snakes, stooping suddenly from time to time for some interesting specimen, and almost at once the two couples were separated. Beech trees were scarce, though there were some beautiful specimens, the whistling and singing of birds were almost continuous and after awhile we decided to try and find the other couple. The voice did not carry very well and it was hard to distinguish an answering whistle from that of the birds. But eventually we got the replies and learned that your mother and Mr. Stover had located a young beech, and so Mrs. Stover went on and I returned with the spade, wandering from the proper direction a time or two, and dug up the beech. It was a very good specimen and I got almost all its system of roots which we bound in burlap with some dirt. It was growing late and efforts to find another were unavailing, and so we started back to the car.

The tree grew heavy but we got there and loaded ourselves in and the tree out on the running board, with me holding it on and your mother driving. As we came in there was a 40-mile gale of course alongside the car, and the leaves of the tree became paper almost before we got home. They let me out with it and by the time your mother was back with the car it was about planted. We do not know whether it will live or not. It will have to produce a new set of leaves. Hated to do so, but trimmed it pretty close. And we are hoping it will live. Your mother also got some wild flowers and I accumulated some wood ticks. After four of them had crawled out of my clothes onto my neck, I went on the back porch and took off my outer clothes and left them there, and the balance I took off in the bathtub and went to bed. Well, my time is up and I must close. Hurry home.

September 30, 1930

The family had a letter from you—Saturday or Friday—which the family much enjoyed. A paycheck is sure one grand bit of paper. It will surely be a glum time when such a missive is no longer dropped regularly on my desk. We are anxious to know your impressions from registration at the University of Chicago and what will be the line of your scholastic endeavors.

Your mother is quite an apt pupil in art and indeed has a great interest in it. I wouldn't be surprised if it were true that "Art" was her bent in life though she has never discovered it. She is, as you know, artistic in temperament with a high sense of beauty, harmony, balance and the like—elements essential in art. If art was her bent, it's just too bad that she didn't get an early chance at it.

One has to work a bit outside to keep warm these last few days. It has been beautiful and bright but chilly when one is inactive. At nights we sit before the fireplace if we are at home. Yesterday we had a golf game, both playing as poorly as possible, each making 68. I did learn what has been the matter with my driving for three years and can correct it, which should cut my score some. The lake there is at least five feet below normal.

Your mother has telephoned asking me to come home early and plant some bulbs she is now digging up. A garden is just like anything else—subject to change. I suppose that's one of its fascinations. At any rate, something has to be taken up and put somewhere else every once in awhile.

Harold and Alice have been here one night for supper since you left and your mother has been in Mattoon once. Nothing else has occurred since you left—nothing out of the ordinary at all. The bank meeting set for the 7th is absorbing all my waking thoughts as the prospects are that we will be whipped and we have not figured out a way to turn probable defeat into a possible victory. The annual church meeting comes next Wednesday night. Do not anticipate a fight there and am not concerning myself much with its affairs. Lots of love. Remember us to Mrs. Ray, Pat, and Mrs. Boulton.

October 8, 1930

I have just read for the second time your letter of Sunday. I read it yesterday noon but without comprehension as the bank meeting was set for two o'clock and I was, of course, keyed up to the limit. I got more out of the letter this morning as my turmoil is subsiding and while I am not yet near enough normal to write anything in answer to it except to say that your activities looking toward your growth bring to us a marvelous pleasure and we are back of you and your program with the full strength of the Kelly-Tolle aggregation.

Back to the bank meeting which is still uppermost in my system, though its force is gradually diminishing, and maybe it will do me good to write you something about it.

The meeting of the stockholders of the First National Bank was called to consider a resolution of voluntary dissolution which the chief examiner of this district insisted be put to the stockholders with the implication that if it were not passed a receiver could be appointed. Judge Dunn and Mr. Jeffries wished to comply with the request of the government agent and pass the resolution. A majority of the stock was represented by Calvert of Indianapolis, Charles Lee, the attorney, and Rufus Alexander, all of whom have been working up feelings, as we understood, for some months against ratification of the contract between the two banks. The call for the meeting limited the purpose of the meeting to the resolution to dissolve.

Up until just before the meeting yesterday, I had hopes that the opposition might be willing to dissolve if the ratification of the contract did not enter into it. And at 1:30 Lee and I went into conference to agree as to the program as far as we could. We agreed on the calling of the meeting to order, the voting list of stock, that is—the proxies—who was to vote the stock, the permanent chairman, the permanent secretary, and upon the form of the resolution for dissolution. Lee then told me that they would vote against dissolution and I knew the battle was lost before I entered into it.

I made up my mind to avoid all personalities and devote all my effort to dispel as far as possible the cloud of intense rumors that has darkened the financial situation here for the past seven months and rendered the polls of the First Bank the more difficult. So I presented the resolution and moved its adoption. It was seconded, and the meeting was ready for discussion which I opened.

I spoke for an hour or more. I was followed by Calvert who read a long paper, again giving currency to the most hurtful of the rumors and dwelling particularly on the one which accredited Mr. Jeffries with having used his political influence to bring the action of the examiner to require the closing of the bank. Calvert gave in detail the misinformation as to circumstances upon which he reached the conclusion that the rumor was probably true. Mr. Jeffries answered Calvert in a fiery address, denying and denouncing the rumor as a falsehood. I was very proud of him, but his face was a deep red and he was worked up to a pitch dangerous to a man of his age. Lee then spoke in appeal to the pocketbook alone for the stockholders to fight any assessment that should be made against them. I answered, probably at this time, Lee and Calvert—speaking for perhaps half an hour. Ben Anderson and S. S. Anderson talked not at length but well, agreeing with me as to the law and disagreeing with Lee. Perhaps a few others had a few remarks to make. Then came the vote, which I had known from the start, and the resolution was badly beaten at 5:39 in the afternoon. Whether I got anywhere in my efforts to quiet the disquieting rumors I know not, nor do I know what the result will be. All seems quiet in town.

It was a hard day and night for me but not nearly so hard as for Mr. Jeffries, who was so worked up he didn't sleep at all. I slept some. Went by myself to a comic picture show, your mother being at her card club. The picture didn't seem very funny. It was "A Bunch of Nuts" or had a title in which "nut" was a part. Maybe you have wasted time on it too.

Well, I have been interrupted several times and for rather long periods, and I no longer know how far I have got. Here was another interruption. Lots of love. Good-bye.

October 16, 1930

We were mighty sorry to have missed your telephone call the night of the 14th. The next morning Ivins told me that you had called at 11:30. That was a bad break, our staying out so late at night after 27 years of married life. One would think that by this time we would have begun to keep better hours. In this day of telephones it's pretty hard to keep the kids from knowing what we are doing, isn't it? However, we were in good company. The Millers and we had gone to Alice E.'s for supper and before we realized it, had stayed too late, not leaving there till about 11:20. The time had slipped away fast.

The 14th was uneventful. Your mother went to Terre Haute. Mrs. Duncan entertained the card club there for dinner and the morning was devoted to shopping. They had lunch at the New Hotel and left there somewhere about 3 o'clock. And as we were out till late that night it was a long day for your mother.

My work is here now and I am giving all the office hours to it. Mr. Jeffries comes in a time or two each day and unloads what is on his mind about the financial situation but on the whole I am pretty well away from that now, which is a relief. The public reaction and the trend now is toward sympathy for the Trust Bank, a feeling which was lacking before the meeting. As that was the result I sought, I am feeling better about it. Your mother and I had a ride of about 30 miles Sunday, mostly off the hard roads. The trees are pretty now and we were south of Route 16. On our way back we picked up four good rocks.

I don't believe there is any other news. I haven't time for much of a letter. We enjoyed your letter of Sunday. After all, you did do a good many things that day although you did need and have a day of comparative rest. Your mother frequently worries that you may be doing too much, but I tell her you are more than 16 years old, have a mind of your own and a good one at that, have a good viewpoint on life and good judgment and if you find you are going too far, you will just draw back, so why worry, and that satisfies her. There is in fact no answer. We are well. Will try to be home earlier than 11:30 hereafter. Appreciated your effort to call us. Remember us to Pat.

October 27, 1930

First, to get Mother's message written down before I forget it. Mrs. Albert Moore has a friend teaching, I believe, in Oak Park High School—a Miss Anthony who is also very well acquainted with Mrs. Ray. She was here Saturday night and the old chow mein bunch had chow mein at Mr. and Mrs. E. H. Taylor's Saturday night. Miss Anthony is quite interesting. A couple of years ago she was in Russia for some time and was good enough, Saturday night, to tell us of a great many interesting experiences and conditions in Russia at that time. She is an associate member of the 19th Century Club of which your mother thinks you are also a member. If so, it would be well to attend the meeting next Wednesday night for something good is on then, and in addition Miss Anthony would like to meet you.

Yesterday after church the Stovers, Tolles and Kellys went out to Rocky Run, about 30 miles from here—a wild place of much interest because of its unusual earth formations, or rather rock formations, and unusual forest and plant life—and there ate a great big dinner—steaks, pies, potatoes, coffee, buns, onions, tomatoes, pickles, etc. After dinner which was late of course, we wandered around up the rocky creek and over the steep hills till dark. It was a perfect afternoon and very delightful. If you had been along the afternoon's pleasure would have been complete. I don't know anyone who enjoys that sort of thing any more than you do.

There isn't any news. Suppose you filled out a busy week as usual Saturday night and spent a part of Sunday trying to collect the pieces of yourself. You sure have a lot on hand and if you find that you cannot physically get by with it, know you will have judgment enough to call it off. Know you have the grit to go through with your plan but sometimes doubt whether your physical strength will permit. There isn't much news here and I have plenty of work now so will have to close this with lots of love from both of us. By the way, as we drove along yesterday we saw a flock of a dozen or two turkeys and probably we can get a turkey instead of a rabbit for Thanksgiving dinner.

November 18, 1930

Mother gave me a box to wrap and mail to you this morning and I obeyed orders. It contained some sweet cakes which in their original state were very attractive. I tried to so pack them so that they would come through without crumbling. What success I had you will probably know by the time you get this letter.

This morning has been slipping away with nothing done. Last night I put the cookies by my hat so that I could not get the one without seeing the other, and so when I left home at 7:15 in the car this morning to have a rattle fixed, I picked up the wrong hat. As I got to the square I remembered the cookies and so went back and got them. Left the car at the garage and as I got close to the office, I remembered the cookies and so went back and got them. Then wrapped them up and mailed them at the post office. Came back and read the papers sketchily, and Mr. Jeffries was in two or three times to talk awhile. Then I remembered a paper I wanted to take to the courthouse and did that. Then after I got back I remembered that it was time for milk, and so the morning is about gone and nothing has been done.

It is a beautiful morning, as perfect as could be conceived. Would be ideal for hunting—quiet and sunshiny. Don't think I will hunt any this year. We had a bird apiece Saturday night which Harold contributed. They were a mighty nice treat.

Are counting the days till Thanksgiving. And it's getting pretty close. You can't be home long, but we are sure going to enjoy you while you are here. Your letters have been more interesting this year than ever before. And each one shows that you are growing mentally by leaps and bounds. Our only fear is that your varied activities may tax and strain your physical capacity too far; so to relieve us of that fear, you be sure to watch yourself closely and if necessary, put on the brakes. Well, I must close.

December 5, 1930

Well, the memory of the Kentucky trip is all to the good. It was a peach of a trip and you made it possible. If I had been driving the first day the chances are we would have been wrecked. That drive to Indianapolis from Harrodsburg through the rain was a peach. Taking out 15 minutes for your call in Lawrenceburg and the stop for gas, you averaged 38 miles an hour, which was going some. The trip was all right—and the first day out will play no part in it as a memory of an unpleasant day. Its memory will simply be as a difficulty overcome.

There is not a great deal of news with us. Alice and Harold will be over for supper tonight and Miss Kimball will eat with us also. She had a very severe blow yesterday and is thoroughly downhearted. Her job was temporary with a possibility of becoming permanent. Mr. Lord told her yesterday it was definitely temporary. While it paid only $100 a month, yet she wanted it badly as she is in debt for her last school year and her parents are very moderately fixed. She had thought the job had become permanent and had so written her mother—not positively but almost so. Believe me, she was downhearted. We kept her for breakfast this morning and bucked her up so her upper lip is stiff and she has a glimmer of hope.

I am glad Miss Rost is to have an advancement even though it comes through pull. Don't know where or how you and I can exert a pull, but we must try to figure out some way to get an advancement for you, too. For the present, fill your present job good and strong. That will be a good foundation on which to base a pull or push forward. When the back wheels of an auto are on firm ground it moves forward. So it is with anything else. I have been mulling it over in my mind since you mentioned Washington in Kentucky. However, I don't want you in Washington without a real salary of $400 or $500, and that is impossible at present.

Am enclosing your muffler. Also a clipping from the Chicago *Tribune* which bears on the subject we were discussing in Harrodsburg. Well, I must close this now. You sure were a good fellow on our trip and made it possible and in every respect delightful. And the best memory of all is of you and your sportsmanship.

Lots of love,
Affectionately,
Dad

P.S. If you get any idea in your head as to advancement, let me know and I will see if there is a stone I can turn.

December 9, 1930

We had your two letters, one to the family and the other to St. Nick, and enjoyed the former very much. The latter will take some considering. It may be you have been listening to Amos and Andy and got some inspiration for the Santa letter from the letter written to Andy by Madame Queen's grandmother wherein she listed a lot of things which Madame Queen would like to have and expected to get from Andy for Christmas. At any rate there are still 15 days before Christmas, and I ought to be able to make up my mind about something in that time. Your mother said about the only thing you forgot to mention was an automobile, but as I reckon it, you didn't forget, but simply wanted to leave an item or two unmentioned so that there would be a possibility of a surprise.

Miss Kimball's job is to end with the week and she plans to go home not having anything else in sight to do. She's terribly downhearted over it. Yesterday we received our ham from Lillian. It is wrapped in cloth and we haven't unwrapped it but no doubt it will be fine about the time you come home from the environs of Chicago. Your mother spent the morning at school in pursuit of the Goddess of Art and after a small snack at home at noon, she brought me downtown and headed for school again. Her duties there seem terribly exacting.

I note from your letter that you are to give some time to resting and sleeping. At your age those details of life are not of very great importance—so it seems—but when you have less than 50 years to go to see a century plant bloom, they become of considerable importance. It's a good idea though to get yourself in good physical trim for Christmas, for we are liable to sit up till all hours listening to the radio or doing something else while you are here, and you should have something in reserve for such contingencies.

Well, I won't prolong this as there is nothing to write. Your mother, Alice and I went to Springfield last Thursday. They dropped out there and I went on to Jacksonville where I attended to a bit of business for my mother, took dinner at Ed Brown's and chatted two or three of the relatives for a few minutes each. Then back to Springfield where I surrendered the car to Alice E., and your mother and I became passengers.

December 16, 1930

. . . At noon I found your regular Sunday letter and while you said that the week had been full of uninteresting things, yet the things you told of were not uninteresting. For instance, when the Spelling Bee was being held by WBBM our radio happened to be on that station, and we were interested enough to let it stay there until the broadcasting of the contest had to be discontinued. Thus we knew that your school was represented but that its representatives were in company too fast for them. Somehow it didn't occur to us that you might be present. If it had we would have been more interested than we were.

Another thing in your letter which we found especially interesting was that you are to come home next Sunday. Is that possible? We had the idea you would not come till the 23rd, and it seems too good to be true that you can get here a couple of days earlier. And then, the length of the vacation—till January 6—seems better luck than one has any reason to expect.

Another thing of interest is your examination next Saturday. I didn't know you and Alice Rost were preparing for the same examination. I thought she was preparing for a teaching examination and you for your university. If my idea or understanding is correct, it was probably not good judgment for you two to study together, for with such an arrangement the one or the other would find herself profiting at the other's expense of time and effort. Sometimes I wonder if we haven't trained you to be just a bit too self-effacing in our efforts to have you a wholesome, unselfish personality. You are positively both of those things, but isn't it just possible that your very unselfishness may prove your own undoing?

Have you yet anything in mind where it would be possible for me to use any influence I may find to get you in a more satisfactory teaching position? I think it should be there near Chicago University, in a high school. Had thought that Mr. Jeffries would be in Chicago before Christmas and through him and Bob I might get a line on something, but Mr. Jeffries abandoned his plan of going. Mr. Hudson is, as you know, in Harvey. Bob Jeffries is in a far north suburb. Can you think of any other leads? We ought to begin to work on this. You wrote of "respect" with just a tinge of irony, but respect—self respect and respect for others—is about as valued a treasure as life can bring and I believe you know and appreciate that fact as well as anyone on earth. So, maybe, I just read the tinge of irony into your letter.

I judge from your letter that you got your ham from Lillian and hope that it was properly cooked. There is a good deal in the cooking of even the Kentucky ham. The one Lillian sent us will be disposed of while you are here. You are just the type to entertain Catholics* and Jews* on Friday and furnish ham for them to eat. Suppose you think you should not accord their prejudices the slightest notice. However, I think you are all right, for a Kentucky ham, properly cooked, is not a meat but a confection. In its curing and cooking it has lost its original character and has become a creature of art. No Jew or Catholic is justified in associating the finished product with the thought of its origin in a pigpen.

Well, I had better quit. Sunday will soon be here and you with it. That's enough good news for any reasonable Kelly.

---

*Emma C.'s 8th grade pupils—Spelling Bee contestants in Cicero, Illinois.

1931

January 9, 1931

Your letter of about midnight Wednesday night, addressed to me at 820 S. Sixth, was delivered to me at the office a few moments ago, and besides being very much enjoyed by me, served as a reminder that I had promised myself to write you a short letter this morning, not that there is any particular news to tell but that you may at least have a word before Sunday.

It is encouraging to have had responses from several of the schools. But I am wondering how you are to get the influence of Mr. Blair, important as that is, unless you are to refer to him. Perhaps, though, after you have made your applications in the one case, and had your interview in the other, you might write to Mr. Blair a short business letter telling what you have done and containing the hidden suggestion that he might of his own initiative take such steps as should seem proper to him to advance your cause. I suppose you can get such a suggestion hidden between the lines of your letter, if in no other way, by asking what suggestion he would make to you under the circumstances, etc.

Your mother and I have maintained our good humor since you left. She picked up a bad cold Sunday and has been fighting that ever since. And as I have had a cold also, we have been a well-matched pair. However, I am decidedly on the mend and I think she is also. She was working yesterday—at home—on her doll's trunk and has become anxious to finish that. So it will be finished soon. After that she has lots of things in prospect to do, and about every day she is ordering a seed catalogue or ten cents worth of seed.

I have written no Christmas letters yet, but the work on my desk is beginning to clear up and I can get to such things. The car hasn't been out of the garage since Sunday. However, the roads have been slick here in town and there is no pleasure in driving. We are still eating minced ham in one form or another occasionally, but the turkey and the loaf of bread we had when you were here are all gone. It seems to me I had something to tell you or some advice to give, but if so, it has slipped my mind. I do know that there has been no event of any interest since you left.

January 15, 1931

I am well. Your mother has been having quite a siege—headache, cold and generally bad time of it. Yesterday she stayed in bed and Mrs. Francis came to see her. Today she is much better and Mrs. Francis will come again, and I think that will mark the end of her troubles. She ate two of my cakes, a cup of coffee, and half a grapefruit this morning and pronounced her breakfast all to the good, and she is very apparently better. Alice E. phoned this morning that she would call, with Harold, after supper and would bring some soup, but I told her I had made a pot of soup yesterday and we were all too well supplied with that article of invalid's diet. I may even have to eat some of it—or rather inhale some of the blamed stuff to get rid of it. My cooking has rather palled on me but I had a dandy noon dinner at church yesterday—fried chicken and everything. As Dr. Alexander said, the chicken must have been raised by a good, kind mother and not an incubator, for it was very tender. Well, these are the items. We are coming along fine and I really think your mother's troubles are practically over. She will be in bed today, but as a measure of precaution rather than a necessity.

January 24, 1931

I really have nothing to write about, just wanted to send my love in my own way. This morning I heard the red bird before I got out of bed, the first time, I think, this winter. I know I haven't seen him. It is almost spring-like. It was just about freezing point last night and the touch of spring was in the air yesterday, and this morning the feeling of spring is very pronounced, but as January is still here and February is yet to come, this can only, with safety, be considered a mild January thaw of a mild winter. This sort of weather one hardly thinks of Florida or Cuba. Rather does one's thought turn to the lake country of Canada—particularly to Skeleton Lake, for one can easily keep warm in winter but one cannot keep cool in summer here in Charleston.

Am sorry your cough is still with you. With present-day knowledge about such things, one ought to overcome it, if one values an ability to go about seeing things and doing things. Your room here is very attractive but if one had to stay in it steadily for a week, a month, or a year or two, the scenery would become too familiar. So perhaps you had better look after your rest and sleep and overcome the cold or cough while it is yet in its infancy. Perhaps also you had better give a Saturday afternoon hour to an examination to see if you had better give up your work and come down here to get in bed for a month or two or three. I am not saying these things in jest. It would be easier for you, as well as all of us, to take the cough now and strangle it, if it is a dangerous one, than to wait till summer.

We are well. Your mother seems now to have all the excess pep in the world. Yesterday she put in about ten hours of constant housework activity and did not seem and was not tired at night. That's some comeback, isn't it? She is calling on Alice E. today. Well, I must close.

January 31, 1931

I have no news to write nor any interesting story to tell. Your mother is coming along very fine—is out at Normal School this afternoon still working on her doll's trunk. I think she hopes to finish it by spring, anyway. The bookend pieces some child gave you she colored green and antiqued so that they are much improved. We had cabbage and boiled potatoes for lunch today. Yesterday morning and this we had buckwheats—all we could eat. The day is murky.

We enjoyed your short visit a lot, were sorry when it ended, but the memory lingers on—one of the worthwhile happenings of life. Were glad of your note that you were safely back. From the terror of some of the news items from Chicago, it now seems unsafe to be around most anywhere in the Loop anymore. Suppose you had better stay in Cicero as a measure of safety—not go downtown at all. If you are inside you might be blown up—if outside, you might be shot. You will have to write a book sometime about living in constant danger of such disaster, the feeling from moment to moment. Well, I must close this. Remember us to Mrs. Ray and Pat.

February 2, 1931

Ground-hog day and the sun is shining down bright and warm, and no doubt the blamed little varmint will become frightened and break back to cover. It's just too bad—or is it? I understand that those who have gone from Charleston to Florida are disgruntled, being subjected to chilly rains and generally uncomfortable weather, while here at home it is perfectly delightful. Really there is no reason, except that it is only February, for not planting a garden. At noon I told your mother I would leave the office at 4:15 and spend an hour puttering around in the yard and garden. When I was ten years younger, I would have gotten in at least four hours work a day of this kind. Now it's an event for me to make up my mind to work an hour—even though I eventually back out.

Yesterday was Alice E.'s birthday. The Millers, at their instigation, your mother, and I had dinner at Bucklers* and then called for a few minutes on Harold and Alice. We then drove out past Lerna to Toledo, then to Greenup, then to Casey and Martinsville, to Westfield, and home. On the way from Westfield home, we met Harold and Alice who had been out in the byways all afternoon. They went on to Westfield, and all of us met at

*Cafeteria in Mattoon.

home for a pick-up supper. It was a very nice day. It would have been fine to have cooked our dinner outdoors.

The three pairs of gloves came in today. They were too small. Your mother sold one pair to Mrs. Thomas and will send the other two back to the store for exchange. When I went home at noon today your mother was just finishing up a lot of dyeing for rugs and the kitchen was a mess, so I went out, got the axe, and chopped wood for half an hour. We had bean soup and milk for dinner. Don't know what the prospects are for supper. Your mother has really been feeling good the past two or three days and is once more full of energy.

Well, there isn't any news.

February 13, 1931

I looked at the calendar a few moments ago. The day of the week is Friday. The day of the month is the 13th. A double negative makes a positive. Two tokens of ill omen in juxtaposition ought to be a sign of good luck, ought it not?

The occasion of this letter is to let you know that I have just mailed a small box, by way of a valentine, I suppose, the contents of which your mother got a lot of pleasure out of preparing this morning. Wrapped with the box are the two pairs of gloves which were too small to fit your mother. You can do as you please with them, and Mother figures that she will do without until she is in Champaign, Decatur, Springfield, Terre Haute, Indianapolis, or Chicago. Maybe she will wait till she gets to Hamilton. Who knows?

We had a quiet, gentle rain about all of last night, and this morning a melting snow blew along for awhile, but the clouds are beginning to break and it is not particularly cold, just a fair exhibition of not very horrid March weather. Tonight we go to the Iknayans' for supper. He is quite a diet shark, as you know. Probably we will have spinach for supper in some form or another. Seriously, however, I imagine Dr. Iknayan is as well-informed as anyone on the subject of diet. Today at noon I was hunting on the radio for some good dinner music. There was a talker at most every station. The one at Detroit was a "dead ringer" for Dr. Iknayan in enunciation, accent and timbre. He quit after a few sentences however, and I didn't learn the subject of his talk, just a hint that it might have been concerned with milk or dairy cows. Last night the radio was hard to leave. About every station had something good to offer, even after the Red Cross appeal and Hoover had concluded. Some nights it's a pleasure to turn it off, but not so last night.

Your mother was restless yesterday afternoon. She brought me to the office and then acted as a taxidriver for a while, picking up her friends and hauling them where they wanted to go. After she tired of that, she went home and a little after four called me to come take her a-riding somewhere, anywhere. Well, "somewhere, anywhere" naturally turned out to be Mattoon, but Alice E. was not at home and it began to rain a little as we started home, and so we came home in the dark and the rain. We had a good supper and a very pleasant evening as she was no more restless. She had a headache, and after awhile I rubbed her neck to snare drum music and her head quieted. Today she is feeling fine.

I wonder if you couldn't do something really worthwhile with the Shaker history. You ought to get a better background than you have or can get from the books* which Lillian has. You ought to know the origin and history of the Sect. There have been several colonies of them, one in Ohio, I think, one in New York, I think, and perhaps one further south. I don't know where you could get information on the subject. Perhaps Lillian could give you some information, and perhaps you can find some of the history embalmed in the records of the Appellate Court of Kentucky in one or more of the cases in which the Bohons were involved following their purchase of Shakertown. One of those suits was brought, I think, by the State of Kentucky who contended that upon the death of the last of the Colony, the land escheated to the State for the want of heirs to claim it. If you could do a big job with the Sect in a big way, it would make school teaching seem a rather small profession. But before you start to write, I think it necessary that you have your background of facts against which your romance can be pictured with due attention to the setting.

Well, I have wandered on too long and must close.

March 3, 1931

I have been neglecting you, and depriving myself of one of the pleasures of life as well, by not writing you now and then, and today I am not to have the pleasure, as I have not the time of writing you a real letter. We just had a letter this noon from you, and your mother was surprised that she had given you the definite impression that she and Alice E. would visit you the coming weekend. The prospect of doing so was very pleasing to your mother and she has been toying with the idea, but she now instructs me to write you that she will have to postpone the pleasure. She doubts whether Alice E. could come at this time at all.

Then, I have been keeping very short of cash and for some reason or other allowed my cash for the month to go lower than I had intended. Financial conditions are still very bad—there has been no improvement,

---

*Journals of former Shaker Colony at Pleasant Hill, Ky.

and the conditions are touching and rocking financial standing of men here, one after another. Now is no time to owe a dollar, for a little debt can take a lot of property. Wealthy men here are finding real difficulty to secure funds to meet such obligatons as they have. I have in my lock box at the bank the $40 you sent me some time ago and the $80 you recently sent, but I don't want to go into that for a little pleasure just now. As I have cut my cash down so low, may find it convenient to go into that fund for necessaries before my next check comes in, but hardly think so. Believe you me, I am going to watch my pennies from now on and get something laid by for a rainy day, then I am going to put padlocks on it and try to hold it, and you probably have seen enough by now to compel you to do the same thing. It will sure be nice for us to have you here next winter, but I rather imagine that if you have the chance at a good high school job you will go to it and get you a real store of cash as a reserve to back up whatever you want to undertake. The idea of your spending a year in trying out your capacity as an author has appealed to me wonderfully, but I doubt whether you could put it over with the $300 or $400 you will have saved by the time school is out, but that would give you a good start.

Well, I haven't time to go on with this letter. Furthermore, I haven't thought the thing through and what ideas I have are half-baked. Just as soon as I get straightened out in my thinking, I will write all about it. Selfishly I want, as does your mother, to plan so you will be here, but when we think it over, we don't want to tie you down till we have to, and maybe when we are so old and feeble that we have to call upon you, you will be so far along on your own road in life that you can make other arrangements for our comfort. Well, goodbye, lots of love to you. Remember us to Mrs. Ray and Pat.

March 9, 1931

It looks as if I am never going to get a chance to write you a real letter. This morning I was late getting up—woke up early enough but the room was a bit cold and I was comfortable so found considerable difficulty getting out. Eventually I built up my courage and now am at the office and have read the *Daily Jim*.

We enjoyed our talk with you last night. Gather from the papers you have had a good deal more snow than we have had, though there has been plenty here. Saturday I was in Moore's grocery store and there was a mighty nice hen there so I bought her and your mother telephoned inviting Alice and Harold over to dinner. Harold said Alice had the flu so of course we wanted to go over and look her over. After dinner yesterday I phoned to a gas station and was informed the Mattoon road was open so that one could get through without chains. We found the information correct with one qualification, i.e., provided one didn't drive partly into the side drift to let another car pass and stop there as I did. We were all right as long as we didn't stop but when we tried to start, the back wheels merely spun merrily. Our stop was short, however. I got out and tried to help by pushing but didn't have force enough. Somewhere during the stop I fell flat without harming myself and then the car behind offered to bump us out, which turned out to be a successful operation.

The snow was blowing in such clouds that we decided our stay in Mattoon must be brief so Harold put our chains on and I borrowed a shovel and we started home—your mother chauffeuring. Before we got to the same place—about halfway along the north and south strip, we found a line of cars stopped, waiting for what we know not. We waited patiently and comfortably for quite awhile and then five or six cars came through from the opposite direction. We thought we were released, but not so, and we waited not so patiently for a time. Then I took my shovel and got out into the blizzard. The snow was still blowing across so thick that cars had to have lights to warn cars coming in the opposite direction. I went up to the scene of trouble and found the way blocked by a dead car which had waited so long for the trouble to clear up that the snow blowing into or under the hood had wet the points (whatever the points are). So I helped push it in the clear. Back of it was a big Hudson which had come up too fast and in stopping, its front wheels had buried themselves in one drift and its hind wheels in the drift on the other side. I left him shoveling and a couple of other men came up to help so I went back to impatient Lizzy. I was pretty cold and had neuralgia from the wind. Pretty soon the Hudson was dug out and I picked up the borrowed shovel and we came on home without further incident. As soon as I got in I took an aspirin tablet and thus prevented myself having inflamed passages in my head which would surely have resulted otherwise. This morning I feel fine and really, except for the fact that my head got chilled, your mother and I enjoyed the drive in every way.

Well, I've run on here and said nothing and time has been called.

March 11, 1931

I think it's right apparent by this time that it is impossible for you to carry the university work and teaching at the same time. Either job is about all one can successfully worry along with and the two together take too much out of one. So it's necessary to cut out one or the other.

We also think that you should not teach after June in the grade school system—to do so would put you in a rut which you will probably not get out of. So that's that.

A good high school employment may turn up before next September and if so and if you accept it, all of your time next winter will be required to get accustomed to the routine.

If the high school work doesn't show up or if it does and you do not accept it, you will be at home which would be a condition much desired by your mother and me. We would enjoy it thoroughly, but we are still active and not decrepit from age—still in the possession of most of our faculties, and the mere fact that we would enjoy you is not to be considered of importance in your outlook. You will probably have enough money saved by June to carry you through your activities for a year, such traveling as you do and such clothes as you may need, and if that is so, in the course of the year you ought to have acquired all there is to know about the history of the Shakers and to have written something based upon that and the diaries which Lillian has. Thus your year might be made far more worthwhile than several years of teaching, or, for that matter, of studying under the university professors. We will not be able to finance your trips in making this study—to libraries or original sources, but you will have funds enough to do some of that. It may be that by writing to the proper department of the government you would find that the study of original sources has already been made by some government employee or board or department.

That settles the business end of the next year and none of us need think any more about it.

We are well. Alice E. phoned her mother this morning that she is feeling well again and wants to go to a picture show tonight—"Cimarron." Harold is planting another large elm tree. This is the second large elm tree for him recently—trying to get shade for the back porch. The beech he put west of the house. There isn't any news.

March 17, 1931

You are certainly blessed with a fine sense of humor and no doubt it has carried you through many a tough spot. Don't lose it. Your letters have been so full of humor—at your own expense—that we have hardly felt the worry which we would have naturally felt pretty strong to have you sick with the mumps. The mumps is singular in some respects. It is at least singular that you should have got them at your age—well beyond childish things, with a serious outlook upon life—to be teaching, to be studying for a Master's degree, to be thinking of writing a book, and then get the mumps. What an anticlimax! Singular, yes, decidedly so. You have been mighty nice to keep us so well-posted as to its rise and fall.

There isn't much news. . . . My mother's tenant has not paid the rent due March 1, and I think I will drive to Jacksonville tomorrow. Hate to lose a day from the office as my desk is piled high and there's hardly room to write this letter. Have little better chance to write than Andy has with his lead nickel. We had dinner with Alice E. and Harold Sunday and spent the afternoon with them—mighty nice, comfortable afternoon. This isn't intended to be a letter and I don't know when I'll get a chance to write a real letter again. The only way will be to just take time the first thing in the morning some day. . . . Remember us to Mrs. Ray and Pat. We sure appreciate what they have done for you.

March 24, 1931

For fear that I may finish this letter without mentioning it, will start it with the information that I received the bank draft for $50 which you sent to add to your savings account making a total of $170. Looks as if you are due for a fine vacation, if you do teach next year. Perhaps it is wiser for you to teach, but your mother and I were rather hoping you would stand pat and not teach at all if you had to teach in Cicero.

Alice and Harold were over Sunday for a chicken dinner. After dinner we sat around awhile and then drove out along the edge of the river across in the valley which you see as you drive down to the bridge at the dam site. There is some water in the river. At the far bend we found Joe Dodson, and I got out and talked with him.

You know he is our chief river man. He loves it, and his occupation is located upon the river's banks. He is a Hutton township man owning a small farm there. His children are all self-supporting. While they were at home he found his occupation somewhat interfered with by the necessity to provide for them, but in the last few years, having only his wife, himself, his "tin-lizzie" and his fishing tackle to care for (and in winter his hunting equipment), he has been able to move into town and devote all his time to his chosen occupation.

He, as you may not know, was a justice of the peace in his township when a fisherman—a neighbor of his—was brought before him charged with the violation of one of the fishing laws of the State. After an exciting legal battle between the lawyers, and intense interest aroused among the large crowd of neighbors and friends, Joe calmly announced that the State law was unconstitutional (a point neither of the lawyers had thought of sufficient importance to even mention), discharged the defendant and adjourned court.

Well Joe was at the bend of the river Sunday, in his best clothes, looking the situation over. I got out and talked with him as I do always when I get the chance, asked him what the prospect for fishing was, and he said it was poor until the river should get high and remain there two or three weeks, for the fish had a long way to come. Joe was down it a great many miles recently looking it over, and everywhere he found winter fishing going on—which never happened before—with traps, three or four to a mile, and last summer in the dry spell the pools were seined to the limit, so the fish have to come up the river for a long, long distance.

There isn't any news. We are well. . . . Take care of yourself.

March 28, 1931

Your mother is all pepped up and all messed up over a furniture job and consequently has no time to do any writing. The library table has been on her mind for many moons and the Shaker chair for more, the former for use as a livingroom table and the latter just for a dressing up, which of course starts with a complete dressing down. I left her this morning nursing the chair and rubbing it down. After she got the many thicknesses of red paint off she discovered that before it was painted it was deeply stained with a reddish stain that is fairly pretty. She will not attempt to sandpaper enough wood off to remove the stain—just enough to leave the job a smooth even one. The table cleaned down to a beautiful color and finish and she is delighted with it. The top is a sort of oilcloth, and that she expects to convert into wood with the aid of paint and varnish.

We have been rather "socialistic" this week—one night the Millers, Digbys and Barnfields were at home for combination dinner and cards, the next night Miss Ford and Mr. Taylor for the remains of the baked ham and good side dishes and for contract bridge. Last night we were at church for dinner, and as each night of the three the dinner was heavy and accompanied by much strong coffee, our sleep has been insufficient and troubled by varied phantasmagorias of disordered minds.

Your mother wants you to write her whether you will be home Thursday or Friday night. She is planning to have a dinner for you Friday night with some of the younger college teachers if you are home Thursday night. So when you get this letter write and let her know.

Your mother and Alice E. are both very anxious for you to take the trip to foreign shores as you are planning. Me? I am doubtful whether you can get by on $500. That is a big sum for many things, but by the time you have paid your R. R. fare to New York and back, and your steamer, second class, to Europe and back, there won't be enough left to wad a shotgun and you will probably have no place to sleep but jail and nothing to eat but turnips. I do not believe the trip would be a pleasure or inspiration without sufficient money to get a bowl of thin soup occasionally and rent a soft bed to sleep in at least once a week. You never did get a full acquaintance with the necessity for money under most all conditions and the wisdom—in fact, the necessity—for a bit in reserve for use in untoward circumstances. So just this time, before you start be very sure that you are sufficiently supplied to assure a pleasant, or at least a comfortable trip all the way.

If you go it will make no change in our plans. I have my route, financially, for the summer mapped out and will follow it unless something serious comes up to make a change. It requires the use of all my income, and as the bank here is lending no money, I have to depend entirely on my income, but I would not feel justified in changing the plan just for a little trip to Europe, and so this is another reason why you should figure pretty accurately before you start. $500 may be enough. I don't know, but if it were I, there would be no comfort in less than twice that amount. All that aside, however, I would be delighted if you can take the trip. Europe has not the charm for me that Skelton Lake has and so I cannot entirely sympathize with you and your mother in your desire to go to strange places and see and do strange things, but if we were all alike this would probably be a tiresome old world.

There isn't any news much. I can thoroughly sympathize with your feelings before, during, and after your examinations. You simply undertook too much, wore your strength down, caught the first contagious disease that came along and played havoc generally. If you didn't pass, it's all right, for the sky has not fallen in yet. So what's the difference? You enjoyed some of your work, learned something about the limits of your strength, and acquired some scholastic knowledge as you went along. What more would one want for his time, money and effort? So forget it and take pleasure in the present and your anticipations for the future.

Lots of love,
Affectionately,
Dad

P.S. I will go into the June term behind (with cases) for the first time in years. The June docket is larger than usual, so it's going to be a continuous grind to get through early enough to look with assurance for a trip north. Am beginning to get really uneasy, for nothing in my life has ever brought the entire perfect pleasure as our trip last year—a perfect thing in the living—a perfect thing in retrospect.

April 21, 1931

The letter with the two checks in the total amount of $50 came in yesterday, and I read the letter, cashed the checks and put the proceeds in my bank box for you. I also wrote to the County Clerk of Sangamon County at Springfield to get a copy of the record of your birth certificate, and when it comes I will send it to you. Let me make a suggestion about your traveling bag for your trip. Just have a 35 cent handle—like the old one—buckled on to the old grip and bring it home for me. It is just the size and of just the right age and experience to travel comfortably on the running board of the Ford, and if we go anywhere at all this summer, I want it to strap to the running board. My nice new bag I want to initiate by giving it a trip to Europe where it can accumulate much practical experience and knowledge of foreign affairs, and also a bunch of foreign labels. Then after a few years it can graduate to the dignified position of a Ford running board. So we will consider the traveling bag question settled as I suggest. You can get the handle at most any place where trunks and grips are sold.

The yard and garden have been taking most of our time lately, as the weather has been beautiful and spring has burst out like an explosion. The country is adorned with flowering redbud and the dogwood is just coming out. In the yard, the hyacinths, and dwarf iris, the tulips, the flowering almond, the forsythia, the buttercups, and a sprinkle of wild flowers have presented a mighty pretty show. Many shrubs have had to be moved, as usual, from where they were to where they now are. Sunday a week ago, the morning, we spent in the hills and brought home a lot of wild flowers, samples of which we sent to Dick. The afternoon, we spent at Rocky Branch with the Thomases. Last Sunday afternoon we took the Millers to Rocky Branch for the afternoon. Had been out to supper two or three nights the week before and went to bed at 8 o'clock, as nearly worn out as we have been in a long time. Through all the busy days lately your mother has planned to clean house the first three days of this week and get it all done in three days and then join with Mrs. Frank Craig to give a dinner Thursday, I believe—maybe Friday. She had a man engaged who was said to be excellent and fast. Well he was a wash-out, doesn't know how to wash white woodwork or windows, can't see dirt, slow, handicapped by a crippled left hand—he has merely the thumb. By noon your mother was pretty nervous, but all the bedding, mattresses, rugs were out on the line and on the grass. By 2:30, it was raining and everything was got safely in except 2 blankets and a sheet. By 4 o'clock, your mother telephoned me with complete discouragement in her voice and I went home. She had already phoned Mrs. Craig and the dinner was off.

Well the man left pretty soon, paid off and with no engagement to come back, and we went to work to get our bedroom in order. While your mother dressed the bed and hung the curtains, I got out on the roof, washed the outside of the windows and put in the screens there for the summer, and when I came in, the room was dressed and your mother was quieted. That room is in good shape, but otherwise the house is wrecked and this morning your mother has no assistant but has set out to spend the day in her own way cleaning house, having sent out distress signals to Mrs. Hutchison and Mr. Butler whom we ought to have engaged in the first place.

It's cold today and I built a fire in the fireplace but imagine she will keep warm at her work. Hate to build another fire in the furnace as I cleaned the cellar yesterday morning for the summer, and a single fire will have it somewhat dusty. As I can't clean it again with a smile, and as the grass is growing fast and needs regular cutting, and as the balance of the garden is soon to be planted, I sure don't want to build another fire. May have to do it though. This is dogwood winter, and blackberry winter is yet to come and probably there will come a day when we just can't get along without a furnace fire. So it goes in every well-regulated family. It's probable your mother won't find time to write you this week, and you know why.

May 25, 1931

This, as you know, was a most important day in the life of the "Widow Zander." However, it is not my purpose to devote any more of this letter to her affairs. When I went home at noon your mother asked me to read the story of the "Black Gloves", and I did so. Am indeed glad you have made a beginning. It is not to be wondered at that the first story was rejected. I have absolutely no knowledge of the character of stories *Liberty* uses. Think I noticed from the rejection slip that it is one of a bunch of magazines perhaps under the same management, one of which was *True Story*. If it caters to the same taste as *True Story* does, it is not surprising that your story got only the usual rejection slip, for *True Story* wants only gory details. On the other hand, I have read short stories in *Harper's* and one other of the better magazines the name of which I do not recall just now, which rely for their interest upon just the sort of neat turn which your story had—something which requires a bit keener mind perhaps than the average or mine-run of readers of current fiction have.

Your story is well-written and the point is well-made—pointed with a razor blade and not with a dull table knife; and your story has a peculiar interest for me, your father, because I can see in it a bit of your own self—an incident told, perhaps almost putting into words, at least into feeling, a succession of disappointments and negations in your life that may assume a large place in creating a feeling of frustration. Nor am I prepared to urge that these disappointments and negations should not seem of large value to you. However, I do believe this: that your life will, in the proper way and at the proper time, work out into a well-ordered, well-rounded whole and that you will eventually find that much which seemed so disappointing has merely contributed to your full development.

Now, how did I get on that? Merely started out to comment on the story. It's a dandy beginning. You of course could not write a *True Story* story which would satisfy the reader of true stories. *Harper's* and magazines of that class do not cater particularly to fiction. At the start I would eliminate both extremes from the list. The class of stories in the *Saturday Evening Post* is good—nothing abnormal, but always of interest and usually well-written. You cannot write the Darky stories or the lawyer stories, or any of the stories pertaining to specific subjects. The standard stories of romance or mystery you probably could do, but it seems to me that you are in daily contact with something—a part of young America in the making—out of which stories of intense interest could be built, perhaps serving a better purpose than mere fiction is intended to serve. There ought to be incidents occurring day after day around any one of which could be woven a story of fascinating interest—not fascinating because of love and laughter in it, but of malice, hate, cunning, etc. Well, I'm not a writer and should not presume to make any suggestions. Am sure glad you have started. Keep up the good work.

Not much news. Your mother went to Mattoon for Alice E. this afternoon. She is to stay the night with us. The four of us were in the woods yesterday afternoon. We are all well.

June 27, 1931

Yesterday your mother was looking up the schedule of your trip with the view of addressing a letter to you somewhere which you would be fairly sure to get, and she told me last night that a letter written now would reach you in Vienna and that she planned to write to you today. So I am taking a few moments off to add my salutation to the letter she is to write unless she is dissuaded by the torridity of the weather here. We have really been gladder of your trip since you left than ever before, for summer has been making it miserable for all those living in the Middle West—the thermometer registering at some time each day for serveral days 100 or worse, the nights hot, and at an early breakfast time the perspiration popping out upon very little exertion. We are investigating the price of army cots and may turn the porch—too hot for day use—into sleeping quarters.

We sure appreciated your letters from New York, the *Resolute* and the

Statue of Liberty. They removed practically all the little uneasiness we may have had about your trip—that you had made your connection in New York and were off to a good, happy start. Your mother and I also sent you a telegram to be delivered at the boat in New York but guess we made some bobble about it, for your letters did not mention its receipt.

Your mother reported yesterday that Homer had bought the roofing business for $6000 which Harold considered pretty reasonable. It's the guy who can get going now who will profit when the good times come along. I think the Monday after you left here we had a card from Pat in New York. She had seen the *Resolute* in harbor on her way to Coney Island, I believe, and was mightily thrilled at the mere seeing of the beautiful boat. She said she didn't think you would be able to sink it. So far as our Middle West papers are concerned, no storms have been reported on the Atlantic since you left and your passage may have been really good. This morning's paper reports a severe storm on Lake Erie and in northern Ohio, 55 mile-an-hour, torrential rains, lightning causing many deaths and much trouble to lake vessels.

I must close this note. Have come to the point in it where I should proceed with my usual line of caution and advice, but you are now beyond the ken of my experience and I find there is not a "beware" or "be careful" I can offer. You have simply put me out of commission as the family adviser, and I now occupy a lower place in the cast of the Kelly family—have had to surrender my high estate as oracle and lawgiver and must admit my incapacity to carry it further. We will say this, however. We are not visualizing anything but pleasure and joy to you on your trip, have not a care in the world about it, but the greatest happiness over it all, and that you are taking it in the company of Alice Rost, to whom we also send the best wishes and hopes for her pleasure on the trip, extending to you both our high appreciation of your nerve in planning and carrying it through.

Well I must close. We are well. All I do now is to growl about the weather and dig into the work here in the office and sometimes after office hours, push the lawn mower a little bit, sweat gallons, and take a cold bath which just about hisses as I plunge into it. Your mother pulled weeds a little after six o'clock yesterday afternoon and the perspiration stood on her face in great drops which watered the ground as they fell almost.

Well, be on your way else the steamer will get away from you on the trip home. There is as yet no promising prospect of our driving to N.Y.

July 6, 1931

It seems sort of useless to write as news what will be old when you get the letter. In these days when a trip can be made around the world in 9 days and news flashes around instantly, letters which are to be read two weeks after they are written seem anachronistic. Yet, when and if you do get this letter, its contents will be news to you and it is therefore to be written.

We came safely through the Fourth, bought nor fired any fireworks in celebration but had to listen to lots of noise made by others who still had money to burn. We had a picnic dinner in the evening at the "Doc" Hite home—eating in the yard. The kids were there, Bobbie Hite and Walter Glassco's two children, and there were some fireworks, part of which were set off, but the older Glassco child got a big surprise and a slightly burned finger from the delayed explosion of some sort of contraption which was meant to be glittering in display but turned out in nature of a bomb, and so the interest in fireworks waned. Then we tried to play cards for awhile, but there was a dog added to other distractions and so interest in that waned also and we all went home at a reasonably early hour, our stomachs, however, too well loaded to permit restful sleep.

Sunday morning we—your mother, Virginia and I—embarked for Springfield to see again the interesting things there, and after doing so went on to the Grove and called on the Smith girls and Jim and Julia Smith for a few minutes. Jim has sold his farm and is to give possession on August 1. Then on to my mother's farm and from there to Jacksonville where I interviewed the tenant, telling your mother and Virginia to drive downtown and get a drink and to come back in 15 minutes, but they found a band concert going on at the insane asylum for the benefit of the insane and for their enjoyment, and so they proceeded to take advantage of the entertainment so generously provided by the State for her incompetent subjects and left me stranded for an hour or better so that we didn't get home till 9 o'clock—of course thoroughly tired out. We did sleep fine, though, and all feel good this morning.

Last week was a full one for Virginia. I suppose your mother will write you about that and our own social activities. Think we must have had a good many things to do for I got very little read in the *Saturday Evening Post* and heard very little radio, the only radio program which I remember being the report of the Schmelling-Stribling fistic encounter which turned out to be a battle royal, with Stribling at the receiving end of a very effective battering machine. It may be you heard this report for it was sent to Germany short wave length.

We have relief from the heat. Yesterday the skies were overcast with clouds and it was pleasantly cool and this morning the thermometer was at 65 and at breakfast I was dignified, completely clothed, even to coat. It got so hot—no relief at nights—that we bought a couple of army cots and slept on the porch a few nights. The cots are a bit uncomfortable for a night or two, but after a little experience the discomfort disappears. Should have had them during the hot spell last year,—the first time however, that we had really needed them as it has not very often been too hot for comfort in our bedrooms, cross-ventilated as we are upstairs.

My work is going good and I will be through with its pressing part by the latter part of July. What is left can be done at odd times before October 1. However, we do not yet know that we will attempt a trip of any kind. If you can get 4000 miles from home, looks as if we ought to risk a thousand, but don't be surprised if you don't see us waving from the Statue of Liberty as the *Hamburg*, storm-battered from her fight with the wild Atlantic, staggers over the rim with her precious load.

Really there is no news—just the usual round of small town stuff. Harold was not well for a few days but is well now, I believe. We stopped there last night on our way home but the house was dark and the garage empty. Harold planned to play 36 holes Saturday and I was interested to know whether he did so and if so, what his score was. He made the 9 holes this year, once in 33 and once in 32, the latter being the former course record, I believe. The ice business has of course been good and I think maybe Harold worked a bit too hard in the heat and it upset him.

We are anxiously waiting your first report. You may have sent a line at one of your stops before Hamburg and if so, we ought to get it pretty soon. Chiefly concerned to know whether you and Alice Rost were seasick. I am betting you were not but both ate your six meals a day, if for no other purpose than to get your money's worth. Well, this sheet is about full and I will stop.

July 14, 1931

The front pages of the papers here are pretty well covered with what purports to be news of Germany's critical financial condition and the danger of a crash of the Government. How much is true and how much the product of imagination we at home have no way of knowing, and I even imagine there is not much evidence of unrest among the citizens generally, though the closing—temporary or permanent—of all the banks would no doubt create a tempest anywhere. I suppose the American Express is prepared to take care of the checks anywhere, and if not the U. S. Representatives will look after the well-being of U. S. nationals, and so we are not worrying about you and Alice. If you are following your schedule you still have ten days in Germany and this letter may not reach you in Paris or anywhere, though there ought to be time if there is a mail ship going conveniently. Your mother has not yet got to the point of writing you. She will possibly do so today.

Virginia didn't leave till yesterday morning having stayed three full weeks during which time of course your mother was real busy, and our living was upset somewhat. This morning your mother said her house needed considerable cleaning as the first step toward our normal household regime. We were over to Alice E.'s about an hour Sunday afternoon. Believe I told you Harold had not been well. Alice E. had Dr. Iknayan make a thorough examination of him some time last week and the Doctor found that his trouble originated with the liver and could be corrected by some attention to diet, as I understand it. Nothing organic or to cause worry. So that's that.

Am still grinding along here at my desk and am barging along fine. In fact, the end of the grind has showed above the horizon as the Statue of Liberty will appear to you on the 8th. Still we are not planning with any degree of certainty to meet you at the dock and you will pull in not knowing, but with your hopes highly aroused, only to meet with a disappointment which can but be keen when you fail to see my misshapen summer hat towering above the crowd and your mother's red head lending an effulgent glow to that part of the great city of the homeland.* Well, you have been disappointed before, and I do not know any way either to assure you that we will not meet you, or to promise that we will. Can only say that the chances are about 10 to 1 against it, but that odd chance I feel sure you will take, as the gambler takes his lottery ticket, and build upon it a foundation of sand as it is, a great and glorious castle of hope. There's nothing I can do about it and maybe nothing I would do if I could because you will have had the hope, and the disappointment is soon over. Sometimes I think there is more pleasure in anticipation than in realization anyway.

We had, as I probably wrote you, the hot spell—day and night. That was followed by a spell of heated days and cool nights. Last night was half and half—hot first, cool at last. No rain. Condition of corn getting critical. Big wheat crop—disheartening price—the lowest I reckon since the seven fat years of Egypt while Joseph was there. The oats hurt some by the heat. That's the crop situation. Farm lands still going down. Nobody wants a farm. The eastern banks worried over their loans to Germany and getting ready to throw more money into the same hole. All the money of this country concentrated in the cities. Chicago and Cook County about "busted"—Chicago paying her teachers in scrip to sell to the money sharks. The government with almost a billion deficit. Everybody feeling poor and scared. Such is the financial situation.

The ice business in Mattoon is still good however, and now that we know what was ailing Harold, we are all well.

So far we have had no letter from you save those written on the boat. This is as it should be for you have no time to write letters. You can do that

---

*But they did meet the boat! J.Y.K. in a brand new hat bought specially for the occasion.

during the long winter evenings when there is nothing to do in the quiet back-country town of Chicago but hold your hands or knit or write letters. . . .

September 25, 1931

I almost quit worrying about your getting into Chicago long after dark as soon as I got you started from home, but your mother began to worry then and worried pretty much all that night about it and occasionally expressed concern thereafter until she got your letter. Never again do you start from here so late. Life's too short.

We did enjoy your visit. There has been nothing happening since you left, just the usual round. We ate dinner last night at Mrs. Ball's and after dinner played cards with Mr. and Mrs. Lantz at our home. Your mother and Mr. Lantz beat their opponents pretty badly, but we enjoyed the game.

I drove to Jacksonville this week, going up by myself and getting my mother's business settled, I think, for the winter. Got back about 5 o'clock. In the course of the day I picked up five "hikers" and carried them to where they wanted to go—just kids looking for work, except one whom I carried to business college in Mattoon.

Alice E. telephoned today that she will take lunch here tomorrow and spend the afternoon with your mother.

There was a lot of rain here this morning and it has been cool for a couple of days. I really think that summer is now over and am glad of it and don't care very much when we have a frost to kill that pesky wire grass that grows up overnight in the yard and keeps me wasting all my spare time cutting it.

Glad you are getting some extra cash out of the Christmas card business. Your school is probably running in good shape now, and possibly making your plans for the day's teaching comes more easily. I think I will pay the insurance when your check comes in. You ought to keep your credit there good with your garage and service station and keep enough money out of your paycheck to pay your obligations there. I am going to try to get McArthur to cut something off that note for the expenses you were put to almost as soon as you got the car out of town. How is it doing? Have any more faults developed?

Well, I think I have told about all there is to tell. Take care of yourself.

October 1, 1931

We had your letter with its enclosed check for $80 several days ago. I deposited the check and paid $300 on my note, leaving myself incapable of paying your $150 note this month. I also paid your insurance bill of $31.20 to Charley Miller and charged you with that amount. I also have McArthur's bill against you for grease and oil amounting to $2.25 and will pay it today and charge to you. As I wrote you once before, I am still going to try to hold him for the $21 bill you had on the car a couple of days after you got it.

Your pleasantry referring to a weekend trip to Kentucky was duly noted—a thousand miles in three days at a cost of $30 for gas, oil, grease and depreciation, and at the cost of your efficiency as a schoolteacher on Tuesday and Wednesday is a mighty nice dream but impossible for anyone over 19 years of age. Life's too short and too full of trouble to permit of such a tax. Therefore, I knew that your suggestion was a mere pleasantry.

Your mother is giving a dinner tomorrow night. I went down to the chicken house down by the Town Branch this morning and bought 5 chickens. The man was good enough to wring their necks and I left your mother just getting ready to clean them. She figured—after I got the chickens home in their headless condition—that she needed only 4 as she was to have only 16 people to dinner instead of 20 as she had planned; and as I have had the second operation on my teeth and am not eating meat, I reckon your mother will be tired of chicken by Sunday night. The two dental operations take care of my front teeth, upper and lower. The recovery is pretty slow and the thing will drag along pretty much all winter, but I also believe that when it is over I will have a good set of teeth—mostly my own "raising."

Other news is scarce. In fact I know of none. My term as chairman of the Church board expired last night, and if it is offered for the coming year, I know how to say "no" and shall say it with vim and vigor.

October 20, 1931

Will Graves and Ruth and Kirtley and Helen dropped in on us one evening for supper last week, I think Thursday. They stayed with us overnight and left early the next morning for home. Will Graves just couldn't stay any longer. When I pressed him for reasons, one excuse he gave was about as follows: He had left no one in charge of the chickens, had merely put two or three bushels of wheat in their feeding trough, and he ought to get home to renew the supply. That was not the main reason but undoubtedly had some weight. You know how people are when on their way home from a trip—they just haven't time to stop anywhere except to eat and sleep. Horses have much the same inclination. The old gray mare never had any special pep to go anywhere away from home, but when she was headed home, her youth was almost renewed. Going away she drowsed along, uninterested, slow, sedate, apparently almost asleep and without a thought in her head, except when she came to a corner the turning of which might be a turn in the general direction of home; then, if you too were drowsing, she would be headed around the turn by the time your attention was aroused; coming back with head up, stepping out briskly as age and increasing infirmities permitted, alert, undoubtedly visioning the quiet and comfort of home. So humans and especially the Kellys, on their way home. Well, we enjoyed their visit, short as it was.

The weather here has been very beautiful for several days. Yesterday I went home at noon and found your mother pretty thoroughly chilled. She had been sewing all morning and the house had not heated much, though there was some fire in the furnace. After lunch she tried to take a nap, but though she bundled up in bed she couldn't get warm, and after awhile she came down grouching about the fire and put on a sweater and your old checked overcoat and went out to work in the garden. I left for the office and a little before 4 o'clock she called me and suggested that I quit and come home. The suggestion suited me very well. Out in the back yard her sweater was here and your cloak there, and tools were scattered around promiscuously, and there was much evidence that she had been busy. After awhile—a moment or two—I heard her slow progress across the Thomas's yard—mostly Mrs. Thomas talking about something or another in her own inimitable way—and your mother came home, pink-cheeked, warm and rosy, and the discomforts of the morning were apparently forgotten, at any rate were not again mentioned.

Well, I've wandered on here without saying much and must say goodbye for this time. We are looking for you Thanksgiving and would of course enjoy seeing you before then.

November 19, 1931

I have been wondering for some time how the Cicero school system was getting money to pay teachers, etc., in the face of the financial situation and tax collecting delays that are general throughout Cook County. I suppose no one can foresee with any accuracy how long the system will be broke. You, along with the other teachers, of course will be more or less inconvenienced by the delay, as your plans have been made with a view to the regular payment of your salary. It will be nice to get your salary in a lump when it does come, but in the meantime you will have to incur some interest charges for expenses of living. Your policy, no doubt, will be to pay as little interest as possible, therefore, to spend as little as possible and when you borrow to borrow as cheaply as possible. The interest rate is 7%, which is plenty of course, but no doubt as cheap as money can be had.

I don't know exactly what your arrangements are with McArthur or how much you owe him. I think the cost of the new car was $550 or $560, and you had a credit of $132 on the old car by reason of the payment of $100 and credit for expenses on it. If this is correct, you owe him $418 or $428 plus interest and I had better make arrangements to pay him as your installments fall due. So please let me know what is correct as to amount in total and the dates and amounts of installments.

You will probably try to sell enough Christmas cards, along with your tutoring, to keep you in change for your minor expenses. Perhaps you will require other money for room and meals. As soon as you get a line on how much you will require for your necessities, please let me know.

I signed the claim yesterday (in your name) for the stolen tires. The claim amounts to $10.80 arrived at as follows: original value of tires, $15.70; depreciaton for about 2000 miles use, $1.57; and allowance for the old tires which were put on in place of new, ten or 15 percent, leaving the amount of claim, if figured correctly, $10.80.

There isn't very much news. Your mother had not been especially well. I had the final dental operation yesterday and expect to be all set for your visit here Thanksgiving and for the special food that will probably be available. Maybe I will open up the mackerel kit again. Have made a sort of tentative arrangement for an unusual meat for Thanksgiving. If we get it, you will not have chicken, duck, goose or turkey but something else—so have your appetite ready for any emergency. You may find only chicken, duck, goose or turkey, but maybe not. Now, you and Pat and Mrs. Ray may have a guessing contest. Wonder if we ought to offer a prize to the one making a correct guess.

Well, take good care of yourself. We are anxious for Thanksgiving and you to come.

December 8, 1931

Shortly after I came to the office yesterday morning your mother phoned that Mrs. Jessie Craig wanted her to go to Indianapolis for a few days—till Wednesday afternoon. Your mother had agreed to go. A little later she reported another conversation with Mrs. Craig. Some thieves had, on Sunday night, butchered 4 of Mrs. Craig's fat hogs and had taken the meat. Therefore Frank might have to use the car. Why couldn't they go in your mother's car? A short time later it was so arranged, and at about 10:30 the Kelly Ford pulled out all bright and shiny for Indianapolis. I haven't heard from them. However, I found your letter of Sunday night at home this noon and was glad to get and read it, though it had no later news than your telephone call.

I suppose a good many will shop as you and Alice did last Saturday—just look and decide what you would like to buy but refrain from doing so because they too do not know what to use in place of money. I can understand how one who runs a car at the same time she is paying for it, merely greeting and saying farewell to money as it passes by, might very well look upon Christmas shopping this year as a desire which must be suppressed, especially where the source of the money has become so barren as the various municipalities of Cook County.

There isn't any news. Hope you acquit yourself well as a witness. The best thing to do is to tell the truth, the whole truth, and nothing but the truth and stick to it. No lawyer can help you to do that. We are anxious for Xmas to bring you home.

December 9, 1931

Your mother and Mrs. Craig barged back from Indianapolis a little after 4 yesterday afternoon. Your mother was tired but enjoyed her trip a good deal. She rested very well last night and is her usual self this morning.

The check for your stolen tires came in also. I enclose it. It's payable to you, of course. I am disregarding your instruction to pay it to Charley for two reasons: first, it is payable to you, and second, you may need it yourself. Charley gets enough profits out of me each year in insurance to justify carrying his account for awhile with us, and I owe him nothing.

There isn't any news. From Dec. 9 to Dec. 23 there are only 14 more days—not long even in prospect, practically nothing in retrospect. We'll be seeing you.

1932

January 11, 1932

Mother told me to write you this morning and I am doing so partly in obedience, but mostly because I like to write to you. Your mother has had an infection around her finger nail for some time. She went to Dr. Iknayan last week and he treated it probably for its ultimate good but making it very sore and putting it out of use for the present. It's the index finger of her right hand, so she cannot write to you as she otherwise would have done yesterday. The doctor also told her yesterday to keep it out of dishwater, a command which also touches my convenience. As a result we are using as few dishes and kitchen utensils as possible. Last night we were to have a cold lunch and as your mother was reading at about supper time, I slipped out and put the lunch on the table putting at our places squares of paper instead of plates. She almost adopted the idea, but I relented and got plates. . . .

The bank questions seems to be ironing themselves out. I may be elected a director tomorrow. At least I have agreed to accept if elected and have qualified for election by getting three more shares—in all, making the necessary ten. Mr. Jeffries I think makes some slow improvement. He attended a rather stormy session last week which put him back some but was downtown this morning for awhile.

. . . The weather has continued mild. I hardly think the thermometer has registered below 20 this winter, so, my first supply of coal will last through January, and that's a record.

January 27, 1932

Because of an enlarged heart, as I have explained to your mother, I am going on a diet outlined by Dr. Bliss and am governing my conduct as is necessary. There are some compensations, for I shall cut no more grass and perhaps next August and September, I shall take a long lazy vacation. However, I lose the right to eat pancakes at all or wheat bread which has not been thoroughly dried or toasted twice, as well as the right to smoke or drink coffee. I also shall accept as few invitations for evenings as possible. I have known of an enlarged heart for many, many years. Your mother is falling into the plan. The only part which might tend to arouse her suspicion was the separate room for me and as to that, my report was that the doctor suggested that it be tried in an effort to get more sleep at night. So that's that.

The banks of this county and Cumberland County agreed to a plan yesterday—put in operation today—which will probably forestall any more failures here. They will pay out no money deposited before today in savings accounts, for the time being or until further notice. Other accounts—that is, active accounts—will continue active where used for necessities of life or business. New accounts are not restricted. This is an excellent move. There is no news.

April 21, 1932

We had and greatly appreciated your two letters written in one day, and I wrote to Mullet Lake to see what sort of entertainment they offer for elderly people who want to fish but not be bothered too much by having to take fish off the hook.

There isn't any news here but the unnoted happenings of uneventful lives. Mr. Drewel is no longer president of the bank. Since he has been president he has sold some stock in a speculative concern in blocks of $5,000, and those to whom he sold are in no very friendly spirit toward him. I do not know what they can do, but think they will do what they can. Frank Johnson is acting as president with the title of executive vice-president. The change seems to have met with very general approval.

Your mother has been having the two front bedrooms and sewing room papered. They ran out of paper for the south front room, leaving the space around your bookshelves, and that cannot be finished until another roll which had to be ordered shall have come. You will be pleased with the new views in the room.

Your mother has a woman helping her clean the upstairs halls and bathroom today. She also has a man mowing the yard and doing other odd jobs around there, such as planting garden, etc. So you see she is pretty busy. The yard is pretty now and will get more attractive right along. . . .

One thing of interest is that I am still putting on flesh. My weight this morning surprised me by passing the 150-pound mark by half a pound. For me to have attained that weight after more than 50 years of striving is to have accomplished the seemingly impossible. Let this be a lesson to you to learn from it that you too, if you follow Mrs. Ray's suggestion as to Ovaltine, can attain a rounded and attractive contour which will stand you in good stead in meeting the vicissitudes of life.

I have bought fishing licenses for your mother and me. Who knows, some Sunday afternoon we may find ourselves down on the banks of the Ambraw with rods in our hands and lines leading to attractively wormed hooks. One never knows when a thing like that will happen and it's always well, as you have learned, to look ahead and be prepared for emergencies. Out of such considerations grew the thought that I should have licenses.

It is right warm today. There is still a fire in the furnace. I hate to build a new one. As sure as fate, if the fire should burn out, it would get cold.

September 14, 1932

We had your letter of yesterday, and before I forget it will answer the two questions. The check came in and I deposited it to my credit. My record shows that you have paid all you owe me except $88.80. That is a small debt as debts go these days, though it is considerably larger by comparison than $88.80 used to be in the good old days before 1929.

There is but little news. Your mother and sister went to Terre Haute yesterday. . . . Shopping was the object. . . . They drove into the garage here just a little before dark last night. Harold came over for supper. Moore had butchered one of Frazier's fat steers a few days ago and we had a steak out of it. Had a steak out at the Rocks a few evenings before at a steak roast—out of the same beef. It sort of ruins one for the ordinary steak we get, to eat a piece of first class beef—blue ribbon meat. Of course a town the size of Charleston cannot support the butchering of such cattle regularly, but it's a treat to have an occasional shot at it. We wouldn't have had this treat except the steer broke its leg below the knee and had to be butchered.

We are well. Your mother has invited her mother to come up and visit us for about a month beginning next week some time. I don't know whether she will come or not but have the feeling that she should not get so far from home. Her visiting days, possibly from the point of view of her own good, are over and she has reached the condition where a quiet life and a contented mind are almost essential to her health. Perhaps a quiet life cannot be had without a contented mind. At any rate the invitation is out.

Well, write to us as often as you can. I seem to have lost my knack of writing interestingly. At any rate it has been hard to do in the last 8 or 10 months, perhaps because there is such a mass of other things on hand—unfinished business the end of which is not in sight, and the result of much of which is yet on the knees of the gods. If affairs go right for the next ten months, I am going to take a full month off. You, your mother and I, and Alice E. if possible, could have a royal good time for a month together, couldn't we—off at some lake—out of touch with everything, even careless whether we fish or not. Well, that's in the future. Remember me to all the members of your household.

October 7, 1932

We had and appreciated your good letter, and while we knew you could do no real wrong, yet there is no questioning the fact that your letter helped us out a lot, and we are sorry that I felt called upon to write as I did. I ought to have and did know that the most you had done was to be careless and indiscreet. Now, let's forget it. I know that hereafter we need not worry. Thanks a lot.

There is no news here. One thing and another keep me busy—some of the things worry in a business way. My October term work is in and is heavy. Yesterday I was out of the office all day—at the bank mostly. Haven't got our money from the Sangamon farm yet. Corn is still going down. Your mother is having the time of her young life fixing your lounging robe. You'll be surprised when you see it again. It'll be a wonder of wonders. Can hardly put it down to get something to eat. . . .

Your little car is of course lost yet. Probably it has perished from the cold, stripped as it probably is. If you get it back, be sure that everything is in apple pie order at the expense of the insurance company. Pardon the short note. I just stole a little time.

October 18, 1932

There are times when one feels as if he would like to get in the little Ford car and just ride till both the Ford and yourself are ready to go back home again. Isn't it so? We wonder how you make out without the little car anymore. . . . It must be a continual lost feeling, and I supposed you plan to get a new one when the insurance company comes across.

Have you made any proof of loss of the Ford? The paper which I sent to you and which you returned to me came from Chicago and I supposed you would send it direct to them then, but I sent it right along and I suppose the delay won't make any difference. I don't know what the proof of loss consists of in an auto case but suppose it follows a fixed course. It's quite a nuisance for us that your car was stolen, for you don't have the temptation to come home strengthened by convenience of travel as you once had.

There isn't much news here. . . . Elizabeth Pasfield and a couple of Springfield friends drove up in the afternoon and we visited them a few minutes at the curb. Along about 6 o'clock Harold, Alice E. and the dog drifted in. They had been to Rocky Ford for steak dinner, to see the beautiful colors, to exercise the dog, and had on their rough walking clothes, but they stayed for a snack of food and Alice E. helped her mother wash all the dishes from the noon meal.

The waters of the Ambraw are very low and as served through the water pipes are impregnated with dregs to such an extent that after washing one's hands they carry an offensive smell for hours. They say that coffee made with it is practically unbearable, yet this is what we drink in this community. If it were just a case of holding your nose till you got the water by, it wouldn't be so bad, but the taste lingers on—and on—and on.

This is the first spare time I have had for a good while. Sent the last of the certiorari cases back to Springfield this morning. There were 60 of them and I was glad to finish. That's the fastest and most unsatisfactory work I have to do—not enough time to do them justice.

Corn is still going down. Have made arrangements to crib all the Jeffries corn and your mother's as well. For the Jeffries corn had to adapt 4 broomcorn sheds to the storage of corn. It was not a hard job. All I had to do was to order the necessary materials, and the tenants put it where it would do the most good. For your mother, her tenant is taking her corn into his own crib. So with these arrangements all made, it looks as if I will not be concerned with any more farm income this year. We can carry through without disturbing the cribbed corn until about August of next year and by that time there may be some recovery. Kinnett sent his check for the rent due last September 1. I suppose the check is good. Haven't got the return on it yet.

Well I had better close this.

October 26, 1932

Your letter was mighty fine and reassuring for me, and I shall not worry anymore. I must confess you had me guessing. It's so easy to get one's head down and so hard to get it up again—so easy to see only the muck and dirt in life and so hard to keep one's eyes on the peaks—so hard to go through it all and yet keep a proper respect for oneself—the very finest thing in creation if one will have it so—the very lowest if one weakens. I thank you for your reassuring attitude and if your affection for us is the life raft which will keep you floating through your depression of spirit, we will have not lived in vain. You are the kind who can carry happiness wherever you go, but you have to keep your own balance as you go else the fine instrument will be destroyed for usefulness. There isn't anything you own—anything you can get from life—as fine as yourself. Thanks a lot for your reassurance.

Now no more lectures—no more discussions. We are on our way. We are well and very happy. We know you will enjoy your Kentucky trip and are very glad you are going. Don't do anything hurriedly. There is plenty of time to do things leisurely and in a dignified way and the rewards for dignity are plenty big. I haven't time for a real letter this morning—just wanted you to know how much we appreciated your letter.

1933

June 1, 1933

Your mother has just laid upon me the pleasant duty of writing you a letter, a duty which though pleasant, I have much neglected in the past year. We had your letter hinting that you expect to inhabit a wee bit of an apartment on the northside and your two cards telling of your pleasant day at the great glorified country fair. I have wondered if you actually contemplate living on the northside, close to the lake, and teaching in Cicero. The two things combined do not quite make sense, for it will be some trip from the place of your abode to the place of your labors. However, whatever the difficulties, proximity to the lake is well worthwhile.

Your mother today had a man working in the yard. At noon she was quite tired enough, but in spite of all I could say in opposition, insisted on his returning after lunch. The yard and garden are preying on her mind much as they used to prey on mine when I was doing the actual work in connection with them. Now, so far as I am concerned they may grow up into a wildwood. I concern myself not at all about them—just see and admire, and by the way, under your mother's management they are indeed admirable.

The bank situation has a brighter tinge. Eisenmayer, the conservator, has been displaced, oozled out of his job, as the morning paper is inclined to put it. His successor is Bruce Rardin of Rardin who comes with the intention of giving us a chance to work out our salvation. Reorganization is now up to the depositors, stockholders and debtors of the bank, and citizens of the community—all of whom will have to help and encourage—and the first three classes will have to make some sacrifices either by waiving a part of the deposits or securing some cash upon their stockholder's liability or debts to the bank. At any rate, we are brighter and more hopeful that all is not lost than we were.

We plan to drive out in the country late this afternoon to see if any plowing is being done. Much rain has put the farmers way back in their work. The ground for corn and broomcorn is not plowed, and it's all but too late—so late that we will spend the beautiful summer hoping for a late fall. Also, the rains spoiled 20 acres of mighty nice clover for your mother. She worries not at all about the weather because she says she doesn't propose to waste any time and energy worrying about what she cannot help. I can't see but what her idea is very good. We have had several days of rainless weather and are hopeful. The ground is still soggy in most places. There isn't any news.

July 18, 1933

We had your letter yesterday containing schedule of your activities for several days and enjoyed it a great deal. Your writing is getting harder to read right along. In that respect you grow more like your dad every day. Sometimes I can't read my own writing.

There isn't a great deal of news to tell. Last week was the annual stockholders bank meeting and I had two hectic days preparing for that, then spent the balance of the week looking over the political situation in our judicial district. The outlook is not good. It's Democratic weather. We can get the nomination, but the war cry of the Democrats will be that Judge is too old. And that is dangerous. We are considering the question whether the handwriting is on the wall or not. Go to Decatur today and may decide the question today.

Your mother has had a new attack of the flu since Saturday. She was up for breakfast this morning and has just phoned me, so I think she is still feeling better.

How is your car coming? Do you want your license plates sent you or are you coming home soon? Charles is still trying to do something with the insurance company.

Well, it's 11:30 and as I have your mother's dinner and mine to get and leave town at 12:30, I had better not try to finish this letter.

September 19, 1933

We have been moving along in much the same old way since you left. No excitement much. The men returned from Washington encouraged to hope that there will be a reorganization rather than a new bank, and the machinery has been set in motion to bring that about if possible.

I had a wire this morning that Cousin Ed Brown of Jacksonville died yesterday. Shall try to go to the funeral on Thursday.

The State Christian Church convention is in session here. There is quite a church full of more than average distinction in appearance.

Mr. and Mrs. Spooner called for a game of cards last night and your mother and Mr. Spooner gave us a perfect trimming—not a break in it.

Your mother's ankle still swells a good deal and I reckon it will be some time in making a complete recovery. Nevertheless it improves.

I think your mother's tenant planned to cut broomcorn today. A rain has been threatening to fall all day and I don't know whether he started to cut or not. It's rather unfortunate to get rain when the broomcorn is down and before it is in the shed. Have you seen the cutters at work? It's interesting—

a scene of great activity—enough men to break, cut and table the brush for 20 acres and thresh the seeds off, and put the brush in the shed all in one day.

There is no news. We haven't heard that you reached your club safely but suppose of course you did. We do not worry anymore about that sort of thing. I feel that you are probably better qualified to take care of yourself than we are. No news from Mattoon. Mother will write in a day or two.

September 27, 1933

The case—tax case—to which you probably attribute the effect of rendering it impossible to get further money for the school system is, I suppose, the one wherein a reduction in valuation of 15 percent of certain classes of property—a horizontal reduction—made by Jacobs was held to have been within his authority and the Cook County Board of Review was held in error in setting aside the reduction. The opinion of the Supreme Court was filed at the April term, I think, holding as above stated. A re-hearing of the case was granted at the June term, and perhaps a second opinion will be filed at the October term. What the final result will be no one can know. But as long as there has been a deliberate expression of the Supreme Court to the above-stated effect, men who loan money will consider that the final opinion will not be different than the stated opinion. Therefore, the valuations upon which tax is based being decreased by 15 percent, the tax will be proportionately decreased, and the amount which can be anticipated by the issue of anticipation warrants likewise. There will thus be fewer such warrants to sell and less money available for the tax-spending bodies such as the Cicero school system. When the anticipation warrants, lawfully issuable, have been exhausted by the school system, there will be no money available for teachers.

Your mother will write you soon. We went to the Mattoon picture show last night, and when the show was out there was a heavy downpour which had been going on for some time and continued for 15 or 20 minutes. When it let up enough for me to go to the car, I found that I could not start it. Someone came to my rescue and wiped off the distributor with my good clean handkerchief and we came home without trouble. Harold and Alice E. were there and I suppose they had no trouble getting home. Alice's cold was better, but she should not have been in a crowded picture show.

The strengthening of the bank proper to meet the requirements of the Reconstruction Finance Corporation for the loan we want is slow and difficult. Paper is hard to strengthen under present conditions when everyone is straining every effort to pull through. Yet we are hopeful of success. As I am informed, the funds of the depositors are not being depleted by keeping the bank open upon a restricted basis. The bank has or should have a good income as interest on its notes, etc. Keeping it open does not or should not exhaust its income. Also, the assets of a dead bank, or other institution, are worth less than the same assets if held by a going concern. Those who owe a dead bank have no particular incentive to pay, whereas if the bank is active, they have to consider that it still has the capacity to affect their fortunes in the future. The bank should be kept alive if possible.

Your mother and I put the lunch and fishing pole in car Sunday, and we found a quiet, secluded place on the river where we ate. After lunch your mother caught ten nice sunfish and I caught one. It was a very happy day.

October 9, 1933

Are you working too hard? I have had a little uneasiness lately for fear you are "overdoing it."

I went out to Walnut Grove Country Church yesterday for services and after services came back and got your mother who had prepared a large glass dish of Spanish rice—steaming hot. We then went back to the church and joined the homecoming basket dinner. Some crowd! Some food! After dinner there was a program which was still going on but apparently drawing to a close at 4 o'clock when we left and came home. Alice E. and Harold got in a few minutes after we did, and about 7 we had a nice fried chicken dinner. Alice E. is well and anxiously awaiting her time. . . .

There is no real news here. We are both well though your mother's leg still swells, and we wonder why it doesn't come through with a complete recovery. It's been a nuisance, hasn't it?

There is no news in the bank situation yet. We are still very hopeful of reorganization. The whole matter is now before Washington, I think, and we believe we will get just treatment there. Well, I must close this.

October 16, 1933

Yesterday was a beautiful day. Your mother and I went to church and from there to Casey where we had a very good chicken dinner at the Blue Bird Cafe. Then we drive home by lonesome country roads. One of them came to a dead end and we had to go back a piece the way we came. The trees are beginning to show their fall colors and the drive was very nice. We didn't have a fishing rod along so we got home at a fairly early hour, some little after four o'clock.

Your mother and Harold and Alice E. were in Decatur Saturday, and your mother started for Terre Haute directly after noon with the Spooners. We were at a reception at Pemberton Hall Saturday afternoon and met Mr. Buzzard and his wife. It was homecoming weekend for E.I.S.T.C. and I reckon was thoroughly satisfactory except that Normal trounced the E. I. team at football. Alice E. called up at noon today just after Mother left. She is well—in good health and spirits.

You know of course I think a lot of my new tackle box and flies. The tackle box has been long wanted and I know exactly how to use it and what to do with it. For 50 years—I think I fished at five years of age—I have wanted a tackle box, but have been forced to content myself with cigar boxes and the like. I reckon if one lives long enough all of his desires will be gratified if he wants hard enough and hasn't too many desires. You sure exercised good taste in deciding to send me a tackle box. Now the flies are tempting. I have never had any fly-fishing and to fish with flies is an art and a science. I am tempted to learn how to do it. You know Loren Digby has been fly-casting all summer, wading the stream of the Ambraw and casting toward shore. He has had some luck and has learned how to cast. Of course it's a bit too cold for that now, but next summer, maybe "me" and my brilliant flies will try what we can do to lure the gamy bass from his retreat.

We thought of you quite a bit yesterday and are quite anxious to get a colorful account of your trip to Michigan, and especially the part which had to do with fishing. I failed to look on the map to see where you were. No doubt your letter when it comes will tell of the drive up, mileage, etc., as well of your experiences.

Mother told me at noon that we are planning to go to the picture show tonight. What is to be shown I don't know but no doubt it has been "touted" as something good. When I go I make it a practice not to expect much except from the news reels and then I am not much disappointed if the show happens to be mediocre.

A few sorehead depositors set out to have some of the bank officials indicted on the theory that they kept the bank open after they knew it was insolvent, and a good many witnesses were subpoenaed to appear before the grand jury, but the States Attorney explained to them that the bank was a national bank and the State had no jurisdiction. So nothing came of it, though gossip was stirred up somewhat. As a matter of fact, the Government contemplates the regulation of banks in a different way than by making it criminal to keep a bank open after it's known to be insolvent. It sends examiners out to examine banks and when the government man says the bank should close, it is closed. The Government recognizes the fact that there may be circumstances under which an insolvent bank should be kept open for a time in anticipation of a favorable turn in its affairs, etc. However, I have never thought that our bank was insolvent, or, for that matter, is now.

Well, I have wandered on about one thing and another and have written little of anything of importance. Your mother's foot and leg are much better. She is back in high heels. We think the low heels delayed the recovery. There is no news.

October 23, 1933

There is no news bearing on the question whether you are to be an aunt or an uncle, as you put it, though this letter may be ancient history by the time it reaches you.

Sunday was uneventful. We set out to call on the Harold Tolles. They were not at home. The house was locked and of course we thought they might have gone to Decatur. We drove around south of Mattoon awhile and came back to the Tolles. They were still gone. When we got home however, we found that they had been driving, had called at our home twice in our absence. This morning I took your mother to Mattoon, and she and Alice E. and Harold set out for Decatur. I suppose your mother will be home tonight but don't know.

There is no real news. Somehow I am sleepy and lazy this afternoon—rather glad I have nothing special to do, and that I can read the new *Harper's* which Judge brought in this morning.

November 9, 1933

Your letter came in a couple of days ago, but I forgot to take it to Mattoon Tuesday night when I called there on your sister, nephew, etc. If it doesn't get too cold during the day I may go over again tonight, and if so, will take the letter to your mother. Alice and Jim are doing fine. Your mother went over Monday night and she and Harold went to Decatur and brought them to Mattoon. Since then your mother has been on the job getting them started right. I expect to bring her home Friday night.

We are looking forward to a lot of pleasure out of you and Betty this weekend. It's cold here today, below freezing and with a high wind. Hard to heat the office with the gas heat. I am wearing a jacket sweater and it is necessary. Think I will eat downtown as the food your mother left at home is about gone. So far I have managed to keep the dishes washed; there is not a dirty dish on the place so far as I know.

There isn't any real news around here. Tomorrow opens the hunting season. Harold, the preacher, Charley and Byron with guns and dogs plan to go out. If it remains as cold and windy as it is today there will be more grief than pleasure out of the hunt. As usual I have had the fever somewhat (for hunting) but have it no longer. It would be more pleasant, it is true, than drinking cold beer out on the lake front, but nonetheless I would rather be inside a house. Am hoping Saturday will be warm enough to make your drive pleasant.

November 17, 1933

Your letter came in today. I have been thinking some since you left about whether or not you are burning up too much energy. It seemed to me that you were a bit thinner and that your face had the somewhat drawn expression which comes from overwork. You have a heavy load—perhaps too heavy—and it may be that you could break under it. It's worth thinking over and perhaps worth a reorganization of your days—cutting out a part at least of the art work, either the dramatic or violin studies.

I pulled a bad one on your mother Wednesday. It was bright and clear in the morning and while it was cold, the day from inside looked good. So I suggested that we get a lunch together and I would buy a hunting license and borrow a gun and we would go up to Sangamon and have a big day. I wanted to shoot that beautiful pheasant I saw there last spring. So we left here at or shortly after nine and reached the farm at one. As we started to eat our lunch, coffee and cold sausage sandwiches, I saw a covey of quail going one at a time from the road hedge to the field hedge about 30 or 40 yards away. So we ate hurriedly and followed them up. I got three good shots and missed them all. Well, your mother walked along for over a mile away from the car. It was real cold with a strong north wind and it made her sick, cold and sick at her stomach, and a mile from the car. I beat it across the cornfield, got the car and drove back and took her to a farmhouse where the women took charge, and then went hunting again. Saw and had a good shot at a mallard duck and at the beautiful pheasant but missed them both, though they looked as big as a bushel basket flying through the air. Then got your mother, somewhat improved, and we drove to Mattoon where Alice E. gave her some bouillon and me some spaghetti. Then we came home. Your mother was cold, but I got her a hot rock and she got warm. Yesterday she was shivery but is apparently all right today, has gone out for a card game and suggested steak for supper. It was a real trip, and grandparents ought to have had better sense. Other than this there is no news.

The nephew is well and now weighs 11 pounds and Alice E. is doing fine. It remained cold here until this morning. There has been some rain today. I think Harold and Charley went hunting today.

By the way, on my trip I demonstrated that I had built up considerable resistance, as I walked about 5 miles in the cold and carrying the gun and drove all the 260 miles without any bad effects except a soreness of muscles.

This letter is just to let you know we are all well. It may also serve to illustrate the folly of going beyond one's strength and might find application in the life of a schoolmarm as well as of grandparents.

Remember us to Betty. We enjoyed her immensely and can see why you and she have a lot in common.

November 24, 1933

The death of Mrs. Horace Tolle (Harold's sister-in-law) occurred unexpectedly night before last at about 8 o'clock. A blood clot had got loose in the blood stream and was eventually carried to the heart, or some other vital place, and caused immediate death. It was a shocking death, of course, as it was entirely unexpected by the family, though the doctor may have had some suspicion, for there had been a previous swelling in Mrs. Tolle's leg which had subsided and which was followed by pains similar to those caused by pleurisy. . . . Such symptoms ought to and perhaps did warn the doctor, but if so he did not inform the family of the possibilities. Indeed, I was told the symptoms some days ago and should myself have become suspicious as I knew the nature and indications of embolism, both from testimony of doctors which I have read and from what I learned about it when Eliza's death occurred unexpectedly from the same cause. . . . The funeral is tomorrow. There is no other news.

Your mother is giving her second turkey dinner tonight. The first was Tuesday night, and Wednesday night we had turkey dinner at the Dunns' and afterwards went to Normal School to hear Elsa Koch sing. Yesterday morning your mother went to Mattoon but was home to lunch, and we then went back there in the evening. Alice and Jim are well.

I tramped the field about an hour yesterday but saw no birds. Did I tell you I have bought a cheap gun, $7.50, and some rubber boots and maybe before the season is over I will be able to hit at least one bird, but I doubt that. At any rate my intentions are murderous.

November 29, 1933

I send herewith the application for the surrender value of your life insurance policy. You will sign it and then acknowledge it before a notary public.

I have done so, my acknowledgment appearing on the reverse side. A. T. & T. stock ought to be as good—safe—an investment in stock as you can make. If you want to take a little longer chance, somewhat in the nature of speculation, you might try out three shares of Libby-O-Ford, or maybe your money would buy four shares.

There is no news here. I have been out a couple of times, by myself, walking around the fields with a gun in my hand, trying to be hunting dog and huntsman both, but have failed to find the birds. Harold and I are planning to go out tomorrow afternoon for two or three hours. We won't have time for a real hunt, but with the dogs we may find something to shoot at. I have seen several rabbits but there was no sense in shooting at them as I didn't want to handle, dress or eat rabbit.

The Comptroller of the Currency in Washington has given us a plan to work out the organization of a new bank here and pay 50% of the deposits in the old bank. If this can be put over, it will turn loose half a million dollars here. It will cost me my stock and an assessment and an investment in the new bank. Though I am not yet certainly informed, I think Washington has required that the assessment and investment in new stock combined shall equal 100% of my stock. If that is the plan, and I think it is, it is fair enough. We will have to work fast to put it over by Christmas. It will almost have to be put over by Christmas because a law, passed by the State Legislature to enable public treasurers to waive part of deposits, ceases to be operative on the change of the year.

There is no further news of special interest. Know you will enjoy your Michigan trip.

December 9, 1933

I enclose herewith the certificate for the share of A.T.&T. Upon the question of investment in any stock, I have no opinion which has sufficient basis to be acted upon. Your information is probably better than my own. Libby-O-Ford may be an excellent buy but the only tip I have on it came from you. A.T.&T. is spread out pretty much all over the world and can be hurt or helped in many places. You know that the only investment that I think I have sufficient knowledge to act upon in my own case is land, and as to that I cannot figure out the end. So you use your own judgment. I am sure it's as good as anybody's.

Our last dinner was thrown last night. It was preceded by hors d'oeuvres, (Is that spelled correctly?) and followed by contract. There were sixteen, your mother helping with the serving and not playing cards. Counting her twice and me four times the four dinners combined were for 56. Last night it was baked ham. The next preceding dinner was quail and the first two, turkey. In between times we have lived high on the remains.

The bank forms came in yesterday—a single copy of each. We are to print them in final shape and send to Washington for final approval before the effort is made to reorganize. I think they will be mailed to Washington today. The plan is somewhat better than anticipated from the point of view of stockholders as we have put up our notes due in three years for only $20,000 instead of the $40,000 we expected. This is better for the stockholders but might not be considered so good for depositors, though it makes little difference to them.

The courthouse has an allotment of government money of about $18,000 for redecoration and repairs, and the workmen are busy erecting scaffolding up the tower on the outside and inside. I think the entire building is to be redecorated. Many of the roads and streets they are hoping to surface with gravel with the aid of government money. Indeed, much of that work is already going on, I understand. The Government seems to feel that much money should be spent for similar projects all over the country, and it will be spent. The edict is that if not spent at one place, it will be at another.

Your mother is going to Mattoon some time today. She just has to see Jimmie every now and then. The recent reports are that he is doing fine on his changed and increased diet. I wonder if he will be so grown that you will not know him the next time you see him. The last reports that I heard were that he weighed all of 12 pounds, and that was several days ago.

There is really no news. Christmas will soon be here, and you with it, which will be fine. At least I suppose you will be here a part or all of your vacation.

1934

January 4, 1934

Dear Girls:*

Mother phones that we ought probably to write you a letter on the state of the family for the particular benefit of you, Alice Elizabeth.

First of course you want to know about the lord of the manor, James Y. Tolle. There is really nothing to report about him. He is very industrious, very hearty and healthy. Very hungry when he is hungry, and that's always at his regular eating time, very little concerned about his mother being away, very much of the opinion that the companionship of his grandmother is sufficient compensation for any slight loss growing out of his abandonment by his mother and father. In fact you need give yourself no concern about the son and heir for he is well and happy.

However, I think he will remember you when you return, for your mother had him in Mattoon yesterday afternoon and when it was time to leave Harold, he showed a considerable measure of displeasure at the idea of leaving his dad. By the way, Harold does not yet (or did not yesterday) know whether or not he would come to Chicago Saturday. He is doing very well, his cold improving satisfactorily and your mother says that if he does not come to Chicago, there is no reason why you should not stay there over Sunday and come home Monday. However, I suppose you have heard from Harold ere now.

There is no news here. We are well. There was a surprise cold wave yesterday and last night, sending the thermometer down to about 12, but I think it will not last long. . . . Mother says for you both to have a good time and forget, Alice E., all the responsibilities you have here. Everything is going beautifully.

Emmaline, I like my pen very much.

February 2, 1934

The groundhog has been able to see his shadow all day so far today. I don't suppose that one has any justification for hoping that he overslept. Reckon we are in for six weeks of winter. As there has been little winter so far, there will be no cause to complain.

There has been little news. Your mother and I went to a dance at Normal school last week and danced. We also went to the president's dance and danced. We also are invited to a dinner dance at the Grant Hotel for next

*Alice E. visits Emma C. in Chicago.

Monday evening. We have accepted and expect to dance. We are dancing right along through life, but I at any rate pay something to the fiddler the following day—not much, just in a few aches and tweaks.

The bank is still unopened. Mrs. M—has thrown a monkey wrench into the machinery which may hold us up awhile. She had filed a suit claiming a preference over other creditors to $3500 of government bonds which, under the plans, are to go into the new bank. As she has a court injunction restraining us from disposing of the bonds in that or in any other way, it would seem that we have to get the injunction set aside before we can go ahead. She really has no case, but she secured the injunction without notice and, until it is out of the way, it must be respected. Judge Cofer and I are going to Danville in the morning to try to get the injunction removed. This will not be a hearing on the merits but simply on the sufficiency of the complaint—a legal question.

The goose we had for the weekend was very tasty. We called in the Hugheses and Mrs. Harryman to help us the first meal. Since then we have been going it alone on the goose, except that on Wednesday your mother had a tea during which she served sandwiches with a filling which was in part ground goose. It is possible that the bird will be finally and completely disposed of at supper tonight as the pickings were getting rather slim last night.

Your mother spent most of yesterday with the Tolles. The young man is still growing, weighs 17 pounds, is happy and cheerful, has blue eyes and sandy hair. He seems to be a pretty fine youngster. I think he will be a big man as he is not fat, but has a large frame.

April 10, 1934

That was quite an experience you had about Kankakee. I can think of nothing much more disquieting than to run out of gas late at night on one of our main roads and several miles from a filling station. Good that there were three of you. Better that a Samaritan came along. At any rate you had an exciting experience and I imagine it will be long before you have that sort of trouble again.

I fear your trip home was depressing. Don't take it so. We are more than content with you, for you are a charming girl, active in mind and body, enjoying life as you go along. You have a sane, sound mind and good outlook on life, and, if my temporary feeling of depression has depressed you, it's too bad and I am sorry. If it has, snap out of it, as you can and will. If I could order a change in you, I wouldn't know what to order. You are perfectly satisfactory.

There is no news. Your mother has been working in the yard again yesterday and today. It's as clean as can be. She sure has got along fast with it. I put an hour in yesterday late, but what I did was of little extent or importance. She has been over practically all of it with the rake. I think she plans to go into housecleaning soon.

May 2, 1934

You painted an interesting and detailed pen picture of the view and surroundings—human and otherwise—as you sat Sunday there by the lake waiting for Betty to keep her engagement with you. I shouldn't wonder if, in time, you will not be able to make a very good living with your pen. Your experience, fine outlook on life, ability to see the humorous and capacity to draw contentment from yourself in most surroundings, combined with your literary attainments, are the source from which may flow a rippling, clear, sunny stream of interesting impressions and reactions.

However, horseriding is more or less of a bother. Horses are dangerous. They are expensive as playthings. As a kid nothing was more pleasurable than bareback riding. Even to ride the old gray mare without saddle or bridle was fun. Nevertheless I remember her deliberately pitching me over her head into a briar patch and giving me the horse laugh after which she stood, staid and dignified, for me to mount and go for the cows. I remember an Indian pony (small horse) racing with me on her back, when a storm seemed coming up, (at such times horses are nervous and full of pep) with boys on other horses, and other loose horses racing with us. I fell as we raced along the bank of the Avenue* (before it was widened—a steep bank) she going at full run. Her front foot touched my chest but never came down, for she stopped in her tracks and withdrew her foot. I remember other things about horses—a dashboard kicked in, a carriage turned over. The sorrel I drove the last couple of years while in Kentucky, could do the 12 miles between Georgetown and Lexington in an hour, wouldn t let any one else drive her, had to get in the buggy on the run. She was ruined by the Negro who worked at the place within a month after I left. I remember the horse that was used when there was a milk route. When you drove her she wanted to stop everywhere along the street where milk was delivered. Horses are interesting but they are more dangerous than you youngsters might suppose. I recall a laughable incident, a Negro riding a mule, just about the bridge on Main street over the town branch. The mule, restive,

**Kelly Avenue* in Georgetown, Ky.

suddenly pitched the darky in the air to light on his head on the hard macadam, the darky not hurt at all, his head not being so easily vulnerable. Well enough of the memories of the past. Not old enough to indulge so much.

Your mother and I rather think you should make your Columbia plans without reference to our plans. I have not heard from Dr. Cole yet. To Dr. Cole I suggested the latter part of July or the first of August or a combination of both. Our plans are not definite, and you make yours. We will accommodate ours to yours if possible. But if you have the Columbia chance, don't miss it.

We were fishing Sunday—had our noon meal over the campfire—saw some nice fish caught, but only caught a couple ourselves. There was one really worthwhile string of fish—4 different kinds of fish. Were out almost all day which left us both too tired. Hereafter we will not do so much at one time. Write to us. Your mother goes to Mattoon, possibly to Champaign today. Housecleaning is about over and she is tired. The yard and garden are well-cared-for. No other news.

May 14, 1934

We had your "Mother's Day" letter and enjoyed it a lot though it did remind us that we had not written to you during the week. Mother had been rather busy last week—in Mattoon a day or two, in Champaign a day, fishing part of a day, doing the odds and ends of housecleaning—and as you know, I am no longer a good or reliable correspondent.

Did I write you that the dust storm reached here the day after the back porch was thoroughly cleaned and its floor varnished and waxed? Your mother was pretty well discouraged over the result, but the dust was easily removed from the floor and furniture and it's all in good shape again.

Alice E. is over today at a luncheon bridge. . . . Jimmie and Josephine* are at home. I built a fire at noon in the fireplace and I suppose they will get along all right. Your mother and I had supper last night with Harold and Alice and got home shortly before ten. We had dinner at the Church where there was much good food and we ate lots of it. Consequently neither of us had a very pleasant night. The weather has been right windy. We had one good rain that was not general all over the Middle West. Consequently the drouth has not harmed here yet.

The chinch bugs are thick. As one walks through the wheat fields the distinguishing chinch bug odor is noticeable. They are here in such quanti-

*Josephine—a maid, employed by the Tolles for a time.

ties that no doubt they will do a lot of damage unless there is wet weather when the new crop is hatching out about the first of June.

The shoe factory here is closed due to labor trouble which we hope will not be a long-drawn-out affair.

The yard at home is mighty pretty with many of the Iris in bloom. The dandelion tops have detracted from the appearance as the yard is literally full of them in places. They give a ragged, unkempt appearance. There is but little news.

May 24, 1934

I am going to call Sunday afternoon in Evanston. Your mother will drive up with me and we should reach your abiding place along about noon of your time or our time—I rather think our time. We expect to use this opportunity to "do" the fair all that we intend to "do" it. In fact, your mother expects to give Sunday afternoon to that job and perhaps Monday and Tuesday. I suppose I will see it Monday and Tuesday. In the years to come I must be able to say that I attended the Century of Progress Exposition. Personally I would be content to say that I saw such parts of it as were in view from an Illinois Central train, but that it seems will not satisfy.

There is no news since you left. I felt that when you started Sunday to Chicago you had got no rest from the trip and that you were thoroughly tired and we didn't really have the usual satisfactory visit with you. Perhaps the drive to Chicago was the most restful part of your trip. Hope that you were not overly tired out and that you took no ill effects as a result. We have not seen Alice E. and Jim since Sunday, nor do I think your mother has been in touch with them. I suppose they are all well, else we would have heard.

It is a rather unpleasant day, the wind from the northeast. In this section any wind coming from east of the meridian is malicious in its effect upon humans. It has long been said, "When the wind is in the east, it's good for neither man nor beast." That saw applies to this section, yet it originated in a far country about the dawn of the Christian era. Malicious mischief would seem rather natural when the east wind blows. Well, we will be "seein" you.

September 21, 1934

. . . We got up early enough to let your mother have a leisurely start. She ought to be in Louisville now having a quiet lunch somewhere, as it's now half past one. With good luck or reasonable luck she might have been in Louisville by noon. She may come home Saturday evening the 29th and will do so if she can.

. . . There is but little news to report. I have my Watson cases coming along better and have some hope—though not especially well grounded—that I may get somewhere, particularly with the partition suit. I was able to learn Mrs. Morrison's home address in Detroit and had her served by copy of the bill and of the process of the court. I think the service is good. At any rate am not making publication service at present. Your mother knows a little of the affair and that I am in some sort of difficulty over it. I don't know yet that I will have to go to Detroit. Mr. Heinlein said he would want to be present and hear her deny her signature on the judgment docket. Therefore, if he takes her deposition I will be present.

. . . I feel somewhat lost without a car, but reckon I won't have to go anywhere for a week. We had a nice letter from you yesterday. You do mighty well in writing to us.

September 26, 1934

The letter here came in today from your mother. She is having a satisfactory trip.

. . . Yesterday morning I found in the larder nothing but milk, butter, two slices of bread and enough coffee for a single cup. That was a close call for a breakfastless day. I am better prepared now.

It's hot here today but bright and clear. There isn't any news. I went to a picture show Monday night—Mae West in her recent production. I am fed up with her acting. This play was of the nineties, glamorous or roaring, as you will, and as usual was more or less a caricature, but when I think of much that is written about the nineties as caricature, I also think of my own striking appearance in long-tailed coat and wide striped trousers and wonder whether "caricature" is not properly used.

I hear that the Cicero Board is not caring much whether the teachers live in that village or not. If so I am very glad.

October 29, 1934

Somehow or another I seem to have passed as a correspondent. I seem to write no more letters than I have to. Wonder what is the cause. No doubt there is a reason but it would probably be of no value to try to learn the Why.

We have been tolerably busy. Wednesday night we went to a dinner and political meeting at the U. S. Grant Hotel in Mattoon. Thursday or Friday night to a card party given by the Eastern Star order at 25¢ a person. There I got a nice prize—a pencil which sells for $3.50. Saturday night Mrs. Marshall and Miss Ellington were with us for supper and cards till midnight. Last night we saw Will Rogers in "Judge Priest." Sunday dinner we had with Alice E. and Harold in Mattoon. Jimmie has a cold but enjoyed, while asleep for the most part, a ride in our Ford. Saturday noon we had a church dinner at the courthouse. Taking it all in all we are circulating fairly *rapidement.* (Is that French word properly spelled and used?) Tonight your mother is having to dinner eight people, I believe, and we expect to play cards afterwards. This dinner seems to have been called for by reason of the fact that a few days ago your mother and I drove out in the country and bought a dime's worth of green beans of the Kentucky Wonder variety. We got so many that it was a hopeless job for the two of us to try to consume them. Hence the dinner.

We had another discussion of my motion in the Morrison-Watson case to set aside the judgment of revival. At the conclusion of the discussion the court decided the matter under discussion, setting aside the judgment and opening up the case to permit the defense to be made. This decision brought me out of the hole I was in if it is not appealed. I do not think it will be appealed. At any rate the advantage is now with me.

As I understood you on the phone the other night, you have received leave of absence from your teaching duties to permit you to attend Columbia. That's fine and whether you ever get your Master's degree is unimportant in view of the fact that you are on your way and will no doubt have interesting life while en route. There is little news here. We have some hope of making a good political showing next week, locally.

November 24, 1934

Your wormy letter came in yesterday and your mother and I got a hearty laugh out of it every time we thought of the picture you drew of your adventures with the crawlers. Indeed the report was so good we are sending it on to Dr. Cole who, we think, will enjoy it as we did. However, though the story was a good one, we both feel that there was a little exaggeration—that maybe there were not quite 50 pounds of worms. That would be a good many worms—even of the night-crawling variety of monsters, prehistoric worms as it were. Just think how many bass one could tempt at Lake Leelanau. . . .

By the way I got five fair-sized night crawlers which invaded my cellar during the heavy, long-continued rain and put them in my bait box hoping they would survive there till time to go north next summer and do their stuff.

Your description of Chicago dusk from the Michigan Avenue bridge was good also. I reckon there is some charm sometimes even in the overgrown gawky settlement there on the Lake shore. . . .

There is little news here. Your mother has shown a few signs lately indicating that she will need a lake vacation by the time June 25 comes again. The good she got last year certainly showed itself strong in the variety and continuity of her activities.

We are coming to a period of stress at home, I think. Every mealtime and at odd times when we are apparently talking or thinking of other things the question of redecorating the home recurs. At present the most intrusive idea is a nebulous plan, nebulous but becoming more and more fixed and tangible, to paint the dining room walls and ceiling with a yellow background and trees, vines and maybe birds and monkeys scattered around. I don't know what will come of it, but methinks I can discern the influence of modern-day art in the idea, certainly encouraged, perhaps initiated by the art teacher who has his studio in your old room.

Your mother is starting out to get one Christmas present ready—for Alice E. That's just a start and no doubt the tempo will become quicker and quicker as the time grows shorter and shorter. What with the stress of Christmas preparation, the redecorating of the house, housecleaning-and-all coming on, methinks I see a real necessity for a vacation next summer.

Well, we will be glad to have you home again and it's not so long now till Thanksgiving. Whether we will have for the big dinner, goose, duck, turkey, chicken, or plain rabbit I don't know. One can never tell. It may be that your mother's repressed want of thirty-odd years' standing will find expression, and a pig with apple in mouth may grace our table.

1935

February 8, 1935

We have been trying to follow you, in imagination, about your daily activities but find that we haven't the background to do that very successfully. So, sometime after your stomach has caught up with you and after you have caught up with yourself and your body with its necessary rest and recreation, just sit down at your leisure and give us a word picture of a day's activities and of the surroundings amongst which your day is spent. However, put that off until the time and circumstance unite to make the drawing of the picture a work of pleasure and art.

We have been a bit uneasy about your stomach, and we do want a true report as to your physical condition. If the trouble continues it may be better for you just to abandon work, spend a few dollars on a good doctor and his prescribed treatment, a few weeks in seeing New York, and then come on home for a rest here till time to go to Leelanau and a good time and rest there till August. This suggestion is seriously made and if your condition is not, ere this, normal again, you should consider acting on it very seriously.

There is no news of any importance. Your mother has put in one day on her rug and now has not more than two days to go before taking it off the frame for binding the edges. In Springfield Monday she got a bargain in yarn and has started to knit it into a sweater. This she does at night when we are at home.

We got a couple of days ago the pictures of your mother, Jimmie and me. They are very good. Alice got some also, I think, and the Tolles brought the other baby* over and had his picture taken by Lynn Sanders. I think Lynn is above the average as a photographer.

There was considerable rain last night and there is a fog this morning. Mother is to cook all the remaining sausage today as the weather is hardly cold enough to take chances with it uncooked. After it is cooked we won't have to eat it except as we want it.

I wrote Lillian to get Fan Rogers' address and send it to you. I don't know what Fan's last name is, but think it may be Jeffries. Don't think I ever met her husband or that I have seen Fan (until Will Graves' funeral) since I left Kentucky, January 1901. Think the man who became her husband came into the picture after I left and that Fan was married later in 1901. I think she is now a widow. She talked to me at the funeral, but I was not quick enough to get in very many words. Her words came too fast and about all I could do was to grin and take it. Well, be good to yourself.

---

*Jimmie's first cousin—Eddie Tolle, whose mother had died shortly after his birth.

February 12, 1935

We have enjoyed your cards and especially your letter and more especially the appearance or feeling that you had that the milk regime was about over for a time. We hope that you are well again. I think your trouble is somewhat a matter of nerves, and the new order of morning rest and a sanely governed life, which now seems possible with you at least for a time, will do wonders for you physically, as no doubt the broader contacts you will make in the International House will be valuable to your mental growth and general knowledge and education.

Your mother has been putting in her spare time, and some time which was not so spare, in working on her rug. Yesterday she got in a full day's work and still has about two days to go before she can take it off the frame. "The last long mile" is the hardest. Today she will be able to give about two hours to it—this morning, but this afternoon there is a bridge or contract session. She will go to Mattoon tomorrow or Thursday and get the book you want from there, and then soon after that we will send the books you asked for.

The Tolles were over a little while Sunday afternoon—all well, and Jimmie showing material progress. His progress is really apparent now from week to week. Sunday with a little China dog in each hand, he was hurrying to the "what not" to put them back and try something else. When both feet were off the rug, they went up and he went down on his back—hard and flat. Was he embarrassed? Well, apparently not, for when he hit, both hands were up and his head was craned forward and up so that both dogs and head were safe and sound. He lay without moving until he gauged the meaning of our laughter (your mother's and mine), and apparently coming to the conclusion that he was not hurt enough to cry about, else we wouldn't be laughing, he turned over and got up in as good humor as before, but just a bit more careful in walking. He had new shoes, by the way, which probably contributed to his downfall.

Well, I had not any business going on in that insane way about the kid, but reckon the nature of grandparents is compelling. . . .

February 18, 1935

I am sending today by American Express prepaid the books you want except one, Chaucer, I think, which could not be located.

There is only one item of big news in the home—*the rug has been finished* and is a beauty.

I brought your radio down to the office this morning so that I might get an early report as to whether the Supreme Court decides the gold clause case today, and if so, the kind of decision rendered. The radio is now blaring away from Tuscola reviewing the news of the day. It will be kept on Tuscola, for that is the station from which this section gets its quarter-hourly reports of the grain market, but it will not be permitted to blare except as I want to hear something.

Alice E. and Jimmie were over Saturday for the day, both well and glad to be here as we were glad to have them. Jimmie still thinks that he is smart. We cut church yesterday but did see Will Rogers in "Country Chairman." Also in the afternoon we took Mrs. Neal for about an hour's ride.

Your letter showing that you are back on normal diet was a real relief. We had been a bit worried about letting you get away in bad physical condition but thought that the new surroundings and interests might quiet you down. Your school program seems interesting. At any rate it will be such a complete change for you that it may well be considered a vacation—and under pleasant conditions.

It is surprising how little news there is to tell. Washington rather "hogs" the play these days. . . .

Well, I haven't time really for a long letter today as there were three items to do, each of which took a little time. One of the lights on your car went bad and I spent a few minutes at the Ford garage about that; second, I wrapped your books and addressed them; and third, I hooked up the radio. So now it's time to be doing other things.

I enclose some of your notes—Milton, I think.

March 30, 1935

The infrequency of my letters is no measure of the appreciation both your mother and I have of yours. I am lazier than I used to be when it comes to writing. Perhaps I am just taking a rather too prolonged vacation after the eighteen years of constant writing I had while connected with the work of the Supreme Court.

I like all three of the pictures you sent us. While posing you seem to have tried to assume a more serious expression than you ordinarily wear and the line of your lips is unaccustomed to you. Yet the picture ought to serve the purpose for which it was taken—perhaps better than a different pose. At any rate, I like the pictures, though I think the one taken at Marshall Fields is somewhat more charming.

Your mother has set out to make herself a party cloak—I think it's to be a party cloak—and I think she had a very good day at it yesterday and planned to finish today, but Alice E. called this morning and said she and Jimmie would come over for the day, and your mother has gone to Mattoon to get them. She would rather have a day with them than any party coat.

The yard is now very pretty—the yellows of buttercups, the yellow shrub hedge, the variegated bed of hyacinths, the green of the grass. I have dug a little for worms—enough to make a place for a couple of rows of peas—and probably will dig more next week. The worm harvest was not very good either in number or size, but I put what I found in the box and am hoping that with good feeding they will grow big enough by July to handle any blustering bass which they may tempt to have a go at them.

Am offering your car for sale. Started the offer at $300, of which $100 would be left with McArthur to be used as needed on a new car. The best prospect so far is a fair chance to sell for $250 plus an old Auburn which might bring $10 to $15 for junk. Mac says he would take the offer if it actually develops because he thinks it a good one, the Model-A's having been antiquated by the V-8's. If that dicker does result in sale, there would be $150 plus junk price of the Auburn which might be enough to get you by till you find work to do or something else turns up. I have no business trying to keep up two cars as it's tax-paying time, and life insurance premiums will also be due before June.

It was quite a relief to win that case. I don't know yet whether it will be appealed or not, but of course hope not. If appealed I will do my best to prevent a reversal, though there is one error in the proceedings which might cause reversal. However, there is a very good reason not to reverse which ought to minimize the effect of the error. Even if the case is reversed, there will have to be a new trial and on a new trial my adversary would have no assurance of winning, so I know he will think at least twice before he appeals. When the first day of the trial closed I saw no chance to win. When the evidence closed at noon the second day, I saw little chance to lose. So I cut my argument to the bone—about 20 minutes—and stressed the two points which it seemed to me would convince any man. And gave little attention to the parts of the evidence which we had fought over the most during the trial. Sure enough, I had gauged the workings of the normal mind correctly and the jury stood 11 to 1 on the first ballot. The one was not wedded to his opinion and came along on the third vote. So there was a quick verdict. However, I learned that I take my client's troubles too seriously and give too much of myself. Some lawyers do that, and a trial to them is a real drain. If I had had anything in the house to drink, I would have taken a substantial shot when it was over. In the bank trouble I promised Ed Chilton who was ill that when the trouble was settled we would have a drink together, as I had refused him many times in 18 years. My promise cheered him a lot, but he died and we never had the chance.

If you will not take it as presumptuous on my part, I would like to say just a word here. I believe I will take the chance anyhow. Drinking is a treacherous thing. An occasional social drink is probably worthwhile, but it's a seductive thing. First one has a fear, but slight familiarity changes that. Then one welcomes the opportunity, then makes the opportunity, then the urge to make more and more frequent opportunity, and so on. You would be surprised. When that time comes, drink is destructive. It was Solomon, I think, who said that at the last, "It biteth like a serpent and stingeth like an adder." That is still a true conclusion, though I think the generation of which you are a part has more self-control than had mine.

There is little or no news. As usual in the February-March season, many people have died. The western dust scattered a mile up still keeps sifting down from time to time. Mother cleaned the winter's accumulation of dirt off the back porch, and the next morning it was heavily coated with dust. Many people suffering from colds and sore throats are inclined to attribute their troubles to dust, though I think they are mistaken.

Several carloads of E.I.S.T.C. folks went to Nashville yesterday and broadcast the story of that institution. Mr. Buzzard, the glee club, the faculty trio, and a number who just went along. We listened and of course enjoyed doing so because we knew them and the school. We also went to the picture show last night but thought it was not worth the price of admission. I don't know just what it was that led your mother to think we ought to go. Well, I must close.

April 6, 1935

I enjoyed your letter a lot. What you said concerning my letters was very flattering to me, and I reckon we all appreciate a bit of flattery. I of course know that you being a rather close relative, might conceivably be somewhat inclined to look upon my efforts in any direction through rather rosily colored glasses. At any rate I thank you for your appraisal, whether it be actually justified or be somewhat warped by your good wishes. In either event I am pleased, for in the one case, it is good to know that you like me enough to permit your judgment to be warped, and in the other that I am really capable of writing something worthwhile.

The car sale is in status quo. McArthur couldn't sell it (or said he couldn't) for $250 plus a junk car worth about $15, even though I had agreed to leave $100 with him to be used in future car purchase. So I withdrew the car from his custody. I am in two minds about its sale. I believe I can sell it fairly advantageously by inserting an ad in the paper offering it. The questions are these, or arise out of these facts: The car has 40,800 odd miles on it. The valves will soon need grinding, its winter of exposure to the weather will soon necessitate painting. The tires will have to be replaced after a few thousand miles. However, it's a good car and still fast. If you teach in Cicero next September, you will need a car. If you get a job in New York City, you will need a car. I suspect that you are getting short of money and may need money to carry you through June. The bank stock is a little difficult of sale though I have not yet tried to sell it. I have not yet cashed your $10 check you sent for the dress, fearing you would need the $10. You and I can borrow money here at the bank on our note, but if you are to stay in New York City till September or till February, or indeed if you need money to carry you to June, it would probably be best to sell something. If you are to teach in Cicero next September, it is probably best to sell the bank stock. If not, it is probably best to sell the car first, then the stock, then borrow. Will you please give me your views.

There is little or no news. We are all well. I am sending you today the buttons in a little box with two handkerchiefs—by mail. Mother is doing some housecleaning—a room at a time. The bathroom and mine are cleaned, though the bathroom is to be painted. The paper for the dining room has come. The flowers are still pretty, no weather cold enough to kill them, no weather hot enough to fade them. I did some digging for worms, and incidentally for the garden, since I wrote you and rather overdid the work, as I have been lazy since then. The next time will not do so much.

April 15, 1935

We had your nice letter several days ago and are glad to know that your finances are not to be difficult—also rather glad that the car is not to be sold yet. While your car was at McArthur's offered for sale, both your mother and I had some qualms about letting it go out of the family, perhaps to an unhappy home or to a hard-driven, uncared-for old age. Somehow it didn't seem exactly right to let that happen.

Glad you should be (that) you are not at home just now. The wintry winds are blowing a gale and have been since early last night. The kitchen is but a shell, nothing but the cabinets and the plumbing fixtures left in it. Even the gas stove has been carted away and the floor is a mess, but there is a brighter side to the picture. The kitchen walls are beautifully done in new paint as is the ceiling, and the cabinets are done by now, and in a day or two a new enameled electric stove will have been installed, and after the floor is washed and perhaps varnished and waxed, it will be an attractive place to cook and eat in.

The library is likewise dismantled, no curtains, no rug, no furniture, no nothing but the telephone and some ladders. Perhaps by now some of its woodwork may be resplendent with new paint and perhaps the new ceiling paper may be on. At any rate, the room is to be papered and painted and perhaps a new rug of Olson make may be ordered, though the electric stove may have shortened the bank account too much to permit the rug just now.

I suppose we will cook tonight on the little electric plate in the dining room, as that and the toaster constitute our only cooking equipment. The dining room, too, is divested of all its furniture and equipment except the table which was too large to be put out without taking a door down. The ceiling paper has all been taken off and the plaster cracks in the wall are repaired, leaving the room scarred and ugly, but it is planned too to bring it out in Easter adornment and the inconvenience of the present may be discounted for the hope of the future.

As all the downstairs furniture is in the big double living room, there is no charm there either. Your mother is, I think, in the china closet in the dining room dolling its sides and back up with new paint and probably having a good time doing it. We hope to have the three rooms finished by Thursday, and after that can at least live comfortably and get the balance of the house cleaned up at leisure though with the winds and the dust it hardly seems worthwhile to do anything about it.

Apart from the turmoil at home there is little news worth the telling. We are all well, both the Tolles and the Kellys. I don't think your mother will come to New York this time because we are spending considerable money and probably will want to economize for a while. We will be glad when it gets and stays warm. There was quite a heavy freeze this morning.

April 24, 1935

I suppose you will appreciate a letter from home though there is nothing of interest to write about. . . . The yard at home needs attention—the grass needs cutting, the vegetable garden needs forking and planting, and a lot of odds and ends there need doing. The painting and papering of dining room, kitchen, and library are finished, but the windows of the whole house need washing, the screens need putting in, and the big living room and halls are untouched. The back porch needs putting to rights for the summer, and the last three days have been beautiful, bright, warm days to whose charm the apple, pear, plum and cherry trees have yielded giving a mass of blossom over the entire back yard. The dogwood, the lilac and the wild crab will be yet a day or two before their masses of color and fragrance are won by the wooing softness of sun and air.

Your mother is lying in the bed in the back room where she can see out the window and enjoy the view if she will, but it may be that thoughts of work undone will intrude to spoil her pleasure in it all. Yesterday afternoon she was at a card party, but a growing soreness of throat convinced both of us that it would be wise for her to keep her bed for a few days, as the throat infection was producing fever and making her extremely uncomfortable.

Really, she and I should be on the banks of the Ambraw today lazily trying to lure some of the finny tribe to our hooks—maybe hoping that not too many fish would respond and make labor out of what should be laborless.

Just here Charley Miller was in to deliver an insurance policy. At least that was apparently his mission, but as a matter of fact he and the preacher are trying to arrange to go to the river at about 2 o'clock today, and Charley may have had it in mind that the temptation would be too much for me to resist. If he thought that, he is not far from right about it, but looking ahead and visualizing what might happen should I go, I think the possibilities which a trip to the river now present ought to compel me to frame a firm "no" and not leave me stuttering between "yes" and "no." The truth is that fishing for bass at this time is forbidden, yet the bass don't know it, and they are just now inclined to get themselves attached to hooks, hooks intended (perhaps made a little more attractive to bass than they should be) but ostensibly intended for other kinds of fish than bass. Now just suppose I should go to the river and a handsome, shining, fighting bass should disregard my lawful intention and come out firmly fixed on hook of mine. What would I do about it? I am free to admit that I don't quite know the answer to that question, and not knowing, I perhaps should not permit myself to be put in the position of having to give answer on the spur of the moment and of the excitement which would attend the putting of the question.

Well I must bring this to a close. . . . Mr. Hobbs said he saw you toward the latter part of his trip and that you were busy and enjoying the whole New York experience. We enjoyed all your letters. Write when you can.

April 29, 1935

Your mother and I were at Alice's yesterday for dinner while Harold was golfing. Had a good dinner and the afternoon slipped away before we knew of it. After a while we went out to the Club and picked Harold up and then drove to the Mattoon Lake and around it over a very rough new road. There were lots of fishermen all around the lake but we saw only one string of fish, four or five small croppies—nor did we see a single fisherman get a bite as we slowly passed. However, we did think of fishing and of the lake in Michigan.

Really we are both rather glad that you are again thinking of cutting off your college work in June rather than continuing it till September for two good reasons, either one of which seems to me to be sufficient. One of the reasons is that we did not get a great kick thinking about a vacation at the lake without you being there, and the other is that we have had many disquieting thoughts about the possibility of serious results to your health should you continue the exciting, active, candle-burning life you are living until September and then step right into just as exciting, active, candle-burning a life teaching in the environs of Chicago for a further ten-months' period. Youth has lots of comeback, but we wondered if going right through the long stretch would not put you out physically for the rest of your life, might cut the corner too closely and wreck the physical machine, even though you have youth and an exceptional fund of pep, enthusiasm, courage, and vitality to draw on. So, if you do decide to go with us to the lake, we will be greatly pleased and really draw much relief from that decision. A Master's degree is much to be desired and one is justified in spending time, energy and money to attain it; yet after all it's a poor thing indeed if one pays for it by exhaustion of pep, courage, and health. At least that is our attitude towards it, and yours is now probably the same. At least we hope so.

The yard has been beautiful with all the fruit trees, the dogwood, the redwood, the lilacs and tulips in full bloom. The wild crab will burst forth today or tomorrow.

The back porch has been cleaned again. Just after its cleaning there was more dust, but not as long continued as some of the dust visitations we have had. Today I put a fire in the furnace again as it was damp and coolish. Your mother is feeling pretty good again and I am well.

May 20, 1935

I know you will treasure the enclosed certificate issued by the Order of Ananias. You may not have earned it, though your night crawler story, even though true in every way, has enough of the extraordinary about it to justify us in the assumption that the facts were artistically enlarged to create that interest which one must arouse to be classed as a good teller-of-stories. You also have a fish story or two, which I used to help induce the Grand Mogul of the Order of Ananias to issue this license, for who would believe, for instance, that you chased a three-pound bass all over the lake and finally caught it in your bare hands. I may have known that the latter story was true in its every detail, yet you readily see how effectively I could use it in wangling this license from the powers that be. Dr. Cole has been a great aid to me in securing this honor for you. In fact, it may be that we have, in our efforts, almost qualified for a like certificate. After he secured it he sent it to me, fearing perhaps that you would resent having anyone think that you had been so inartistic in your telling of tales as to leave the impression that your tales were enlarged—that you might feel that your artistry was being impugned. However, I am sending it on. No offense is intended, as you know. I have always regretted that I have never been able to so embellish a tale as to make it worth the telling, and the ability which I lack I admire the more in others and if you have or should show an especial ability in that line, I would be correspondingly pleased, for the trait would stand you in good stead should you ever take up the writing of fiction and generally, as you go along, will furnish entertainment to your friends and associates.

There is no news, no where, no how. It just rains. All this month it has rained—10 inches of solid water have fallen over this section since the month opened. Corn and broom corn are unplanted, ponds all over the prairie, the river out of its banks, the earth a mass of mud. The spring flowers have come on in their seasons, spreading their beauty of color and scent to the soggy world, beaten and pelted by rain, finally fading almost as useless as the flower which wasted its sweetness on the desert air. To go out and cut the asparagus I dress in rubber-boots and coats. In the meantime, the housecleaning has gone on. Nothing much left now but a final coat of varnish for the kitchen floor (the third) and then wax on it.

The Tolles three were here yesterday afternoon—too rainy for golf. They are all well.

We rather think it's best for you to stay in New York till September. It does seem as if it would be considerably wasteful to come back this summer. You sometimes write as if you do not think of coming back again to Cicero in September. I suppose your place there is on ice for you. I rather think the car should be insured, else it might be stolen and burned at a total loss even though not in use. We have used the new car little this month because of the rains, and yours sits out anyway. Don't know when we go to the Lake but think we will be back here before August 1. I don't believe I care to be up there in this sort of weather and I have heard that sometimes rains there last three days.

Well, I reckon there is no news to write.

May 24, 1935

Though the enclosed letter was dated the 19th, it didn't reach home until today and I found it there at noon. I judge that it ought to be sent on to you. Your mother phoned this morning before she went to Mattoon that there was also a letter from you which she was taking on for Alice to read. The house is cleaned now and the sun has been shining off and on today. I let the fire go out a couple of days ago but built it again yesterday and it's still too cool to be comfortable without a fire—a radical difference from weather conditions this time last year. Corn ought to be planted, but practically none has been planted and even without rain, it will be several days before planting can start.

I wrote to Dr. Cole that we would take the cottage for the period till July 27. Don't know when we can go, but the cottage is at our disposal at any time after June 3 when Dr. and Mrs. Cole go there.

Your mother had a letter from Virginia (your aunt) yesterday giving a rather discouraging report of Garnet's health, and last night she wrote to him renewing her invitation to visit us at the cottage. I do not think it very wise to take a sick person that far from home, but suppose he and Leona will not accept. Your mother is going to learn today whether or not Alice E. and Jim, Jr. can go. I do not think they will be tempted until the weather grows warmer.

I do not think your bank stock should be sold now. The book value is $137 a share but there have been no sales and no demand. Therefore, when you want money you will have to borrow. The bank here will lend on your note signed by your mother and me, and you can pay the note as you earn the money next winter. . . . There is little news.

June 12, 1935

You should have been here this morning for breakfast, for we had good coffee, of course, and along with that there were the best of sour milk cakes and butter, all drenched in real maple syrup. I fear that I may have overdone it and that I will be drowsy and listless all morning, but at that I will be satisfied. Thanks a lot for the syrup and especially the thought back of its sending.

There has been no summer here so far and no promise of summer. It is still spring—wet and chilly. A trip north does not attract as it did last summer. However, we are tentatively planning to go on the 23rd—your mother and I. We do not yet know that Alice E. will go then, or, for that matter, at any time. She wants to go but has not yet indicated that she will be able to arrange it.

Was in Jacksonville and at the farm in Sangamon a few days ago—made the trip alone without tiring especially, so I am apparently in better physical condition than a year ago. On my way back—just a few miles this side of Pana—a lot of cars and people on the road, the people centered about a body lying on the slab, so aroused my curiosity that I parked and walked back along the string of cars to see what it was all about. Someone in authority was going through the clothes to see who he was and what he had—a few dollars, identification cards from various lodges, etc., keys, and the usual line that a man carries—a Springfield man, James T. Davis. His wrecked car off, through the guard fence, down the embankment over the farmer's fence, upside down—a complete wreck, the left chest of the man broken through and gaping open where the heavy guard rail had gone through. Not a very pretty corpse did he make there on the slab, an unpleasant memory perhaps but certainly instructive as to the immense power in an automobile traveling at high speed. I believe even I drove a bit more carefully the rest of the way home.

Night before last Mrs. Shaffer called your mother wanting her to go to Indianapolis yesterday. After considerable hesitation she agreed to go, and so they set off about 7 yesterday morning and were back about 6:30 last night. It was a good trip, restful to your mother, though a like trip would have tired me a lot.

The yard has been beautiful but the weather too cold to really enjoy it. Likewise we have had little good from the use of the back porch.

There is no news.

July 3, 1935

It seems impossible to find time to write to you or to anyone else. Here it is one o'clock on a day when we decided to do nothing but run into town for a loaf of bread, etc., and write to you and Alice E. And perhaps dip into the lake for a few minutes. So far all we have done is to write Alice E. a hurried letter designed to aid in getting her, Harold and Jim here safely and quickly without missing the road, and we have been in Traverse City and have returned with part of a watermelon, a box of strawberries, bread, vegetables, three metal leaders for hooks, and four sinkers.

I was taught yesterday that a strong leader is as essential as a strong line when an over-weighted fish is being brought unwillingly toward an anchored boat. You may remember that last summer I bought some catgut to make my own leaders, using a more slender hook than the regulation snelled hooks. Well, yesterday I was using one of the homemade snelled hooks when a big bass took a liking to the wiggling mass of Charleston night crawlers which were dangling in his neighborhood. By the way, the many night crawlers your mother and I got some days before we came up did not live long enough to be brought to this delightful climate, but those we caught the night before we left came through in fair shape and immediately became active and fish-luring upon being placed in the worm box here. They lasted until yesterday.

To return to the homemade leader on which the capture of the big bass depended yesterday. All those in the boat were at once apprised of the impending climax and excitement was supreme. I had been fishing quite a bit out from the boat, and once before when bringing in a small bass—one that weighed say a pound and a half—he had broken water, jumping about a foot out, and while it is pretty to see a fish so break water, yet he does it in an effort to shake the hook loose and oftentimes succeeds, so I was holding the end of the rod down close to the water to make it more difficult for the fish to jump. The net was reposing, or had been, on the front end of the Doctor's big boat and your mother had passed it back to the Doctor's capable hands. The net is a good one, a square-nosed, bamboo handle, long enough for any emergency, bought here—not the inefficient kind that you bought in Decatur. The bass was grudgingly yielding to the pull, slowly coming along, almost a tamed bass, yet having in him capacity for one more supreme effort and the woe that effort produced. After it the line went loose, and on being brought in, there dangled the hookless leader broken at the hook. Last year I lost the big bass by a broken line, this year by a broken leader. So I bought this morning some more metal leaders. This was wise, for your mother has already had a leader cut by a pike, and I have caught a pike on your rod which is equipped with a metal leader. The Doctor also caught a pike yesterday and we saw one—in fact the Doctor had him hooked for a moment—which must have been 26 inches long.

The pike this year are more voracious than they were last year. They seem to actually fight harder than last year and when in the boat, we almost want to get out, as you about did last year. I think I had to hold you and the pike both at the same time. At least that's the way I now remember it, and you were harder to hold than was the pike. Your rod seems the lucky one this year. I venture that two-thirds of our fish have been caught with it, and your mother and I are getting superstitious. We expect to have a controversy before long as to who shall use it.

When we got here there were myriads of may flies and the fish were living high, their food dropping like manna from heaven right on their plates. It was hard to persuade them that anything else was fit for food. Most of them were simply not interested, though we did succeed in keeping the table supplied after the first day. One bass I remember tipped the scales at a little less than two and one-half pounds.

Yesterday was a bit overcast almost all day. The Doctor and his wife had just returned from Wasseon where they had been on business for a couple of days. The night before, a fishing trip had been planned with luncheon taken along. The overcast sky kept us near home during the morning and the fish had not yet got very hungry, but we came in with enough fish from that string for two days. Then about 2:30 we headed across the lake and settled near a weed bed, moving here and there, having an occasional bite and catching two or three fish; then another move, and all of a sudden, excitement in abundance, something doing every minute for a short time, bass and pike and lone rock bass uniting to give us a good show, one big fellow following the worm right up to the surface without biting, another leaping a foot or more out of the water in sheer anger, disappointment or what you will, at missing the bait at which he had grabbed, the bass leaping to shake the hook, the bass breaking my leader in his last supreme effort, the pike which Doctor caught actually for a moment out-swimming the reel till the line went slack, the big pike with his whole head above water when he was lightly hooked, the missed bites and the fish actually caught—as handsome a string as one would wish to see, weighing a total of 11 pounds—then home across the three miles of almost motionless water to give as many fish away as possible, to clean the balance, to cook supper and to eat it at about 10 o'clock, and to bed so tired as to be all but helpless. That was yesterday.

The Harris-Gray families came in several days ago. Ann will not be here for some time. She is at Interlocken. Betty and the men went back Tuesday or Monday to return today, I believe. They have a new motorboat. I have written this letter without telling much news and now haven't time to write a newsy letter as I planned. Your mother will probably have to somehow find time to write you. I can only write an incident now and then.

July 12, 1935

I have read the data you sent concerning Madison and found it quite interesting. In thinking it over, I believe I approve the Madison plan of having the teachers take a real part in the civic life of the community, that it will make their services of considerably more value to the community which pays them and create a feeling between school and patrons which is much to be desired. I think that under Mr. Lord there was a real weakness in the school here in that respect, and I think I see signs that something of the Madison plan is now being followed here. For instance, last night there was a chicken dinner at a little church about 11 miles northwest of here which your mother and I attended. We found there a large table occupied by faculty people, and I noticed that they did not leave directly after eating but were doing their best to be sociable, though I noticed too that they were finding it hard to do so.

The Wayne Hughes are back. I dropped in to see them the other evening. Your mother was playing cards in their neighborhood, and I went around to take her home and, while waiting, called on the Hughes who were a bit unsettled in their house, not having got quite all their furniture back. Wayne Jr. had just dropped two quarts of milk and Nancy Gay was cleaning up the mess, which was on the living room rug.

Your mother canned peaches and tomatoes yesterday and finished up the peaches this morning. She then went to Mattoon to play golf with Alice E. I told her that despite her poor assortment of clubs and despite her lack of practice, she could and should beat Alice E. She was rather doubtful.

I called on and was examined by Dr. Iknayan a couple of days ago. The sedentary life I have led in the last few years has brought my heart down till it's about normal in size, and there is nothing to fear from that except I must not exercise until it beats hard and fast as it used to do. . . . I am getting along fine and think I will build back to a satisfactory condition. . . .

I have been thinking somewhat about the possibility of completing your Master's degree this winter without affecting the efficiency of your school work. It may be that there are night classes, or more likely Saturday classes, and it seems to me that perhaps an hour a week perhaps on Saturday might equal a summer term and if that is so, and you find that you can carry both your work and Columbia work, it would be a result highly to be desired to leave your summer open for a vacation. You will sure need it. This suggestion may have no basis in it. It is also true that you should not endanger the success of your teaching merely that you might have a vacation next summer. The suggestion is merely for your consideration. Well this will have to be just a note. It's lunch time.

July 14, 1935

I return herewith the note and co-makers' statement and agreement. There is little news here. Harold left Thursday morning taking with him a number of nice bass, part of which he caught. In fact he caught the limit (5) Wednesday, the largest of which weighed 3 pounds. Dr. Cole, Harold and I spent most of that day fishing, each catching the limit and throwing back a good many bass which were under 10 inches long. We have had little luck since then however. Alice E. and I tried yesterday and a long time today with little success. Yesterday we drove to Charlavoix and had supper there.

Jimmie is a great boy but a handful. In fact your mother and Alice E. hardly are a big enough team to handle him. Vacation has taken on a very different complexion since his advent. It's now pretty late in the evening, and Alice E. is in her room with Jimmie, trying to get him to sleep quietly. Your mother is working on a crossword puzzle and I am trying to write a letter to you which will be of interest while I am too tired to get what little brain I have to work. Betty was down the other night and we had time for one rubber of bridge before a late bedtime.

Your varied activities no doubt keep up a perpetual interest. They are really interesting to read about—as you write of them at any rate. No doubt as you engage in them it is with an ever renewed interest.

Well, I am not going to write a letter tonight.

July 19, 1935

Am sending you two pictures taken here after Jimmie came on to run the family. Harold was here only till Thursday morning. The Doctor and I were determined that, if possible, he should become interested in fishing. The first day, Tuesday, was given to getting settled, though Harold and I were out for a time with little success. Wednesday, however, the Doctor got out the big boat and we chugged up to the place where you chased the bass around an acre or two of lake. Not a bite was had there, and about noon we came back close to home where you caught the pike and off and on had good sport the rest of the day, each of the three of us catching the limit. One of Harold's weighed 3 pounds. He took enough fish home with him for the whole Tolle family and also took, I think, a high regard for the sport of fishing.

Alice E. has had little luck, but I am hopeful that she will still get some good fish, though it is harder now to get any fishing done as Jimmie always requires one attendant and there is much more to do about the house than before. Alice E. and her mother are at the Harrises' tonight playing cards. Alice E. did not go till about 10:30 when Jimmie went to sleep.

I have been under the weather today, my stomach having played me false, but expect to be okay again tomorrow.

There was a strong wind all day and the lake was too rough for comfortable fishing, though Dr. Cole's son and his girl were out several hours. The waves were real high and the boat shipped a little water occasionally, I think, but they enjoyed it. The day has been hot. There has been more heat here than last year. Have had some trouble getting worms but have supply for several days on hand. Some sort of animal, a skunk I suppose, tried to get at them last night but I don't think he succeeded—at least I hope not.

Cherries are ripe, and today we had a box of strawberries, the last of the season I suppose. We also got a box of raspberries today. Traverse City is crowded for the Cherry Festival. Doctor and I slipped in and out yesterday morning and this morning in our quest for worms. Driving was difficult and the city was hot. Tomorrow is the last day of the festival. There is little news. Jimmie is crazy about the water, and Alice E. likes the place as well as we do.

July 29, 1935

We got back home Saturday night having come through in fairly good time, considering that Jimmie was with us, from the pleasant temperature of the Leelanau country to the seething climate of central Illinois in summertime. I find plenty to do around the office here and have been wading along in the mess of it all day long.

At home the yard has a good heavy growth of grass. In fact I think quite a large haystack will be cut from it, and the weeds and grass have hidden the vegetable and flower gardens. The most serious objection to a vacation is that when it ends there is the return to the grind with the accumulated duties of the vacation period. We were indeed sorry that our time at the lake was not longer. Your mother would really like to spend the two months of July and August there, and I would enjoy it myself. I spent a few moments today telling Charley Miller of the good fishing, etc., and trying to make him envious or rather sorry that he had not been along. The vacation would have been better had you been along, and the folks you met there, the Harris and Gray families especially, were sorry that you were not with us.

We are wondering about what time you will be in from New York and how much or little time you will be with us. I suppose you will write us when you know. I think we have some pictures which you will be glad to see, especially of your mother and her 4-pound bass and of Harold and his string and of course pictures of Jimmie in various postures. Jimmie loved it there, especially the lake, and I think he couldn't quite understand it when he waked up at home Sunday morning. We saw them at Mattoon Sunday evening about 6 o'clock and Jimmie was running around all over the yard as active in the heat as he was at the lake. He is such a heavy and active child that he keeps his mother pretty well worn out most of the time.

I haven't time for a real letter today. This is just to let you know that we are home and well. The battery in your car got a short circuit while we were gone and burnt itself up. Had to buy a new one at a cost of $7.50, I believe. Lots of love. We are anxious to have you with us again.

September 4, 1935

Here is a letter which your mother opened thinking that because it came from Madison, she might find it of sufficient importance to wire contents to you. As it dealt only with an offer of rooming quarters, I am simply mailing it.

Last night the Millers served the fish which Charley brought from the North. One was a 10-pound muskie, another a northern pickerel or pike or whatever the proper name is—not many bones. It sure was fine to get some more good fish. Mr. and Mrs. Digby, Mrs. Brown, Mrs. Barnfield, Mrs. Williams, Frank and Mrs. Craig and Bonnie and Byron were the party, and there was just enough fish—we licked the platter clean. Charley and his two companions employed a guide—Lake of the Woods, Canada—and as a result had a great fishing experience. Each caught a muskie; they also caught 10-pound lake trout—plenty of them—also the northern pike or pickerel, and a few bass. They brought a good many home. I played one rubber of bridge after dinner last night and then went home, your mother coming an hour or so later.

Your mother phoned just now that she had had three more cards from you making seven in all. Thanks for writing. There are two things we want to ask: one is your route after you got in the Pittsburgh neighborhood. Your mother wants to know if you went through Pittsburgh. We figured you could save distance by cutting north of Route 40 somewhere in the Pittsburgh neighborhood and we both think you did that, but we lost you in that neighborhood. Also, you fooled us in Ohio as we expected you to spend the night at Columbus. The question I want to ask is "What happened to the cow?" Did she die without benefit of clergy, or did she live long enough to make her Will, etc.? Also, what effect the fright had on the nerves and appearance of the little brown Ford? By the way the car is insured. I don't know whether there is any insurance on the car itself for damage resulting from collision or upset. Have just phoned Charley, and he says there is no insurance against collision and upset resulting in damage to the car itself—just insurance against loss by theft, etc., public liability and property damage to others.

The more I think of it the better pleased I am that you go into the new place with a new car. It gives you a standing at the start which should help. I also feel sure that you will make good with your teaching and that the move is a good one. Of course I ruined to some extent your vacation and am sorry, but I hope you, in your long ride alone, got a hold again on your nerves and will pull out of the depression caused by my sickness and be none the worse for it. I am well and about have my strength back. The fish dinner and rubber of bridge had no ill effect. In fact I feel stronger this morning than ever, even for some days before I went to bed.

Your mother is canning tomatoes today—got a half bushel for 25¢, which was a real bargain. The sun is shining, though it is still fairly cool. The furnace fire went out last night and the house was not uncomfortable this morning if one wore a sweater.

There is no news. We miss you like sin, but will get over that in a short time. Are still doing crossword puzzles.

September 10, 1935

It is very pretty weather and when I tried to reach your mother a moment ago by phone to find out whether she had heard from you or not, I got no repsonse. So I conclude that she is in the yard as she planned to be today.

There is little news here. I am getting along all right and while I am taking things rather easily, yet your mother and I did see Rogers in "Steamboat 'Round the Bend" Sunday, and the picture show "All the King's Horses" last night. Harold and Alice were also over for the show last night, and they and Jimmie called on us Sunday evening.

We are of course anxious to get a good letter from you when you become settled and squared away at your work, but until then we do not want you to burden yourself with writing much to us. By the way, whenever you want the title to the car, let me know and I will send it and direct Charley Miller to transfer the insurance to your name. . . .

Somehow I don't seem to have anything to write about just now. The home life sails on upon an even keel. We are still interested in crossword puzzles. I have caught up with my *Saturday Evening Post* reading. My brief is on file in the Appellate Court. Have been working slowly on a partition suit, which I ought to have started even before I went north, to partition a tract of land, part owned by the Jeffries estate, part by Judge Dunn, and part by various others. It's the land at Oilfield. Your mother and I went to Marshall last week to get some information needed in that suit, and got it at Westfield. Still have to go to Oakland to get information there and then should have all the information necessary to complete the complaint for the suit. The title has been complicated itself for 30 years, and by assignments, deaths, etc., the suit is a rather complicated affair with defendants from Los Angeles to Indianapolis, and from Nome, Alaska to Hollywood, Florida. Americans are nomads, are they not? In the old countries, I think people stay put very well all their lives. In America there is continual change in habitat. You are a pretty good illustration—from Charleston to Lexington to Cicero to Oak Park to Chicago to New York City to Madison, New Jersey—and yet a youngster. Your wandering feet have trodden the muck of Illinois, the bluegrass of Kentucky, the hills of Missouri, the sands of Michigan, the rocky ridges of Canada, the sidewalks of New York; the charms of Germany and Austria are memories of personal experience, and in speeding cars you have traversed Indiana, Ohio, Pennsylvania, Maryland, Virginia and West Virginia. Yes, you have the itching foot.

Well, this letter seems to have run itself out and I will close. Just wanted to let you know that all is well with us.

October 2, 1935

Your letter with the enclosure (Betty's letter) came in this morning. It was delivered at home. You did very well considering that you had written a flock of letters before you came to mine. Indeed, your choice of words and arrangement of them has improved quite a lot since you left the conglomerate structure of English or American as it issued in and around Cicero for the purer language atmosphere of the cultured and sometimes miscalled effete East.

Your mother is still in Kentucky. Alice and Harold dropped into the office yesterday morning, and Alice said that she had received a card from your mother saying she planned to be home Friday or thereabouts. Will be glad to have her back though have encouraged her to stay away as long as she is enjoying herself.

We had a rain—steady rain—for about 24 hours last week, the latter part of which was accompanied by sufficient wind to lay the broomcorn down, flat in some cases, not so bad in others, but bad enough in any case to about double the cost of cutting to the farmer and taking about all of his needed prospective profits. Mr. Hudson had started to cut your mother's broomcorn and had worked the gang about an hour when night came. The next morning the rain came. The wind followed that night. His corn went down least of any that I have seen or heard of, yet the cutting cost him at least $100 more than it would have had there been no rain and wind. He finished cutting yesterday afternoon—has a good crop—the earlier crop and the late crop matured together and his shed is overflowing. Think he had to borrow shed room for a little of it.

I borrowed a car and went out yesterday afternoon as he had been in the office in the forenoon and had left word that he would need a shed and where on earth (that is, in the neighborhood) could he get it. When I got there he had found a shed which he could use a few days. The beans are not going to produce much of a crop but the corn is excellent.

Now that I have told you the farm news, it would seem that there should be something else to write about, but there is not. I have not gone out at night, except Saturday the Millers took me to Alice Elizabeth's where we had a mighty good supper and visit; therefore I have no gossip to tell you. The office has been quiet and I am in good health. Really, Christmas won't be long in coming. After a month comes in, it's just a short time till it goes out. On that theory October is about gone. Then there is left just November, for after November there is really no time at all till Christmas. So we will be seeing you soon. But in the meantime drop us a line as you conveniently can halt a few of the fleeting minutes.

October 11, 1935

Your letter came in yesterday and your mother wrote you yesterday also. So you know that she eventually did come back from Kentucky. She phoned me a few minutes ago that she would come down in the car and pick me up—that she would bring her knitting with her, park in a convenient place, and knit and watch the people go by until I was ready to leave the office. She is now parked in front of Alexander's—in *media res* as it were—knitting and watching to see what and whom she can see.

Charley Miller was in yesterday and I told him there should be collision and upset insurance on the car. So it is now insured against accident to itself where the accident results in damage of more than $25. The first $25 of damage in any accident is not insured. The adding of this insurance is the only excuse I have for writing a letter so soon after Mother's.

There is really no news to tell. I might write of the corn and broomcorn price prospects but will not. I might tell of the weather, but it has been so unattractive lately that I haven't anything nice to say about it. I can say that I am mighty glad to have your mother back. She is very well. Was very sleepy last night and about 7:30 decided she couldn't sit up any longer so to bed we went, and she actually got in 11 hours sleep and wanted more. I think she is merely reacting from the Kentucky trip. Today she has been out and around in the car a considerable part of the day and is as chipper as one could wish.

Well, I won't keep her waiting any longer.

October 17, 1935

It is very embarrassing to forget a name at a critical time. However, in some cases there is an absentminded way of avoiding the embarrassment of being discovered in the lapse of memory. Foolishly, during the time I have been in Charleston, rather too much absorbed in work and too little in people, I permitted my mind to acquire the habit of non-retention of names. In that respect it is as faulty as an ordinary mind at 75 years. As a consequence I have devised a system which works fairly well part of the time, that is when I have not forgotten both names. If both names are gone then the situation is of course hopeless. When but one name is gone, after a moment or two of chatting with the forgotten man, I direct his attention to Mr. Jones whose name I have in mind and say "May I introduce you to Mr. Jones," or some such sentence—simply in an absentminded way—and usually the forgotten man comes across with his name, whereupon I am slightly confused and slightly apologetic, but he can never know for sure what was back of my slip. However, one should never let his memory of people and their names slip as I did.

We appreciate your sending of the candy which will probably come today. That which you brought in August was of the best and we have enjoyed it thoroughly. The 14th was a warm, beautiful day, and in celebration, your mother devised the plan of going to the woods for our supper—the plan contemplated a boiled supper, boiled in our two iron pots over a camp fire. It also included the entertainment in the woods of the Dunns, the Stovers, and the Ashleys—also the Tolles if they could come. So your mother had a busy 14th getting everything ready, the big pot, the little pot, the coffee pot, the cabbage, the onions, the meat, the carrots, the potatoes and a pan of apple dumplings (the latter cooked at home), and about 4 o'clock she and I went out to a sylvan retreat out by the river, out by the stone quarry, out by the old Ashmore river-bridge, where you will remember the little stream trickling across the woods road and falling over the ledge of limestone down into a clear pool below, and then trickling on into the river where now the foliage is painted with fall's most artistic colors and the leaves are dropping one by one, carpeting the ground with rustling color in their disintegration, to nourish the trees from which they fell. After a time the pots were boiling and the Ashleys drifted in to help keep the fire going and prepare the feast. And after there was no daylight left, when six o'clock had come and gone, the Stover car with the Stovers and the Dunns came cautiously round the bend, in its very careful, hesitant approach showing clearly the uncertainty of its driver, who had been wandering around the neighborhood of the old Ashmore bridge looking for a gleam of firelight and seeing none until the moment his auto lights showed around the bend. Well, the dinner was all that a woods-cooked boiled dinner should be; and replete with food and content with the world, we sat around the fire and talked till the full moon was high among the trees, until the fire was low and all of our wraps were in use, and then home and to bed. It was a pleasant way to celebrate the anniversary. Again the 14th had come and gone without rain or storm, the same as it has done every year beginning with the year of our marriage.

On Sunday the 13th, the Tolles, the Millers, Mrs. Barnfield, and we had cooked our supper at the same spot, bacon and eggs, coffee, etc. It was Jimmie's first picnic and perfectly he entered into the picnic spirit. I wish I had his picture sitting straight up on a blanket—as straight as if a shingle were tied to his back—there by the fire, eating his cream of wheat, calling for a second dish, eating his bacon as a special treat, eating his other food as big as life and as hungry as a wolf. Your mother wishes she had his picture stamping along, swinging along, striding along the woods road back deeper into the woods, leading the women on a tramp back to the farm gate while Charley and I, directed or rather watched by Harold, tried unsuccessfully to catch some sort of a fish. Alice E. said that before Jimmie reached Mattoon he was dead to the world, that he remained dead to the world as he was undressed and put to bed and that he didn't stir till time to get up on Monday. He says he had a fine time at the picnic and we could see that he did. He is plenty old, plenty husky and mature for that sort of sport and I suppose that next summer, he will get a lot of it.

Your mother was at a tea yesterday afternoon with Mrs. Andrews. In the morning she had been working in the yard. This morning she is to work in the yard and have her hair washed and this afternoon to go to her card club. This evening we plan to take in the Bushton chicken fry and tomorrow she is driving to Hoopston to a women's "Old China" meeting with Mrs. Buzzard who is to deliver a talk there on "Old China." What is in prospect for Saturday, I don't know. I ought to go to Springfield soon and suppose we will go next week sometime.

There is little news. . . .

November 5, 1935

. . . The letter and the $10 check came yesterday and you now owe on your borrowing from the bank $15 plus some little interest. We enjoyed your fine letter—the one in which you told of your impersonation of Mae West. The whole letter was exceptionally good, making the happenings you told of stand out vividly, and evidencing the fact that you still have a large, saving sense of humor in spite of the experiences which have given you the courage to face lions if necessary. There is little news with us. The Taylors (E.H.) and your mother and I took supper with the Albert Moores in Springfield Saturday night. The Taylors spent the night with the Moores and we (your mother and I) went to Elizabeth Pasfield's for the night. Sunday we had chow mein at the Moores', for which the Millers drove up; home shortly after 8 at night. Had a nice time, but both a bit tired by the trip. Your mother is in Mattoon today, as Alice E. is giving some sort of an entertainment, a luncheon or tea or something.

I suppose you were asleep and did not know of the earth tremor in your neighborhood when it occurred. No one felt it here and I suppose it did not extend this far.

Had a letter today from Mrs. Cole. She and the Doctor are well and are planning for next summer at the lake. We have made no plans yet.

I don't know if I have written you fully of the crop situation or not. It seems to me you made some crack about that in one of your letters. This is the situation. The broomcorn is in the bale waiting for a buyer. The price is not what it should be, but enough to give a profit. It was a fair crop and a fair quality. Your mother has 30 acres of good corn and I have 20 that is Indian corn. All Indian corn was left a bit soft by the early freeze, but shucking is beginning now. The damp weather is injuring it some, as the heavy rain and wind before the freeze bent it so that some ears are in contact with the ground. There were not enough combining (threshing outfits) machines to take care of the big bean acreage in the few days we have had, so more than half of the beans are still in the fields. They may yet be saved if the weather turns favorable. Beans cannot be threshed if they are damp. A heavy dew puts them out of condition until 9 or 10 o'clock of a clear day. There was a big acreage and few machines. Your mother's 30 acres are still in the field. In spite of the seeming impossibility there will be considerable corn on the Sangamon farm. It is soft and will dry chaffy and of light weight, yet there will be some corn there to sell.

Well, there is nothing more to write about just now. I believe I will send you Lillian's letter.

November 18, 1935

I guess I got so interested in the leaves from the law magazine as an aid to your English work that I forgot to put my letter in and the renewal note for McArthur's note which matures tomorrow. It is now owned by the bank and I intended to send you two notes for your choice, one a pink note like the McArthur note which retains a lien on the car and the other the regular form of note to the bank—a green note like the one enclosed. I had the two notes and wrote a letter about them and I can't lay their loss to Mr. Farley, for you got the law magazine leaves.

The $65 check came in today and I have paid the $15 balance plus $1.63 interest on the note you gave the bank and have taken that note up. That left $48.67 of the $65 which I have paid as follows: $5.57 interest on the McArthur note and $43.10 of the principal, which leaves $275.00 still unpaid. The note is due tomorrow. In renewal I prefer that you give a straight note to the bank which I will sign with you, rather than the pink one like the one you gave when you bought the car, for that one kept a lien on the car. So if you will sign the enclosed note and return it to me, I will sign it and take up the McArthur note.

The enclosed paid note you may tear up when you have received it.

We are well. The Tolle family was over for a cold lunch last night. Alice E. and Jimmie are coming over tomorrow evening and spending the first two hunting days with us, and I think we will have Jimmie a day or two next week. I hope to go out and catch me a pheasant Wednesday. That is the first hunting day. Hoped to have E. H. Taylor with me but he cannot get away from school. It is longer from September to Christmas than I supposed it would be, and you are not a bit more anxious to get home than we are to have you here. There is no news.

P.S. I will thank McArthur when I see him.

November 27, 1935

I don't believe I have written you for some days. I ought to report that I received the $25 check of the State Auditor and it has been applied on your note, leaving a balance of $250. There is also some auto insurance which has not been paid. It is charged to me, and there is no pressing need for early payment. The bank stock is not yet easy to sell, but if you really want it sold, I guess I can take it over and then sell it at my leisure so that there will be no necessity to sacrifice it. At any rate it is worth enough to pay the note off here. There is little news with us.

The Tolles take dinner tomorrow with the Tolles, Sr. We are having some folks in to eat with us—the Parkers and I think four others. The turkey has been delivered at home and all the fixings are there and apparently the dinner will be a good one. Sunday night we served pheasant to the Andrews, the Burruses and the Scruggs. Sunday noon dinner at *Bucklers*—Mrs. Jeffries hostess. Monday we ate on the remains of the pheasants. Tuesday noon, quail. Tuesday night, a big dinner at the church which I attended while your mother was at the duplicate whist club. Today we are not eating meat, but from the appearance of the turkey I think there will be plenty left to run over the rest of this week and far into the next before we finally have turkey soup. Jimmie was over Monday night to give his folks free rein for a dinner and card game they were having, and Alice E. and Jimmie were over the first two days of the hunting season. I was out hunting on three different days last week and attended the Don Craig funeral Saturday afternoon in Mattoon. Altogether living has been strenuous and I am pretty lazy and no account.

The bean crop was finally harvested. It was not much of a crop but brought in some money—about $4.35 an acre. The corn is being shucked. It is turning out well here in Coles and is worth 45 cents a bushel. The broomcorn has not been sold and the market for it is weak.

Glad you went to see Kate Graves. I have not seen her since I left Kentucky. Thought a lot of her and am of course sorry that there could not have been some association through life. Glad you liked her. I wondered if you would. One never knows what effect time will have on a person. She used to be the jolly, fun-loving sort. I haven't the slightest idea what her life has been, or its effect upon her.

The sun occasionally shines now. In fact it has just broken through for the first time today. There are still clouds in the sky, but appearances are that they may all drift away.

Sign the enclosed bank stock certificate on the back at the X mark in the presence of a witness and return to me. We are all well.

December 10, 1935

I enclose a letter from Mrs. Krueger which was enclosed in a letter to your mother. We have both enjoyed reading Mrs. Krueger's letter to you. I sent you your auto title yesterday special delivery and Charley sent the insurance policy.

There is not much news. Your mother, Alice E. and Mrs. Jeffries were in Champaign yesterday—all, I think, upon Christmas shopping bent. It was a beautiful day and the weather was bright and pleasant. Today it is uncomfortably raw and windy. We are all well and would be marking time to your return were it not now, as it always is at this time of the year, that your mother is busy with so many things on her mind that she can hardly let herself go to sleep at nights. Besides the many things looking toward the coming of you and Christmas, she has certain places to go during the week: yesterday to Champaign, today to Mrs. E. H. Taylor's to lunch and cards, Thursday to Mrs. Frank Craig's to lunch and cards, and so on. I think there is also a show to see today or tomorrow, and what else is in the cards that have been dealt, or will be in those to be dealt, I know not, but this I know—that the outside activities coupled with the speeded tempo of the pre-Christmastime have got your mother stepping high, wide, and handsome.

Your letter yesterday was a dandy, and we were particularly glad to know that you had taken a little time off to sleep and rest and had got a quick response from an overworked and insulted stomach and nerve system.

Jimmie is still smart. I believe he thinks we have all been spoofing him about Santa Claus; can't see how he could come down a chimney or get his sleigh and deers on the roof. At any rate Jimmie will have no more of such foolish talk—has definitely barred it from the family chatter.

December 14, 1935

A few days ago your mother attended a picture show—I have forgotten the name but Martini was the singer and hero—as a guest of Mrs. Taylor. I believe I wrote you that Mrs. Taylor was having a lunch and card party. The fact was that she had a lunch and theatre party. At any rate your mother was so pleased with the show that she insisted that I go at night. I was not averse as I have heard Martini on the radio and had been so pleased with his singing that I really wanted to see what he looked like. All this introduction but leads in a verbal way up to the meat or the reason for writing this letter. At the show I sat next to Mr. Koch and learned from him that his niece or daughter, I never did quite learn which, who teaches in New Jersey, is coming through to Charleston next Saturday, and that she expected to have the train stop for her here. The way to insure that it will stop is to tell them, when you ask for a ticket to Charleston and they tell you the train does not stop, that you will go on the Pennsylvania to Terre Haute unless the train stops here. At least that is the understanding I got, though perhaps the arrangement should be made beforehand. You can learn as to that. . . .

Winter has not been severe so far. We have a load of wood for burning and will keep a fire in the living room while you are here, unless the weather gets too cold and we have to close the draft up the fireplace chimney to keep the house warm.

1936

January 18, 1936

Mother planned to write you today but I believe she missed doing so as she gave me no letter to mail to you. I suppose you are at a theatre or something this afternoon, for you said in your last letter that you had the urge to see a show and this is Saturday.

Well, the Chenaults—David and Katherine, Nancy and Emily and Virginia Corbin—came in Tuesday afternoon and from then on out it was a busy week around 820 South 6th. At noon I found your mother just about too lazy to have an interest in much of anything and I am just about the same way. There has been some playing of cards and something of this and that pretty much all the time. This morning the visitors left, planning to go home by way of Indianapolis. I hope they changed their minds before getting out of town and that they went south on 130 for the roads are slick clear across Indiana, I learned this afternoon. We sure enjoyed their visit, and I think they were not dissatisfied.

Mrs. Rogers* died a few days ago. Your mother and I went to the funeral yesterday afternoon, while the rest of our household went to a show in Mattoon. The Appellate Court decided the Morrison-Watson case yesterday affirming the judgment of the Circuit Court which was another victory for our side in that case. I hope there will be no more battles.

I enclose your bank dividend. Spend this great sum carefully. The bank statement is a good one and the book value of a share of stock is $142, though it is not yet being sought as an investment. There is no news. Your mother and I will probably lay up tonight and tomorrow to recuperate from the unusually intense activity of the passing week.

January 23, 1936

The thermometer is 45 over there by my desk so I am backed up against the gas stove using the typewriter desk. Yesterday the wind did blow and the snow swirled and darted around, restless as the spirit of a departed sinner is thought by some to be. The thermometer when I left home about 8:30 yesterday morning was ten above and when I went home at 4:30 was fifteen below. During the night it fell two more degrees, but your mother gathered up most of the blankets on the place, and with them on our bed, a good fire going and no windows open, we slept comfortably and well. You know at our house there is considerable fresh air that finds its way in without open-

*Mrs. Rogers—Harold Tolle's grandmother in Mattoon, Ill.

ing any windows. The snow which was blowing around had fallen the night before and the sun shone yesterday and is shining today. There was a radio announcement yesterday evening that there would be few schools open around Chicago and none in Chicago today. In one school apparently the children were to stay all night, for the announcer said that the children there were comfortable and being well cared for.

There is little news. The David Chenaults and Sissie have come and gone. They went home by Indianapolis and had icy roads to that place and a few miles south. Across Ohio they found heavy snow and reached Lexington about 4:30 P.M.. There they were marooned until Monday by drifted snow. They made an effort to get to Mt. Sterling Sunday but after eight miles gave it up. We enjoyed their visit and I think they also enjoyed it. Alice E. and Jimmie were over one day and night this week. Your mother ordered her yarn last Saturday by letter to the yarn house. She will write tomorrow. . . . .

I have wondered if you were caught in New York by the big snow last weekend. You had written that you were hungry to see a play, and it seemed more than possible that you had gone in just in time for the traffic troubles which the snow caused. Hope you were not so inconvenienced. Well, while my back is warm enough, my hands are cold and I believe I will quit, especially as your mother plans to write you a newsy letter tomorrow. I don't plan to run for office. The result would be too uncertain. Tuesday the Republican candidate for city judge in Mattoon was soundly beaten.

January 30, 1936

Your mother is sitting there in the northwest corner of the office where it is not very warm, knitting on a round needle, using a greenish sort of yarn. She has had a right unsatisfactory day. The thermometer was only 10 below this morning and she felt that she should go to Mattoon after she got the dishes washed. After a while she phoned me that the car wouldn't start and a garage man was coming out to start it. The car had to be towed to the garage, and time went by. A thermometer in the sun showed 10 above. So about 11 she started. On my way back to the office from lunch the air was pretty full of blowing snow and I heard that it had been announced by radio that a blizzard was on its way, and as it looked as if the blizzard was here, I phoned to your mother in Mattoon and advised her that she better come home. So she got in about 3, somewhat disgusted with her day. She only saw Jimmie about half an hour and didn't half have her visit out—and it is bright and quiet outside.

Yes, I got your bank dividend. Thanks a lot. You and I are now square. There is little news. I enjoyed the letter from George Prewitt. I reckon it's a good thing for the weather to get too bad for us to get out much. Mother says she cannot remember whether she wrote you that newsy letter which in my last letter I promised you she would write. In fact I do not think she did write it. So you have the promised news yet coming to you.

We were out to dinner Sunday with the Jessie Craigs. The Funkhousers were there also. A wonderful chicken, oyster, etc., dinner. About 5 o'clock we came in to the show, "Tale of Two Cities." From there to the Millers' for a few minutes and then home to fix the fire. The thermometer only went to minus 15 that night. The car was sure stiff to handle. . . .

The yarn you sent is pretty. Mother is trying to use a skein a day, though she hardly expects to do her stint today. Alice and Harold are going to the President's ball tonight.

February 14, 1936

I suppose if I should paint you a word picture of Winter's conquest of central Illinois, it would fall short of protraying it as realistically as your own mental picture of his conquest of the East. We have not had the drifted snow to the extent that other parts of the Middle West have been afflicted, but there has been the slick road and cold weather to such an extent that we have used our car little and your mother's rides to Mattoon have been infrequent. I have had to shovel coal more heavily than usual and have bundled up more than usual coming to the office and many times have had to walk with the extreme care of one walking among eggs, but we have kept warm, and with us there has been somewhat of pride in watching the thermometer and the weather reports to see how many days in succession the thermometer would pass the zero mark. We have not been really inconvenienced, but many people have, especially in a hundred or two homes where the ground has frozen below the surface water pipes and they have been without water for a considerable time. This occurred all around the Winter Corner and in other parts of the city. I think the city has been making some progress in thawing out surface pipes by the use of electricity in some way. Thawing them by building fires on the surface was found to be too slow and ineffective in view of the great numbers of frozen pipes.

Your mother's skirt is finished. She tried it on yesterday. It fits nicely and unless it stretches too much will be quite satisfactory. She has only 5 hanks of yarn left for the waist and figures she will have to knit fast to come out even.

Alice E. is having the reading circle today and planned to send Jimmie over for the day, but a new cold wave with snow is blowing in from the northwest and I doubt whether she will risk sending him over, especially as there is a film of ice on the roads—not much but enough to make driving uncertain in spots.

We received the picture of the boat and of various parts of it. The prospect of the big boat ride is exciting. I won't admit that I can ever be so fortunate as to get such a boat ride until we have warped away from the dock and are headed downstream to wave goodbye to the Statue of Liberty, but I get quite a kick out of anticipation "anyhoo." You say there are many things to do before we embark after we reach your section. If it is reasonably possible to do so, I would like to see Kate Graves. Except for Paul Prewitt there is practically no thread of communication between any friend of my youth and me. That all ties have disappeared probably has arisen out of some defect in my make-up. Perhaps I have been too exclusively concerned in the circumstances of my own immediate place. Whatever the cause, I would like to see Kate.

There is little news here—an explosion yesterday in Mattoon, probably from leaking gas, which wrecked three downtown buildings and killed one and injured several people; a man burned so seriously here yesterday that he died. He was using kerosene to start a fire.

Your mother said this morning that the older Weir girl is to have a party today to announce her engagement. Harryman is now married to Miss Ewalt. When and where the wedding occurred is not stated. Mrs. Wyeth says that Bobbie emphatically denies the rumor that she and Byron are to be married. There is another rumor that a young Mattoon attorney, Mr. Werden, who is associated with the Craig and Craig office, is deeply interested in Miss Barnfield. There is one less dog in the crowd which has been making our yard a place of rendezvous. He fell before a policeman's gun. Had been living on the Thomas porch and tearing up the cushions there.

This is all the neighborhood news I can think of. Your dress will be pretty. You and your mother will make a charming picture together on the boat in the new outfits.

February 28, 1936

This is your mother's birthday. She says she is 49. Birthday presents are barred because your mother says we are going to spend some money in preparation of the proper wardrobes for the boat trip. The bathrobe she made for me the first year we were married won't do, she says. The old slippers are not good enough, and so on and so on. I should worry. It's her job to get us ready. She brought me to the office this morning on her way to Mattoon to pick up Jimmie and relieve Alice E. of his care while she prepares today and this evening gives a dinner party or something. Jim always seems to enjoy entertaining us and running our house. He is quite the master of the situation at 820 South 6th and becomingly bears and exercises his authority.

Today is a beautiful day, freezing as yet, but with the sun shining as brightly as it is, the air will be balmy soon. The freezing morning had the feel of spring in it and I feel sure there will be no more bitter cold.

You must have got quite a kick in seeing and hearing the three youngsters of your Chicago days. You didn't say whether you looked them up behind the scenes but I suppose that you did not, though no doubt they would have been tickled also to have seen someone out of their Chicago experience.

The boat trip is beginning to loom larger as the time draws near. I really expect to gain a lot of repose from it, and I have thought all along that you, if you will while you are on the boat seek rest and repose above everything—not be much concerned in the boat activities—will gain a benefit that you are probably seriously in need of. You may expect me to take full charge of you and forbid this and that to you with all the assurance of a political dictator, and that, if you should show any inclination to disobey my mandates or circumvent them, drastic steps will be taken to enforce implicit obedience. It has been long since I have thought it needful to advise you or direct your course, but in this case, after your long period of labor without vacation, I intend to put you back in the old role of the obedient child, at least until I can see that the ravages from constant work have been repaired. Probably, I will be able to turn you loose a day or two before we get back to New York, but I anticipate that it will take at least eight days for the sea air and me to get all the weariness out of your bones.

Your mother is deep in knitting. When that is done she will proceed to something else for the trip. Just now all her spare thoughts are concerned in finding and buying the proper coat for the trip. So far, the one at home suits her better than any she has been able to find in the Charleston stores, so her mind is turning to Champaign, Terre Haute, Indianapolis. I imagine that when the car rolls out of the garage to head east with us that we will be prepared. There is little news. The streets, or rather the parkways, are badly torn up by the workmen hunting gas and water leaks, and more will be torn up. They are getting worse and will probably be bad in appearance all summer in many places. Take care of yourself—rest all you can.

March 14, 1936

I wonder if you got over your sick spell quickly. Have had a feeling that you have been dragging ever since Christmas and have feared that you would catch a cold while in a run-down condition. Hope you are coming along all right now, that you make it to the 10th and then the boat ride, with nothing to do and nowhere to go, will put you on your feet in good shape for the last long mile to June. Your mother and I had a touch of something—I think it was caused by onion sandwiches with milk which we ate for supper Sunday night. I pulled out of it a day or two before your mother did. She was sicker and madder than I was. However, she is well enough this morning to go to Mattoon. Just had to see Alice E. and Jim. We were not really ill—just nauseated and headachy. The trouble may have been a slight touch of Jim's summer flu.

We were in Mattoon when Jim surprised himself and the rest of us by giving an excellent illustration of a very seasick person. In just a moment's time and without any warning, which we had sense enough to heed, a stream issued from his mouth with considerable power behind it, and at once the chair, the rug, the hardwood floor around, and his mother were a mess. Jim was scared, as it was his first experience in that line, and cried for a while. We should have been warned, as at supper time it made him disgusted to look at his soup with a crouton swimming around in it and he ordered, with disgust in his voice, his grandmother to take the crouton out. Then he refused to eat anything, and I hurried through my meal and roughed him around the living room and his mother came in and took him just in time to save me from the deluge which I had stirred up or rather undammed. Last reports Jim was hungry again and the Mattoon folks are well.

There is little news. Mother has the rest of the yarn and is crazy (she says) about the buttons. Thanks for the instruction as to clothes. This seems to be a social affair as much as a boat ride. Apparently I will have no need of rough clothes. I get the impression from something I saw in the *Chicago Tribune* that the boat will be loaded to capacity, and if so, there will be a fair-sized town on board so far as population is concerned, for the *Georgic* is a big boat. Well, I must close.

April 27, 1936

We haven't written you as we should. Two nights in Washington with the Colvins, one at Natural Bridge, two at David's* and one at Helen's. Home about 4 o'clock Sunday afternoon—a good trip you gave us, not particularly a restful trip but surely a change from the customary routine. Found the Tolles well and glad to see us, much interested in the trip. Should have written you along the line and as soon as we reached home, but many good

*David Chenault, brother-in-law—Mt. Sterling, Ky.

intentions have no fruition, and such was the case here. Also we would like to have a line from you. Did you have an unpleasant reaction—too tired to think and work—or was the result just the opposite? I am at the office rather feeling swamped and in no mood for writing a letter. Therefore this is not a letter but just a notice that we are at home well and in every spare moment living over the trip with you.

April 28, 1936

Your card from old Greenwich was a surprise. I rather thought that for a week or two you would be adding to your hours of sleep whenever possible and reveling in memories of the boat trip, but am glad you had pep left for the Connecticut visit.

You remember Theodosia Newman, of course. Have had some business dealing with Mrs. Newman recently and find her a very sensible, interesting person in spite of her facial expression which I suppose fell to her by nature and not by volition. She was telling me that her daughter had ulcers of the stomach and she, being put on cooked milk as a diet, drank so little of it because she disliked milk, as to lose weight fast enough to break her health down almost. A man at the People's Drugstore told her of a remedy to the use of which he attributed his life in a case of stomach ulcers. Theodosia bought a box or bottle of the tablets at three dollars a box or bottle, I don't know which. In the box are tablets for 30 days—three a day. She used that box and half another box and is completely recovered. The name is PHUNDER'S TABLETS. You might investigate. If they are as good as Mrs. Newman thinks, you can save the cows a lot of work.

Your mother has gone to a luncheon at Mrs. Andrews and I ate down town at Bill's. Tonight we go to a school dance. There is a dinner in the offing next week for both of us and I think a couple of bridge meets for your mother this week. Saturday night we are to have Jim in charge of us. The housecleaning is of course untouched.

Don't know just how much we wrote of our trip home. The roads were bad for the most part till we hit the Kentucky line—full of chuck holes and in places almost no roads at all. We were forced to drive slowly most of the time, though we did very well from Georgetown home, thank you. If we haven't written of the trip we will tell you about it sometime or maybe write you. Don't know how lasting the impressions of the drive will be. We are well.

May 4, 1936

I am sending a set of the cruise pictures. Most of them are very good and they are swell reminders of the joys of that trip. Your mother is in the throes of housecleaning, and of course I have at times to conduct myself very carefully around home for the present—to be extremely diplomatic. No matter how careful I am it is natural that there should be some denotations now and then during housecleaning periods.

I don't know whether we ever wrote you of the trip home or not. From Madison to Washington was a long two hundred and odd miles because of the curly roads and the innumerable chuck holes. We had a nice lunch somewhere along the line, and with Colvin's instructions to guide us, had no difficulty in driving to the door of his apartment. Had supper that night at the dining room of Colvin's apartment building, and breakfast Mrs. Colvin served. Spent the day seeing Washington under Colvin's guidance, the Supreme Court building, the Capitol, the Congressional Library and various other sights of interest—a well-spent day with lunch at a large department store, supper at a French place, its name being the French word for snail. None of our party of six cared to try the snails, but some who were there were eating them with relish. It was an interesting place to eat, a good meal with white wine to make it better. The next day we spent an hour at Mount Vernon and three at Richmond in the rain, seeing a good many things of interest there after we had walked several blocks looking for a place where Virginia ham was served. By the way, we found such a place and your mother had ham, but I preferred steak, and when we got to Kentucky there was plenty of ham just as good as Virginia ham. The same day we were in Richmond we drove on to Natural Bridge through the Blue Ridge, seeing the most beautiful sunset framing in flaming gold some mountain peaks. From Natural Bridge we drove the next day to Mt. Sterling—miserable roads from Richmond to the Kentucky line for the most part—stopping for lunch with the Lloyd Smiths at Rainelle and reaching Mt. Sterling about 8 o'clock. There called on Mother Chenault and spent the night with the David Chenaults. Lunch next day with the Garnetts* and dinner and the night with the Davids. The next morning to Helen's where Lillian and Ruth and Buddie and her two girls met us. Sunday we drove on to Charleston, having had our lunch somewhere in Indiana and reaching here about 4 o'clock. Such is the very condensed log of our journey.

This letter has been spoiled by interruptions. Had intended to write a real letter, but several things have come up to destroy the continuity of my

*Garnett Chenault, a brother-in-law—Mt. Sterling, Ky.

thoughts and put me in a frame of mind out of which no good letter can grow. Alice E. and Jim were with us yesterday and you know we enjoyed that. Your mother took Jim to Sunday school but your mother did not enjoy the lesson prepared for the infant class. Jim didn't tell me whether he enjoyed it or not. We are well. We cannot tell you how very much joy you gave us in the trip and your company. You are a good sport to have around—not looking so much for your own pleasure as for the pleasure of others.

May 7, 1936

Glad you changed your room. Almost slipped up on you, didn't it? I send with this a letter from Aunt Nannie, a newspaper clipping, and a letter to you from me which has already become fairly well-traveled. I wrote it after dinner at the Natural Bridge Hotel and one to Alice E., sealed the two letters and addressed them. Your mother had the stamp supply so I took the letters to her for stamps. She wanted to read them, so I directed a couple more envelopes and gave them to her. As you know, the Scotch in her ancestry is sometimes the prevailing force, so in this case I reckon she decided to put one over on the Government and save a penny on each letter. At any rate, they were mailed each bearing the post office symbol of two cents. Alice E.'s was delivered to her and I think she still owes the postman a penny. Notice of yours was left with the mail at your door but you overlooked it, so the letter sorrowfully came on to Charleston. What may have been of news when it was written is news no longer.

Mother is still cleaning house and are we in a mess! Yesterday I made an excuse not to go home at noon, but today she forestalled that by phoning me directions to come home at lunch. I was suspicious but went. She did have a nice lunch on the back porch. While I was there, I might as well put in a few screens and did. Nothing more needs mentioning. It was nice and restful sitting on the porch eating lunch leisurely. The foliage has all come out since our return. There are splotches of color. The birds are much in evidence, and I conclude from that fact that cats are scarce in the neighborhood.

We enjoyed your letter and Betty's. Can see why Betty would feel a bit lonesome since the Grays and Harrises are not so constantly planning their pleasures together, and can well understand why she finds it so nearly impossible to replace your companionship. There's a real reason for that to be found in your nature and dispositon.

We are well. Were at a card party and dinner last night at the Andrews' and I am a bit sleepy. As you may recall I was always sleepy on the boat with no time to sleep. Now after one night of late retirement I find myself sleepy. Suppose there is something in habit. . . .

May 13, 1936

Well, tomorrow is your birthday and this letter will not reach you until the 15th. Your mother and I have wanted to send you a "little something" but have not been able to think of anything you would need or would find sufficiently unusual to give you a thrill. Of course we have thought of the hats of Nassau, but there is no way for us to now get a dozen or so of them, and so we are finally at the point of sending you a small check with the instruction that you use it to get you a little something or other for yourself. . . .

Mrs. Wyeth (Grace), Mrs. Watson of Champaign, a tall stately blond, Miss Harris and a Miss Tillitson, I think the name is, called Sunday afternoon to view our back premises. Your mother was up with Jimmie taking a nap so I did the honors. Miss Tillitson said that she had been doing some work for the travel bureau of Columbia at the time you engaged our passage, and I believe she said that she had some correspondence with you relating to it, or at least prepared or typed the letters or something relating to the matter. She said that the matter only impressed itself on her at all because from the correspondence it appeared that your mother and father were going on the cruise with you and they were from Charleston. She spoke of the Mr. Van- "Something" whose name she didn't remember—the booking agent whom we met, as you will remember. She seemed struck with the thought that the world is small indeed—that she little thought when the matter was up at the travel bureau that she would soon meet the parents. My impression is that she did not meet you. At any rate she did not think she would know you. Wasn't that a wonderful trip? It was certainly kind of you—good of you to give it to us. There is nought but pleasure in its memories, and though I still have an occasional qualm that we let you spend so much money on us, yet I cannot—never could—find it in my heart to criticize that big expression arising from your generous and happy nature.

Alice E. had a bad sore throat Sunday, so Jimmie was brought over and has been with us until this morning. Alice E. is some better and Harold and she thought it better that Jimmie be brought home to sleep in the other room there. Also Josephine was with us, and now that it is determined that the bad throat is not scarlet fever or something serious and Josephine is needed in Mattoon, both have gone there. While here, Jimmie had a stomach ache. (Never breathe it, but he had been given strawberries and bananas and his ache was a natural result.) The ache occurred while we were at a dinner party at the Thuts' and Jimmie got in his crying, beyond Josephine's control. So your mother left her dinner half-eaten, and I left the party right after dinner. When I got home Jimmie was asleep, the doctor had gone and all was peaceful, but it was too late for me to return to the party which had adjourned from the dinner table to a sleight-of-hand performance at Eastern Illinois. Inasmuch as I really missed the like performance on the boat, I was anxious to see this one by a professional.

There is little other news. Much of the housecleaning is done. Nothing has been done in the flower garden. We are thinking a lot of you at this your birthday time. Of course your mother has not had time to write and that's one of the reasons for this delayed letter. . . .

May 20, 1936

The weather has really been delightful in the main—rains as needed and in between sunshine and shadow, the rapid clothing of the bare landscape in green, interspersed here and there with splotches of color where flowers bloom, such as is now the beautiful backyard at 820 South 6th where the iris, the poppies and other flowers in lesser numbers, are almost enough to satisfy the eye of a painter looking for a symphony in color to transfer to the canvas. But in the country the rows and rows of corn have shown their green through the brown of the soil, and wheat and oat fields are a solid green, of course. We ought really not to want to go anywhere under weather conditions such as have been here. Furthermore, there is a well authenticated report that the Ambraw is just right for channel cat and croppies.

Just so far I came with this letter and then had to go out in the country for an hour, and so the letter will proceed on another theme. Alice E. and Jimmie recovered from their attacks of the flu, and while that was going on, your mother went on with her cleaning and by Saturday had the house clean to the kitchen and the curtains hung, and in the main the yard was trim. So early Sunday morning we picked up the three Winters and went to the Sangamon County farm. After dinner at noon we called on several people, and at Elizabeth Pasfield's your mother had a bad coughing spell and lost her voice. She had had a slightly sore throat for a day or two. When we got home she went to bed and is still in bed taking lots of Dr. Iknayan's medicine and I think wearing out the flu gradually. Alice E. brought Josephine over this morning and cleaned up whatever dishes were in the kitchen, and I have no trouble much getting meals for your mother, though it leaves little time at home for recreation. I think however your mother will be up and around in a day or two.

We haven't heard from you in a week and know how busy a time was ahead of you, so are not worried at all. You know it really is not a long time before you will be heading west and really the summer will be half-over before it gets here. As I grow older the months go more and more quickly. Well, someone has just come in and this letter is hopeless.

June 1, 1936

Your story of the picnic was a good one. Congratulations. We enjoyed the picnic a lot through the story.

There is little news here. Alice E. and Jim were over yesterday and we had a good day. Our impression has been that you have engaged the Cole cottage this year. Consequently we have done nothing about that. However, in talking it over we wondered how we got the impression that the cottage has been engaged. Let us know if you have attended to that. Also, it's about time for your mother to know your plans. Will you all leave from here, or will you join them in Michigan? If you go directly to Michigan, you all ought to make your arrangements to reach the cottage the same day. I have forgotten when your school adjourns for the summer.

Your mother and I attended the tea on the college lawn yesterday for the graduates who were there in cap and gown. It was a lawn tea with grape juice and cookies instead of tea and wafers. The day was beautiful, and indeed the weather has been exceptionally nice. Today there is a rather high wind and the air is pretty full of dust particles. The WPA street work has kept considerable sand and dust around on the streets, and much of it is now in the air. They have been re-laying street right around this office corner ever since I got back from the east—four days a week, and sand and dirt on the street drift into the office with every puff of wind. It's astonishing how long it takes them to get anywhere considering the number of men working, but I suppose the work just has to last till election.

Your mother is getting along very well, has not full strength back yet, but coming along and getting ambitious. I just talked her out of giving a party or so, or think I did. Frequently when I think I have her convinced, her plans go right along.

June 10, 1936

Was mighty sorry to be away from home when you called last night but last night was "bank" night at the picture show, and you mother was determined that I should go. I think she fully expected my name and number to be called for the $175 which was the amount standing ready to be awarded to someone by Lady Luck. Naturally Lady Luck could only favor one, and so my number was passed over with all but one. However, the show was a good one with a few murders, a love story and many comic elements most of which were supplied by Butterworth. The name was "Angel-something," perhaps "Half Angel."

It seems to me there is little if any difficulty about the Lake vacation and I am sorry my letter was disquieting. I had not planned to spend all the time there this year. Last year I thought it too expensive, not in money actually spent, for we can live there as cheaply as here, but in loss of business at the office and in other respects. So my plan has been to go there and back weekends as I can, while you, your mother, Alice E. and Jimmie will be there all the time. I rather think it will be foolish for you to come home before going to the Lake for we will probably be there two or three days before you get there from Detroit. I think we plan to be there the evening of the 26th. Your conception of the law business is in some respects correct. At times proceedings may be delayed to suit a lawyer's convenience, but for all that, the "Law" long ago earned and gained the reputation of being a jealous mistress who if neglected will promptly bestow her favors upon more attentive suitors. I have ever been inattentive, and she has responded in keeping with her reputation.

Your mother had had quite a time for herself since we got home from our beautiful trip: first housecleaning, second the flu, and third a sort of recurrence of the flu which, while not at all serious has been trying. I have been nurse, cook, dishwasher, yard "oversee-er" and what not, though Alice E. has been over several times to give me a fresh start. We have gotten along very well, and when my cooking has palled on me, I have gone to a restaurant. Your mother has had to put up with my service and in the main has made little complaint, though there may have been many times when she felt that complaint was justified. She is now downstairs part of the time for her meals, and should pull out rapidly, though being too steadily at home is trying on her nerves of course.

Now quit worrying about your summer. We will notify Dr. Cole in a few days when we expect to be at the Lake. The vacation will work itself out satisfactorily to all of us I think. Will be awfully tickled to see you and will enjoy being with you, as I always do. You are a cheerful cuss and being with you is like a tonic in the springtime. So here's mud in your eye for a happy summertime, both at the Lake and in Charleston.

July 8, 1936

The only thing about this weather which has any tendency to make me content is that you four are somewhere else. If it's hot there, you can at least go down to the beach and stay there. I about got blistered from the sheets last night. At least they were hotter than blood temperature. At supper last night at the restaurant table with Mr. and Mrs. Heller, she said she played bridge yesterday afternoon. Bob and I went out on the prairie yesterday afternoon to some harvest fields. There was a very good breeze out there and the heat was not so oppressive as in town. Corn is of course being hurt, curling in the heat, but I think it can stand three or four more days and still produce some corn, though the crop is probably already cut. Broomcorn is also hurt.

I had the radio on the other night while I was reading and after a time realized that the program was advertising the boat *Roosevelt* and its daily trips to St. Joseph, leaving Chicago at 9 o'clock your time and costing, as I understand it, $1.50. That seems to me the proper second leg of the journey to Traverse City. No doubt I can there get a bus for Traverse City. Had worked over bus schedules quite a bit that day and had decided that they would be altogether too complicated to mess with.

Am still watching grain markets—wheat and oats. They have been booming of course. Haven't sold the Sangamon wheat, as I get a chance there to hold a little while after threshing. The oats, however, have to go in at the market when delivered. Imagine that the oats are already delivered and that the wheat is in process of delivery, as there has been no rain to interfere with the proposed schedule. Am up on law matters for the month or practically so but cannot come to the Lake this week.

Imagine fishing with you all is largely a matter of getting food. However, with the success you have been enjoying and the possibility of the big bass biting at any time, you must find some sport in it. How are the worms holding out? Suppose, when and if I get there, will have to bring some worms along, as those you had, if still alive, must be getting pretty tired.

There is no news here. I think I said, Alice E., in one of my letters, that I saw Harold the day I went to Sangamon, and he was well. How does Jimmie take to the water this year? Is there any prospect of his actually learning to swim this trip? Imagine that girl, I have forgotten her name, who swims so well and who likes Jimmie, could teach him a few lessons. You might suggest it to her. If he starts right it will make him a better swimmer than if he just learns as I did to dog-paddle slowly along, at great expense of strength and energy. Jimmie ought to be an apt pupil if you make him feel that in taking lessons from her he is being highly favored. In other words, show him why. He can understand.

Am sure glad you, Alice, are getting along all right. Have not heard how the lowers are coming but suppose all right. Dr. Tym* had been rather well tamed when I saw him and no longer was anxious for early payment. Take awfully good care of yourself. Don't any of you tire yourselves out. I can't rest up there as I should because of the call of the finny tribe, but the call does not come so loudly to the rest of you, and you will or should get real restoration from your rest there. I can't say I am sorry you are not here. True, I miss you a lot but am so darned glad none of you is here that the weather doesn't bother me. You hit it exactly right again when you engaged the cottage this year. It's perfect.

Well, Jimmie, how are you getting along there at the Lake? Are you taking good care of Mommie, Mother and Emmaline? Have you learned to swim? I wonder if *Vivian* (just remembered the name) won't teach you to swim? She is a dandy swimmer. If she would give you a few lessons I believe you can learn to swim. She knows how to swim right. Have you watched her swim? Watch her once. Maybe, if you ask her nicely, she will help you to learn. If you learn to swim right, won't Daddy be proud? You are a big boy now, big enough to learn, I think, if you could get Vivian to help you learn. If she will help, do everything she tells you, just like she tells you, because she is a dandy swimmer and knows how. Pop, Mommie, and the rest of us can swim just a little but not very well, but Vivian knows just exactly how to do it, and I believe you can learn if she will help and you try hard.

Well, I must close. Have a good time all of you. Rest as much as Jimmie and the fishing worms will let you.

July 10, 1936

Your telegram has just been phoned to me from Decatur. Me for the Resort Special when I come, which will probably be the last of next week. I fear it was a mistake to send you the *Courier* with its ravings about the weather. I am getting along all right, taking a good many cold baths at nights, and so long as the water holds out, I will get along. I rather think though that I will sleep on the porch tonight. So far I have not put a cot out there but surely will tonight, for it is cooler there than upstairs. This evening I think I will go to the theatre as it's economy day and it's cool there. Monday night, and Sunday night as well, Jeanette McDonald is to be in the picture with Gable and I shall also want to see that. Really, the *Courier* reports of the weather are not exaggerations. Yesterday and the day before it was 105 here in the office at 5 o'clock in the afternoon. Today it's 108 at 4 o'clock and of course will continue to get hotter till 5 as the sun will continue to get in its work on the west wall and windows.

Corn, broomcorn and beans have come thus far, but no doubt have been

*Dr. Tym—Charleston dentist.

hurt and yield will be curtailed. They can stand very little more. We had some rain night before last, but it evaporated or disappeared fast, though no doubt it did some good. It was purely local. They say the crops still look fresh in the mronings though by night they are sick. I was out on the prairie Tuesday afternoon and corn was then pretty well curled by the heat.

Harold phoned last night. Said he would phone Homer today or try to phone him. Did not know whether Homer had returned or not. I told Harold I was going to the Lake the latter part of next week. Wheat and oats prices receded for a couple of days and I got cold feet yesterday and sold wheat for $1.00 and oats for 30¢. They went up again today.

You know I was never so happy over anything than that you are all at the Lake. Thoughts of that Lake at the door, its cooling waters, its sunsets, the busy, lazy life, the fishing, etc., etc. will intrude occasionally to make me dissatisfied here, but I really am getting along all right, and, like the corn, will be able to stand a few days more. I feel sure that when I do get up there again, I will enjoy it as never before.

September 12, 1936

I had your letter containing the two newspaper clippings, one about babies and the other about books, and drove over to Mattoon after office hours. The baby clipping was read to Alice E. and Harold, and both your letters by Alice E. They are well and I stayed for supper. Alice, having been out to her reading circle where she had some sweet slops, was not at all hungry and I ate her supper, not that she didn't have plenty for all of us, for she did, but she couldn't and didn't eat a bite of anything.

It seems to me from the tone of your last letter that you are still feeling more than a bit squeamish about having destroyed a first edition of a mammoth work which was apparently so painstakingly made and so complete as to almost necessarily be valuable in a reference library. I am still squeamish, but I also still want to know just how serious the act of sabotage* was. When you find out, let me know. It would be difficult of course to restore the work, but it could probably be done as nothing has been thrown away, and the detailed drawings of plants, animals, etc. were cut out or rather removed in bulk. Replacing the pictures and sections and rebinding would restore the substance. I don't think though that I will ever recover from the feeling that I never deserved a swifter or harder kick.

Had a card from your mother. She is homesick and I expect somewhat discouraged. I try to keep her cheered and write every day. The railway

*Steel engravings cut for framing from an old volume—later learned to have been valuable first edition.

agent phoned me this morning that the bookcase is in, and I will try to get it set on the back porch today. There is no place to put it except next to the radio, and your mother has not said she wants it there yet.

Helen asked if you want the Encyclopaedia.* I wrote her that I think not but asked her to write you. She said that oil is showing at the well being drilled 1½ miles from the Texas land and they were somewhat excited over the situation. I wrote her that hurry was not yet called for on our part—just to wait and take the speculation ourselves rather than now give a lease to some speculator. One had wired offering to give $15 an acre for the first year and a dollar an acre for the next five years each. That is of course the offer of a speculator who would hold until the field is developed and then sell the lease.

There is no news. I am well and perfectly content, though homesick to see her, to have your mother at Mt. Sterling so long as she thinks she is doing any good.

September 17, 1936

The article with reference to banks and government bonds is one of the things I have been concerned about for a good while. The situation is thoroughly understood at our bank here and I have talked it over with Jack Claar and have, as far as I am able, impressed my views with reference to bank ownership of government bonds. Shortly before we went to Kentucky, I went through the list of such bonds owned by the bank here. In the main they are short-term—so short-term that they may well be considered as cash, and the bank, if government credit began to slip, could do no worse than hold till maturity and receive their face value in money of such value as money then has. Whatever the value of money, a dollar of it will pay a dollar of deposit. If the bonds are held to maturity, the loss to the bank will be only the small premium paid for them, which will average less than a year's interest. Jack is watching the situation and if government credit fails, he plans to dispose of the few bonds which are of a little longer maturities and, as he said, some morning he might come to the bank and sell all his government bonds. There are some phases of the "reformed" banking law which are disquieting. One is that it seems to give the governing authorities power of life or death over individual banks. If such power exists constitutionally, we have the stage laid for central banking to an extent never, to my knowledge, reached in foreign countries. I understand the authorities may

*First printing of the ninth edition, *Encyclopaedia Britannica*, from Kelly home in Georgetown.

require any individual bank to keep its entire deposits liquid or cash. If that is true and it is constitutional and the power is without limitation that the requirement must be based upon a reasonable cause, a bank may be destroyed, because if it must keep its assets in cash, it cannot earn money to pay operating expenses and obviously such bank would buy government bonds till the cows came home, or do what else the authorities required rather than submit to destruction, and the entire policy of the individual bank could be forced by a central authority. That would be central banking with a vengeance. I am sure that no single policy dictated by anyone would suit all local conditions and am opposed to real central dictation. This is one of the things which may be corrected following the November election and the elimination of the present administration from the picture.

Had a letter today from Mother. She will probably come home next Tuesday—that is, if her mother holds her own. She says to tell you she hasn't time to write you, but will do so when she gets home. She wouldn't take anything for the opportunity she has had being with and caring for her mother these two weeks and more.

Alice E. phoned yesterday that the cradle* had just been delivered. She didn't know it was on its way, nor had I. So your fight brought results, as I told you it might. Had a letter from Lillian asking for the Shaker records and the next one who goes home will take them to her. We are all well here. Lots of love to you. I always feel better after being with or having a letter from you.

September 21, 1936

I am interested to hear your account of reaction to storm warnings—your reaction and others. Also, how much of a storm was it where you had your hat at the time? How would you have liked to be in its path on the *Georgic*? It seems to me there are times when I would not care to be on the ocean.

Alice is over today with her girl and Jim. Josephine has quit to be married in November, I believe. I have a girl here also to clean the house under Alice's direction, and Alice has a new girl. This is her first day. The house wasn't very dirty and they expect to have it finished by the middle of the afternoon. Your mother plans to come home tomorrow with Tandy** and Julia who will stay with us a couple of nights. Her card also told me to put the Haig away.

Mother Chenault seems to have improved quite a bit as she sat up in bed

*A Kelly family heirloom.

**Tandy Chenault—brother-in-law from Mt. Sterling, Ky., and wife, Julia.

without assistance last week. I suspect your mother's visit had something to do with the improvement. I hope she is not badly tired. Sure has had a hectic summer in some respects. I saw the cradle yesterday—or rather this morning when I went over to Mattoon for Alice. It is pretty and well cared for—in good condition.

It's hot today. Had a few cool days and don't expect any more real hot nights, but today is unpleasant because of the heat, though otherwise it is pretty. It's still dry and the river almost gone, almost nothing but a memory and some pools of green scummy water. How they get the water looking clear and fairly good to taste I cannot quite understand.

The Tolles took me to Newton for dinner yesterday. As usual the dinner left nothing to be desired. I went to a Charley Chan show last night. I always enjoyed the Charley Chan stories, and the actor who takes Chan's part makes them live. I think it was "Charley Chan at the Race Track" or some such title.

There is not a bit of news and I am hot and tired, so this is not going to be a letter. Alice and Harold have some of the pictures from the Bob-Vivian Longneckers, and are invited to visit at the Lake in October. They are thinking of the Lake with longing. I had a letter from Dr. and Mrs. Cole which made me homesick also. I enclose a handkerchief which they sent with some things of Alice's. The bundle was tied with an old fishing line. Can you think of anything more cruel?

September 29, 1936

I don't remember when last I wrote you or what news I told you. I believe I did ask you your impression during the advance of the hurricane from the South Seas upon New York, but how far I carried the home news I have forgotten. So will begin at your mother's return a week ago this evening. Alice was over Monday and, with the help of her girl and one I hired here, got the house in shape. By the way she has lost Josephine who plans to be married in November. She had a new girl a week ago but dispensed with her Saturday. We knew that your mother was coming Tuesday with Tandy and Julia and that they were bringing chicken for supper. So at ten minutes to six as they had not showed up I got in the car and started around the corner to buy steaks for supper. At the corner your mother came around me driving Tandy's car, and so I parked in front and met them at the back door. Tandy had driven most of the way and his top speed seems to have been under 40 and for that reason the trip lasted from 6 to 6. Everyone was in good shape, and we (Alice E. and Jim were with us) had chicken broiled by Julia, Kentucky-style, which was undoubtedly the best chicken I ever ate.

There is an art to it. The meat was tender and the flavor was perfect. Tandy and Julia were with us three nights. Thursday we drove to Island Grove with Harold and Alice and had supper, and Friday morning Tandy and Julia started for Kentucky at 6 o'clock and reached Lexington at 6 o'clock in the evening. We all enjoyed their visit.

After they left your mother slept most of a day and a couple of nights, complaining some of being tired and wondering why. In the meantime we stewed and fretted about where to put the bookcase, measuring here and there and always coming back to the west wall south of the radio. Sunday night Charley and Ariel dropped in as we started to eat and ate with us. And we measured some more. Careful measurements showed that the case would fit in, with nothing to spare, between the register and the kitchen wall in the library, and yesterday morning your mother was thoroughly tickled to have the bookcase. We uncrated it Sunday and it was on the back porch. The rain was falling steadily and it was pretty cool. When I left home Monday morning, she was intent on getting to work to refinish it. About 10:30 she phoned for me to send a skilled carpenter at once, so I sent one out to do some little adjusting about the case. About an hour later she phoned me to come out at once and help get the rollers in and bring the case in. I did that. Last night the case was three-fourths cleaned and the house smelt to high heaven of wood alcohol and your mother was enthusiastic about the case. It is pretty. When that is done, she is going to redo your mirror, then the table in the library, then upholster the couch by the radio, then re-cover her pillows, and so on *ad infinitum*. It's quite a schedule, but she is enthusiastic and feeling good. Her mother is much better—I think the result of the regimen your mother followed while there and tried to establish for the others after she left.

There is little news. We are enjoying being home together. Haven't had a letter from you for some days but hope for one today.

* * *

*While I was attending Columbia University, I was one of a class of 150 or more students taught by a team of professors. One day our leader, Dr. Watson, announced that for the few remaining minutes we would separate into groups according to our political beliefs. Those who held with the plan as set forth by Republicans were to meet on his extreme right; Democrats, middle left of the auditorium; Communists in the balcony on the left; Socialists, back left; Laborites, here; Cooperatives, there. After assembling we were to set aims for ourselves, points to be looked up before the next class meeting. At that class meeting we were to discuss in groups for the first hour. Speakers were to be chosen who during the second hour would be allowed to defend

---

*Explanatory interjection written by Emma C.

their ideas. The following week the Democrats and the Communists would have a go at it in a panel before the entire class; the week after that, Republicans and Socialists; and so on down the line.

I, of course, joined the few of us who were Republicans, choosing as my special topic the handling of relief. And because I had throughout the course asked my father questions stirred up by teachers and students; and because he had answered those questions with painstaking care to keep me on the straight and narrow Republican path; and because I voiced some of those answers in defense of my special topic, they chose me to represent them on the panel.

Writing the speech was easy. I merely copied word for word excerpts from my father's letters.

Result: A perfect onslaught of questions from a thoroughly aroused class, an onslaught under which I crumbled pathetically while my worthy Socialist opponent sat back in unquestioned ease.

As I sneaked off the platform and down the aisle toward the nearest exit, I was stopped midway by Professor Clark who had notebook in hand and pencil poised. "Miss Kelly," said he, "did you write that speech?"

"No," said I.

"Would you mind telling me your source?"

When I told him, he said as he put his notebook and pencil away, "Well, I just want you to know I have never read or heard anywhere the Republican point of view so clearly expressed."

Now forty or more years later, recalling both the student attack and Professor Clark's praise, I believe the Emmaline letters may be of some historical value.

* * *

October 11, 1936*

Things useful to man have a value. Man will work mind or body to get them, if there is no other way. Some men will take them by force (steal). Men will accept them as gifts.

The greater the desire, the harder is the work, the stronger is the incentive to take by force, the more enthusiastic is the acceptance of gift.

The second element, stealing, may be eliminated as an economic factor. It is forbidden by one of the ten commandments; all normal people since civilization began have agreed that it should be forbidden.

The third element, acquiring things by gift, within proper bounds, should not be eliminated. A gift helps the giver morally. Frequently, it harms the recipient. One naturally wishes to give food to a baby, or to anyone who is in need and has not the physical or mental ability to create or earn those

*In response to a question from Emma C. about a course in political science she was taking at Columbia University.

things which he needs. One also wishes to give to benevolent enterprises in which he has become interested. There is an open question as to how large a gift or inheritance one should be permitted to leave to another. Heavy taxes are now being laid upon gifts and inheritances above specific amounts. Putting limits upon gifts or inheritances may serve a useful or destructive purpose.

The former is illustrated by the fact that frequently children of a successful man have been of no use to the world or to themselves because they have been ruined by the gifts of inheritances for which they did not have to work. All that they succeed in doing is to ruin themselves and distribute their gifts and inheritances without producing a thing of value to satisfy any want of man, aesthetic or physical.

The latter is illustrated by the result which follows when a useful business, productive of employment and of useful things is hamstrung or destroyed by excessive succession taxes, that is, taxed out of existence. A useless gift is one which results in breaking down the moral stamina of the donee and a useless distribution of the gift. Whether a gift will be useful or useless depends upon the donee. The donor would not make it unless he expected a good result. His judgment of the donee may be wrong. However, who can exercise better judgment or give with more care than the man whose ability and energy created the thing which is to be given? Certainly not the political agent.

However, but few people can hope to acquire by gift those things which they feel are necessary to satisfy their wants. If all receive by gift, there will be no creation and wanted things will soon be exhausted. Therefore, the process of creating must go on. The land must be tilled for food, the mines must be operated, wells must be bored and pumped for fuel and oil, factories must be constructed and operated to adapt natural things to human wants, and a transporting and distributing system must be provided.

The economic-social question is not, How can the service of men's wants be accomplished with equitable distribution to all? but, How can the service of men's wants be accomplished with equitable distribution to the greatest number possible?

It will no doubt be admitted without discussion that nothing human was ever perfect and that there can never be equitable distribution to all. It is the nature of some men to shirk and of others to do more than their share. The thief is the ultimate shirker. At present the penalty imposed upon the thief is confinement. The penalty imposed upon the shirker who merely slights or steals time from his work is loss of capacity to get what he wants. He loses his job or his crops are poor. He hasn't earned his bread by the sweat of his brow. The inducement now sought to be offered to men to do their share perhaps cannot be more clearly expressed than in the four words, "Root hog or die." Under the present competitive profit system a man must use what he has of mind and muscle if he is to have what he wants; the better his mind and the stronger his body, if he is not a shirker, the more of his wants will be satisfied. But if he shirks, he pays the penalty. The motive has a powerful result in human action. Actuated by that motive new things useful to men are thought of and created. Short cuts are conceived and perfected to create more quickly and with less human energy things which men want. Until today things which men and women in the United States want can be supplied more quickly and with less human effort than anywhere else in the world, save possibly in the South Sea islands, where nature is beneficent and wants are few.

Can government supply a more effective motive than the one which is expressed in the homely phrase, "Root hog or die"? I think that psychologists will agree that there is no stronger motive. A man who is not at all influenced by it might be too lazy to make a stroke to keep himself from drowning if he should find himself in deep water.

In government (politics) some men are always found who delight in power over others, and in them the ambition for power is the primary motive for action. Such men also find their places in the present system. Others will be sufficiently moved by the desire for peace. Such men also find their niches in the present system. Others are moved by the desire to create. Such men find their places in the present system. Others will seek the easiest way, the places where work and responsibility are the least burden. Such men are far down the line, as a rule, in the present system, but in politics, owing to political pull they might be too highly rewarded.

Under political control some will do the full share of work that comes their way to do. Others will be content to feel that whether they do well or ill, government is obligated to see that they are not without food, clothing, and shelter. From such as these the motive furnished by the idea that one must work to live will be taken away. What is left is not half a man. How many of us fall into this last category no one knows. Until someone knows or has more than a fair idea, it would be the height of folly to try it out on a nation of 130 million people. If it must be tried let it be in some small state (not Illinois) as a proving ground.

Futhermore, what hope is there that, if government takes over business, all jobs will not be given for political reasons and not for merit? Such has always been the case. Such is the case now. What can happen to so change human nature as to assure that jobs will go to the efficient and *not* to the mere political worker—a factory worker or foreman, a farm worker—all appointed by political methods? What a picture of confusion and inefficiency!

Of course the blind or otherwise disabled and incapacitated should be cared for. If they have property of their own, it should be devoted to their care and comfort. If father, mother, child, brother, or sister has sufficient income above his or her own requirements for necessities and reasonable luxuries, the care of the disabled father, mother, child, brother, or sister should fall to him or her. The state, not the nation, should furnish proper care and comfort to its disabled citizens—disabled by natural physical or mental deformities, by fortuities of life or the passage of time—where none of the other proper sources of support and comfort are open to such disabled persons.

In all provisions of law for the betterment of citizens, thought should be given to effect upon morale. The feeling of independence and self-reliance should be inculcated as far as possible. Effort should be encouraged. Men should be taught to try to excel. A law which guarantees security without effort would be deadening. What motive will actuate the majority of us stronger than the desire to provide for our own needs and wants and the needs and wants of our families? What stronger motive to conserve capital to be used in useful production, whether it be invested in stock or bond of a corporation great or small, or private business? Government dissipates funds which otherwise go to useful enterprises—enterprises which produce. A tax collected has always been spent, very frequently unwisely, with the result of removing the funds from industry which could have used it to produce things of use to men.

Investment in government bonds produces nothing—merely permits the Government to spend more than its income for mere government and takes the savings of the people from useful production. About $35 billion of capital which might otherwise have been usefully employed is tied up in United States Bonds. A great mass of other capital is tied up in cities and states. To the extent that this money has gone to reasonable and necessary Government activities and economically created things which the people want, such as roads and battleships, it is justified, *provided* there was no reasonable tax which could have been levied to pay the expenses.

Whatever money a government gets it usually spends wastefully and spends it all. Every new responsibility which a government takes over results in a bureau with a lot of self-important functionaries, useless except to draw their salaries and to become pompous and overbearing. Red tape becomes twined and intertwined in, around, and over the activities of a government bureau until one having business with it loses all patience. The wonder is that a government department ever gets anything of value done. Frequently red tape can be cut for a political friend, seldom for a political foe, and politics makes its way into all government activities, no matter whether they pertain to the humanities or general government activities. I suppose that politics has little to do with military matters, though politics and graft may possibly find their way into the purchase and supply of military equipment.

Government can control the acts of its citizens. It can declare by proper enactment any act which is detrimental to men to be criminal. If the Government attempts honest enforcement of a criminal law, it will be successful, as in enforcing the law against murder, provided the people are in accord with the law. However, the Government cannot prosecute and jail a very substantial number of its citizens as was disclosed (admitting the honesty of the Government's efforts) in the national liquor legislation and the history which followed its attempted enforcement.

Under the profit motive, the tendency of private capital is to continue rushing into private productive enterprises until a time comes when the country can no longer absorb the product at a price which will give a reasonable profit to the invested capital. When that time comes a depression follows which, if left to itself, squeezes out great masses of capital. However, when much capital has been squeezed out, the same machinery of production remains. It can still produce the same amount of useful things and no longer has to earn a profit on as much capital as formerly, for much of this is gone. It goes into operation producing goods and returning a profit upon reduced capital; the goods can be sold cheaper and more widely. The cycle starts and goes its rounds. After each cataclysm goods are cheaper and more widely distributed. . . .

October 13, 1936

The interesting letter concerning your grandfather's 9th edition *Britannica* and other things, written some time ago, was here when we got back from Kentucky last night. I hope you have written Helen that you want the set of books, though she was at Mother Chenault's funeral and neither she nor I mentioned them. If you have not written her you had better do so soon. If you have her send them here, I have a place for them as I brought six of the sectional book cases, which were at home, down to the office. We could not have brought them home with us as we had two chairs, and a lot of other things in the car, and we also brought Aunt Nannie to stay here till Thanksgiving.

The night before we went to Kentucky an old-time severe cold started to dig in on me, and I was in the main rather miserable and a threat to everyone. I am about well but will have to fight a cough for a while. Hope I didn't leave any germs with anyone there—tried to be careful. Your mother stood the ordeal in good shape. She and Aunt Nannie are inclined to talk things over, and I have instructed your mother, for Aunt Nannie's sake, to change the subject when Aunt Nannie starts it.

We loafed along the way coming home, spending a couple of hours in and about Madison. As we ran into a couple of detours later the trip home was a long one in a matter of time and tired us more than it should, but we all rested well. The car, however, had two flat tires this morning, both from nail punctures. One of them had leaked on the way home but we had it pumped up and came on in.

I will try soon to write something more in the way of suggestion to meet the "Red menace." Just now my head is thick. If you will always keep in mind the human element—motives which actuate—effect of ideas psychologically and effect of action psychologically—you can answer much. If you will require the "Reds" to give a concrete suggestion for improvement, the weak spot can be picked out. The ideal, physically, is that everyone should have what he wants and do what he wants to do. When everything is done automatically—by pushing a button—then we may reach the ideal, design and build a bridge by pushing a button—no one to mine the ore, move it to smelter, make steel, move it to the site, place it on foundations put there without human effort—all by pressing a button; teach a child deportment and his ABC's by pushing a button. In such cases physical perfection would have been reached. Another case: a machine to automatically compose and record music, to produce ideas and put them in books. Nothing in all the world to do but push buttons—no "hewers of wood and drawers of water." Even then would not the psychological intervene? Some of us would want the work and high honor of pushing buttons. Others of us would shirk the job. No program which has been suggested and tried during the world's history has met with the success achieved in America, where men have a measure of freedom and have been permitted to retain the fruits of their initiative and energy. Nature itself has made human equality impossible, for some have better physical or mental inheritance than others.

Well, there is no news. Saw Ruth and Warfield at the funeral also.

October 15, 1936

It was another beautiful 14th. I suppose that, if we live long enough, there will some day be a 14th of bad weather, but to date that has not occurred since 1903. Your interesting letter of Monday, expressing good wishes and so forth, came in yesterday. The book also came but I have not yet examined it.

You are up against a difficult situation in your work at college. In some recent indictment of the trend of teaching in the American schools, one of the most serious charges, as it seemed to me, is the tendency of the teaching to slur or abandon those subjects which train the mind to accuracy, such as mathematics, the dead languages and the like. A mind trained to accuracy is a valuable asset in practical life, and a cultural training is also essential to the full development of the possibilities of living. Education seems in the process of abandoning these things for discussions which in their nature can reach no conclusions, an example of which you are finding in the school work you are doing.

In starting, in your discussions, you may admit certain things as facts. It is obvious that it is desirable that there be no poverty in the world; that if all land capable of being farmed were farmed scientifically, in the absence of failure of crops from natural causes anywhere, sufficient food would be produced to supply the needs of all the world for food; and that if all the equipment furnished by science and capital were manned with all the manpower available, other needs of all the people could be supplied, and if present equipment is not available to do that, then there is sufficient manpower—surplus—to create sufficient equipment; that it may be desirable to supply every person with what he wants, whether it be books or Lake Leelanau bass.

You may, it seems to me, fairly conclude from these facts, which for the sake of argument you admit to be true, that it is highly desirable that all the resources of the world, equipment and manpower, be put to work to produce things, whether books, music, pictures or food, autos, or fishing equipment, and to distribute those things when produced.

You may admit as a fact that the capitalistic system fails in both essentials, i.e., it does not produce all the things possible, and it does not distribute equitably what things are produced.

At this point comes the difficulty. In the history of the world no system has been devised which has gone as far in production and equitable distribution as has the capitalistic system under the free competition allowed in the United States. There may be a better system, but before any particular substitute is agreed upon, one must be very sure that all elements which enter into the premises are true and are considered. Otherwise we find ourselves in the situation of Aesop's dog which, passing over a plank bridge with a bone in the mouth, saw the reflection in the water below, made a grab for it, and lost the bone he had. The dog misjudged his premise. He judged or concluded that the reflection was a bone and that he could take it from the other dog. That particular fable and the picture in McGuffey's have given me many a pause in life.

In a complicated subject such as social economics there are many elements to be considered. Indeed, human nature generally is a big factor. The nature of the individual, where it differs from the mass, must be considered. No mind is big enough to comprehend all the elements to be considered, to assure itself that the premises are true and comprehensive, and to deduce what the results of all the combined elements will be. It may be that perfection will have to be attained by trial and error.

If it be admitted that perfection can be attained in no other way, it would seem the height of folly that the big dog (130 million people) should drop its bone and grab for a shadow, that 130 million people should risk what they have on somebody's guess from unknown and untried facts. If a bone is to be risked, let it be the bone of a smaller body (a state for instance) where the result of error will not be so widespread. Many reforms have been worked out by states. When they succeed they eventually reach national scope. How can a reasonable man conclude that he must gamble with the welfare of a whole nation by discarding all that we have for a theory which no man can know will be practical.

Well I have spent more time than I should. Lots of love.

October 23, 1936

Your mother and Aunt Nannie have gone to Mattoon to the birthday party of Jas. Y. Tolle. I cautioned them in as strong language as I am capable of to get home before dark and fully expect my caution to be disregarded. There is little news. We are well and wasting considerable time at night by tuning to political speeches—the real talent, not the *minor* speakers.

The class you fell into is surely an effective propaganda machine. However, I think you are fully capable of taking care of yourself and will do so. From one sentence of your recent letter I believe that you are about to make a serious error.

There is an old Southern story which I have often used to fix a point. It deals with an old Southern darky who had been fishing for his dinner, a dinner which was also to be his breakfast. At long last he had landed a nice mud catfish, big enough for his combination meal, and singing contentedly he set to work to prepare the fish for cooking. Naturally, as you know from your own experience with pike and the like, the cat was squirming and flopping around in the darky's firm grip until the old man became impatient and interrupted his flow of song of thanks to address the fish something to this effect: "Now looky heah, what you all squirming and flopping about? I ain't goin' to do nuthin' to you, only gut you." All that the communist or the autocrat (fascist or nazi) is going to do to the United States citizen is just to gut him of his political, civic, and religious liberties. The difference is he is hiding his purpose, while the old darky had nothing to hide.

You may take certain things to be facts because, without exception in history they have always occurred under certain conditions. Given the conditions the things will recur because human nature cannot change until humans become supremely altruistic, that is, until the ideals advocated by the Christ are attained. They have not been attained yet.

Government has never, ergo it will never, voluntarily surrender power which it has once seized.

The communistic theory, however good as a theory, must surrender to the autocratic. Witness the events following the efforts in France in the 18th century and in Russia today. Ancient history is not needed here, though it is enlightening in the connection.

However good the theory of the socialist is, the administration of government based upon it must be in the hands of men, and as long as men are what they are, favoritism, dishonesty, and all the injustices of which men are capable will exist in its administration, whether it be in duties belonging to government or to executives or to workers on farms or in factories. The man higher up will often be simply an autocrat awarding the preferred places because of favoritism or other improper motives and not because of merit—punishing his enemies, rewarding his friends. Government has and, in the present state of human nature, will act upon this basis in performing whatever function has been laid upon it or assumed by it. The long fight for civil service reform has been our effort to make government efficient and just in this respect rather than merely a system for distributing the spoils of office as favors.

These and other truisms have, in my judgment, no real answer. But getting back to the point I wish to make as it grows late—the loss of the essential liberties which you indicate you do not fear at the present time.

These essential liberties were the ideas which men fought and died for during the age-long struggle between people and their governments. So far as we are concerned they were won, or a chance to win them was won when England was defeated—really the first chance which had ever occurred that I recall just now, barring Greece and Rome. The decadence of those governments is history, the facts and their reasons.

The American leaders, whatever else they may have been, were avid students of political history and to them fell the job of trying to devise a system of government under which the essential political and human rights might be forever assured to their people. They rightly judged that a pure democracy would fall to pieces, too weak and inefficient to be relied upon in the face of a determined effort of ambitious men to break it down and to usurp authority. (Rome and Greece gave forceful evidence that this was so). They sought to and did create a government of delegated powers, reserving to the states or people all powers not delegated, and, in excess caution as some thought, providing a bill of human rights by the first ten amendments, which rights the government could in no way violate. They hoped that the government could not be broken down by men ambitious for power.

You think there is no danger. I think there is. If ambitious men would be as fair to us as the darky was to the catfish and tell us that they were only going to gut us of our human and inalienable rights, among them the right to life itself, it is obvious we would not permit them to assume the autocratic power to arbitrarily deprive us of life, liberty, property, or the pursuit of happiness in our own harmless way; would not permit them to break down our form of government or to change it in one iota while allegiance of men and women is being bought by the expenditures of our substance in willful waste and riotous giving where it will do the most to weaken opposition. Therefore, the ambitious and designing men proceed by indirection and deceit, nibbling a little here and a little there, boring from within with an announced and proper motive but with the effect of eating gradually into our political foundations, restrained only by an honest and able Court, whose members are old, enough of whom will die in the ordinary course of such events within the next four years to enable a designing executive and a subservient Senate to so stack that court as to cause it to surrender to the executive. If that occurs, then our form of government is gone and with it our inalienable rights are held at the mercy of an autocrat with arbitrary power of life and death over his subjects.

Jefferson understood and said that eternal vigilance is the price of liberty. It is as true today as it was then. Government always grasps for more and more power. I believe, as firmly as I believe that I have less hair on the top of my head than I once had, that it is the intention of the present executive to break down our form of government, or he would not have cowed Congress into submission, demanded and received from them the enormous fund which he is spending apparently for political reasons, required the passage of laws, however much they might seem to offend against the Constitution, given vent to his tirade following the Supreme Court decision of the U.R.A. case, advocated unconstitutional laws for emergency purposes, stated that the purposes have now become permanent, and so on *ad infinitum, ad nauseam*. In the meantime in his campaign evading the issue his acts have raised, distorting facts, raising up, in fact preaching class hatred, giving public funds as the Romans did of old for public favor, in every way known to the astute schemer trying to reach the point where he will be powerful enough to complete his coup d'etat. My judgment is that our form of government is being subjected to the severest test it has ever had to undergo, that our personal freedom is endangered, and that if we have ever another chance to vote for a president (if Roosevelt succeeds himself), it will be under circumstances where we will not dare to cast a free vote. If we lose the presidency to him and win even the lower house of Congress we would still have some hope. But the chances are that the head of the ticket will carry Congress with him, for not all the senators are up for election and it's too heavily Democratic to be won by the Republicans.

We have to judge a man by his acts.

October 30, 1936

Casually you throw this at me: "I also want you to explain to me the functioning of the economic machine and its significance in relation to domestic and world economic and social problems." Thanks a great deal for the compliment and all that. Of course, you know that if I could actually give the answer to that one I would merit election as President of the United States of the World. The economic machine is a complex affair. Money is a part of it—a token of value, a medium to simplify exchange of things. The machine requires many attendants or operators, one looking after one part, another some other part. It is operative throughout the world. Theoretically it offers to all a sufficiency of the necessities of life—to the specially gifted and industrious special reward, to the less gifted or lazy a less reward. For its proper operation it requires men who will dig ditches, and men who will plan and create machinery, and men of all grades and capabilities in between, actually furnishing something for each grade of men. The ditch digger will always be necessary, just as will the great executive and the mechanical-minded and the scientist. The machine is engaged in producing things for men to use and in distributing things for men to use. The driving power over men is that more is distributed to men who are qualified and industrious.

The machine is subject to abuse or misuse. Where possibility of misuse or abuse develops, it seems to me proper for Government to make misuse or abuse criminal. That is done when it is made criminal to steal the product of the machine—to get it, without working for it, by fraud or deceit. Many examples could be cited, but these glaring ones are enough. There are many methods of misuse that are not so apparent, and gradually the use of such methods could be condemned as criminal. I am not going on with this. Suppose Government appropriated the machine. Who is to condemn its misuse or abuse? Answer that and you will have solved a real problem.

I believe I will add this. The economic machine is a machine designed to produce and to distribute things which men want. It requires capital—capital for investment in stable enterprises as well as for the most adventurous wild-cat oil wells and blue-sky projects—men of conservative tendencies and men who are gamblers by nature willing to risk all their money—or for that matter the inventor willing to risk all his future—men all the way in between: men to own cars and men to drive them, men to dig ditches and men to use them, men who like snails and men who like sole, men who want diamonds and men who would feel disgraced to wear diamonds. It's a magnificent machine, abused and misused here and there, throttled at times by Government—still supporting Government as a necessary evil, at times—and if ever displaced by Government, still necessarily surviving or reviving when Government has failed as a substitute.

Think it over.

October 31, 1936

We appreciated your phone call a few nights ago, perhaps more than you can realize, though maybe you wanted to hear our voices as much as we wanted to hear yours. We would far rather have that pleasure than flowers, candy or whatnot. Thanks a lot.

We are anxiously waiting for the copy of your speech. Send it along as soon as you are finished with it. I will keep it and return it to you if and when you want it again. Know you have got a big kick out of your radical class and believe that you have done a good job in your answer to radicalism. Wish your speech today was to be broadcast.

Tilford showed up here. I have not talked with anyone who heard his speech at the Democratic (?) meeting in the courthouse, but while he was speaking his mother sat in Republican headquarters obviously distressed. I understand the Doctor is backing his son in his cause. That is absolutely contrary to the Doctor's background and is hard to understand. Of course, Tilford has a good salary, and I am told that his sister is also on the New Deal payroll at an excellent salary.

There is little news here. It is necessary for one to avoid political discussion at home as much as possible because Aunt Nannie is a bit touchy. Have not even had the nerve to get by radio as many of the speeches as I wished because of that situation, but have heard most of the top speakers at least once—New Deal, Republican, and Democratic. Heard Colby only once and Reed once. Would like to have heard both of them the second time. Do not care to hear Landon often. Am with him heart and soul on the main question, What is to be our form of Government? and nothing he can say can make my support for him any stronger. Do not care to hear the President at all, though I have listened to a number of his tirades against classes and his sophistries. I hardly think he can fool the majority this time, though he may do so. But enough of politics. You have heard all you need. I have had all I want. Indeed your ballot came in this morning and your job is done. I am ready for the question as I have been these many months.

Just here I went down to buy some cottage cheese and butter at the farmers' market and see what happened to my scrawl. I didn't, however, buy some cheese from each—just bought from one. Do you remember that when you are in the market you just cannot resist?

Saw Mrs. Fred Moore a few days ago. She said among other things that a Miss Kern whom you met, I think there in Chicago or Oak Park, was on ship with us to Bermuda. Such is life. By the way, I suppose that Mr. Compton never showed again. Boat acquaintances are notoriously as temporary as the trip itself.

We are all well. Jim was over a few days ago with Alice E. Jim put in a hard day's work helping your mother rake leaves and ate like a harvest hand. He is certainly sturdy and efficient for one of his years. There seems no limit to his endurance during the hours of being awake.

Your mother sends her love. It's hard for her to write and I have been negligent. I think Aunt Nannie gets on her nerves somewhat at times.

November 7, 1936

I read last night Garet Garrett's article in the *Saturday Evening Post* of this date dealing with the so-called problem of youth or youth problem, however it may be termed. As usual when Garrett writes he has something to say. His impression is that there is no problem. There seems to be a problem when you consider youth as a class. There is none when individuals are considered. A quotation from your Dr. Watson is in the article. It would pay you to subscribe for the *Post* to get Garrett's articles.

May it not be that all of our problems—class problems, or most of them when broken down—are problems of the individuals whom someone has placed in a class and in whom class consciousness has been engendered?

I have been thinking of some homely illustrations within my own kin here in Charleston. You remember John, the fisherman to whom you told your Kankakee fish story and who immediately responded with a better and thereby deprived you of qualification as a member of the Ananias Club, a distinction which you earned later, however. John, as you recall, owns forty acres of poor land, marginal land. His children are now good citizens taking their places in various parts of the United States. They reached good places in the social economic order, and their background had nothing in it but the marginal forty acres and John and his wife. John was near the river and to him the call of the river was irresistible. He knew the habits and customs of the fox and was not deterred by the offensive weapon of the skunk. He was the man who deprived a beautiful red fox of the skin your mother wore for so long. And John knew the river, knew it in flood and drouth, knew its every hole and shallow up and down for miles, knew its banks, its moods, whether it roared as its yellow flood passed or gently rippled and gurgled a song of peace along the way—knew and loved it—whether its bosom were ice-bound or rippling in the leafy shadows protecting it from the hot summer sun. He it was who knew when and where and with what kind of bait what kind of fish could be caught if any could be caught, and, when fish could not be caught, he did not try, but often could be found on the bank just looking, apparently communing with the river of his love. John was always happy and content. Your mother and I, and perhaps you also, have come upon him at mealtimes there at the river, with his sufficient, though meagre, equipment and food supply, always with coffee, his fishing and his meal occupying all his attention. John is still with us, still a happy and successful man, still has the forty acres, and still content to take what little the forty can give provided he is let alone to tend the river, to catch such of the finny tribe as he needs for sport or food, to chase and bag an occasional varmint—to let the world wag as it will. John as an individual has been successful. Had he been placed in a government-made class what would have the advantage been?

You have heard of or seen Axe-handle Pete—for a long time our only factory—shuffling his big flat feet along the sidewalk and carrying three or four axe handles—good ones too—in town on business and pleasure bent, a stooped, aging, unkempt specimen of the human race, highly endowed neither physically nor mentally, his business the making and selling of a few good axe handles, his pleasure—after his meagre lunch of bananas, or crackers and cheese or the like, on the steps across the street from my old office window, or at some other place of vantage considering the sun and the season—to shuffle into a cafe where coffee would be served to him without cost, as much as he could drink and as often as he wanted it; with no ambition, no wants save such as the sale of two or three axe handles in a week or two could supply, no desire to acquire what schools or governments have to offer, content to make a few axe handles and have his regular spree on coffee. Pete was a successful man according to his capacities, considered as an individual. Could government have handled his case better as a member of a government determined class? I think not. Pete has reached the age when he ought to be able to retire from his business, and to him the old-age pension is luxury, though I think it does not reach above fifteen dollars a month. The factory has, I think, closed permanently and Charleston will have to content itself with machine-made axe handles. I see Pete now just about as often as I used to see him when he was in active business—active for him—about once a week, still shuffling his way along the sidewalks, with no axe handles now, dressed a little differently now, and maybe shuffling along with a little more assurance, dressed a bit startlingly in that he wears and has worn for some time a bright plaid (red and some other color) shirt, which may or may not have been washed since he got it. He is still happy and content with life. I think maybe he gets his whole meal at the cafe. At any rate I see him no more eating his frugal repast across the way. His one added pleasure is to leave a few nickels at the restaurant to be used to buy someone else coffee sometime. Naturally the town is happy that Pete has a pension.

You probably never saw or heard of Pete's brother. I don't remember his name but will call him Dick. Dick, too, was of the underprivileged, yet he lived almost in seclusion a happy and successful life commensurate with his desire to live and enjoy. Dick did know what made the wheels of a clock or watch go round or fail to go round, and when I knew him, his office or shop was on the second floor of the Hopkins building, hard to find around the hall from the stairs. If you knew it was there and hunted along the dark hall long enough, you could find it after awhile, and there would be Dick, bent over his bench if circumstances required him to work, or merely resting if he felt that way about it, always however with time for the visitor, clocks of all ages and in all conditions of decrepitude littering the floors and furniture. Indeed his office at times was almost a graveyard for ailing clocks, but one could get his clock fixed in time, if one went around often enough to finally get Dick to understand that one wanted his clock fixed. But one knew that when Dick fixed a clock it was fixed, and no one knew so well as Dick how to fix the clocks of the past generations. Dick had few wants, either material or spiritual. He did become a picture fan early in picture history and, until the management gave him a pass some years ago, I suppose he had to work a bit harder to get money enough to attend all the shows—and he did attend them. I suppose Dick now is on a pension, too, and if he is, the town will think that he has earned the right to retire. As an individual he solved his problems successfully. Could better results have been reached had government handled him as a member of some government-fixed class? I think not.

There are other examples here of interest, but it is lunch time.

We are all well.

November 7, 1936

The letter I mailed you yesterday may be a confused thing for it was written without continuity in the writing. The result is probably that there was little continuity of thought and perhaps inaccuracy of statement—maybe also there was inaccuracy of reasoning. If so, you will find it.

In the past campaign, as in that of 1934, my chief concern was the outgrowth of my fear that our constitutional form of government is to be weakened and perhaps destroyed, and in my view all else was subordinate to that.

When the Revolution closed, there were here thirteen free states or governments, each supreme within its own territory. They had united for rebellion in a loose compact. They realized that none was strong enough of itself to long remain free. As separate, ununited sovereignties, each had to fear its neighbors as well as countries across the waters. Events during the Revolution had demonstrated that the Confederation under which the war with England had been fought was too weak for practical purposes. Therefore, there was a convention which constructed our Constitution and offered it to the thirteen sovereign States. The offered Constitution was full of compromises. The weaker states feared the stronger, and there was the bitter controversy arising out of the fear most of the statesmen of that day had of the power of a dictatorial government. In other words the central government had to be given enough power to make it a success, but it should have no power to limit the inalienable liberties of the people. There were other subjects of controversy also and where agreement could not be otherwise reached, compromise was effected.

The Constitution as presented by the convention did not sufficiently protect the rights of the people to win the approval of enough states to make it effective, and before approval could be won, the first ten amendments were demanded and assurances given that they would be adopted. These ten amendments have come to be known as the Bill of Rights. These rights were probably protected, in the main, by the Constitution as proposed, but there was a contrariety of opinion as to that, and the specific protection of the amendment was demanded and given as the prerequisite of ratification. The 11th Amendment was of later adoption, but is properly to be considered a part of the Bill of Rights, for it added a safeguard to the rights of states with reference to suits in the federal courts.

The theory upon which the Constitution goes is that the government is one of purely delegated authority—delegated by the States or their peoples—and that the government has no power save such as had been specifically delegated, or such as is clearly implied in the delegation. All other powers were reserved to the states or to their peoples. The Bill of Rights merely assures that nothing in the body of the Constitution shall be taken as authority to the federal government to infringe certain mentioned rights which were considered essential to human liberty. (Incidentally, as you know, the States also have adopted constitutions. The difference between a state constitution and the federal is that in the former all powers are in the state save such as have been delegated to the federal government and such as the state constitution has reserved to its people.)

The federal Constitution, for the purpose of this paragraph, may be divided into two parts, one of which concerns basic principles, and the other the machinery of government. A basic principle, if correct, is not affected by the change of time or circumstance. "Thou shalt not steal" is good for all time. So any correct principle. Practice may show that machinery is faulty or changing time or circumstance may suggest change of machinery. If a principle which I consider basic and correct is attacked, I have the reasons which cause me to think it basic and accurate in my mind, and the attacker must show me wherein I am wrong and he is right. If improved machinery is sought, I also like to know wherein is the improvement, though I have not as firm opinions about machinery of government as I have of basic principles.

The 12th Amendment was to correct a defect in machinery which clearly developed in the first presidential election. The machinery of the electoral college system was deficient and was corrected.

The 13th, 14th, and 15th Amendments wrote the results of the Civil War into the Constitution. In part they never ought to have been written at the time, for the North was mad with victory. They won the war amendments. In part they are good. The provision in the 12th section of the 14th Amendment, "Nor shall any state deprive any person of life, liberty, or property without due process of law," had more far-reaching effect than had been anticipated and has resulted in more litigation in the federal courts of appellate jurisdiction than all other provisions of the federal Constitution combined. At least that has been stated as a fact and my own reading of federal cases leads me to think the statement is true. Nevertheless, the provision was a good one.

Somewhere about the time of the Spanish War, Congress sought to lay a tax on incomes. The act of Congress was held unconstitutional by the Supreme Court. Thereupon, the 16th Amendment was adopted to give the federal government power to tax incomes. I have no particular fault to find with this amendment. A just tax on incomes is desirable. (I won't discuss here the question whether both state and nation should have and exercise that power.)

The Constitution provided that senators be elected by the legislatures of the States. Under this provision there were instances of men buying legislatures—by money, political influence wrongly exercised as by promising government jobs and the like—to elect their senators. The 17th Amendment was adopted to return the election of senators to the people under the mistaken notion that a stronger senate would result. This was a political mistake, just as it was a political mistake to give the nomination of candidates to the people through direct primaries. The reasons why these things were mistakes appeared in practice. Theoretically they were not mistakes.

The 18th Amendment was also a mistake. It was a mistake in theory as well as practice. Theoretically no mere police matter should have cumbered the Constitution. Practically it endangered the people, as was implied by what Mr. Taft said about it before it was adopted when he expressed the thought that although it might eventually be successfully enforced after fifteen or more years of earnest effort, yet it would bring disrespect for the Constitution and incidentally for all law. While the 21st Amendment sought to correct the error of the 18th, yet it could not do so for between the 18th and 21st damage had been done in the respect anticipated by Mr. Taft (in moral thinking as well), which will not be fully overcome in the lifetime of anyone now living, probably.

The 19th Amendment gave to women the right to vote. I have no view on that which I would spend any time trying to maintain. It's just, of course. Whether it has a practical value, I don't know or care.

The 20th Amendment amended the article relating to the beginning of the presidential term, etc., an amendment purely of mechanics, desirable and made possible by improvement in transportation and communication since the Constitution was adopted—by going from the horse-and-buggy age to the age of the auto.

From what I have written you can yourself see how very little there is to the loudly pressed argument that the Constitution has been amended many times and that there is nothing sacred about it. Amendments to substance have been few. Such amendments have not always been better events, for if principle is correct, no amendment can better it. Amendments should never be adopted in times of high passion among the people. They should be deliberately and sanely considered before adoption.

This concludes what I have time to write this morning, except that in my judgment the proposed amendment relating to child labor goes much too far. It is so general in its terms as to permit the Government to reach down into matters which are purely of family concern—such as a farmer boy working on his father's farm.

We are still well. Jim is with us today. He and his mother were raking leaves. He is very industrious and, when such a chance offers, tries to earn his living. I hope that no instructions at home, in school, or anywhere else will tend to destroy such high ideals as he might naturally have. Lots of love. Glad you are interested. You won't, I know, follow my reasoning blindly. You will think for yourelf. That is as it should be.

Let me give you the caution not to take your work or experiences at Columbia too seriously. It isn't worth anything, in the Columbia surroundings, except the good you can get out of it for yourself. It can be and will be very valuable to you if you do not take it so seriously that you feel that the burdens of the world are on your shoulders.

November 8, 1936

I am delighted that you had the nerve to go through with your part in face of the hostility of the crowd. I know how naturally it comes to you to efface yourself in a crowd and how naturally you prefer not to assume a position of prominence. . . . And I know that you have always had the nerve to go through with whatever you deem your duty to undertake. In other words, you have something of the spirit of a crusader. We are glad for all these things even though we know that the crusader is likely to meet many unpleasant experiences and shorten his life by sapping his vitality by the very earnestness of his feelings and efforts. We wouldn't have you otherwise if we could.

What you say of me is so flattering that I cannot accept it all, though I am somewhat—indeed much—gratified merely by the fact that it has been said. . . .

I may have been wrong in my estimate of the seriousness of the situation which confronts this country as a result of the election. At any rate, I shall watch developments without worry. It should be interesting in any event.

Fear you have set me a job to comment sensibly on the quotation from Dr. Clark's book, *Introduction to Economic Problems for Students and Teachers*. The first sentence is "To the economist, value means simply the ability to command something in exchange." In other words, the value the economist considers is "sale" or "exchange" value. Trade, exchange, or sale value needs no definition. It seems to me what Dr. Clark intended to say was that, to the economist, the generic term "value" is used to mean trade, exchange or sale value. To that we agree.

The second sentence of the quoted text is "Until conflict between amount and value is solved, it will be impossible to carry production as high as it should be carried." The meaning of this sentence is not apparent, though no doubt Dr. Clark knew the idea he intended to convey by the words chosen. It assumes there is conflict between amount and value and upon that assumption bases the assertion that until the conflict is solved, it will be impossible to carry production as high as it should be carried. Not knowing what is the meaning of conflict between amount and value, I cannot know whether the conclusion (assertion) follows or not. At present, sale value is based upon supply and demand—that is, theoretically. In some cases, where it is to the public interest that there be a monopoly—that is, in the case of recognized public utilities, such as electric supply—the public through government has taken control in an effort to fix prices to the consumer upon a basis fair to producer and consumer alike. In some other cases where industry has not been considered to fall into the class naturally calling for monopoly and called the public utility class, monopoly had long been attempted by the industry. Up to 1933 the government recognized as a basis for action that monopoly should not be permitted, and criminal laws were long ago enacted to prevent monopoly. One of the complaints of farmers is that the industry manufacturing farming equipment is virtually a monopoly in that it is able to limit production to the demand, both in good times and in bad, and thereby maintain their prices at all times. Of course limiting production of machinery to demand for it in bad times throws many men, who were employed in good times, out of work. By that process the industry is enabled to save its investment, though for the period of the bad times profits disappear and its surplus fund is probably depleted. Monopoly is, I think, admittedly improper. It destroys competition. Whatever good there is in our system requires free competition. No industry should be permitted to so combine its units as to destroy competitive production or marketing of its goods. The Constitution, state and nation combined, furnish plenty of power to forbid monopoly and punish its practice.

Admittedly, the prevention of monopoly does not solve all the difficulties inherent in the system based upon free competition—profit and loss—for at times demand is such that industry so increases production that supply outruns the capacity of the consumer to buy. In such cases our present system destroys much capital, though in most cases the machinery of production is left intact to be used later. This rule is not invariable for in exceptional cases the machinery of production is destroyed, either destroyed or dismantled before it has an opportunity to come into use again. To date in our system the failures which have resulted in periodic depressions arise not from overproduction in the sense that more has been produced than the people could or would use if they were able to buy to the extent of their wish to buy, in which sense I think there has never been overproduction (at least no one can prove overproduction in that sense) but such depressions came, I think, from the incapacity of the people to buy all that industry was prepared to produce. In other words, the competitive system has not failed generally when sufficient funds were available to buy the things which industry could produce. If my opinion is right, then the problem is to devise a new system or a modified system, more practical than the present one designed to reach the ideal. If the ideal is to supply every whimsical want of man, I won't quarrel with that—at least not for the sake of this discussion.

It is apparent that many things are to be considered before any change is made, for any change reacts upon the life of the whole people for good or ill. It has lasting results. A false step, in my judgment, cannot be retraced any more easily or with less permanent results than it can be taken.

Can anyone say what effect the money system which we have now has upon the problem of production and consumption? Can anyone determine in advance what effect a change in the money system will have upon the industrial system?

Suppose the Government be given the job of producing all things, on what experience of history can be based the theory that the job will be as well done as under our system? Will science be as well encouraged? Will inventive genius find as full expression in the production of new, better, more prolific, and easier methods of production? History shows the contrary. This point can be enlarged indefinitely.

How far should Government go in regulating business? It seems to me it could well go farther in preventing monopoly. There are no doubt many laws which should be enacted by Government (State or Nation) to restrain improprieties in the production end, including in the term "improprieties" injustice, etc. The blue sky laws of the states—maybe also S E C of the federal government—are valuable to correct the wrongs they were intended to meet, i.e., sale of improper securities, etc. There are valuable labor laws looking to social betterment. Others can be enacted as their need is disclosed. (Incidentally, the proposed constitutional amendment with reference to child law goes too far, but I will not discuss that now.) No one, in my judgment, can yet show that free competition is not a better system of production than state government production nor that the powers of government are not sufficient to forbid and prevent the improprieties of the system.

The other end, distribution, is difficult. At times, in my thinking, it has seemed that theoretically to reach the ideal I assume earlier in this letter, the money system must be scrapped in its entirety. To scrap that destroys the free competitive system. It also brings to an exchange system our dealing with other people. It does many other things the consequences of which are incalculable. My mind is not big enough to see the end. I am not ready to scrap or seriously change the money system.

However, this letter has wandered far from the text you sent. . . .

The second paragraph, "A most important duty for the present generation is to see that full information is available regarding all occupations in all industries and that opportunity to enter occupations be provided as equally as possible." I wouldn't class that as an especially important duty. Something might well be left to the individual. Many industries train their own men. In all but the exceptional cases their men are selected upon merit and not pull. Merit in industry means ability to do the job. The present system results in many square pegs being in round holes, but would any other plan result in less of that difficulty? If there is something better it has not been suggested. Industry has always been well manned. The next sentence, "Economic welfare consists in a balanced abundance," is probably another way of stating the ideal that everyone should have what he wants, which I will not try to controvert. It merely states something as a fact which may be open to controversy.

The fourth paragraph starts with the proposition that unrestrained private development may be a perfect method for opening up a wilderness and conquering a new continent, which by the way, is more of an admission than need be made as to any man-made system. Nothing in the way of a social or political system devised by man can be called perfect—will never be perfect—until all men do unto others as they would others do unto them. Taking into consideration human nature, all that can be said is that some systems are better than others. It neither follows that private industry is good or bad for our present highly interrelated economic structure. Admitting that the job of development is complete, which it is not, yet there is adventure now to be had on the industrial frontier of the chemical laboratory and in countless other lines. So far as industry is concerned, the frontier is not gone. It may be true that the production of too little rubber in the East Indies may upset industries halfway round the world, but the production of too much will not do so in any way that should be permitted to count. All that will happen is that those who have bought rubber too high (speculated) will lose some of their capital. The consumer will get his rubber at less cost, which is all to the good. Industry expects loss as well as profit and should be organized to take the loss when it comes. If, as stated by the text, industries were combined into large industrial groups (I take this to mean that each industrial group were made a monopoly) and if output were definitely so planned as to make the product from each unit of industry equal, the text says we should have the actual advantage of the present system without the disadvantage. This part of the text concerns production and price only. It would make a monopolistic system with power to fix price, which a little thought shows is the destruction of competitive systems. Power to limit production and fix prices should not be entrusted to any man or set of men, industrial or government, so long as any personal profit by way of monopolistic practices or graft is to be had by exercising the power inequitably. The production end under our system is not the weak spot. The suggested alteration offers no remedy for existing bad conditions in the production end and gives more power than any man or set of men should have.

I don't understand the first paragraph on the back of the sheet. If any man thinks that "marginal returns" in one industry can be made equal to returns in others, he, it seems to me, has not considered the practical difficulty. The AAA program was, I think, based on some such idea as that. In agriculture the planner has to take into consideration wet planting or dry, wet or dry seasons of growing, good or bad harvest time, bugs and all the natural conditions the world over, and such men as think they can do that and are willing to try, gamble with the food supply of the world on a mere guess, when never in all the world's history has there been more than enough food for all. Again here, let the production be as great as possible and let our chief concern be with proper distribution. What does it matter if capital destroys itself from time to time? Things are what the people of the world want.

Of course it is better to abolish the need for charity than to give charity, as the text suggests. I add the proviso that in abolishing the need for charity we do not destroy character. There are many cases where help should be given as pure charity and the recipient impressed with the idea that it is pure charity—for the good of his soul. In the subject suggested here, what is to be done, if anything, should be done only after complete consideration of its effect upon humans, and in considering humans, the effect upon each class of humans should be considered. From how many of us will charity, demandable as a right, take away even that which we seem to have? This and other questions, which will occur to you, should be considered.

The next question is "Who of us feels any compunction of conscience from receiving large amounts from changes in money value?" In the first place it is, and always will be probably, an open question whether money values change or commodity values change. I believe of course that commodity values change generally at any rate, according to law of supply and demand, and that therefore money will buy more or less at one time than another—that is, when money has a fixed definite base such as gold. One who has goods takes his loss when values decline and his profit when they increase. That is all there is to it. Stacks of books have been written about it, theories are plentiful, but in the main the laws of supply and demand will work their will and, in my judgment, no amount of tinkering with supply or changing money standards or values will break down those laws.

I agree with Professor Clark's suggestion that one of the most important economic needs of the coming years will be expansion of the moral code until it includes social consciousness and the duty of every individual to play his part in a planned and orderly economic life. I qualify the suggestion by insisting that the planning be by the free individual and suggest on my part that a moral social consciousness cannot be inculcated by governmental action looking to the taking of the home, for example, which I think I earned by hard and steady work, from me and giving it to the man (or set of men) who failed to play his part in a planned and orderly economic life. Such a man, if he was able to lead such a life and did not, is probably entitled to charity, given as charity, but not as his due.

In your letter, Professor Graham's quotation is "The unemployed should be put to work for themselves—providing necessities. Nothing made by unemployed should enter regular channels of trade." This may be true. It is certainly true that Government with power to tax generally should not enter into competition with any industry unless Government wishes to destroy that industry as a private affair and enter into it as a government affair. It is probably true that tax money should not be paid to unemployed to produce goods in competition with private industry. I think government competition is unfair. It is the destruction of some for the benefit of others. A government which engages in that can hardly hope for expanding any desirable moral code.

The last suggestion is to use all the people to do all the work and shorten hours. Has Professor Graham any suggestion as to how that can better be done than by the slow, laborious, discouraging method followed with us, a method which with all its faults has produced some remarkable results when comparisons are made with peoples of other countries? I have no suggestion to make of a better method than we have. I think insuperable flaws may be found in any suggestion thus far made by any thinker.

In all my thinking, I start with the proposition that we have nothing, man-made, which is perfect, just as I look upon myself as far from perfect. When a suggested change is made, the question I ask myself is first, whether the change is of practical nature; second, does anyone know, or can anyone show convincing reasons why or how the change would better conditions, considered in the light of human experience and with a fair knowledge of human nature? If a betterment is not shown with a considerable degree of certainty, I refuse to accede, because I know that something once taken into the body—social or political—can with difficulty, if at all, be eliminated.

Well, I started this letter yesterday and stopped and started many times both yesterday and today. It is probably not very good or thorough, but maybe there are some suggestions in it which may give you starting points for ideas derived from your own thinking.

Jim is still with us, but Harold is coming for him this afternoon. Jim has had an active, busy time for himself. Your mother has had an active, busy time for herself.

November 16, 1936

We had your letter Saturday—the one in which you told of your long-delayed buying spree. We thought it was long overdue and are glad you finally got to that horrid task, or if not horrid, then dreaded task. Also glad your Chicago friend is now to be located in New York.

There is little news with us. Aunt Nannie is still here and I suppose will be till after Thanksgiving. For Thanksgiving, the three Chenault men and their families and Virginia are invited. If they come, of course there is not sufficient sleeping outfit at home and we will have a full house indeed. It might be that we could sleep in relays, a part sleep while the others run the radio and converse in Chenault style, though I doubt whether that would be a practical solution. There are at least a few difficulties in an arrangement of that sort.

If I have not sufficiently covered—sketchily though it may be—the ground you would like me to cover in connection with your class work, you may make suggestions. I find it a bit difficult to select a point for discussion and write about it, unless I feel it will have some interest for you. I wonder if you would care for a brief statement of the system of government as outlined in the Constitution. I believe I have already written briefly of the amendments.

It developed during the Revolutionary War that the Articles under which the States had confederated were not sufficient. The Confederation was simply a confederation of states with little strength in itself. One of its greatest weaknesses grew out of the fact that it had no independent income but in that respect was dependent on the States. There were other weak spots, and it was clearly not efficient as government. I suppose a discussion of the

Confederation and its failures, and the reasons for them, would not be of very much importance to you just now, except that as part of the background out of which the Constitution grew, it had become apparent that any central government to be erected by the free States, to be of value, would have to be endowed with considerably more independent powers than had been created by the Articles of Confederation. The problem for the free States was to create a central government in which should exist all the powers necessary to constitute an effective government for the purposes for which it was needed, and at the same time to reserve from it the innate, inalienable rights of the people, and to preserve for the free States as large a measure of sovereign rights as could be done and at the same time give to the central government the sovereign rights which it was necessary that it should have.

On the question as to the extent to which the States should go in surrendering sovereign rights, there were two schools of thought represented in the Convention, or rather there was a division of opinion of rather wide extent, one set of thinkers wishing to make the central government far more powerful than the other set was willing to concede should be done. Let's call the former the radical element in the Convention and the latter the conservative. Hamilton was of the former. On the question as to the protection of the inalienable rights of the individual there was somewhat of a like division as on the question of sovereign rights. The views of the two sets were compromised as far as possible by the Convention itself, and as a final inducement to the conservative element to secure the ratification of the finished work of the Convention by sufficient states to secure its adoption as a basis for government, the first ten amendments—the so-called Bill of Rights—were agreed to.

There was also the necessity to put into the hands of no man, or no set of men, all the powers—legislative, executive and judicial—which it was necessary to surrender to the central government which the States wished to create, for out of the centralization of all such powers in the hands of a single man or set of men had grown the tyranny of history. The power to make, execute, and enforce laws, granted to or usurped by an individual or set, is clearly tyranny, because the law—its execution and enforcement—is at the will of the individual or set. It is not a government of law but of men. The individual or set favored with such a grant of power, or acquiring it by usurpation, is the government. And historically speaking, a government of men had never, except where the monarch was by nature so inclined, considered the rights of individuals.

There was also the fear, which the smaller States held, that in the central government to be created the larger States would infringe upon the rights of the smaller States. In formulating the Constitution this fear had to be met. The equal representation of the States in the Senate was one of the compromises effected to dispel this fear. The number of electors from the various States in the electoral college was also based in part upon compromise to dispel this fear, giving to the States a somewhat unequal voice in choosing a president when number of inhabitants is considered. As you know, each State has in the electoral college a number of electors equal to its representation in the lower house plus two, the number of senators, so that smaller States, population considered, have the advantage. There was also a protecting provision inserted permitting the levying of direct taxes only in proportion to population. In mentioning these instances of compromise I am not intending to say there were not others for the same purpose. These have occurred to me as I have been writing.

A careful reading of the Constitution will show the practical provisions intended to separate legislative, executive, and judicial departments and the checks sought to be put on each. The legislature ordinarily needs the executive approval to make a law, though in case of veto a large enough majority can dispense with such approval. The legislature also has the power to tax and to appropriate money. The executive appoints certain officers, but with the advice and consent of the Senate, and may make treaties with foreign powers. But treaties require approval of the Senate by two-thirds vote. The lower house has power to impeach, and the Senate is the court to try impeachment proceedings. The executive is Commander-in-Chief of the Army, etc., for which the legislature is the master of the purse. It is apparent that the surrender of the legislature to the president removes a great many checks—in fact, almost all of them. Furthermore, the judicial branch as exemplified in the Supreme Court has nothing much to sustain it except the power of reason. It is dependent on Congress for money to operate, among other things, and upon the good sense of the people to maintain its judgments and sustain its authority. In the early days it came in conflict with the President and Congress, and the power of reason won its fight. Can it so maintain itself now if the executive and legislative are combined and the people consent to its destruction? Of course not. Is it worth keeping as a check upon government? The people in the final analysis must decide. It is, as it seems to me, hardly fair to make them decide under stress, or to so impregnate the body politic with conditions growing out of the enforcement of unconstitutional laws as to make it seem to the people too inconvenient to return to the constitutional checks.

However, my time is up. This may suggest some things for you to work out to your own satisfaction. As you read the Constitution you will note the provisions preserving the States, particularly the 10th Amendment: "The powers not delegated to the United States by the Constitution, nor prohibited by it to the States, are reserved to the States respectively, or to the people."

By court construction the dispute between the then radicals and conservatives as to a rule to be followed in construing the Constitution was early settled by the Supreme Court to the effect that while the United States got authority only by specific provision of the Constitution, yet if for the attainment or the exercise of a specified grant of authority it was necessary to exercise powers not specifically granted, the grant of such necessary additional powers would be implied. This rule is, of course, the basis of authority for a great many things which the United States has done.

But so much for today. Alice E. and Jim were over to lunch. They are well.

November 27, 1936

Mother and I had our dinner yesterday with the Parkers. The Lantzes and the Fred Millers were also there, and so after those who had to take a nap had done so, we had a few hands of bridge. Yesterday was very unusual in my life because I didn't come downtown during the day. Your letter containing the newspaper account of Mr. Kepple's life and death came in today. It was apparent that he was not in the best of health when we met him. I have no doubt that he was an interesting person to know and that Mr. Compton will feel his loss keenly. Please convey to Mr. Compton our sympathy for him in the loss of his friend. You would probably be surprised to know how often your mother and I have thought of the very pleasant few moments we had on the boat in the company of Mr. Kepple and Mr. Compton. They were, we think, both men with whom we would find a real pleasure in more frequent association—pleasure and profit, not of the money kind, but social and educational.

Hope you have enjoyed your Boston trip, and imagine the article from the *American Bar Association Journal* which I sent you was a real preparation for your appreciation of Boston and its environs. Your best message was that you will be home on the 19th. That's the only Christmas present we want out of you. Your name goes in the pot on that date, and the Christmas turkey will be plenty big so that no one will have to hold back that you may be supplied to your stomach's full capacity. So forget any other Christmas present, and it may be that we will not have anything for you, either. We don't know what, if anything, you need or want and so very likely will not get you anything at all.

Have had no urge to write anything on political or economic subjects recently and no doubt you are surfeited with those subjects by now. I think my distaste may grow out of a suspicion (probably unfounded) that the recent campaign may not have been what it seemed. There was all along considerable wonder expressed that Landon had been nominated. Since the election, the engagement of a Roosevelt and a DuPont has been announced, and only today the announcement is made that Mr. Boettiger (Roosevelt son-in-law) has been employed by Hearst as manager of the Hearst Seattle paper. The DuPonts were heavy contributors to the Republican campaign and Hearst embarrassed Landon rather seriously by his enthusiastic support of Landon and condemnation of Roosevelt.

Glad you have got you some new clothes. I also bought a rather nifty suit the other day. Your mother is still economizing about clothes for herself, but is planning to put a bit of money on some of our chairs and perhaps on some new paper and paint. There seems always plenty of places for money and one has to pick and choose how to spend it.

There is no news. Aunt Nannie went to Kentucky last Friday. Jimmie's dog is a springer spaniel. Last Saturday, Charley Miller, Byron, Harold and perhaps another were out on their annual hunting trip together, so the dog, Jimmie, Alice E., your mother, Mrs. Miller, the gun and I all went hunting on my 40-acre tract after dinner. Didn't see any game, but Jimmie and the dog had a good time and learned something about game. However, both were young and couldn't take it very long, but they walked more than a mile through the cornfield and along the fence rows. They were well-pleased with their trip and all in and very sleepy as a result. I understand that Jimmie and his dog have thoroughly hunted around the garden, back of his home and Mrs. Tolle's home. Sunday was a beautiful day and we all enjoyed the outing.

December 3, 1936

The story of your Boston trip was well-told and we got a lot of pleasure from reading the story. Harold brought Jimmie over yesterday afternoon late, and I sent the letter on over to Alice E. for them to read. Your mother was at her card club meeting with Jessie Craig yesterday afternoon and came home with the prize—a handkerchief. She was at the faculty club bridge Monday and came home with the visitor's prize. We were at a card party with Miss Johnson and Miss Weller Saturday night and brought the men's prize home. I think we had better stop playing bridge. I don't know whether Jim is to be with us tonight or not. After we went home he helped me stack some firewood in the back yard and was ready for bed rather shortly after supper. However, he waked us up this morning sooner than usual—said he wanted his breakfast, but in the show-down was not very hungry. He has a bit of a cold which may affect both his sleeping and eating.

We are enjoying *Gone With the Wind*, a fascinating story, telling of beauties and horrors with an equal perfection of language. It will be some days before I will finish the story, but it is so interesting that both your mother and I read it as we can, alternately. I had it last night for she was occupied with Jimmie, but she is a couple of hundred pages ahead of me.

There is little or no news. I didn't hear Tilford when he spoke here but suppose his views were tempered somewhat by the locality. We are not too radical generally around here. The Bible story may not be divinely inspired, but there is much in it which tallies with human experience. The incident telling of the consequences of the forfeiture of the right to live in the Garden, among them the prediction that man would gain his livelihood by the sweat of his brow, and the story of the building of the Tower of Babel, which was frustrated by failure of men to understand one another, a prediction fulfilled by all human history (the failure of the tower followed by the failure of all human plans designed to reach perfection) are but two examples of the many causes for wonder if the Book be ascribed entirely to human inspiration.

I suppose you have, in your studies of the relation of government to society, had in mind that a government is an institution designed by man primarily as an instrument to be used to protect the governed from one another. My basic view has always been that the people which is least governed is best governed—that is, least governed when the purposes of government are considered and given effect. If a government can be devised which will make all the governed happy, that is the ideal, the tower of Babel. If that ideal may be reached by giving all power into government's hands, who can reasonably object? No one, of course. If a single step can be taken in that direction by giving an added power to government, can anyone reasonably object to the taking of that step? The trouble or difficulty arises out of human nature in most cases. What is sauce for the goose may be sauce for the gander, but what is one man's food may be another man's poison. You know the mere flavor of an egg is rank poison to the body of Will Gannaway when taken with food. So likewise what is pleasure to me is a bore to my neighbor. To surrender a specific right to the Government may be easy for me, while the same surrender by my neighbor may deprive him of all that he deems worthwhile. Therefore, when a surrender is proposed, I insist that if such surrender has been tried before, it shall have been proved successful. If it has not been tried before, upon what is the hope based that it will be successful—how far will it meet the demands of my nature, how far my neighbor's, etc.? How sure are we that we will all talk with the same tongue? Well, enough along this line.

It won't be long now till the 19th though it has seemed long since you left us at Mt. Sterling. We have in a plentiful wood supply and will keep the fire going while you are here. The wood man brought twice the supply I ordered and after he had it unloaded I didn't have the heart to make him load up again.

1937

January 20, 1937

I don't believe I have written you this year. Isn't that a record of some sort? Am getting along fine—have just been lazy and not inclined to do what was not compulsory. Thanks for the copy of your paper. It was excellent—sane in a welter of impulse-born gush vehemently advanced as logical and desirable. What did Kipling say in his poem about him who is able to keep his head under all circumstances? Read that poem when you get the chance. It's a good poem to read once in a blue moon. Again, I say your paper is the product of a sane mind. Your style of writing is showing considerable improvement. No one ever is perfect, you know. The style here is excellent.

Mother has been fixing up the wicker chair she brought from home for the north bedroom. Bought herself a remnant of material for 35¢, some cotton padding for 9¢, and used about a nickel's worth of thread, and now has the chair beautifully upholstered. She also has back all her furniture from Mattoon except the piece we call three-cornered. Has made up her mind not to paper or paint for a year anyway and is happy to have that job off her mind. Jimmie has the flu and is tolerably sick but I reckon will be on the mend in a day or two. The flu went through the entire Tolle tribe, they say. Mother has not been over yet to bring it to Charleston but is getting restive.

The buy of the 60 acres on the prairie is still unsettled. The deed has been signed, but there is a flaw in the title against which I have drawn a contract for all of them to sign. If the contract is signed up I will accept the deed, pay the money and rely on the contract for protection. Lands have been increasing in price and any one of the 16 signers of deed may balk and refuse to sign the contract.

There is little news. It has been wet and gloomy; for a while this afternoon couldn't see the town clock because of fog.

January 28, 1937

This is income tax return time and my correspondence with you has been badly neglected. *Mea culpa.* However, there has been but little news of real interest. Everything else seems to have become of small importance beside the violence of the Ohio. Alice E. and Jimmie are both improving. I suppose your mother has written you since Sunday. We were in Mattoon for several hours that day and your mother helped Alice E.—nursing, etc.—for the time we were there. She has had a threat of cold the last few days but is fighting it hard with fruit juices, etc. She is covering the top mattress of the little daybed. Got the material Monday, I believe.

Mrs. Colvin will be in town Saturday and your mother is giving a dinner for her Saturday night—sixteen people, I believe. From the dinner I believe we plan to go to the President's Ball. Friday Mrs. Allen has asked us to a turkey dinner and yesterday your mother was at her card club, so you see there is plenty doing. I am well, as we told you on the phone. Of course, we have not heard from Jim Kelly* in Louisville or Tom** in Cincinnati though we suppose that they are all right. Tom lives in the hills and his office is above the water level. If he has remained at his home he has been affected, of course, by lack of water and lights and perhaps has had other inconveniences. We do not know where James Hugh lived; his place of business, 18th and Magnolia, was of course under water. James Hugh is, I think, skilled both in swimming and in the management of motorboats and he may have been of service. We have had snow and sleet and of course much rain in January.

We hope you find yourself able to make the seven points between now and summer, and then with only five to go, you will feel pretty easy; but if you could make the five this summer, that would put a long road completely behind. However, as to both the seven and five, health comes first. An M. A. is not worth endangering health.

I saw Bobbie Wyeth a few days ago. She and her mother are going to Florida soon but I suppose will wait until the Ohio has subsided. When you have your papers typewritten, have an extra copy made if it doesn't cost more. I like to read them. You said quite a lot when you said that it is easy to write if there is something in the mind worth saying. Under the same circumstances, it's easy to speak also.

Well, I will have to call this a note and not a letter.

February 5, 1937

I have just re-read your second paper, the one bearing the heading, "How Education Can Compete with Business." On the first reading I was left with the impression that it was written with tongue in cheek—that it is somewhat satirical. I wonder if you intended it that way, and I wonder what the teacher thought of it—if he was able to see the satire if satire there was. Your first paper made, or suggested, the idea that success or happiness grows out of the ability to do some one thing well and in doing that thing, and that teaching should consist of training the individual to want to do and to do that thing. The second paper, it seems to me, while in it there is the

*Nephew of J. Y. Kelly.
**Brother of J. Y. Kelly.

probably solid idea of fitting the subjects taught to the nature and tendency of the individual—individual and not mass training—yet links such training up with the idea that success is to be measured by commercial value, and further, that commercial value be the whole end of education. May it not be that, in an all too material world, education should have the higher duty, along with the preparation of the individual for his encounter with forces dealing with the material, also to inculcate a sense of the ideal—the things of the inner man as it were? May it not be that too much stress laid upon the material will tend to destroy honor, for instance, or integrity? I wonder if you intended by the paper to argue that education should be commercialized to the extent suggested, or were you merely having some fun?

In the paper you use this expression: "They will find that business makes an appeal to almost every other attribute of man but his intelligence" which, I think, a little narrow, for business serves and appeals to every attribute of man, including his intelligence. For instance, when business offers you a book or offers the intelligent a book, business appeals to intelligence for a reason why it should be bought. In selling some books an appeal to intelligence would be hopeless, but not so with other books. Business must be intelligent also to appraise human needs and wants, to educate the public to want more of old things and of new, to make and dispose of things at a profit so as to justify the existence of business as a service to men. Schools offer education as their product—education to develop and supplement natural endowment. They are selling their product to the masses. They are successful as salesmen of their product. They have the entire youth of the country sold and in their hands to help or harm. Will it help or harm to teach them that success is purely material? Can a country ever produce a contented population on that basis? I think the ants and bees have perfected a material civilization for themselves. It takes no thought of the individual or of anything but the material. Man is, I think, capable of combining both the material and spiritual into his life; and being so capable there can be, I think, no perfection which disregards one part of his nature. However, I may have your paper all wrong.

The article by Dorothy Thompson seems reasonable. Yet I wonder if a slight modification might not be possible. I note the suggestion by someone that in case of war abroad our selling can be put on the "cash - carry" basis; that is, we will sell to anyone who will bring us our price and take his purchases from our shores—acknowledging the fact that the high seas will be dangerous in war and that it will tend to keep us out of war if we have nothing on the high seas to be harmed by a warring nation.

Well, I haven't told you any news. We are well, as no doubt your mother's letter told you. Also no doubt she told you of her activities recently. Am glad you are going to an occasional show. Don't forget to mix pleasure with business, else you will be a dull woman.

February 20, 1937

I thought from your cards that you were not especially well and was glad that in the third card you said you were feeling better. I want to make a suggestion. I bowled when in college and was more than fond of it. Nevertheless, it was not the sort of exercise one of my build needed and I have no doubt it did damage. It may be that it is not good for you. It's a bit more strenuous than it looks, and the exercise to the body is not uniform. I believe, if I were you, I would drop that particular thing, though it is fascinating.

Alice E. is with us for a week to give her a rest. She is in the rundown condition that flu, not treated with due respect, sometimes leaves, but nothing seriously wrong, though we had Doctor Iknayan give her a thorough going-over today, just to reassure ourselves.

There is little news. Mother's party campaign will rest for a week anyway. She has had three so far, plus her club with two extra tables. I think she has three or maybe four to go.

Believe I told you there is considerable oil excitement around the Texas land, and somebody must, or ought, to go down. Tom, Kirtley, James Hugh or myself. So far we are all trying to put it on the other fellow, though Corpus is a beautiful place to be at this time of the year. The gulf coast, fish, oysters, and all that goes with the climate there.

March 3, 1937

Four weeks ago yesterday the goundhog came out of winter quarters, looked around and went back in again for six long weeks of hard winter weather—so it was said. Today I sit at my desk by an open window with my coat off and the radiator turned off, and the sun shines brightly. None of the four weeks has been hard winter, but at times considerable fog, a bit of rain or snow now and then, rather light freezes some nights and the last few days warmer and more spring-like and the robins waking us with their morning calls. I know that the groundhog has himself admitted that as a weather prophet he is unreliable, for I saw him along the roadside between Louisville and Shelbyville as I flashed by in the Ford.

Had quite a trip. On the way down stopped at Louisville to see James Hugh but he was on the way from Georgetown to Louisville and I went on. In Georgetown found Lillian and Helen deep in the throes of the necessary effort of trying to decide whether to lease the 100 Texas acres for oil development. A young man from Houston was there trying to get the lease for the Costa Oil Company. He called me from Cincinnati Sunday and I went down to meet him. I spent the night at Kirtley's and the next morning drove to Mt. Sterling, stopping on the way to see Virginia and Tandy and Julia. Had lunch with David and Katherine, saw Garnett and called on Aunt Nannie and was back on my way to Georgetown. Ruth had come in from Florida in the meantime, and so back to the lease question—Ruth and I wanting to lease, Helen not caring much, Lillian wanting more time, and Kirtley oppressed with the thought that whether we leased or not the land would be developed and we might as well hold for the big gamble of development. Eventually, about 10 o'clock at night, we called in a notary and signed—Lillian with the reservation that she could withdraw upon return of the lease to Georgetown. Next morning the young man and I went to Louisville where I abandoned the car to him and went under James Hugh's care. Had lunch with him and Billie*; then they went to the office and signed the lease, and took me a long drive through the recently flooded sections. Then dinner at the dining room of the Mayflower apartments where they live. It's a toney apartment hotel. Then cards till bedtime and they put me up there in an apartment much larger than theirs. The next day the young man and I came on to Charleston where your mother and I signed the lease and I mailed it special to Tom, and phoned for him and Cora to sign and take it with the young man to Georgetown, there to deliver it (if Lillian hadn't changed her mind) to Kirtley to give to the bank with draft for $2,500 to be sent to bank in Houston for payment of draft and delivery of lease upon payment of the draft. I was pretty well worn out, and I know the young man by the time it was over—if it is over—was pretty tired also, for he had been on the job for a couple of days and was on it a couple of days after I dropped out here. This lease may lead to development, and development may lead to some oil. He says not much oil is expected, for the formation is not very good for it, but we have some hope, meager though it is.

Your mother is still going along in her entertainment program. Last night we had cards at the Cavinses' across the way. This afternoon your mother is at Mrs. Frank Craig's at her card club. Friday night she had a dinner, and another dinner next week closes the program, I hope.

There is little news. We are all well. Hope you have a fine time during your Easter vacation. We sure had us a time last year.

March 11, 1937

I wonder how many letters you have written to us and how many we have written to you since you went to school in Lexington. You have been an

*Billie—wife of James Hugh Kelly.

interesting and faithful correspondent and at times I, at least, have not written with regularity. There is little news to tell you today, but I don't recall mailing a letter to you from your mother, and so, in the interest of regularity, I will write a short note.

Alice E. and Jimmie are here—have been here two nights. Alice E. is finishing a paper for the Reading Club and will deliver it Friday. In the meantime your mother has had charge of Jim, who, by the way, is not at all well. I don't know what is wrong with him. Such time as he seems to have pep he is very active and somewhat excited I think. Then when his pep is used up, he is all in—had a chilly feeling about supper time last night—I think a chill—was very fretful and seemed miserable and I think was. He ate little and had a hard night, and this morning his face was white and his eyes tired, though he was in good humor. He was in bed when I left, and the plan was to keep him there—how successful the plan, I don't know. Your mother goes somewhere to a luncheon today.

March, for the most part—temperature the last two or three nights well-below freezing but most of the month well-above and a day or two actually balmy. What snow has fallen has disappeared quickly.

It won't be long now before your spring vacation. I believe your plan is to spend it in New York where you will have enough leisure from your school work to make it a real vacation. I hope you enjoy yourself thoroughly. I have not written you any suggestion for your guidance for a long time, and, of course, once in a while have to show that I think I am still wiser than you in some respects—that is the privilege of age, is it not? My suggestion is that you watch your spending. If 90 cents can be made to do as satisfactorily as a dollar, save the 10 cents in order that you may "begin to get started to commence" the accumulation of an emergency fund, or asset of some kind.

I hope your optimism as to oil is well-grounded. I am not particularly pessimistic, neither am I very optimistic. Of course, the Texas people wanted a lease else they could not give 2500 bones for it and spend a lot to get a lease. Of course, they think they are getting their money's worth and that they will make a profit besides, but if oil is there, it's six or seven thousand feet down in the ground and no one has seen it. If they find it, well and good; if they don't, well and good. Life's too short to worry about whether it's there or not. I suppose, though I have not heard, that the lease has been delivered to the oil people and the $2,500 paid, and I am not worrying about whether that has happened or not. I do think, though, that you would be wiser and truer to yourself if you would save a bit, not spend on the spur of the moment, get to be a bit of a miser. I know you are too unselfish to ever get very far as a miser, but you are a good enough actress to play the part fairly well if you really set your head to it.

Well, it's dinnertime, and the lecturing of age to youth must stop, for even the aged listen for the dinner bell.

March 17, 1937

I used to think, when I was concerned with such lowly matters, that this is the day to plant potatoes. We, of course, know that it is Erin's day to wear the green. At home today we are not so happy as we might be for Jimmie is making a very slow recovery from whatever it was that ailed him. He has lost considerable flesh, and I noticed him wobble a time or two while he was up for a short time last night just before supper. Also, Alice E. is sick, had fever yesterday and has a headache and backache this morning. Whether she has fever this morning I didn't learn before I left home. Your mother, therefore, has a rather heavy load and she is getting pretty tired and nervous. Maybe I will have to take the job on in a day or two. Am a bit out of practice as a nurse, cook and housemaid, but once upon a time was quite experienced in all those arts and no doubt can do very well if necessary.

We enjoyed your letter which we received yesterday—were particularly interested in the character of the writing you are to do during your vacation. Was in St. Louis a few years ago and saw across from the office, where my business was, some relief workers—a great crowd of them—with measured tread of slow tempo, carrying small shovels of dirt a half block and then returning for other small shovels of dirt, an apparently useless job. Sometimes, I imagine, it seems that the work done for the teacher, with no particular object in view, is of the same character as was the St. Louis job. But work such as you are to do during vacation has a real appeal because it has a practical as well as an educational use. I believe you and I agreed that the one and only necessary rule to successful writing is that the writer have a thought to express or a fact to tell, and then to tell it naturally in simple words and with sentences of simple grammatical construction. An attempt to copy the style of another is usually fatal. "B" natural and your product won't "B" flat. This, I think, we have discussed before. I saw a sentence yesterday in *Saturday Evening Post* (March 20) from the pen of Justice Holmes—a letter written to a young Japanese—which was to the same effect. At least, I saw the thought expressed, and I think it was in that article. By the way, I think you will enjoy those letters, or rather the article quoting from the series of letters, written by Holmes to the young man.

There is little or no news here. No need for you to worry about the sick. They are under Doctor Iknayan's care and are not seriously ill. Jim, we think, is well on the road to recovery, and I think Alice E.'s fever is from a cold, which as usual has affected a sinus. We will get along all right.

March 29, 1937

It was nice getting the Easter box of candy yesterday morning at breakfast time—nice to know you were thinking of us. We, too, have been thinking and talking of you and the boat trip a lot lately. It certainly is a pleasant memory of a pleasant time—and seems as though we ought to be going to Bermuda and Nassau again this year. We never thought of anything we would change about that trip, and while, if we should go again, we would not see the same parts of the islands perhaps, except, of course, the beach at Nassau, yet for the first trip I can think of no desirable change anywhere along the line. . . .

I suppose Mr. Compton has been thinking of the trip also. At any rate his invitation to you at this time probably arose out of remembrance. We will be interested to hear where you do actually spend this vacation—the White Mountains or New York, or maybe no telling where. You have always been more or less unpredictable, and for ought we know, or at least should be able to guess, you may be flying to Los Angeles or boating to Havana. Your mother sent you an Easter letter, special, to the International House which should have reached that address not later than Sunday as it went out of here noon Friday—was deposited in the post office in time to go out at noon.

Alice E., Jim and Harold were over about an hour yesterday for Jim to hunt Easter eggs which were hidden here and there in the back yard. He did very well with a little help now and then and after awhile had all ten of them in his basket. Jimmie is well and Alice E. is herself again. We have had several cold days but today is bright and warmer with the feel of spring in the air again. There isn't any news. Nothing seems to be happening.

A few days ago I got to the book *Man the Unknown* and find it fascinating. I have read it too fast—have not finished it, and should read it again more carefully. Have talked of it so much that both Alice E. and your mother want it. When Alice E. is through with it, I think I will read it to your mother and talk it over as we go. It's in a class by itself and if you have not read it, of course you will. While the concluding chapters are visionary and his proposal may be not possible of attainment, yet it is a high vision calling for the best that man has to offer, if the vision is worthwhile and capable of being made a reality. Thanks for that book also.

I am not sufficiently well educated to get all the scientific data in the book, but Carrel has attempted, with considerable success, to write down to such as I, and I understand enough of it to get the basis for his vision,—and I think its value. . . . After reading the book, Man is still the unknown, but the impression left is that he is a marvelous production whose origin and purpose have not been learned by the scientist, so marvelous a production that though he is literally made from the dust of the fields—except perhaps the part of him which is life and the power to think—the human mind cannot conceive it possible that he, like Topsy, "just growed."

Well, we hope you are having a royally good time this vacation. We are glad of your increased salary for next year. Perhaps you can save a part of the increase—the call of the shoes and whatnot may not be so insistent. One can never tell. I know it is hard to save money and the easiest thing in the world to let it go. I wouldn't have you a miser for all the gold in the Kentucky hills, nor do I want you to consider property of no value even if it does look as if taxes are going to get it all pretty soon. But enough of this.

April 8, 1937

Well, little old New York seems not to have been without sufficient charm to effectually dwarf the White Mountains. The description you wrote of your experiences, colored by the brush of humor which is large in your equipment, was very entertaining, and we enjoyed your account of your experiences and especially your reaction to them. It was like you to lose some of the novelty of the surroundings of your flight over the city because of your interest in the humans around you. I think you exemplify Pope's conclusion, given in his "Essay on Man," that "the proper study of mankind is man." I reckon Pope was right, and I reckon also that considerable of your charm comes from your practical adoption of the conclusion. By the way, if you have not read the essay, I think you will find it's entertaining both in substance and in the stately poetic vehicle used by the author.

Your mother is worried—about the yard work first, for there she has a very poor worker (your father) to help out and the yard is a mess with most of the grass roots pulled out of the ground by the frost, the trees needing trimming, the wood hauled back from the back porch, a small garden patch to fork and plant etc., etc., etc.; second, about the housecleaning, time for which has come, with closets to clean and re-arrange, wallpaper to be cleaned, paint to be washed etc., etc., etc., and most of it to be done by herself. My advice not to worry is of not the slightest value or effect. You know how that would be. I think there will be a strenuous time around home for five or six weeks. I wish we had a smaller house and grounds at this time of year, but there are other times I am glad we have a large house and grounds.

There is little news. The Tolles and the Kellys are well. And here I close because there was a long interruption and I have an abstract of title to examine today. The letter is therefore incomplete.

April 16, 1937

I seem to neglect my writing to you more and more and I know no real reason for it. It is especially careless of me because of the fact that we look forward so interestedly to your weekly letter and we know that you, so far from home, are even more anxious to hear from us weekly. I reckon it will be with you as it was with me. My weekly letter home was pretty regular, just as yours are to us, but I could not count with the same certainty of hearing from home.

There is little news. I had three small dead trees in the back yard, an elm and two blue plums, which I had succeeded after much effort in grubbing out last fall. Off and on this winter I had speculated on a method of reducing them to firewood, had tried the dull axe once and concluded that it couldn't be done that way—by me; had borrowed a bucksaw and tried that and decided it couldn't be done that way—by me. What to do? Well, we have been going to this revival meeting at the Church pretty regularly and likewise a Mr. Bankson—an ex-preacher of considerable age and of fixed opinions—was going also. Now Mr. Bankson has long since given up the thought of earning his living by preaching, and he has been a big strong man. Though he is old and has a small pension, he is still a strong man who glories in his strength. It was he whom we employed to dig the ditch from the street in which to put the sewer from the house. Now as you know a ditch starting below the street level is pretty deep in the ground as it comes through the yard—and costly. So I tried to persuade Mr. Bankson to bring it up rather sharply as he came along, to the necessary final level of the basement floor, but no, that didn't suit him at all; he had dug lots of ditches, laid lots of sewers, and lay it right—as he understood it—he would and did. His opinions in all respects are firm and unyielding. However, he is a good axeman and prides himself on the amount of logs he can convert into chunks in a given time; so after trying out the saw myself, I told him my difficulty and he said that he would be over the next morning and take care of the situation. He came, with axe and saw, as we sat down to breakfast, and in an hour the big sticks were little sticks and he was on his way with a half-dollar in his pocket and my big winter worry was over. So it has been with a good many things I have worried about in the past and no doubt so it will be about a good many things of the future.

You know, we are not inclined to attend revival meetings and this has been no exception so far as inclination goes. Nevertheless, we have attended this one fairly regularly—and that is unusual. Perhaps the reason is that there has been little general interest. We figured we would attend the first two or three services and then when interest had grown and crowds were good we would drop out. The trouble has been that the interest did not grow and the crowds did not come, and so we are still attending. The meeting closes next Sunday night.

Most of my yard work has been done—by your mother. The other day she had a considerable batch of leaves raked up by noon and when I got home she sent me out to move them. She figured that we would burn them that night, and as it was somewhat cloudy and it was apparent there might be rain before night, I figured I would burn them as I moved them. So I set fire to the first load—there where the garden would be if there were a garden—and put a second load on it, then the third load I dumped a little away from the fire—all this was on a pile of brush I wanted to burn—but the wind was high and the last load caught fire and a load your mother had piled up caught fire, and when I got there, grass in the imaginary garden had caught fire and was encircling the young seedling peach trees we had set out there. It was hot and I set to work with the rake to control it. There was no danger except to the peach trees and I hated to work hard. Whether the trees were hurt or not I don't yet know, but I should worry. They were seedlings anyway and probably their fruit would be about the size of English walnuts. The yard does not look bad, for your mother has given it a good cleaning and there are considerable splashes of yellow in the shrubbery and spring flowers.

The spring has been what is known as "seasonable." There has been only one hot day; that was the day I had the grass fire, of course. Yesterday was bright and cool and today is bright and cool with large promise of turning warmer. Lots of love. We are inclined to think the postponement of your final Columbia work is a good plan. How much of that thought grows out of the wish to see more of you this summer than we would otherwise see, we don't know, but however much it may be, we think your idea a good one.

April 22, 1937

The days certainly slip by fast—just about two months till vacation and fishing time—and cherry time too—on the lake in Michigan. It is a beautiful day here, but the wind is straight from the north and it's not quite as warm as it looks, but it's spring at that, and in a few days we will be able to see nothing but the trees from our home windows.

Your mother is all excited today, for Alice E. is giving a party and so Jimmie is coming over this morning to spend the day and night and to go to the circus tomorrow with your mother. Won't she have a grand time of it! Last night Dr. and Mrs. Greer entertained with a dinner at the U. S. Grant Hotel in Mattoon, broiled chicken, etc., and then we came back to Charleston for a card game which began about 10 and ended at 12:30. The yard at that time of night in the bright moonlight was very pretty—all harsh tones softened by the night light. There is little news. Night before last the Charley Millers had us to chow mein supper. Agatha is down here for a few days and the dinner was just a family gathering with your mother and me added.

There is no oil news. You are not wise to get excited over the oil prospect in Texas, for the tract of land has only 100 acres in it and it is divided six ways. Also, the territory all around the Drummond tract of which this 100 acres is a part has been drilled and drilled and drilled for 30 years, and while there has been an immense amount of gas, no oil of any consequence has been found except in the last well at the southeast corner of the Drummond tract, and that oil, after flowing a few days, was displaced by salt water from below. I have never heard whether they had been able to shut out the salt water or not. If oil should be struck on the 100 acres, the one-eighth royalty would be divided among the six of us and there wouldn't be a great deal for anyone. So just forget it.

I don't want you to be broke. It's not a good condition and destroys peace of mind. If you need some money, let me know. We had the $6,000 for your mother's interest in the Kentucky land. It came in yesterday, and with it and some other borrowings we paid the note we had given to the bank when we bought the 60 acres here in February, so while I have no money, I have credit to carry us through till some money comes in and if you need some money, let me know and I will borrow it for you. From the last letter you wrote, I get the fear that you are actually being embarrassed from lack of funds and I don't want that. It's not good for your soul. Or maybe it is good for your soul. The book you gave me Christmas, Carrell's *Man, the Unknown*, has considerable incentive to thought in it. One thought impressed is that man's body suffers from lack of being subjected to hardship, and perhaps a little financial worry is good for the soul too. I am inclined to think that economic security is or has a tendency to be on the destructive side.

I ought to drive to Springfield and view the farm up there to see if the wheat came through good enough to save and whether the plowing is being done, and maybe I will do so. I wish that farm were here in Hickory Township, Coles County, or that my interest in it were out and in land out in Hickory. We now have an 80, a 60 and a 40 in Seven Hickory, scattered pieces of land with no houses to insure or keep up and if we had another 60 of the same kind there, we would have more income and less bother.

Well, we are all well, and there is nothing much to put in a letter or for that matter to tell you if you were here. Your mother and I have our Illinois fishing licenses. Maybe we will get out on the riverbank some day for a dinner and a little fishng soon. I hope so. Now there's always a little job or two to do at home at night, and all in all it's hard to get to the river. By the way, did I tell you that Jimmie brought me over a dandy fishing knife a few days ago, one which rivals Dr. Cole's in desirability? In fact, I think it's named "Fisherman's Delight" or "Fisherman's Favorite" or something of the kind. Am anxious to flash it on Dr. Cole and make him jealous.

April 30, 1937

Somehow from your last two letters I have got the impression, maybe more than an impression, that the next two months seem long to you. Aren't you glad you don't have to teach a summer term too, or for that matter, go to Columbia for a summer term? I reckon as you say one's work does pall at times, but I do hope that your feeling is not the result of any physical ailment and that it comes merely from natural boredom from the day-after-day grind.

How are you anyway? Are you really well? Maybe you had better cut the teaching about June 1, or if you think you should, now or anytime. If you were here you could pitch in washing woodwork, waxing floors, cleaning wallpaper, washing curtains, etc., etc. Your mother is in the throes of house-cleaning and is pretty much a wreck at times when I get home. Last night we went in the rain to the picture show, Katherine Hepburn in "Quality Street." Tonight for dinner (formal) and cards to the Cooks. Your mother had promised to do very little today and I think all she will do is to wash a lot of curtains. At least I found her at that job at noon. Maybe you don't know, but at housecleaning time, nothing a man can say or do can change the customary routine in the slightest. I still try halfheartedly but with no hope of success.

Well, this is to be just a short note, started late in the afternoon because I have been wondering if you are really well. If you are overtaxing your strength, you had better give it up for the balance of the term and come on home. I promise not to break a leg and you won't have to nurse me on that account. But if you are just blue and despondent, get the upper lip stiff and it won't seem very long till June 23. So write me, and if you wish, I will meet the plane in Terre Haute or the train in Mattoon. (I think you can get plane to Terre Haute, but maybe not.)

May 17, 1937

Your mother and I had the day all planned yesterday and it went as planned until dinner time. I taught the Sunday school class, we went to church, the first part at the Christian Church, and the last at the Presbyterian where the Masons were attending in a body, then home to a very light meal, more a weekday lunch than Sunday dinner. About the time lunch was ready Jimmie called and said—very excitedly and with a wealth of words—that we were going fishing, that he had a lot of worms and that they would be right along. So we ate and I also dug some worms and by the time the equipment was ready, the Tolles drove up and off we went to the river. There was little luck—just a few small sunfish, one of which was put back in the water—and Jimmie was called to do some more fishing. His re-catching of the little fish was marked by his appropriate shouts of triumph, and all was well with the world. Then home, where we cooked a picnic dinner out in the back yard and by the time we had eaten that, it was about dark and time for the Tolles to go home. The afternoon's work your mother and I had planned in the back yard had been discarded at the sound of Jimmie's voice over the phone.

This morning your mother is picking up the housecleaning where she left off when Jim and Billie Kelly (James Hugh) came last Thursday. We enjoyed them a lot. They were here about twenty-two hours. I hope your mother can get through the balance of the work without overtiring herself. There doesn't seem so much to do, as the last twenty-four hours before the Jim Kellys came, were hectic and saw much done. Indeed your mother was as far along Thursday noon as she expected to be last Saturday night, but she was about a wreck and, I knew, "had been places." She is planning to drive to Kentucky some time this month and hopes to take Alice E. and Jimmie with her and will bring back David's two children for a visit of two or three weeks.

There is little news. Had a letter from the Coles a few days ago. They go to the lake early in June, and we are to come anytime we can and stay till July 30. I suppose we can't get there until the last of June at the best. You still have better than a month of teaching. We are anxious to hear as soon as you learn how you got along with the final work of the Columbia term, though we know, of course, that you will have no difficulty. I think your mother had some newspaper clippings to send you about the laying of the cornerstone at the new building at Normal and perhaps others, but if so I didn't bring them down. She has nothing on her mind except housecleaning and suggested that if you are to get a letter, I had better write it. Therefore, it's my first activity at the office this morning.

May 31, 1937

Well, May is done and but three weeks till school teaching is done for the summer and you will be headed for Michigan probably. There is little news in Charleston. Last Monday your mother, Alice E. and Jimmie drove down into Kentucky. It seems that Jim had a boil developing on his thumb, the one he maltreats at night, and it must have been pretty bad Monday night as your mother wrote that she and Alice E. were up all night, and on Tuesday they went to a Lexington hospital which they expected to leave Friday. Since that postcard I have had no word and, of course, suppose that everything is okay and that they are finishing their visit. When they left, the plan was to return here on the coming Thursday, June 3. Whether the sick spell has made any change, I don't know.

Though I was alone here yesterday I had a rather busy day: Sunday school and church, dinner downtown, in the afternoon two hours work washing and waxing the floors in the back bedroom and hall, the newspaper to read. Then I went to the picture show "He Met Her in Paris" or "It Happened in Paris" or some such title, a very good play, right comic at times with Claudette Colbert in the stellar role. Then supper downtown, home to read a while and to bed. On my way home from supper I saw Mrs. Shaffer, her younger daughter, her husband and their dog sitting on their porch, so went over and chatted them a few minutes. They asked about you and, as so many people do—probably partly for politeness' sake and partly from interest—whether you will be home this summer. Somehow I have never quite got it through my thick head whether you will have all summer or merely a couple of weeks between your teaching duties at Madison and studies at Columbia. And so I answer that you may or may not be home depending on etc., etc.

The yard is very pretty now. I eat on the back porch, breakfast, and almost every day, one other meal. This morning there was a little woods thrush in the bath. It was there yesterday, too, and the day before. There is a deep red rose with many blossoms just to the north of the drive to the garage door, the Oriental poppies are full of brilliant red, large blossoms, the large shrub bush north of the kitchen windows almost at the north lot line is a big snow ball commencing at the ground, for the limbs are weighted to the ground, on around over the top to the ground on the other side. The iris is in bloom scattered all over the yard.

Your mother left just as she finished housecleaning. It had been too cold to really enjoy the outdoors, and she rather hated to leave just as it turned warm, and to miss the yard while it is yet beautiful, before the heat and dry weather make it unattractive. When she returns she is expected to bring her two nieces, Nancy and Emily Chenault, for a two-weeks' visit and, of course, that will keep her busy. All in all, she will get little pleasure from the yard this year.

It is hot now during the day and last night I was uncomfortably warm most all night, was awakened twice—once at midnight with the idea that someone had slammed a door in the house, but the light was on in the kitchen of the neighbor's and two young people were in there; and again at three o'clock when the crowd at the neighbor's were upstairs rather noisily preparing for bed. Both times had some trouble getting back to sleep, and during the night dreamed of dead men and dreadful situations and difficulties and was in rather heavy sweat most all night, so this morning am a bit washed out, as it were.

June 14, 1937

This is Monday and it is hot and sticky. One would think that the rains are not yet done falling, though for a good while now no day has seemed complete without its quota of rain. That, of course, is not quite true, for on Saturday we four, your mother and I and the two nieces, went to Springfield where I left them and went on to the farm and to Jacksonville. I promised to pick them up at the Leland Hotel at two but was an hour late and they, having seen all the points of interest within walking distance, were well-fagged. So I put them in the car and went to the monument which the girls inspected from outside and in, then on to Charleston by 6 o'clock. Saturday was a bright bracing day. For three of the wet gloomy days last week we had a fire in the living room and would have been very uncomfortable without it.

Do you realize it's but a dozen days till you are free and can come home? And when you come we sure expect to enjoy you. Our plans for the Michigan trip have not formulated themselves yet. It may be none of us will be ready to go before July. Alice E. was saying last night that she thought she would not be ready until some days after we usually go. What your plans will be we do not exactly know, though we hope to have you here a while before we go north. Your mother and Alice E. need rest and I have no doubt you do also—a good, long, real rest. It may be, if you are only going to take a couple of weeks vacation, that you should spend it all here. Really, that could be restful for all of us. I don't yet know how my affairs will shape up for the trip north, but hope I can control them. . . .

The Tolles were over for supper last night. . . . Jimmie shows no evidence of his thumb infection except a slight show on the thumb.

September 8, 1937

I am enclosing two clippings concerning Tilford Dudley, in both of which you will be interested. I suppose his wife is the girl who was rather occupying his thoughts at the time you saw him. I met him and her at the Ford garage. He said he was leaving town as soon as he had paid his garage bill. I wonder if there is any unfinished business here in which you are interested and about which you wish to know. Your mother has been working up to a luncheon today in honor of Mrs. Tom Marshall. There will be eight people including Alice E. Jimmie will also be there—a lone male among eight females. Ruth Dunn is one. Have heard the names of the others but have forgotten who they are, except of course Mrs. Marshall, Sr.

It has been cool since you left, has not rained yet though it is cloudy, and I do not know whether the broomcorn is yet being cut. The weather predictions are for no rain until tomorrow. We haven't had a card from you yet but expect one today. Didn't expect to hear yesterday. Harold lost his golf match three or four down and two to go. You just can't have everything, it seems. We haven't been down to the oil fields. Suppose the notion will take us some day all of a sudden and we will be on our way without a thought—just the notion.

Nothing of interest seems to occur to me to write about. In a small town interesting things are not happening overly frequently—at least if they do, news of them does not reach us. Whether the Walkathon still continues I know not, nor do I care, except I do not like to think of the Charleston-Mattoon road being all cluttered up with cars at all times. There is a chicken dinner somewhere close tonight or tomorrow. The indications are that we will not attend. I will close. We have missed you a lot, and it's a long time until Christmas.

September 24, 1937

We received the letter enclosing the check for $24—#1 of your bank checks. The money came in mighty handy as I am still short, but even so, I was, I believe, more pleased that you have a bank account than to get the money when really needed—or rather when really convenient to have. We have been much interested in the furnishing of your apartment and appreciate your telling us so much about that. The certificate from Columbia was also pleasing. So taking it altogether, your letters have been very pleasing. The certificate is in my safe.

There is little news here. Sunday we went to church, had dinner at home, then to a picture show in Mattoon—"100 Men and a Girl" or some such title as that—Deanna Durbin, a good show. I can think of nothing unusual happening Monday.

Tuesday afternoon the Millers and we drove down into the oil section. It was interesting, a busy place, with offices of the various producers of oil machinery and equipment located any old where in residences, old shacks, new shacks, centers of oil derricks here and there, a derrick with a drill going in a backyard, sidings of railroad loaded with oil cars, a very expensive development of what promises to be a very productive oil field—the air laden with dust, and the occasional clean, rich smell of oil. From Clay City we drove north to Saylor Springs, then west over a dusty bumpy road to Lousiville, [Illinois] in Clay County still, then on Route 45 north of Effingham where we had a good supper, each eating half of a well-broiled small chicken. It was an interesting hard trip and I still think my lungs are full of dust. . . .

The broomcorn is to be baled today. It will bring a poor price—perhaps not more than $75 a ton, and there may be 2½ tons, maybe not so much. Yesterday I sold two crops of beans at 85¢ to be delivered when they are harvested. I don't know when that will be.

Had a letter a day or two ago in answer to one I had written to Tom in which I incidentally asked about the well which was being drilled in Texas in June when I last heard. Tom said the well had been drilled to six thousand feet and was a dry hole, and that he understood that another well would be drilled in the neighborhood. If so, it's almost time to hear from that well also, but we don't even know whether it has been started. So far I haven't invested a cent here in the oil gamble and am not as interested as when you were here.

Your mother yesterday made a slipcover out of old material for the satin covered chair. It was her first try at a slipcover and was a success though it took two or three hours longer than she expected it to take. Well, take care of yourself.

September 29, 1937

Your letter came in a few days ago and as usual your mother and I were much pleased with your account of the simple things of your life, touched, as is also usual, with deftly applied tinges of cynicism and colored with humor. It has sometimes been said, or rather the thought expressed, that the ability to see the humor in one's own life and conduct is a safety valve for him who is so equipped.

There is little news here—news of little things: for instance last night it occurred to me that our wedding anniversary is getting near and somewhere back in my mind was stored knowledge of the fact that many moons ago your mother's watch had gone on some sort of strike, and that it would cost $3.50 to get it working again; that your mother had decided not to have it repaired at the time but would keep it in reserve, expressing the hope that it be fixed for the anniversary. So this morning after breakfast, which was a very good breakfast if I do say it myself who shouldn't, I went to her dresser and searched it thoroughly for the watch, but my eyes were not good enough and eventually I had to call "Min."* The watch was in a covered basket on the dresser which I had examined twice.

Just a little while ago your mother called me, her voice rich in joy and gladness. She had gone out and found a beautiful glass goblet of some pattern or another and had paid 10¢ more for it than the owner had asked. Sunday she and I went driving. It turned out we were going down into

*Wife of "Moon Mullins," cartoon character.

Hutton to definite places. One we found after inquiries along the line in various homes, in none of which did your mother find any glass, nor did she find any in the house she had set out to find in the first place; then on for the second place she was looking for. Her directions as to that were bad, nor did they improve as we went along; indeed they seemed to grow worse, and I don't think we ever came within miles of it. At any rate we eventually got back to Charleston and had a ham sandwich at Rogers Drugstore. It was however a beautiful day and the forest leaves are beginning to take on their gorgeous colors. . . .

Your suggestion that I write my appraisal of Mr. Roosevelt if I can do so without prejudice contains such a large qualification—the "if" clause—that I hesitate to undertake it, for it is hardly possible that I can have come this far, looking upon his acts with ever-present suspicion both of motive and result, without being shot with prejudice.

Perhaps a little review of the things which caused me to suspect, would be apropos. There were two such things. The first was his refusal to collaborate with Mr. Hoover during the period between his first election and his assumption of office in an effort to stem the tide of fear, intensified somewhat by his election, that was bringing financial America to disaster. I excused Mr. Roosevelt for that, at the time, though Mr. Hoover had offered to let his successor set the course to be followed. I thought that perhaps there was sufficient reason for the refusal, and I did not suspect that there was any lack of integrity or motive in the refusal.

The second item—the one which actually caused me to look with suspicion upon every act and utterance of Mr. Roosevelt—was the taking of the oath of office in which he swore to uphold the Constitution, followed by the inaugural address in which I understood Mr. Roosevelt to intimate in unmistakable language that, if something were deemed necessary to be done, he would not let the Constitution stand in the way. I believe I can truthfully say that not till then did I suspect the integrity or the motive of the man. I know I can truthfully say that since then I have first looked for the "nigger in the woodpile" when considering any of his acts or words, and expecting to find the dark man, have usually convinced myself that he was there.

Until shortly before the congressional elections of 1934, I vacillated in my judgment between the conclusion that Mr. Roosevelt simply didn't know where he was going and the contrary: that he was an exceptionally shrewd, cunning man who had set himself a goal to reach which required the overturning of our system of government. Before the election of 1934, however, my judgment had become fixed, and I believed that Mr. Roosevelt intended to so modify the Constitution as to eliminate many of its safeguards designed to prevent the concentration of power in the hands of any one man or set of men. At that time I thought it was very necessary to weaken his hold on Congress somewhat, and—something I have never done before—I offered my services as a speaker to our candidate for Congress. In my talks I stressed the danger that seemed apparent to me—making no use of the soft pedal as the National Republican Committee was doing but putting the blame where I thought it belonged, on the head of the government. Our candidate was beaten and the President had a much larger majority in Congress after than before the elction of 1934.

I then thought that within the following years, the President would probably have a chance to pack the Supreme Court by filling vacancies which might naturally be expected to occur by deaths among the judges. However, that did not occur, though laws were enacted and passions aroused the effect of which cannot be eradicated from the body politic. The election of 1936 came on, and its result was such that the Democrats having won most of the Congressional seats and the legislative bodies of most of the states, Mr. Roosevelt had it within his power to have secured such constitutional amendments as he might have proposed. I believed that within the four following years, without constitutional amendment, he would probably have the opportunity to appoint successors to enough members of the Supreme Court to change constitutional construction to suit his will. In my thinking of him, I had reached the conclusion that he had planned to bring about such financial and social conditions, such class passion, that there would be nothing left for America but an authoritarian government centralized in the Executive in Washington and that probably the result would be as he planned it. I had long before abandoned the thought that he was a man of good intention who didn't know where he was going. I also had concluded that he was a man of real determination who was also vindictive and would destroy anyone who might block his course, if he could.

Thus, you see, I cannot speak without prejudice. I am hopeful now that the weak spot in his character, the unguarded heel, has developed. It almost seems to me as if the old adage has been again exemplified, viz: "Whom the gods would destroy, they first make mad." Roosevelt must have been mad when he proposed to prostitute the Supreme Court—and pursued his intention. . . . He must still be mad in seeking to defeat those who beat him. He must still have been mad when appointing Black to the Supreme Court bench, Black the inquisitor of the Black Senate Committee willing to use his inquisitorial powers to besmirch character. Mad for power, mad in his estimate of his own importance and strength with the people. What he will do with the Black mess I can't imagine. I think he will not hesitate to advise impeachment if he thinks the mess is hurting him. Yet he will be hurt if Black serves on the bench.

Well, I must bring this to a close.

October 14, 1937

Your postal and the subsequent letter telling of your football weekend and the Sunday dinner have come in. All in all it was a busy and interesting weekend for you and made an interesting story for us to read. Have no doubt that the dinner was delicious, and well-served, and the company scintillant.

There is little news here. Your mother is riding her hobby harder and harder. Am beginning to wonder if she is not taking it a bit too seriously. When we go out in the car she wants to stop at every likely looking house; as like as not when I go home at noon or in the afternoon she has one or more excursions to report, and occasionally a piece or so of glass added to her collection on the dining room table. Furthermore, she has cleaned out the music-magazine closet and has some glass there. And she has lots of lines out fishing for information as to the probable location of glass. Amongst her acquisitions, I think that she has a few of the pieces considered more valuable, together with quite an assortment which she would be willing to sell or trade. However, she doesn't let her purchases run into much money—doesn't know enough about values to offer much in the first place, and then she, of course, doesn't want to get much money into the collection. In Springfield the other day she was offered two celery dishes or vases for $5 in her "Ivy and Snow" pattern but of course wouldn't buy at such prices. The "Westward Ho" pattern is out, chiefly because the goblets are being reproduced. I haven't heard of anything being reproduced except in the "Westward Ho," but the reproducing puts that particular pattern out. It's nice of you to think of trying to pick up a piece of glass for her in the East, but, we think, not advisable, for the price would be dealer price, and that, in the East, is probably higher than here. However, when and if she visits you in the spring, you and she can probably have some pleasure going through the shops together.

We drove out to the north farm just after breakfast and from there on to the elevator at Filson. Comes the time to sell some corn and the price has been going downhill. Sold, some days ago, twelve-hundred bushels at 50¢ and should have sold more. The best I can get today is 44¢ and it won't be long before it will be time to deliver corn. I have no cribs and will probably deliver as the corn is shucked.

This evening Alice E. and Jimmie will spend the night with us. Sunday we have dinner at the U. S. Grant Hotel in Mattoon with Mrs. Marshall. Mr. Hudson, the tenant on one of the farms, gave us two pumpkins, three squash, some sweet potatoes and turnips this morning. So runs life in a small town.

October 18, 1937

Your letter with the five-dollar check came in today. Thanks. I imagine I am completely paid up now. Don't overpay. I didn't keep a memorandum nor have I in memory the amount. But you must have paid out by now. Alice E. wrote you a letter some days ago while she was at our house, and you should have it and all the news with her by this time.

There is no news with us. Yesterday, being Sunday, was a busy day, starting Saturday night with a table of bridge at home, the Spooners being with us. During the evening Mrs. Ray called from Emily's. They had planned to come round to call but backed out when she learned we were not alone. Sunday I went to Sunday school, and Mrs. Ray and Emily called on your mother. Then Mother came to church where Mrs. Marshall picked us up for dinner at the U. S. Grant Hotel. After dinner back to Mrs. Marshall's till near five, then two and one-half hours at home, then to Lee Lynch's with Ruth Dunn to coffee and cake and to talk or listen until ten. By the way, Lee Lynch is out at the *Courier* with much Irish fireworks, in the course of which he tossed a typewriter into the wastepaper basket. Emily also lost her job and Lee is working for the morning paper. Said he had already drawn about 400 new subscriptions for his new boss. There is, you see, some excitement even in a small town. There has been the usual run of auto accidents, one Saturday afternoon in which a car was struck at 5th and the Big Four made a complete scattered wreck, one piece going into the waiting room at the station 150 yards away, going through a window and knocking plaster off the other side of the room; but the occupants will recover. One of them came down still sitting on the cushion on which he was riding and which apparently left the scene with him. He has some broken bones and internal injuries which are not expected to be fatal. He was conscious and wanted to know where his watch was. The other occupant was not too dazed to want to know what became of his hunting dog which had been in the car. I have forgotten the names. Do not know the people.

We have had almost continuous rain since early Saturday night, and while not raining just now, the clouds are still heavy.

October 20, 1937

It surely was good to hear your voice last night—a totally unexpected pleasure. We could almost visualize you in your apartment, and that is better than thinking of you talking from a telephone booth.

I ought to have looked up something about the aviation companies when you first suggested them, certainly when you suggested the buying of United

Aircrafts at or below 20 for a long-time investment, but I did not and consequently do not know whether United Aircrafts is a holding company, such as is General Motors and was Insull's Middle West Utilities, or a company producing aircrafts, or in either event what its capitalization and debts. A holding company may be a good investment, depending on its investments and their relation to the clear value of the net assets of the companies held, or it may be a very poor investment, depending on the same things. Many holding companies organized before 1929 found themselves loaded with far too heavy investments in their subsidiaries. However, I really have no money to invest and it therefore will be impossible for me to take advantage of the bargain prices in stocks, though I am sure there are bargains on the counter. Thanks a lot for your interest. I really wish I had some spare money now. I think I would follow your advice on investment. It's usually the case when bargains are to be had that I have no money. A fellow really ought to keep a fund for the buying of bargains. I did manage to get some land at reasonable price, but I usually do not have funds on hand. It is said that the Jews generally have money on hand for bargains, though you know of a case or two where they have been caught in the other position—furnishing the bargains for others to buy.

We are well. Mother is at her club this afternoon. We may go to Springfield tomorrow.

October 29, 1937

I believe that neither your mother nor I have written you a line this week. Your mother has had a bad cold which has kept her feeling bad all week but is getting better and beginning to take a more rosy outlook on life. We now make coffee in one of those new-fangled glass electric coffee outfits and really it makes delicious coffee. This morning we left it on a bit too long and it was strong enough to float a battleship but still delicious. It is always clear.

Last night I was at the discussion club at the college. Mr. Seymour gave the lecture, a speech prepared for a teacher's meeting in which he made a lot of didactic statements upon which he based the conclusion that there should be no constitutional limitation upon the power of elected offices. There was considerable discussion following his address, but he was of the same opinion still, as were the rest of us.

Tonight is the occasion of the Hallowe'en parade around the square as a part of which many and varied prizes are given for the best costume. We might have a box seat here at the office and if your mother were well, I think I would get Jimmie here to look it over.

There is little news. I think they will start harvesting 20 acres of our beans today. It is late and we had promise for a very early harvest of that crop, but the promiser started at his home and worked all the crops of his neighbors and then down the line to our 20, in spite of the fact that we were the first to engage him and he promised first service. However, it's pretty weather and if it holds so tomorrow and nothing breaks on his machine, we ought to get beans in. I think they are harvesting the Sangamon beans also—perhaps started there Wednesday, for I phoned then and had the promise that they would start them.

I saw Jimmie in his new suit. It is dandy and he looks fine in it and is proud of it. Haven't seen him since Saturday, his birthday. I think your mother laid the groundwork for her cold that day not dressing warmly enough and being chilled while in Mattoon running into stores.

We had the dead elm tree at the northwest corner of the back porch—15 or 20 feet from the porch—and the small hickory tree removed a few days ago.

You know there is a squirrel or two who like it around home, eating our pears in the summer, or rather eating the seeds and throwing the pears to the ground, drinking out of the birdbath, scrapping with the blue jays, and generally conducting themselves as happy and busy squirrels. One of them was quite interesting when the trees were being cut. I think he had neglected his hickory-nut harvest for more enjoyable things during the pleasant weather. At any rate, there were a good many nuts under the tree which he had made no effort to store for winter use. So when the men got to the hickory tree he stamped and scolded on the roof of the house—kept up a continuous chatter trying to drive them away. However, though he didn't save the small tree, yet when the trees were cut into firewood, the limbs dragged away and the men gone, the big nut tree was still standing. I think the squirrel must have thought that maybe he had won a partial victory; yet he must have thought too that the victory might be only temporary, for at once he came down and began to harvest his crop of nuts, carrying each one far enough away to be out of danger and burying it for winter use. When I got home at noon he was so absorbed that he had no time to bother with me as I walked back and forth near him—seemed to know that I was very unimportant in his life and went right on with his work. By night when I got home there was not a nut left uncared for, and I have not seen the squirrel since. . . .

November 11, 1937

For some days I have been wanting to go to the farm in Sangamon and I have also known all along that the hunting season was to open on the 10th.

So on the 9th, I secured a hunting license and a box of shells and on the 10th, after arranging for Andy Bolin to rake leaves (you will remember Andy) and knowing that Jimmie would be over to superintend the affairs of home, I set out early for Sangamon.

After I got to the farm I put on overalls and the hunting coat you gave me, shouldered my gun and put out across the field, through all the weeds along the ditch which runs through the farm, along the hedgerows. My low shoes often came untied and caught and held innumerable weed seed, and just as often I sat down to clean them out and tie the strings. Along one hedgerow there were the fresh tracks of a man, and it was apparent that if any birds were there, he had flushed and scattered them, and so I guess he did, for when I turned down another hedgerow and had gone about the distance of the flight of a quail, as I laid my gun down and was sitting cleaning my shoes, the familiar whir of a bird came from directly behind and by the time my gun was recovered, cocked and fired, the bird was far beyond shotgun range and went on unscathed.

After trudging around three or four miles through the field and being ready to quit, all worn out, I watched the combine harvesting beans for a time. There is still about 2-days work in the beans—a very poor crop by the way. Then on toward Pleasant Plains to get some farm measurements the Gov't Agricultural Control Organization had made of the bean field, then back and to Alexander where I had a late excellent dinner of delicious baked ham, mashed potatoes, kraut, baked beans, and the poorest coffee possible. Then to the elevator where I arranged for delivery of a part of my corn there—I sold 600 bushels of my part some time ago at 50¢—and for the division of the bean money small as that will be, between the tenant and ourselves, then on home about 5 o'clock.

When I got home Alice E. was there. The account of the day at home was interesting. Andy had come about noon, but before then Jim had been busy working steadily, in his own way, with more regard to pleasure than usefulness, raking leaves, gathering hickory nuts, doing the thousand-and-one things which to him seemed important to do about the yard—all with your mother's full connivance and assistance, though your mother should not have too much exercise and is under the doctor's care. Doctor Iknayan passed twice in his car yesterday and, though he did not stop, it was very apparent that he was disgusted with your mother's disregard of his advice, for both times she was apparently busy with the leaves. She tells me it was more apparent than real, however, As she has to see him this morning, her medicine having run out, she expects quite a lecture. After lunch Jim had no interest in a nap and spent the whole afternoon, raking leaves, running through the piles Andy had made—apparently to Andy's disgust—using every muscle in his body, doing this and that important thing.

At long last, about half an hour before I got in and just before his mother had come for him, he and your mother went to the Thomas garage to put up the rake they had borrowed—or rather your mother did—while Jim ran on to the Thomas pool where he almost at once made a big splash, how he knew not, but splash he apparently did, coming up with algae in his eyebrows, and fear in his heart. . . . I guess he called once but he had been calling all day and your mother, putting up the rake, disregarded the call; but a more urgent call came a moment later, and there he was out of the pool, bearing evidence of what had happened. Of course he was sent on the run to the kitchen and there divested of his clothes, then to the bathroom for a bath. The day was warm and the water was only tepid and he was still cold, so to bed under blankets while the three of them talked the situation over.

He expressed surprise at the coldness of the water, wondered what the fish thought about it, and made the resolution, of his own volition, that next summer in Michigan he was sure going to learn to swim *underwater*. I reckon that he thinks he can swim on top now.

When I got home and learned the story, I roared with laughter, and he lay and watched me with serious eyes, trying to read my face and decide what to do about my derisive attitude concerning the momentous adventure, and so I had to quiet down and tell him of my falling into the creek when a kid, when there was ice along the edge and I was three miles from home. After a while Jim made up his mind that my laughter was justified by my experience, and so the day was ended on a proper note and as he got into the car he made the unusual demand to kiss me, as an expression I suppose of his full understanding.

Your mother was in excellent shape last night. Tuesday she was at a card party. Today she is to eat dinner—Mrs. Messick hostess—at a country home, an old-fashioned dinner, where the farmer's wife is undoubtedly about the best cook in the world and serves the best and most varied assortment of food on these special occasions—takes great pride in her ability to cook. I have eaten there a time or two in the old days and know whereof I speak. . . .

There is no news with us. I am well as my drive (260 miles) and my long walk of yesterday testify.

Well, Christmas is getting fairly close and we want you to come even though your vacation will be short, if you can do so. From September till Christmas is a long time to not see you. Still you may have a chance at other arrangements which will be better for you or more to your advantage. I can't say we would not be sorry if that were so. Still we want you to do what will be more advantageous in your own life. In spite of what I have said, we will be horribly disappointed if you are not here Christmas, and you know it.

November 24, 1937

We had quite a spell of real winter weather, unusually severe for this time of the year, but today the wind is in the south, the sun is bright in the sky and it is very pleasant. Tomorrow the Tolles are coming over for dinner, turkey, oysters, etc., etc., and we have also asked Mrs. Marshall and Mrs. Grace Wyeth who would otherwise be alone. I hate it that you are not here also, but of course there is no hope of your flying in tomorrow for the weekend. After dinner I am hoping that Harold and I and his dog may go out for a couple of hours of hunting. Have a place to hunt arranged for, and if Harold brings his dog, there will be some prospect of getting to shoot at some birds, if nothing more.

Your mother came downtown this morning to shop for dinner tomorrow, and about 11:30 Mrs. Thomas telephoned from Moore's grocery that she had fallen and her ankle was hurt and I should come drive her to the doctor's and home. Sure enough she had slipped on a green leaf on the floor of the store and had fallen full length. The doctor said she had strained an ankle (right ankle) ligament and bound it up for her, and we went home. The doctor told her to bathe it in hot water several times this afternoon, and I guess she will do it once anyway. I left her messing around in the kitchen getting ready to stuff the turkey. She said her ankle does not hurt, being protected by the binding.

There is no other news. How did you get the idea we were not going to see you this Christmas here in Charleston? It's true in a letter I did try and be very self-denying and tried to convince myself we would get along if you didn't come, but before the letter ended I found out that it just wasn't in me to be so self-denying as all that, and that I would be horribly disappointed if you didn't get home Christmas.

Bob Jeffries and Jack Claar got home from Texas yesterday. They were supposed to be hunting and Bob told me a deer had been shipped home here. It hasn't come. I don't think he knows that it was shipped or that it was even killed and I seriously doubt whether they really went hunting. At least they were in Monterey, and maybe they were just vacationing, not interested in hunting, and merely had a promise someone would ship a deer home for them. I guess I will never know.

Well, I will close this letter. It's really not so long as it was to Christmas, though it has been a long time since you left here. You will have to write us of your Thanksgiving day, for we are interested to know. Yesterday noon I went home and your mother had a sheepish grin on her face, the grin she always has when she has had a ride on her hobby. Sure enough, in a few minutes, it was out. Some farmer had advertised farm implements for sale, and she had gone out beforehand to see what was to be seen and had bought an old German-made china shoe for 15¢ and a more modern cakestand for

25¢. She isn't inclined to spend much but does enjoy looking around for prospects, enjoys meeting and talking with people. This time she beat Mrs. Taylor who visited the same place some time later in the morning and was chagrined that your mother got in ahead. Well, I will close now.

December 2, 1937

It was good to hear your cheerful voice the other night, and it's good to know that the days are slipping by toward your homecoming. Owing to our excitement at having the phone call from you, neither your mother nor I was able to remember afterwards whether you are to leave New York on Wednesday or reach Mattoon that day. So between now and then, when you write, tell us in black and white when you leave and what train we are to meet, for if we get confused we are liable to meet all trains for a couple of days.

Today Alice E. is going to a luncheon in Mattoon and so she brought Jimmie over for the day, and at noon both he and your mother were thoroughly happy. By the way, your mother's ankle seems about all right, though of course she is a bit uncertain in walking and favors it a bit—still has a bandage on it during the day. Imagine she will overdo a bit today and by night the ankle will be hurting a little, but it's doing nicely. I am well, and your mother also is in better physical condition than she was and is getting back quite a bit of pep.

Tomorrow night Mrs. Taylor is entertaining at the U. S. Grant for dinner and cards, and from appearances the weather will be nice, though the weather is really uncertain at this time of the year as you know. We have had two cold spells this winter—more cold than usual—and once the roads have been bad. However, we had no occasion to use the roads when they were bad.

There is no news of the slightest importance. The second test oil well in Texas has not been started. Your mother and I went to the church last night for a chili supper and after that to the picture show—"Styles of 1938" I think was the name. It was in technicolor and the costumes were considered beautiful. There was a showing of a scene, purportedly from the Cotton Club, which seemed more torrid than artistic, the omission of which would, I think, have detracted nothing from the show. Well, I was interrupted and it's growing late.

1938

January 12, 1938

Here the month is nearly half gone and this, I believe, is my first letter to you since you left. Simply shows how lazy I have grown to be, acting on the motto that what is worth doing at all is worth putting off until tomorrow.

Jimmie came to visit us last Thursday, I think, and was with us until Tuesday. His grandmother showed him such a good time that he hated to go back to Mattoon when his mother showed up to take him home. He called up your mother this morning and told her that the next time he came over he intended to stay a week. He certainly expects to be entertained and to be the center of all activities when he is here, and yet one misses him when he is gone, for he is an attractive kid to say the least.

Your mother is attending her club this afternoon. Maybe she will learn what the big fight was about over New Year's Eve. You will probably recall that "the war" was on before you left, but then as now, she was not a combatant—not even on the sidelines. She has had enough remarks and incidents brought to her attention to know that there was probably a battle royal and that some hard feeling is left, but how the sides were lined up and what it was all about she can only guess. Perhaps she will learn today. This evening we go to the Arthur Craigs' for dinner and an evening of rook, perhaps. I planned to go to a Mason meeting about 8 o'clock, but will miss it if I can.

Bryan Tivnen, a lawyer of Mattoon, died and his funeral was at the Catholic Church there this morning. It was a long service lasting from 10 till almost 12, but really worth the time, as a bishop conducted it assisted by 18 other prelates and a few boys, I think. I saw a high Mass service once before, in Georgetown upon the death of the priest there. At any rate, it seems to be a big event. Should have counted the number of vestments put on the bishop at the opening of the service but at the first didn't realize that so many were to go on him, and so I reckon I will never know how many. One of the men on the stage or rather the rostrum was the master of ceremonies and was very busy keeping the players in place and directing their movements. He was really an interesting part of the show. The choir was excellent. I didn't see it as it was in the loft at the rear, but the music was far above the ordinary. Indeed the last hymn was a beautiful thing as sung. I don't know the title of the old song, but you will recall it from the line "Jesus is tenderly calling me home" which is prominent in the song.

There is little news here. A cold wave is on the way. In fact, it's cold and raw now and it will probably be real cold tonight. Your letter was especially good to get because it showed that you have your spirit back and maybe the grind between now and vacation will not be so trying on you as you feared it might be. We were right uneasy when you left here, and were down ourselves. What's the use of your being away from home a minute—or a school term anyhow—longer than you want to be? This is a good home in a way. It's your home any old time you want to use it as such. That I think you know, and you will not hesitate to come home when you are ready.

I enclose the bank check for $6. Wish you and I both owned more stock than we do. You will note the prosperous condition of the bank from its statements which I enclose.

January 31, 1938

It's always an entirely unexpected event when it finally dawns on me that your voice is coming through from Madison.* It seems so casual to answer the phone, just as one does day after day, and as altogether eventful to find you on the line, and so it was yesterday evening. Thanks for calling us.

My sickness—Monday, Tuesday, and Wednesday in bed—almost a loss of voice, some fever, tolerably uncomfortable, but under the efficient care of Dr. Iknayan. Thursday at the office half a day, Friday almost all day, Saturday in Decatur, and yesterday in bed until time to dress for dinner in the evening. Mother had three couples in for dinner and they left about midnight, but I feel pretty well this morning anyway.

We didn't hear from Jimmie yesterday. Mother was planning to go to Mattoon today, but I think I have talked her into not making the needless exposure of herself to the measles. In her youth she was exceptionally subject to that disease and had three attacks. She may still be subject to it. She was exposed to it Thursday when she was in Mattoon, but that is enough chance to take in the absence of necessity.

There is little news here. Mother told you there is some Texas news, of not much importance I think, but still interesting. It was contained in a letter from Donald W. Moore of Houston and dated the 24th of January as follows: "You and the Kelly heirs will undoubtedly be glad to know that we are starting a well immediately on your land in the Drummond subdivision of San Patricio County, Texas, to be located 330 feet out of the southwestern corner of the 100-acre tract. This well will be known as the Donald W. Moore #1 Kelly estate. We own the west 50 acres and Sinclair Prairie Oil Co. owns the east 50 acres. We will probably drill this well to a depth of 7,000 feet unless we encounter production at a lesser depth. You will undoubtedly hear from some people in regard to purchasing some of your royalty or mineral interest. In this regard, I would suggest that you convey this information to all the heirs and that before you agree to sell any or all of your

*Madison, N. J., where Emma C. was teaching.

interests, either individually or collectively, that you contact our office, as we would be interested in purchasing some part of your royalty interest if you desire to sell, and likewise will be glad to give you the information on the well at any time. It would be my idea at the present time that this royalty is worth about $50 an acre base price. What we call "base price," I mean based on the entire 100 acres. In other words, if you sold one-half of your royalty at $50 an acre, you would get $2,500." (The $2,500, of course, is for all the half-interests of the six heirs.) "You or some one of the heirs may receive various propositions within the near future, if you have not already received them, but in this regard, bear in mind that a cash transaction is about the only way that you should dispose of any of your mineral interest if you desire to do so, and anything can happen on the spur of the moment in the drilling of a well. Please rest assured that we will be glad to give you information at any time and likewise would be interested in buying in case you desire to sell."

As I said, the letter is interesting, but I don't think that oil will be found. Still I don't want to sell any of the royalty, preferring to take the chance myself, as the interest is small and it cost us nothing. You know I have wanted a small gamble in oil, and here it is, my total present value there, on the base price suggested in the letter, being about $800. A wise man would probably take the cash, if he could get it, and let the other fellow take the chance, but I do not feel disposed to be wise. What do you think? If the well actually is started, the total value of my one-sixth interest may possibly arise to $1,600, but that would be the extreme limit until the well comes in as an oil producer—if and when.

February 23, 1938

We too had an exciting day Monday—excitement comparable to yours concerning the Honolulu offer. By the way, about that offer, if the school is good morally, financially, and scholastically, you might be foolish not to take the offer. What liberty will you have? Are you to be tied too tight to permit you to enjoy the advantages of climate and sea that are there? Of course, your conduct will, in a girls' school, probably be more bound round by the rules of decorum than is necessary now in the average American city. At least I suppose so. Make your investigation thorough.

On Monday the postman brought me a card from Ruth from Fort Myers, Florida, saying she was leaving Fort Myers for Miami and would drift up the East coast and home by about March 1; a card from Lillian saying a Mr. Myers had been there wanting to buy half-interest in Texas royalty; a letter from Tom saying Myers had offered $7,500 for half-interest and that the last issue of *Oil Journal* had stated that the well was down 2,500 feet. A little later a telegram was delivered from Moore, drilling the well, saying it was down 5,600 feet Monday morning and asking if we cared to sell quarter-interest. I wired to Ruth at Fort Myers asking to be kept informed of her telegraphic address. The telephone company reported she had checked out of the hotel on her way to Havana and left no address. I wired to Moore telling of the offer, having made up my mind to sell half of my interest for $1,250. Moore wired late in the afternoon a long message, saying I misunderstood the offer, that it was $3,750 for half-interest. I tried to get Myers in Ohio by phone but couldn't reach him, and on Tuesday morning wired Tom he may have misunderstood the offer and that I was not interested in $3,750. Also wired to Moore that I was not interested and proceeded to forget it, being glad to take the gamble anyway. A letter this morning from Lillian with copy of letter from an oil agent asking if we would take $7,000 for half-interest. It is not an offer and before it can be accepted, or made a sale, the well will be either worth something or nothing. The drilling has averaged 350 feet a day, and while they are more than a mile in the ground and necessarily go slower, yet they had only 1,600 feet to go Monday morning to reach their extreme objective, and, of course, they may reach the end before the 7,000-foot depth. The first wire I had from Moore said the well looked good. It will seem strange after thirty years to have no more oil prospects in San Patricio County, Texas. Ought to have called you by phone to tell you this, but you can get a little delayed excitement out of it.

We are well. Your mother at her bridge club. The rug she is working on is not hooked but braided—of woolen cloth, planned in the course of the years to reach the dimensions of 9' x 12'. It is to be her *Magnum Opus* (Is *"Opus"* neuter in gender?) in the rug line. She has material prepared to bring it to considerable size. A funny incident connected with its planning had to do with the thread to be used (stop me if I told you this in my last). She had been using for rugs of the braided variety a large size cotton thread at a nickel a spool. Here common sense eventually had sway, and she switched to linen of the variety used in harness making. She brought me down early the next morning in the car to get it from, or ordered by, Frommel. I asked her if she had the money for the twelve spools she wanted. Yes, she answered in a tone which might have been backed by a million dollars or a producing oil well. So I left her talking the matter over with Frommel. The next time I saw her she told me the story. After picking the size, she asked if they could get a dozen spools for her. Then they must have thought she was a millionaire for a moment, but in a moment or two Frommel caught the difficulty, and after explaining, she left the shop with *one* ball of thread at $4.50—one pound of thread, with the agreement that what was left Frommel would take back by weight. She didn't pay for it, of course, for she didn't have—very seldom has in fact—as much as $4.50.

Well, I have written enough. Had your letter at noon. Were you told of teacher-training, the gift of the fiddle case, etc.?

March 11, 1938

It has been quite some time since I wrote you. I think, however, that your mother has kept you fairly well informed as to the incidents (all minor) in our day-to-day life. I have had nothing to write about.

In addition I have been submerged in the difficulties of various other people, in seeking to make correct income tax returns to our all-powerful, insatiable Government. Have been doing a lot of work in this regard for very inadequate compensation. I have been drawing income tax returns for a good many people since 1917 but have never come to the point where I can class myself as an expert, for I never know surely that a return is accurate. Part of this comes from the fact that the law is changed from time to time and part from the fact that the department changes a ruling from time to time, at times seeming to have no better basis for the change than that in the particular year, or maybe the particular case, it will give the Government more tax. Had an exaggerated example of that the latter part of last year. A business had for 1917 figured its inventory on cost basis. That was during the war-end, in 1918. The government field agent came around and investigated the 1917 business—not unusual—and decided that the cost should be the average cost during the year. The business was dealing in grain. So the income was refigured, and the department sent its report back here based upon average cost. And so the reports for the subsequent nineteen years following the Government instructions. But the field agent came around, I think in December, to investigate the correctness of the 1936 return. His conclusion was that inventories should be at market price for the close of the year, and he pointed to a department ruling as the basis for conclusion. Figured his way the change made an increased tax of a little better than $300. Of course, as it seems to me, this should have been the method used all during the years. It's quite a task to get average cost. However, any method is fair if it is never changed. It may be unfair if changed. In this particular case it worked out without much loss to either the taxpayer or the Government, for the taxpayer was saved about as much for 1937 as he lost in 1936. I made a rather well-considered guess as to the final result before I agreed to the change, based upon the fact that there was little grain handled in the drouth year compared to the big year of 1937, and therefore 1937 profits would probably be large on the old inventory basis.

Well, a letter from home should have nothing to do with income tax. There is indeed little of interest to tell. This morning Mr. Butler cut some limbs and brush and burned them. He also smoothed up the final section where the garden used to be and sowed grass seed there—all things which it is high time to do.

Work on the rug has languished for a couple of days. Wednesday noon your mother went to her bridge club at Mrs. Frank Craig's, ate chicken salad and what not, played her game and for a change won the prize, came home without appetite but ate some steak, potatoes, etc., and then we went to a picture show which was so depressing as to leave us with little light in the mental firmament. Then to bed, and your mother had a hard night, but came down to breakfast. Shortly afterwards, I called Doctor Iknayan, and he dosed her and she has been in bed since. I think she is sitting up a little this afternoon and is all right, and our guess is that the particular food she ate Wednesday noon was just the food which her stomach couldn't handle at the time. I think her trouble arose from a combination of stomach and maybe nervous situation which made a rather poisonous mess.

Called Alice E. last night. She, Harold, Jimmie and dogs are well, though Jimmie's vaccination is sore at the moment, or was last night. The river has had plenty of water in it a good part of the winter, and there should be plenty of fish this spring and until the seines get in their undercover work at low water. Haven't bought my license yet but will do so soon. Know a dandy place where the farmer has and will supply some good country ham and, if need be, I will get some minnows for bait.

There is no news from Texas. I hoped to be going down there about this time but have been unable to get my desk clear enough to leave it for ten days or two weeks. The well ought to be finished—good or bad—by now. I wrote asking Moore to wire me, my expense, when the well was finished, and that was when the well was about 5,800 feet which was on February 24, fifteen days ago. Am not worried about it whether it is good or bad. In fact, have put it almost out of my thoughts since then, but occasionally wonder what-the-Sam-Hill is delaying the finish.

Have had 473 feet of 8-inch tile put in out at the last 60 acres we bought, and am going to have 80 rods of hedge pulled right away there.

Well, I must close and I have told you very little. Indeed there is little to tell. Lots of love. Keep your chin up, and don't let these last long months get you down. I still think you have earned a year's rest, but that is up to you to decide.

March 18, 1938

The sun has been an infrequent visitor here this year, but today it is doing a beautiful job of shining down on us and at noon today your mother said that this is the first day that has all the feel and appearance of spring. She and Jimmie spent the morning messing around in the back yard, raking up leaves and what not. However, I think Jimmie had spent the morning digging and looking for fishing worms. He had a goodly supply when I came home and I promised him that before supper we would drive out and look at the river. He wants to wet a line, and your mother had promised him that I would buy me a fishing license and we would drive out and fish, but the river is high and swift—maybe out of its banks—and I told him that we could look at the river, but if it was high with a swift current I wouldn't go near it, for if I should fall in, the swift current would carry me away as I couldn't swim in such a current. He seemed satisfied with the explanation.

There is no news from Texas. When I went home the evening of the 14th I thought I could finish up all on hand on the 15th and told your mother we would start to Texas on the morning of the 16th, but on the 15th one matter developed complications, and it may be ten days before I can leave here. So I wrote to the man who is putting the well down and asked him to write me the situation. Have not heard from him. As I have said before, it isn't well to count on getting any oil money, and we don't propose to make any changes in plans because of the possibility of the well finding oil.

Your mother asked me to write you this afternoon because she had been called on the phone by Mrs. Hite who told her she had received a letter from Mrs. Ankenbrand wherein it was suggested that the more politic and wiser course for you to follow is to ask for a year's leave of absence from Madison rather than sever your connection there entirely; that by asking for a leave of absence and getting it, you would be in a much better position to secure employment there or elsewhere than if you simply resign when the year is up. Your mother wanted me to write today because Mrs. Hite also told her that you have an engagement with the Ankenbrands soon and it might be well for you to know their view before you see them. I think the letter of Mrs. Ankenbrand had some reference to a possibility of your being employed in Honolulu for a time, and that Mr. Ankenbrand thought if you had that employment on a leave of absence, it would give you prestige; whereas, if you had it merely as one having left a previous appointment, you might have some difficulty securing a job in the States afterwards. I am writing this merely as a suggestion for your consideration. The source of the Ankenbrands is such that one is inclined to give some credit to it, being that the matter is one of school custom or politics—a matter about which I know nothing of any importance.

Your letter came in this morning. I read it under the confusion attendant on the preparation and consumption of a meal whereat young James Y. Tolle is present. Shall read it more carefully tonight. I got the fact that you have again been with Mrs. Wilson*—I must so call her for I have forgotten

*Mrs. Ross Kenyon—formerly Mrs. Lester Wilson of Charleston.

her present name—and that you enjoyed your visit very much, that part of it was at "Onrees" where you had a delightful dish amidst charming surroundings and in her sparkling company. Also, I got the fact that you have the opportunity, which you are accepting, to hear three lectures by the world's highest Shakespearian authority. Your life has certainly been interesting. I envy you no part of it, but it is always a source of pleasure to me that so many and varied experiences have come to you. Would that all had been pleasant, but it needs to be that some are not. One of the few things of the latter kind in your life that I really regret is the experience you have had and are having with your mixed class. I believe that has done more to depress and discourage you than anything that has happened. I can't tell you how to overcome the difficulties which the class offers or the things it's doing to your spirit, for I don't know how, but I sure hope you find a way to subdue that particular class before you surrender it. If you can in some way get a victory there where it is almost hopeless, you will do no end of good to your soul. There must be a way. I know that you have worried and thought over it no end, and maybe have done so much of that, that a way, though clear and simple, would not be recognized. I am pulling for you to find it. Perhaps if you would put it all down in a letter for me to read, it may clear itself in your mind as you write, or something may occur to me as I read. Is that worth trying or not?

Jim was with us last night and I think will be tonight.

March 21, 1938

You are, of course, interested but will not be very much pleased to know that the well prospects have blown up. I had a letter this morning from Moore in which he broke the news in the following language, to wit:

> It (the well) is a dry hole, plugged and abandoned, at a total depth of 7,002 feet. Surely sorry to give you this news, but we thoroughly tested everything that had a chance and, in addition, ran an electrical survey of the entire hole to ascertain whether or not we had passed up anything. The well is high, and in fact, everyone figured high enough to make a producer, but it just didn't. I personally am firmly convinced there is an oil field in this immediate vicinity, but which way it would be hard to guess. I would say, offhand, either southeast or southwest.

And that is that. I am glad that I did not spend any money on the strength of it and I suppose no one else in the family did.

Your mother has again had another little spell but has promised to be very obedient and not overexert herself on the rug, housecleaning, or gardening, or in any other way. I hope she lives up to her promise.

There is little news. This is a beautiful spring day and it is warm. Yesterday also was beautiful. Just a few days of this and we are all inclined to believe that there will be no more winter, but looking backward there is too much in the past to give us a firm base for such a belief. The farmers think they will be in their fields by tomorrow afternoon if there is no rain. There has been much rain and the fields are still a bit too wet.

I have reliable reports that fish were being caught at the river yesterday. Jimmie spent all of Friday getting worms and was disappointed that we considered the river too high and muddy yet. As it turned out his hunch was better than our reason.

April 11, 1938

We made some calls yesterday afternoon, got home about 6, were called to the Thomases' for a snack, went from there to the Normal School to see the faculty play (free), found the auditorium crowded, stood around awhile, and then went to the Colemans', where we remained until 11:30. As we got home I wondered whether or not you had tried to call us.

There is little news, just picking up the loose ends after our jaunt through Texas. We sent you a few cards along the way but of course told little of our trip, and it's really too long a story to tell in a letter while there yet remains the hope that you may be with us this vacation. By the way, every time I begin to let myself hope that you will be here at Eastertime, the condition attached to your coming intrudes; that is, that your coming is based on the proposition that your plans call for you to be somewhere else next summer. Still I hope that you do come this Easter.

I don't know whether I wrote you anything about the oil well or not. It is abandoned and probably dry. The closest land owner, living on and owning adjoining land, thinks it a dry hole. However, that it is dry does not condemn the land except where the drill pierced it. There probably will be at least one other effort made in the neighborhood, not on our land but near, for it is thought by the oil men that there is an oil pool in the immediate neighborhood. The rest of the trip I will not write about until I know whether you are coming home or not. We did jump into the surf of the Gulf, we did acquire a sunburned bald head by fishing a couple of hours in a small row boat in an arm of the bay while the sun was apparently hidden by clouds, we did have a fine trip, saw many things at many places, had many pleasant experiences and few unpleasant ones, driving in all 3,059 miles, and we did get home in a cold wet rain which was with us all day and caused us much disgust.

Mother is at her wits end for gray woolens to finish out a gray strip in her rug. She told me to tell you that if you have any discarded gray clothes (woolen), bring them home with you. I think she especially mentioned a particular skirt.

The river is far out of its banks, as high as it ever gets, I think. The farmers have planted nothing—not even oats or clover. They have not been able to do any spring plowing.

April 29, 1938

I feel that I have neglected you this week and your mother has the same feeling regarding her own failure to write you. It's been almost a week since you left and we have heard from you and you have not heard from us. I am sorry. We were also critical of ourselves that we did not force a sleeper on you for the trip. You must take some of the blame for that, for you refused to tell me about your financial equipment. The $5 was all that we had with us, and the decision to force it on you was sudden and without a thought as to whether it was enough or not. After I got back to the car though, it occurred to me that $5 wouldn't get a sleeper unless there were considerably more to go with it, for to use a sleeper you also had to have a more expensive ticket. Am glad it did a little good though. Don't ever do that again. You take too much reserve strength out of yourself and it may cost plenty in later life.

Your mother has been doing just what she pleases to do, and so far has not overtaxed herself—mostly in the yard in the mornings and sleeping some in the afternoons. Sunday afternoon we three (Jimmie, as you know, was with us and, as you will understand, was the instigator of the activities) went fishing. We had to watch him too closely because we feared the current in the river, and he was soon restive, and fishing was not satisfactory for me, nor successful for either of us. So we walked in the woods for a while looking for wild flowers and found a land terrapin with the initials R.K. carved in it. The date also had been carved but so poorly that it had caused a part of the shell to scale off and could not be read as to date. I think the carving was done by a Kelly, for I found the creature in the woods on the farm which once belonged to Larb Kelly. Jimmie was a bit afraid and apparently at first not much interested. Turned it loose when I got home, and when Jimmie wanted to investigate further, he couldn't find it, and I had to do that. Then he ordered it locked in the back porch and shortly after a pick-up supper went to bed and to sleep. A little later Harold and Alice came and decided to take him home. Harold brought him down wrapped in a coat or something, and at the foot of the stairs he began to wake and soon got his eyes open far enough to see his dad, and they opened wider, and as he was carried out the door he realized what was happening and in urgent tone said to his dad, "Wait a minute, wait a minute!" After a moment's pause he went on to tell his dad to get the terrapin and take it home—and something else of less importance to be done. I hear he is having a fine time with the terrapin, for it's turned loose at night and has to be found the next morning, etc.

We are all well. The road building* is coming along slowly. Mrs. Goodwin cannot keep her hands off and makes extra work, but no one can stop her. Her son tried to work on it this morning but soon gave it up. She must have been busy all morning, for there's quite a mess left. There is evidence around the yard (I started this letter before and am finishing it after lunch) that your mother may have been too busy this morning, especially as she is going to luncheon and bridge and for bridge tonight also. She said she hadn't but manages to keep me uneasy. Hope you are rested by now.

May 11, 1938

Well, May 14 is rolling around again and with it and with the daily thoughts of you, the remembrance that the 14th is your birthday. Would like to send you some worthwhile material thing just to let you know that we think of you in some more practical way than just in terms of respect and love, but as usual the pocketbook has a pinched and haggard look and the small item has to be measured in terms of comparison with the poor old family exchequer. May your birth anniversary be very happy and may you become happier as the future years roll along.

There is little news with us. Jimmie is with us—was last night and will be tonight. He is much less trouble when few people are around and is really an interesting and busy little fellow inclined to be obedient and reasonable. It is about settled that your mother and Jimmie will be the Michigan visitors this summer. That will leave you and me without a car, but I reckon we will get along. It has been too cold here the last few days for comfort. It always seems offensive for the weatherman to bring his cold spells this late in the spring after we have had some delightful weather, after we have changed to summer underwear, and after we have let the furnace fire die. Have rebuilt the fire several times this spring and hope this will be the last time.

Your mother and I were in Sangamon County Sunday at the farm—dinner at a country home, country ham, etc. Then we drove on over to Salem Park. It was a beautiful setting there, with the reconstructed cabins

*A driveway serving three neighbors and being built by J. Y. Kelly.

and so on set in a hill which was deeply wooded around. A beautiful park. The wind was cold and strong all day and we were thoroughly chilled but suffered no bad effects otherwise.

The roadway to our garage is finished and we hope it will withstand any flood that may come. Am now at the business of getting the weeds out of the lawn in my spare time. That has been a bit neglected since we started the Michigan vacations. It won't seem very long now till you are home and we are certainly glad you are to be here this summer.

Mother says buy a sock or something with the two dollars.

May 16, 1938

Old Mother Nature strikes in many ways, sometimes after giving her rattles of warning, at other times as the copperhead. Continued feeling of "laziness" in you is, I think, fair warning because it is rather opposed to your nature. A time or two I have felt that you ought to take a rest by coming home and loafing, but you felt that you could carry on, and you were right in the estimate of your strength and determination, for you did succeed in carrying on in spite of being sick and wore your sickness out. You were right this time, but don't take chances any more. I rather think you can do yourself a lot of good here at home this summer, no summer school, no outside activities—well, practically none—nothing to do but laze and sleep the days away, except for the little housework that is necessary with only two lazy people around. As a matter of fact, if you begin to feel lazy again, there is no *real* reason why you should wait until the end of school before coming home. If you should come earlier you would get a better start on the lazy life. When you were home in April you showed that you were your old self again, and I don't want you to wear yourself down before coming home. Am really mad at myself for not exercising my parental authority with a stern ban on your making a long train trip, either coming or going, without a sleeper. That was a fool thing for you to propose or me to permit. We will have to see that you do cut out the foolhardy things. Carefully chosen food, plenty of rest and sleep, and no worry about your business or pleasure are called for, as you know. You will find it difficult to forget the old saying, "This time don't count." As a matter of fact, each time of overexertion, overwakefulness, overworry does count, and the philosophy of old Rip is no longer yours to follow.

This is to be a busy week for your mother and Alice E. Each has plenty of social events scheduled for the week—invitations out—to satisfy anyone. I fall into one of them, a dinner Wednesday night at the Dr. Shaffers'. There is little other news. The yard is still pretty and we are just coming out of a cold, raw spell which seems to me to have lasted pretty much forever. The new building, Health Education, was dedicated Saturday and there was a big dance that night with seven or eight hundred people dancing. Your mother and I didn't dance but spent $1.10 to sit in the balcony and hear the music which was the kind we shut off when it comes over the radio, the jazzy kind.

I am glad you know what made you lazy, doubly glad the dangerous situation is over, and glad that you have sufficient determination to live up to the rules of the game and thereby win a complete and permanent recovery. Have an idea that a quiet life here is just what the doctor would order—no temptation to fish or swim or overexpose yourself to the sunshine, no need to accommodate your convenience to the whim or convenience of anyone, not even a canary or a goldfish to worry about. Whether you will wait till school closes or not, I do suggest that there is no need for you to spend a week in New York after school closes. Why worry about that, and what's the end to be gained? Doesn't matter whether you get a new job or not, or even keep the old one, or even that you have any job or not. The rule requiring you not to worry forbids that you care whether you teach or not.

May 19, 1938

I haven't any news to tell you, but airmail is to be picked up at Charleston today by plane. This may not happen again. Also, unless I can find another envelope like this, there will be two stamps on it, for I got the wrong stamp a few days ago when I bought two for the two envelopes which I had, and put them on the envelopes before I found out about the special stamps for this week.

Your mother went to her card club yesterday, and last night the Dr. Shaffers had us for dinner and cards. Also, your mother had to turn down a luncheon invitation at Mrs. Ball's. Today she has luncheon at U. S. Grant, Mattoon. Tomorrow she also has a luncheon date somewhere.

The yard is at its best, plenty of rain, luxuriant foliage, deeper colors than usual in the flowers. I believe the Paris flower-loving women will be in Charleston today looking over the beauty spots of Charleston, and our yard is on their schedule.

We have had an oversupply of ham recently. When we were in Sangamon recently we ate at a country home where fried country ham was served. Then for last Sunday your mother brought home a nice large section of ham for baking, and some of that is still in the ice box. Tuesday night we had dinner in the country here and fried country ham was again the basis of the meal. Last night Mrs. Shaffer served delicious baked ham. So, all in all, we are inclined to feel that, while in each case the ham was tops, we are ready to turn to something else.

Hope we have a letter from you today. Don't forget that you are to drop down for a little rest every chance you get—also, that you are not to enter into all the possible activities which come along. Give yourself a break more frequently than just now and then. I am inclined to think that this is the most important rule for you to learn and *practice*.

Save the special stamp and envelope.

May 22, 1938

I fear that Essie* will be unable to get possession of her cousin's goods without legal proceedings, which will be more costly and accompanied with more bother than the goods may be worth. I take it that the appointment of a conservator for the cousin by an Indiana court would be necessary, then Essie and her sister would have to prove up their claims in the court which appoints the conservator and come at the goods as creditors collecting their claims. For that reason I would suggest that Essie get in touch with an attorney in the county where the goods are located, tell him the facts, and seek through him to get something done without court procedure. It may be there is a member of the American Bar Association in the county. While such membership is not a guarantee of integrity or ability, yet it is something or another. It may be that there is already a conservator for the cousin. The records in the county where she lived would probably show. The conservator is, of course, entitled to possession of all the ward's property and must eventually account for it.

There is little news here. The flowers, unusually colorful and profuse this year, have taken several beatings from heavy rains, and still there is much color and charm in the yard. The grass—mostly white clover this year—is growing all the time, the ground is soggy and the sun has been seldom seen lately. We have had already about our annual supply of rain, and I hope the evening-up will not come during the crop-growing season.

Your mother is well though she had too many parties last week. Alice E. has also been too active socially, and they both may profit, if they will, by a rest at the lake. Alice E. and Jimmie came over for lunch yesterday, or rather dinner, for we had our dinner in the middle of the day. Harold was at the golf grounds.

---

*Esther Tress, who shared an apartment with Emma C. for one year in Madison, New Jersey.

September 7, 1938

I see from one of the enclosed forms that Kentucky University is using WPA for a project relating to old grads. It is a truism that money which easy comes also easy goes. States, municipalities, even universities, guided by men have the attitudes of men. Under the old system, which will someday again be the new system, it was just as much a truism that a man to whom money came hard found difficulty in prying himself away from it. Under the mass psychology which has been developed, the latter has ceased to be a truism, for in the minds of the people there is no assurance of a future to be secured by industry and thrift. The best that can be hoped for is that Government will see that everyone has provision for sustenance, clothing and housing until the accumulations of the past have been dissipated, and that one's own life will not outlast the debacle to come. Many of us still have hope for the future based on industry, thrift and common sense. But the other idea is widespread.

There is little news here. Your mother has written you a time or two I think. We had a card written in Chicago and were pleased that you enjoyed your visit there so much. Your mother is helping today with a flower show, largely by using Mrs. Thomas's flowers. With reference to which Mrs. Thomas gave her instructions before leaving on a three or four-day trip, the excuse for which was taking Jo* back to her school work.

Thank you very much for your good note and the $10 left on my dresser. Of course, just at this time I have many uses for the $10, still feel selfish in accepting it. Guess I will just consider it a loan which I will try to repay if and when you are in need of money. I hope you have big success in your teaching this year, particularly in the discipline problem. Feel that if that problem were solved, you would lose your distaste for your work.

I did enjoy every bit of your stay at home. It was longer than usual and, by that much, the better. With your painting as recreation I have the feeling that you enjoyed it also, as much almost as if it had been a summer spent in new surroundings.

September 19, 1938

I have been negligent in writing to you and have little excuse to offer. Have been more or less busy about the trivial things of home and office and

*Josephine Thomas.

perhaps have been wasting too much of my time. There has, however, been little to write about.

Eva and Bob were here and we called at Cavins's to see them. They were at breakfast on our back porch the next morning. We enjoyed seeing them a great deal and they both look well and happy.

Have had the sky picture you want out there framed and will send it as soon as we can get it suitably wrapped for sending. It is now hanging on our living room wall and adding a bright spot to the rather dingy wall space. It hung in my office half a day and I showed it to Frank Craig. He asked if it were a Paul Sargent.* Of course, he is no better judge of pictures than I am, but he did think it pretty. In the language of the day, I think you've got something there, and am anxious for you to make painting your hobby for the winter. As a hobby it may be a bit expensive, but my belief is that you will go much farther there than in any business enterprise. I do not believe that you or I have the first quality required for success in the business affairs of the country. We both see the other fellow's point of view too clearly to deal with him successfully. If an advantage is to be had by either, you or I would give the other fellow the advantage. Think that one over and see if it's not so. In the painting line I think you have a real natural advantage—your make-up is artistic and not at all commercial. The more I look at your pictures the more attractive they are to me and I propose to have the finished bridge picture hanging in my office as soon as it is framed.

Have been cutting out the columns you want from the Corpus Christi paper and send a couple with this. Had a lot of them but lent them to Lee Lynch, on my suggestion, telling him they had interested you and me and might interest him. Didn't tell him so but I thought, by suggestion, he might be led to a gradual improvement of subject matter in his column. He said he would return the clippings as I told him that you wanted them.

A furnace fire was about necessary last Friday and Saturday and our furnace was ready Saturday night. The thermometer was down to 46 this morning, but the day is bright and clear and the atmosphere is not nearly so heavily charged with moisture though rain still falls with the slightest restraint at times.

We had hoped to cook a meal yesterday out in the open with the Tolles, but the weather was too bad. So your mother and I had hamburgers at home after attending church. Your mother's throat is better and she no longer talks of having her tonsils out—and the recurring discussion as to my teeth is at present at rest. So now the discussion is as to papering the living room and getting new curtains—and the rug is to the fore again with plenty of material at hand. No braiding has been done as yet, but material is being

*Paul Turner Sargent—Middle western artist.

prepared, cut into strips and rolled into balls. The close of winter should find the rug much enlarged.

We are both well.

September 30, 1938

I have a lot of "Crows Nest" items from the Texas paper on my desk but think you are more interested in Gipson's column. The "Crows Nest" is frequently in two columns, and after cutting them out, I have them rather mixed up. Suppose the fitting them together would be an occupation something like knitting or solitaire or a method of passing the long winter evenings—with nothing else to do and no place to go.

Alice and Jim, your mother and I were at Springfield yesterday. They spent the day buying a couple of pairs of shoes and I walked around some 3 or 4 miles through the cornfields at the farm. All of us came home tired having had a big day. Tonight your mother and I plan to go to a picture show, "Boys Town," I think. Your mother wrote you of the fish fry at the river. Charlie Miller caught the bass, I cleaned them, and Mrs. Miller fried them. I ate far more than my share and was not a bit ashamed of making a pig of myself. The end justified the reputation I earned, whether I received it or not.

There is little news. Mother was hard at work for an hour or two looking for a specific remnant, which she didn't find, and had planned to put in the afternoon on rug work, but someone called for a fourth at bridge this afternoon so the rug will wait till later. The weather has been ideal. I have walked considerably on all the farms this week and know pretty well what corn and beans will come off. Saw a pheasant out on the north sixty.

This noon as your mother and I were eating on the porch, a small woods turtle, terrapin, came slowly and sedately from the Thomas neighborhood, following the path. Where he was heading for we never learned because we couldn't stick around long enough to find out. I first disturbed him, and he went into his shell. About 10 minutes later his head came out and he investigated the four corners of the horizon devoting about 5 minutes unmovingly to each. Then a dog came along, and he became only a shell. The dog sniffed him over but not knowing anything to do about it finally left, and we had to quit also. Our back yard yields many pleasant surprises in the course of a summer—especially noticeable this year because of the long period during which the weather was nice.

Well I didn't intend to write a letter but wanted to get my money's worth in stamps. We have been anxious to hear to what extent the storm affected Madison. There must have been some wind and much rain.

October 7, 1938

Comes the time when absentee voters, who are as interested in the November election as I am interested, should apply for their ballots. On the theory that you are still a voter here and are a Republican still interested in voting for the good of the country as I see it, I am sending you an application for a ballot. It is to be signed by you on the line following the cross mark before a notary public who will sign on the line above the written words "Notary Public." Then mail the application to Elmer F. Elston, County Clerk, Charleston, Illinois.

I send herewith a few more of the clippings from the Texas paper. Your account of last week was good. I got a very good picture of it all, especially of you sitting out in the open with your easel on your knees and brushes scattered around, doing your best to get a record of the picture before you. By the way, I have your completed bridge sitting on my tall desk. Your mother won't let me have it framed for fear my taste would not be right, but I am getting familiar with the picture and like it better as it becomes familiar. It's really a good picture.

Your mother went to Indianapolis this morning—driving her own car. Said she would drive carefully and not too fast.

There is little news here. We are well and have had and are having the *perfect* autumn weather which Illinois does furnish, I imagine, as well or better than anywhere else on the face of the globe. The fall colors are well on their way, and if there were a bit of a frost would ripen fast. They are coming slowly but with the beauty of coloring of the master painter of them all. Lots of love.

The new supply of vitamins came in on time. Thanks. We are persistent at taking our vitamins.

October 27, 1938

After thinking it over we decided you ought to have your own fiddle if it could be arranged without too much trouble, so I toted it to the express office and learned what it would cost to ship it insured for five-hundred dollars. I also learned that it would have to be boxed, and toted it down to the Muchmore and Irons shop which was closed. I then toted it back to the office and let it rest there awhile, then back to the shop which was still closed, then back to the office, then to the shop, and then home with it where it now rests in the closet from which I took it. After thinking it over in the light of my experience, I think you better just borrow a fiddle till Christmas time. I tried for a week to find the man to frame a picture and failed, and I might have the same experience with the fiddle.

There was an amusing incident in the home yesterday, the overpowering odor of which lingers on and will be with us a month or so, I reckon. For several days I have been ahungered for boiled navy beans, and so day before yesterday, I saw a bag of new-crop beans in the grocery store, some of which I had with me when I got home. Also had some pork chops for supper—one too many chops—and there was the proper combination all suggesting to your mother that the only proper thing to do about it was to soak the beans overnight and on the morrow put them in a pot and have boiled pork and beans. So far so good; that is, the beans were soaked and by noon they and the chop were in the pot—the economy cooker of the electric range—and at noon the power was turned on full blast to bring them to a boil, as I later learned. Then your mother went to her bridge club and I to my office. At five I went home, and as I went up the steps in front there was a reek in the atmosphere, a reek of things burnt. The house was, of course, cloudy with the smoke and overpowering almost with the reek of it. There was nothing to do but carry the cooker out. The meat was all consumed, the beans black cinders, the pot red hot, the odor in the house offensive. Really I think it will be months before the odor is gone—the curtains, the rugs, everything absorbent absorbed it. There were a few creamed turnips sitting on the stove which we ate for lunch today—burnt bean flavor and all. It's bad enough to smell—bad enough without eating the smell too.

A wire came in today that three from Mt. Sterling would be in tomorrow. One will be David's wife, another Emily, who I think arranged the trip so Dick Williams could escort her to Eastern Ilinois' Homecoming. The identity of the third is not known, maybe David or Aunt Nannie or Virginia or Leona.

Well, I have been so long interrupted in writing this letter that the inspiration is gone and I hardly know what I have written. There is a question, though. In one of your letters you said you were sending something and that you were anxious to know whether we recognize it. Whatever you had in mind failed to show up, and with much curiosity—unsated—we await its coming or your further word that its sending was vetoed or postponed.

At Homecoming there is to be a big Bar-B-Q put on by the school with the help of skilled men from Kentucky or Tennessee imported for the occasion, the big pits, the roasted beeves, and sheep, etc., and a crowd of five thousand or more expected—so I hear.

October 28, 1938

Even as I wrote you yesterday that the package you sent had not come, it was sitting at home between the screen and front door, and this morning we had a treat for breakfast. Will try to have a few left when you get home

Christmas. The filets of fish looked good to me and, so we found them this morning. Thanks a lot.

I think I wrote you all the news yesterday. It's now 3:15 o'clock and the Kentuckians ought to be about in—that is, if they left Mt. Sterling at the crack of dawn. Your mother plans that we shall go out to the college tomorrow and try for a Bar-B-Q sandwich for our noon meal. I really would like to have one if the meat is tender. It's been many a year since I have had a piece of meat cooked—in a whole carcass—in a deep pit, as the plan is to cook the steers, the sheep and the hogs tomorrow. Your mother also plans, I think, to have the whole crowd go to look at the dance and hear the music tomorrow night. That pleasure I would willingly forego, but I reckon there is no use to try to evade it.

November 3, 1938

I have just mailed the quilt. I guess mother has written most of the news. There was too much pork at the Bar-B-Q. My sandwich for meat had just a fat piece of side meat. I reckon a pig is almost all fat, judging by the number of complaints I have heard. Most people wanted beef or mutton but most people got pork. I did finally get a sandwich with beef in it, but it wasn't especially good. Would have been better, no doubt, had I not exhausted my appetite on the pork.

The house still bears the odor of burnt pork and beans, but it is gradually growing less offensive. Eventually it may become so faint that it will not be offensive at all.

The wind is pretty high today though the temperature is still delightful. It was 61 on the porch at breakfast time and is warmer now of course. The reports are that a storm started a few days ago in N. E. Canada and that it will be felt in Chicago and, if there, probably here. The quail hunters are hoping that there will be a rain before the season opens on the 10th, else the dogs cannot get the scent. So they will be pleased with a change provided it brings a rain, and the rest of us cannot justly complain, for in all my memory there does not remain a recollection of so fine a fall as we have had. We ought to have been out of doors every day—fishing would have been pleasant whether fish were caught or not—and looking back I feel we have not made much of our opportunities.

Did I tell you that I now have the shady side of the bridge hanging in my office? As I feel about it, the picture is mine for keeps. I think Alice E. wants it, but let her try and get it. Really, I like some of your pictures as much as any pictures I have seen. Maybe I am not well-educated artistically, or maybe my attitude toward the artist who painted them prejudices me, yet

I like them very much. They soon became among the familiar, pleasing things of my surroundings.

November 9, 1938

This day dawned bright and crisp after the heavy cold windy rains of Monday and the marrow-chilling breezes of election day. The county candidates who were Republicans won, but the Democratic candidate for U. S. Senate also won. The Republicans gained some members in the State Legislature and in the lower house of Congress. The results generally seem to be too mixed to be a determining factor in the 1940 presidential election. So there may be two more years of uncertainty as to whether or not we will remain a Republic.

There is little news here in our family. Your mother, Alice E., Jim and I went to Springfield Monday, your mother and Alice to exchange some shoes which they bought on their last trip but found unsatisfactory, and I to go to the farm, and Jim as general source of pleasure mingled with a bit of annoyance now and then. All purposes were carried out except that it rained too much for me to get to the farm, though I went to Alexander and got a report there of what was being done at the farm. As usual the seasonal work on the farm was far behind the neighborhood. It's nice to know that I will have a new tenant there next year. Also, four antique shops were visited in Springfield and one in Decatur and your mother spent 50¢ and Alice E. bought a wine glass. Sunday afternon your mother and I, with Miss Watson in the back seat, drove over beyond Paris, and your mother went into several homes trying to find "Ivy and Snow" glass, but the neighborhood seemed to have been well-combed and while many old families lived around there, they were not disposed to sell anything. Furthermore, none of them had "Ivy and Snow." That pattern is hard to find.

I plan to go out early in the morning and, acting as my own bird dog, try to find a pheasant to shoot at, or to shoot. Very seldom is my license productive of game of any kind, but I always have hope enough to buy a license. This year my fishing license produced no fish, though I held a pole several times in places fitted for Jimmie for fishing. I heard this morning that bass in the river are hungry and giving the fishermen considerable sport, but I reckon I will not make a try for them. It's a bit too cool to sit quietly on the bank.

Your mother was at a card game yesterday afternoon from which she brought home the first prize. I think that the picture show "The Great Waltz" is on today and we will probably see it tonight.

Well, I guess I will close, but before I do there is an item to tell of, which will interest you. Mrs. Albert Moore was in town yesterday and called on your mother, who reports that she was much interested in your painting, thought that your work showed real talent and was insistent that you keep it up for your own pleasure, even if you sought to make nothing of it commercially.

November 28, 1938

Glad the violin came through in good shape. The papers say that your section of the country has been going through some stormy weather. Well, we have had a bit of weather ourselves—after the almost perfect summer and the perfect fall. About a week ago quite a snow came along this way, and it was pretty cold and grew colder till on Friday and Saturday nights the thermometer hit along about 10 above. The snow has not melted yet but the wind is out of the southwest, and while its front end is chilling, by noon with the sun shining the snow ought to be on the way out.

We appreciated your Thanksgiving telegram. Through one thing and another we neglected even a letter to you for that day and are sorry, though we did have you persistently in mind. Our noon meal was at the Frank Craigs' where there was a magnificent bird of noble proportions, beautifully colored by the heat—a model for the artist's brush—surrounded by everything necessary or appropriate to make one, in the eating, forgetful of experiences of the past, regardless of consequences, and after the eating, lethargic and careless of what the future might bring. We went home about 5 o'clock and lounged and dozed till near 8 o'clock when we freshened up our faces and went to the Colemans' where there was a goodly crowd of school people, and about 11 o'clock, another noble meal was served which was based upon a delicious baked ham. Suprisingly there was no bad result from either meal though Friday and Saturday we ate rather sparingly.

Your mother is bitten by the entertaining bug. She has it in mind to catch up with all the accumulation of obligations extending over a period of a couple of years. Her start was last night—a buffet dinner served to Judge and Ruth Dunn, Ike and Mrs. Miles, Dr. and Mrs. Iknayan, Dr. and Mrs. Dudley, Mr. and Mrs. Thomas, and Mrs. Marshall. The dinner was based on baked ham. When I left home this morning your mother was planning a dinner for Wednesday evening. The ham was a large one and a big part is left already prepared for the service. Then later in the week, the Colvins are expected and if they come we plan a turkey dinner for some who are the especial friends of the Colvins. That is as far ahead as the plans go so far.

We are perhaps more anxious than you that the 22nd of December come, not that it brings Christmas closer, but that it brings you closer. We have a turkey engaged to fulfill his destiny while you are here and are all set to enjoy you as much as we always do. One of the great compensations for your being away has always been the knowledge that you will be back after awhile, and we have the joy of the anticipation of that, the happiness of the event, and the memory that it leaves behind.

Well, there is no way to hurry the calendar along. Take good care of yourself, and hurry on home. That's Christmas present enough for us.

1939

January 12, 1939

There has been so little happening that can be made to sound interesting that there is little use to write except that you may know we are getting along all right. I didn't go to the roast pig dinner last night at Mrs. Craig's else I could give you the firsthand story—of course not as enticingly as Lamb did, still well enough to make the reader want roast pig. Your mother went of course. The dinner was the outgrowth of many years of effort and talk on her part gradually inspiring Frank with the desire for roast pig, and so at last Frank was ready. The time was right, the pig was right, and Frank was in the mood to give rein to his artistry in its preparation.

He chose a pig at the start of its life, dedicated it to its noble fate, left it unvaccinated, fed it choice foods after its mother quit the job, killed and dressed it himself when it weighed something over 30 pounds at 6 weeks of age, manicured and pointed its ears (overlook the propriety of the word "manicured" as applied to ears), curled its tail, dressed its skin to immaculate white, and surrendered it to the bakery for roasting with a cob in its mouth. (Incidentally, the necessity for stuffing it thoroughly so that it would hold its shape, and scoring the hide so that in the roasting it would not, in contracting, separate itself from the body, was overlooked, and the appearance of the pig, after roasting, was disappointing. Still the pig was there for all to see, its odor was there inciting to desire, its flavor was there in complete satisfaction of desire and in complete vindication of the great essayist.)

I was sorry of course to miss the great experience after the thirty-odd years of anticipation, but long ago I learned how to relegate to an unimportant niche in the brain the memory of disappointment such as this was. Your mother brought some of the pig home with her, as well as the card prize. I shall in the privacy of the home get the flavor of the pig, but its glamour is gone. It is now nothing more than roast pork. . . .

Have figured out what caused your mother's cold in spite of the Haliver capsules she has been taking. While I was still completely absorbed in contemplation of the soreness and otherwise disreputable condition of my mouth, she tended the furnace a few times. Once, after shaking hot ashes down into the ash pit, she scooped out two buckets of hot ash, something I learned long ago never to do. I can't do that without afterwards suffering seriously from the contact of the gas and hot ash with the nose and throat passages. There is no doubt in my mind but that the effect was the same on your mother as it would have been with me. She is just about well now and felt fine this morning.

Scott Rogers shot himself at the store very early yesterday morning—did a perfect job, a hole through his head, perhaps so well done that there was not a moment of consciousness. His health was bad and had been for quite some time and probably he was finding it difficult to make a financial success at his new location. There may have been some family disturbance, or rather, difficulty of seeing eye to eye with his son. Suicide of a prominent person is always somewhat disturbing in a small community. . . .

Enjoyed hearing your voice the other evening. It sounded good—strong and happy—and made us happy. You knew of course that you would find us at home, had me positively located. My mouth is still uncomfortable, but nine days have passed and it won't be long before I will be measured for a new set of teeth. Am already tired of soft foods and it will be quite a while before I get the new set, and quite a while after that before the gums will be hard enough to permit chewing; still, time is passing just as fast as it ever did, and after enough time has passed, all adjustments will have been made and the present inconvenience and discomfort will be a feeble memory from an unimportant niche.

The weather has been delightful, not cold, bracing part of the time, almost too warm part of the time. In fact, once at least the temperature all but hit 60 degrees. Your mother is working again on her rug. It's a long way round it as you know. If she abides by her resolution to build a 9' x 12' rug, it will evidence a determination almost unknown to human beings.

January 19, 1939

We got the letter with the ten-dollar check some days ago. Enjoyed the letter and appreciate the check. Think I will cash it, as I can use the extra ten just now. Mother says, however, that the napkins are to be paid for by us and under no circumstances are you and Alice E. to eventually stand that expense. Mother is also much pleased with the tablecloth and napkins and began the hemming job last night. Just now her daily stint is to get one round done on her rug. One round now takes four and one-half hours so it is a real stint. The rug is 8'6" x 5'10", and it's a long way round it.

My new teeth went in yesterday afternoon. They are still of little use, except as ornament, but I think I have an excellent job. Dr. Trexler was the dentist, and I really believe that he is unusually careful and exceptionally skillful. Was able to sleep with them last night and did very well, but at one time I almost yielded to the temptation to take them out. Instead smoked a cigarette and went back to sleep. They are a mouthful or seem so for the present. Tonight we are to eat dinner at Hites'—the second invitation there since the teeth were out.

. . . . We have had gloomy weather with two falls of snow both of which were damp enough as they fell to cover trees and bushes with white and make the landscape beautiful. It has not been very cold, but the wind is in the south this morning, and probably the snow will melt today. This is the time of the year when I want the ground solidly frozen, for my coal pile is low and if the ground is not frozen, the truck will cut in. In the fourteen years during which only half the coal supply could be laid in at a time, luck has been with us and the yard has not been cut up. The yard is soft now, for the snow fell on it when it was thoroughly thawed and the snow has kept it from freezing. Still have a week's supply and probably will have our usual good luck.

The Tolles are well, or were the other day. Your mother drove over with Jimmie early Wednesday morning and stayed until noon, by which time the snow had frozen, and she had a difficult drive home but made it without accident and no unpleasant result except the strain on her nerves, which made her a poor bridge player at her club that afternoon.

Every once in a while I think of the suggestion I made last summer or at Christmas time that next summer you go down into Kentucky and paint pictures of your mother's and my old homes. It still seems a good way for you to spend some of your vacation, and the folks down there seem to want to see something of you.

We are curious to know the good news which was expected at the teachers' meeting the other day. Glad you have the periodic recreation of the orchestra. It's good for you.

Well, I must quit writing now, though it seems to me that this is a poor letter—unsatisfactory at least to me.

January 25, 1939

I don't believe that we have written you a letter this week, and though there is no interesting news to tell you, I fear if you do not hear you will imagine that one of us is sick and will worry. We are both well. I am trying to break in my lower teeth, visit the dentist every day or so to have him grind off a place that is hurting. It seems that lower teeth are rather easily displaced, that they have a tendency to float around, and one has to learn to ride them with his tongue. They also seem to find plenty of places to chafe, and as the gums recede no doubt they will have a growing tendency to be vagrant. The uppers seem to be well-anchored. It's no small undertaking to remove them, and as they are firmly fixed, there is little chafing. Think I am doing better than most, but have certainly learned that in buying teeth one should trade at home as I did, for it gives a mighty good feeling to know that in case of misfit or pain the mechanic is only a couple of blocks away to set it right.

Your mother is busy with her rug but took a day off yesterday to attend a luncheon and card party after giving the morning to the doing of general odds and ends around home. She brought home from the party a new piece of bric-a-brac to clutter up the house for dusting. Today she has given to making herself a skirt. Before I could get lunch she mounted the table, and I measured the distance from the table to her skirt at a point 13 inches from the table all the way around.

We have had and are having very unsettled weather, wind and snow several times lately, melting and freezing, sloppy and slick. It froze hard enough for me to get my second supply of coal without cutting the yard. I have had the same good luck fourteen times in the fourteen years we have lived in the remodeled house. Every year I have been uneasy, and every year the weather has been favorable.

The newspapers have reported severe storms in your neighborhood and we trust they have not inconvenienced you. . . . Your mother was at the Tolles' once during this uncertain weather but had a hard, slippery drive home and is not as trusting about the weather as usual. She was asked over by Alice E. today for lunch at the Dinner Bell and a picture show, but had no confidence in driving conditions remaining good and declined. Sometimes it is not so foolish to look to the future, to contemplate the possibilities of troubles coming.

Well, this was to be but a note when I started, for I had nothing to tell you except that we are well.

February 9, 1939

The days roll by with regularity—as one grows older it seems the tempo of their passage has a regularly quickening beat. It would seem also that a sense of monotony would follow the regularity of the passage of time and of the routine of living day after day doing pretty much the same thing, thinking the same thoughts, meeting the same associates, and in general following a well-defined path—followed for years of days, as it seems, through changeless scenes.

But monotony does not come—the family life built into nature as much as the need for food, the home itself with its very imperfections endeared by long custom, the accustomed associations, business and social, grown into a part of man himself, the unnoted small changes in routine, in associates by reason of death or departure infrequent but with occurrence as regular as the coming of day and night, the gradual changes of thoughts and interests—and almost in a few years the whole scene is changed. No, there is no monotony so far. For instance, a little thing like the changing from nature's grinders to a "boughten" set can pretty much fill the entire outlook of a man.

Speaking of teeth. I had a comparatively easy time—so much easier than anticipated that almost there was a sense of disappointment. Had only 14 teeth to be pulled, only one of them leaving any bone fragments to work themselves out, the new uppers holding themselves firm in place, the lower steady when glued-in for an evening meal, practically without pain. Such is the record. There was of course, plenty of discomfort for a time, but not too much nor for too long.

We are still going out to dinner—last night to the Art Wyeths' again. . . . Again I had a good enough score to be awarded the men's prize, the fourth in the five starts this year. This of course resulted from fair grade of hands and excellent partners.

Have seen two pictures this week. "Robin Hood" and "Jesse James" on successive nights. If you have seen the pictures you know we have had plenty of fighting and sudden death for a long time to come. The Robin Hood picture was the more interesting because of the beauty of its setting, the glorifying of Robin's purposes, and the use of old-time equipment, especially the bow and crossbow in fighting.

Your mother has been doing some necessary winter housecleaning. She had to quit the rug for a time because it crippled her hand.

There really is no news.

March 7, 1939

It's been nice to have the flowers around the house and Mother appreciated them a lot—and the memory. And I have also enjoyed them. Your letters were also good. There is little to tell.

On the 28th, a rabbit sat all day at the root of the big hackberry tree just off the back porch. Occasionally he was startled by something or other, such as the grocery boy, the slamming of a door or other threatening event. Nevertheless he held his place, twiddling his nose now and then until late in the evening, some time after Alice and Jimmie came over to supper and to spend the night. Alice and Jimmie decided to stay two nights and did, but expect to go home this afternoon. We enjoyed them, and I think being here has helped Alice. She seemed to enjoy her meals a lot—eating away from home is good now and then.

Today the sun shines brightly but the wind has a rather raw edge. It's good to have the sun, though, for the winter has brought almost a record number of dark days. The red bird call has been going on, I guess all day. I heard it at daybreak and till after breakfast and again at noon. There cannot be a great deal more of winter and as usual, we enjoy the first harbingers of spring.

If the weather holds, we will drive up to Springfield tomorrow, a trip I have been dreading for some time. It's easy enough to find a day good enough to go to Springfield, but in an open winter, such as this has been, it's hard to find the mud roads free from mud, that is, free enough to make the driving seem feasible to me.

I seem very sleepy this afternoon, and nothing worth recording breaks through the fog. Believe I could drop my head on the desk and sleep. Know for sure that I can do no successful office work and probably shall take Bob's *Tribune* and drowse while I try to read it.

The four of us went to the picture show last night. There was the newsreel, some sort of comic which was inane, one of Walt Disney's pig-and-wolf shows which was very good, and the Charley McCarthy show. This is the second time I have seen Charley and I think that is enough. Prefer him on the radio. I wonder if Bergen is a better ventriloquist than those of my younger days. A ventriloquist show was not objectionable to our folks, or I saw several at Chautauquas. I don't remember which. At any rate, they seemed more marvelous to me then. Seeing Charley and Bergen in pictures destroys some of the illusion. On the radio Charley has an individual personality, apart from Bergen, much of which is lost in pictures.

We are all well. Were very angry that you went to New York in the dead of winter without a cloak but apparently you didn't have pneumonia—so it's all right again. . . .

March 17, 1939

We had lots of pleasure hearing your voice. Also enjoyed the letter you wrote before you called and the letter after your call. You have been good to us. I don't know what Mother will do with your check but rest assured it won't be spent easily. There is really no chance of using it to visit you this Easter—a thing we would want so much to do—but it just cannot be done.

Your mother has done some housecleaning after saying for weeks she would do none until June. The big living room is cleaned—fresh curtains, washed woodwork, and cleaned paper. The old paper she decided, after getting her bank account going, would do for another year as there are rather more pleasant ways of spending money. She has been pretty tired several times but comes back strong. Last night she was all in, so she soaked in hot water, and I took her to the restaurant for supper and saved her some of the after-effects of overwork.

March has had one perfect day—several which were really good for March, and several which have been cold and disagreeable—one big rain over four inches in a couple of days, which was pretty general and sent streams in these states out over the bottom lands. We drove out a couple of times to see the Ambraw as we like to do when it is in raging flood, and as we also like to do in summer when we can get to closer contact with it. Jimmie was along once and was just as interested as we.

I have stuck close to the office since I came back from Texas almost a year ago, and must get away for a few days this summer, somehow. In a one-man office everything stops when the one man is gone. I have no plans at all. The water, fishing, is the most attractive. Still it is pleasant to get in a car and just drive without any set destination. After the first day or so, the whole thing becomes routine, except the shifting scenes and people. But it's a carefree experience, taking one very much out of touch with all that goes to make up his usual surroundings and mode of living. For a single person it would be lonely; for two or more it is not so.

Well, this is just to let you know we are all well and appreciate your thoughts and kindnesses a lot.

March 25, 1939

. . . . Since it was decided that your mother could not come East this Easter, we have both been more homesick to see you than usual, but time will run along pretty fast now and June will be here soon. So if you won't let the teaching get you down, we will try not to let longing to see you get us down. In fact, I know how to take it, but your mother fusses a bit. She is planning to go to Kentucky with you this summer. I think you both will enjoy that. It may be that I can arrange my life so as to go along but make no plans or promises.

This afternoon there is a big afternoon tea at home—a shower for Lucile Thomas who plans to be married in April. I think 24 were invited including Jimmie and Alice. Jimmie is to stay the night, and your mother will find all her time occupied being entertained by him. The entertainment he offers her is something rather strenuous as he has an abundance of life and energy—pep, to you.

We have had three days of almost summer heat and several of the double yellow flowers were in bloom last night.

April 26, 1939

Not that there is anything much to write about, but simply that I am in the mood for a short one-sided chat with you. After the seemingly interminable and miserable weather which April seemed intent on presenting as long as she held sway, we had several days of beauty—the thermometer rising well toward summer heat and vegetation and blossoms almost exploding in their hurry.

Yesterday your mother spent the morning in the yard, and for two hours we worked there together in the evening, and as the result—dead branches have been removed and burnt and much of the trash scattered around has gone as smoke with the wind. The rabbits seem to have centered on our back yard as headquarters this spring—three old ones and at least one youngster. The rabbits found some of your mother's tulips at a time when tulips must have been good food for them, for they ate the buds of almost all tulips in the prize bed. It's nice to have them around—there is hardly a time when at least one is not out in the open—but one has to put up with their natural instincts as we do with squirrels when time comes for them to take the seeds from bushels of green pears or rob bird nests. I wonder if they ever have any inhibitions to curb them.

. . . . Your letter telling of your spring vacation in Washington, D.C. was most interesting, and we appreciate to the limit the part the Colvins had in it. That was one of the nicest things I know of, and I shall certainly let them know how much we appreciate their courtesy and kindness. . . .

There is little oil news—none that affects us. Time is surely passing on the wings of the wind. Only a few days until May and then but a month until June, really not long until you will be out of school. It's actually true that time seems to hurry faster to one who has passed the meridian of life, faster and faster as his sun goes to its setting. . . .

May 9, 1939

Such a short time until May 14. How we would like to swoop down on you that day and spend the day with you in real celebration which does not necessarily contemplate anything more than being with you. We are thinking of you so much, hoping that you are thoroughly happy and that each recurring birthday through a long future may find you happy.

We are well. Your mother has pushed herself too hard, mostly in housecleaning, and is pretty well worn out with a bit of trouble in her throat, but she is taking better care of herself now. We have had some really nice weather, a beautiful mass of blossoms on the apple trees, the dogwood, and redbud, and especially on the wild crabs. The lilacs are coming now into full bloom. The big white lilac is not so good and I think it needs nourishment in its old age. We ought to give its roots considerable fertilization this year but whether we will get to that, I don't know.

We drove to the Rocks Sunday and gathered a big mess of wild greens, which we had yesterday noon with jowl, cornsticks, buttermilk, potatoes, coffee, and cherry pie and cheese. . . . The river water looked at the proper stage and just the right color for fishing, but we were out only for greens. I have my license for fishing but so far have not used it. There were two big high-water periods at the river, and there should be some fish there.

The country is beautiful now—not so beautiful as your part of New Jersey, still beautiful for Illinois. We drove down to the Tom Lincoln home later yesterday afternoon, not to stop but just for a drive over the new road from here. It's a broad road with a fair surface, but it would have been dusty except for a rain in the afternoon.

There is little news—just the short and simple annals of the small-town resident, in his own well-defined rut and doing the same habitual things day after day, just as I have no doubt the big city dweller lives the life of a big city.

We saw Alice, Harold and Jimmie a few moments Sunday. Jimmie will be, I think, a nature lover. He likes worms and rabbits and birds and pretty flowers and splendid views. He likes the water, the nearness of the river, the digging in the ground. Toads and snakes interest him and are not horrible, food that "Mommie" likes is good to him, and he is interested in everything that is pleasant to her.

Well, congratulations on your birthday. Many more happy days to you wherever you may be or whatever you may be doing. . . .

May 23, 1939

As the time when we hope to see you draws nearer, it seems there is less and less urge to write, for I have the feeling that I will see you soon and then we can talk.

It is dry here and is getting pretty hot during the daytime. This morning at breakfast it was 70 on the back porch where we sat and ate our breakfast. The beauty of the yard, the glory of the flowers, the flashing of the birds here and there, red birds, jays, hummingbirds, catbirds and thrush, threshers and so on, and the play of the young rabbit made the breakfast of strong coffee, toast, and eggs a feast, and the experience, if it were an unusual one, would have been an event to be stored in memory and recalled to mind when thoughts turn to the memorable events of the past.

This noon I will eat there alone, for your mother goes to a luncheon where Mrs. Reat is the guest of honor. She is to be sent on her way to Alaska for a year or more there with her daughter, Ruth. Your mother has also one or two other luncheons somewhere this week. She is feeling better than she felt for some time. As you know, her throat became infected and the head passages clogged, and she was rather miserable. Think her trouble started in Kentucky where many of the folks were affected by somewhat similar trouble. It is impossible to persuade her that her tonsils are the danger point and probably cause the arthritis from which her hands suffer at times and should be removed. It is probable that she is convinced that the tonsils should be in a jar with alcohol, but it is impossible to get her to the point of having them out. When she is well, she hopes that her troubles are over, and when she is sick, of course, the tonsils cannot be safely removed.

There is really no news. The Tolles are well; Harold had his company-sponsored trip to Kansas City and there delivered his speech without embarrassment.

June 5, 1939

Well, a prospective trip in our family is always a question for long consideration resulting in decisions which, once made, are subject to overnight changes—so that a fixed plan is slow of maturity. I told your mother some days ago that I would go east if I could get a few matters put over until after our return. One of the matters worked itself out. Another was put over until June 29. The third may go over but is still undecided; that is, it may go over and may not. Nonetheless, I planned a trip to New York via Montreal, Quebec, and New England, and I figured that the expense would be all the money she has saved this winter. That expense led her to decide that we would not take the trip. She is still talking about a fairly straight drive to Madison, and of course the return will have to be fairly straight as I am due here on the 29th. I doubt that we will make the drive—still the matter is not firmly decided. What do you think? If we make it, I am suggesting a trip on the way to New York which would carry us through Cumberland Gap, up through Virginia, with perhaps two or three days in that State, which would be a fairly direct route as compared to the Canada-New England one.

. . . . The yard is still pretty and the weather delightful. Have not had much too hot weather. Mother's dinner-card party Saturday night given on the back porch was delightful, although the women all kept their wraps on and three of the tables at cards moved into the house after awhile, and someone started the fire with the material which was in the fireplace and said that it was pleasant sitting by the fire. I was at one table all evening—the one which stayed on the porch—and was not too cool.

I am feeling pretty well this morning, and I think your mother needs some rest and maybe will quiet down in her activities for a time. I hope she does. When I know anything more about a trip east, I will let you know.

June 17, 1939

. . . . We have had a few pretty warm days, then about a week when it was decidedly too cool, the fire started. And now too hot. Such is the normal flow of the weather in Illinois.

We are not going to do much right now about the fire—will have the attic and roof repaired and the wiring put in order, or rather we have already had the wiring fixed, but the balance—papering, painting, etc.—may go until a more convenient season. Summertime is no proper time to be concerned about such things. We had the urge to paper and paint earilier in the season but turned it down and don't propose to do it now, even though the outside is a bit more unsightly in spots and some of the paper is in worse shape than it was.

We really have no plans for the summer. It's been so comfortable at home that we haven't been tempted much to leave. Jim is thinking a lot about the lake and feels confident his Mommie will find some way to take him. Alice would, of course, be better off without him, for a part of the summer anyway. He is quite an active young man and one who has him in care has really got something that is or becomes almost exclusive of other interests. He has been taught to expect grownups to give him their attention at his volition. With it all, he is so very attractive that one doesn't care much, especially if one is a grandparent.

As you say, it is something to have to go to school on the 24th, especially as the 24th is a natural holiday—a Saturday.

There is no news. Your mother drove to Indianapolis yesterday taking Laura Winter and Mrs. Shaffer and bringing Dick Winter back. Miss Ellington had taken Dick east for three weeks, I think, showing him Washington and vicinity, the Fair, etc., as well as the English King and Queen—quite a notable trip for the youngster—and they picked him up at the railroad station in Indianapolis and brought him home.

It won't be long now before you are home for which we are duly grateful.

September 23, 1939

Your mother is on the home stretch on the cabinet this afternoon. It has had its coat of shellac which has been rubbed down, and this afternoon the final coat of dull varnish is going on. Killing that bear has been a long arduous job for her and I have got in a few strokes so that I may be able to say with a modicum of truth, "*We* killed the bear." The cabinet is turning out to be a good piece of old furniture and probably worth the efforts put on it. After it was cleaned to the wood, heavy sandpapering was called for followed by much sandpapering with fine paper. I think it will look well in the house. The Tolles plan to come over tomorrow afternoon to help move it into the house.

You must know the Tolles have a new car, of course. It's a Dodge and real nifty. Ours, I think I told you, is a Chevy. We went to Sangamon in it a few days ago and like it fine. There is a big baggage compartment, the gear shift is on the steering wheel and the emergency brake at the left hand, which leaves the front seat clear for leg and foot room—three passengers can ride comfortably there. The back seat is also wider and there is a general feeling of roominess to one who has been so accustomed to a 1934 Ford. We have had the garage doors changed to swing out instead of in. Until we did so, could not shut the car inside the garage.

Tomorrow I believe we plan to cook steaks out on the river with the Millers—at noon. Your mother and I had planned to eat at Newton until the Millers suggested the steaks.

There is no news here. . . . The weather has been beautiful, cool, sunshiny, dry. It really gets too cool for comfort at night sitting around on the porch or in the house so your mother has been crawling into bed to read. Last night she did that, but when I went up a short time later her light was off and I reckon she was asleep—said today that she didn't hear me come up.

When you write let us know what your new address will be. Know you will enjoy living there* but still dread the long hours of commuting, the early rising, the late retiring.

October 4, 1939

I found your letter at home when I got there this noon. Also a note from your mother telling me what to eat for lunch—among other things pumpkin pie. She said last night she was going to make the pie and maybe take one to Alice E. So I suppose that is what she did.

Yours was an interesting account of the narrow escape you had from sleeping in a deserted apartment. By this time I suppose you are settled, and I think you will really enjoy the change and that it was a good idea to make it.

There is little news here. The cabinet is in place and the upper part set with glassware. It fits in the room as if designed for the purpose and is in better proportion than the cabinets we saw in Kentucky.

Your mother had two finds lately, both of which are in the cabinet. By one of them she added very materially to her chosen pattern at a most reason-

*61 West Ninth Street, New York City.

able price. Suppose she will tell you what was in that find. The other added most materially to your chosen pattern in colors—large red pitcher and glass, milk glass, and a sugar bowl or bowl of some kind. Also a decanter and four wine glasses, Venetian, with figures of boy and girl done on them in colored and milk glass. Also two ordinary-sized glasses of some pattern and some other items which are not so striking. Really her display took on suddenly quite a large growth both in quantity and quality—just as she was ready to put a display in the cabinet.

I hope to go fishing tomorrow afternoon with the postmaster. The weather is beautiful and do not expect a change. October has always been considered the best Illinois month, and as you know, beginning in 1903 there has not yet been an October 14 which was not delightful. Let us know how you like the new arrangement.

October 10, 1939

Your mother didn't go to Decatur yesterday but is going today. Harold reported that Alice E. expected her mother up yesterday and wanted her to come, but it's just as well that the visit was delayed for a day. Monday Harold had first reported that the baby—still unnamed—was extremely ugly. Last night he reported, after he had again returned from Decatur, that the baby was not so bad as he thought. The weight was 9-1/4 pounds, the time of birth a few minutes past 10 o'clock Sunday night. He is fat and apparently a husky, lusty youngster.* That's all I know. Your mother will write more in detail tomorrow.

There is little news except the baby.

October 18, 1939

We are not writing you as often as we want to write and when it comes to offering excuses, it seems that there is none which is sufficient. The facts are that every day seems full of one thing and another and the writing just doesn't get done. Alice was in Decatur on the 16th at which time Alice E. was doing all right. The plan then was to go back to Mattoon today and I suppose that plan still holds though we did not hear from them yesterday.

The weather has been beautiful and is yet so. I was in Danville Monday and my Sunday school class had a wiener roast last night at Fox Ridge. I

*Dirk Tolle, born Oct. 8.

forgot it until near nine o'clock which was too late, and am much embarrassed as to an explanation. There would seem to be none.

I think I wrote you that Osborn Ferguson, who married Virginia Jeffries, and I are to office together. The offices are being redecorated and are in much confusion. I am writing amidst a confused clutter of desks, chairs, and bookcases but we hope to be all arranged by Sunday. There is some hope that the combination of older and younger man may produce more business than either could attract alone. We are not partners, but each can be of service to the other, I think.

There seems to be no news to tell you. We are well, though both of us need to quiet our nerves a bit. You know how that is. At times one's nerves seem to jangle a bit—get out of order as do telephone wires now and then. Your mother is to be at a party this afternoon and perhaps have luncheon before bridge. . . . Don't know whether we will go to Mattoon about 5 o'clock or not—think not, as there will be the whole Tolle family to welcome Alice E. and the new baby and a couple more added could be of little service if any. Alice has an excellent girl, and your mother is to go over every morning for a while to teach the girl how to give the baby a bath and other things.

We enjoy every one of your letters so much—you perhaps cannot understand how much.

October 27, 1939

Your mother reported last night that Alice E. was still improving—in fact getting along all right, but she plans to go over to Mattoon to be in charge during the days until Alice is able to take full charge. I have been taking as much off your mother as I can and have been cooking as good a meal as I can to be ready when she returns at night. However, it has been a trying time for her and she should not overtax herself in preparation for the winter.

There is little other news. We got to a formal dinner at the Grant Hotel in Mattoon tonight and tomorrow night another at the Spooners'. The office is now finished and is quite the most attractive office I have been in. My work place is the second office, the one I had so many years as Judge Dunn's secretary. Over my desk is the picture of the dam. It has enough color in it to suit the office exactly. The walls and floors are redone as well as the woodwork and the tops of my desk and table revarnished. All unsightly files are under cover. For them I got the walnut cabinet of a radio and had shelves and back put in. The front is closed with walnut doors. Your shelves are relegated to Jeffries'* back office, practically out of the

*Owner of the office building & Ferguson's father-in-law.

picture to be used as storage shelves for stationery, books, old paper, and whatnot.

The temperature has been high—76 at 6 o'clock this morning. It has been raining some the last few days, and rain was very much needed as the approach to winter has been dry indeed—a perfectly beautiful fall. Only once I think has the temperature fallen to freezing with two or three light frosts, the leaves beautifully colored, but a high wind last night took a great part of them off.

November 9, 1939

Not that there is much news to tell but just to chat with you, one-sided chatting. The Tolle family goes along fine. The conclusion seems to have been that Jimmie has nothing on Dirk. I continue to think of the name as "Dirke," as I was first told, rather than Dirk as it is.

There has been little rain and the ground is still thoroughly dry. For the most part it has been clear bright weather, but some has been of the chilling type, especially one northeast wind which came on just after I had my hair cut and chilled my head around the edges to such an extent that I got a head cold which has bothered me some but not to a serious extent—I think because we have been taking a Haliver capsule every morning.

Your mother is on reception committee for a meeting of Women's Clubs at Eastern Illinois this morning at 9 o'clock. She doesn't care for club meetings particularly and is inclined to, and does, shirk attendance when she can. Yesterday was her bridge-club meet. Her bridge has not been so productive of prizes for a year or so, but yesterday she won, and a few days ago she won a prize at an evening bridge party, so maybe she has her mind on bridge again.

Jim is to be with us Friday night to gather the hickory nuts that have fallen since he was here. The squirrels get many of them taking them from the tree and storing them in the ground, or eating them, but the crop was heavier than usual and Jim will get a good many. Have ordered storm windows for the three double French doors downstairs and think the temperature in the house will be easier to make it comfortable in windy weather.

November 15, 1939

Don't believe we have had a letter from you this week, but you probably have a letter to us on the way. Really there is no occasion for me to write you. Nothing of note to tell—except that you wish to know of our states of health from week to week. . . .

Sunday the Frank Craigs took us to dinner in Indianapolis with the Lippencotts. On the way home we had some delicious catfish at Montezuma, Indiana, on the Wabash.

Monday your mother was in Mattoon while Alice E. was in Indianapolis for the day—or rather mother went to Mattoon about 8 o'clock in the morning and got back at 5:30. We planned to go to the picture show, and as she was tired, she parked in front on the right side of the street at the curb, parking lights on. Usually when she does that, I take the car to the garage if we have as much as an hour to wait before using it, as I like to save the battery. But forgetting that Monday was the 13th and being a bit lazier than usual, I didn't do so that time, and so as we were getting something ready to eat near 6 o'clock, Davis Garner, all excited, came to the door and told mother that a drunken man had just busted in the back end of "your pretty new car." We hadn't heard the crash but Mr. Thomas, in his kitchen, had and was out there when we got down the steps, as were some college boys. The junk car had knocked our braked car about its length forward and had then been started and hit it again and was hooked onto the bumper, and the man couldn't get away. He was pretty well loaded, had driven up without lights, had not seen our red lights, and was doing his best to get away, insisting that he knew what he was doing. I reckon he knew pretty well that in his condition he should be somewhere else. Eventually, Mr. Thomas and the boys freed his car. In the meantime I had called the Chevrolet people and they drove our car to the garage for repairs.

Still the jalopy wouldn't start for the old man, and at his request, I called for a wrecker from his garage. Then went out to tell the old fellow, but his car had vanished. He got it home safely—scaring a woman driver on the way to his home out of ten-years' growth by turning directly in front of her. He still had no lights.

He is 72 years old, gets relief groceries and old age pension. Of course, he ought to be taken off the highways, but I can't bring myself to believe that it's up to me to start proceedings against him. The police have all the facts and know that various traffic laws were violated in such a way as to bring danger to other users of the streets. They are police officers. I am but a private citizen. Our car was damaged about $30 worth about the back end and I hate to lose the $25 which the insurance does not pay. Imagine that when repairs are completed there will be nothing to show that the car was ever damaged. Reckon we have been pretty lucky with our cars so far.

Well, I think I have told you all which might have the slightest interest for you. We plan to see a picture tonight, I think.

December 1, 1939

The days slip by and it's surprising how each one brings along enough of little-consequential things to almost fill it up and each week enough of out-of-ordinary things to make the whole week a week of rush and activity.

Last Friday afternoon Kendall and Warfield drove in for the weekend and, of course, that was a busy time especially for Alice and Alice E. Harold and Kendall hunted Saturday. Your mother and I and the Chinns had dinner in Mattoon Friday night at the Tolles'. Your mother, Warfield and Alice Elizabeth had lunch Saturday at the Dinner Bell and all of us were at the Tolles' for the noon meal Sunday, after which the Chinns left for Kentucky.

This weekend the Davises,* Billy and Bess, are to be at the Millers' and we are to have them for dinner Saturday night or Sunday, I have forgotten which. I think the Millers have us Saturday night and our meal is Sunday, and so it goes. I don't know when we have had a quiet weekend.

I was at the Sangamon farm last Wednesday. As usual the trip took the whole day. The Hugheses have a card party tonight and there are a couple of parties already on the calendar for next week. At my age these things take more out of me than they once did.

A few days ago your mother had a cinder blown into her eye and after suffering several hours and working with it, scratching it around in her eye and inflaming the eyeball, she had to go to the doctor. That night the eye was so painful she didn't sleep, but the next day it improved and is well. She was washing the windows and cleaning the house yesterday for the weekend and will finish that today. She planned to go to Mattoon today, but it's a rainy, drizzly day, and she may not go as the car was washed a few days ago and is still clean.

Sorry Kentucky didn't stand up better in its football fight with Tennessee. Heard the broadcast of the drive which resulted in the first touchdown, but after that was busy with other matters until after the game had ended.

Now that the second Thanksgiving** is past, it isn't long until Christmas. Do you yet know when you start for home and how long your vacation will be? I hope a full two weeks. I believe the Teacher's College has only ten days.

---

*Former Charlestonians—from Chicago Heights.

**Roosevelt's change of traditional date.

December 11, 1939

I rather think we missed writing you last week. Your mother kept planning a letter and I kept waiting on her until the week was gone. Yesterday she went to Mattoon just after breakfast to take care of Dirk while Alice E., Harold, and Jimmie, and Eddie went to Chicago to see Field's display of toys and various other things of interest to children and grown-ups. The travelers are to be gone until about 10 o'clock tonight. Your mother planned to write you a letter yesterday, but as any number of things may have interfered, I will write also or anyway.

Your mother plans to drive to Indianapolis tomorrow taking Laura Winter with her and be gone for two days. Jessie Craig called by phone yesterday wanting to go along with Mrs. Arthur Craig, I think she said, and I referred her to the Mattoon phone number and suppose she called and made the arrangement.

There is no news with us. Miss Johnson and Miss Weller entertained seven tables of bridge, starting with turkey dinner. Yesterday noon I had turkey dinner here, went home afterwards for the afternoon and then to "Barricade" at the Will Rogers theater. Slept a little better than usual last night and feel more rested than in some days.

The weather has remained delightful. Really, most of the days a fellow could be out on the river bank fishing—a little cool perhaps but dry, and with a little extra clothing, not at all bad. Still haven't been tempted. The hunting season closed last Saturday. I didn't even buy a license, but we had three messes of quail.

Everyone now is looking towards Christmas—the various Thanksgiving days having been duly celebrated in accordance with the wishes of the individuals. The 23rd is not far off, and we will be at the station in plenty of time before your train gets in. As we understand the arrangement, your train will stop here. That's an excellent idea. In the old days, before autos took the cream of the traveling public, towns the size of Charleston were really revenue producers for the railroads and were considerably more than mere way-stations, as they now are. I don't see how the railroads are to survive unless they are permitted to meet auto competition by a flexible rate schedule, a thing they cannot do so long as a government bureau—slow moving incubus that it always is—retains its present control.

Glad your financial affairs are looking up. You must have adopted a system or something.

1940

January 16, 1940

Much of the snow which was on the ground here when you left is still on the ground, dirty, in places in the form of very sticky ice. Some additional snow has fallen and there has been some melting. We have had the car out only once since you left, though the state highways are clear. I thought that I would have to use it yesterday, and as the Goodwin driveway was very slick ice all the way up, I connected up Cottingham's driveway—from where he had left off covering with ash—to our back yard using two big buckets of ashes in doing so, covering enough of our own ice-covered premises to permit the getting of the car out of the garage and off the premises. However, I caught a ride to Danville with Jack Kincaid and so didn't use our car.

The weather has been cold and our coal supply was about exhausted. Arthur Craig didn't have the kind I wanted so I told him to send me a jag of another kind to tide me over until his carload of Kentucky coal should come. This afternoon your mother called me by phone, a bit of excitement in her voice, and told me that only a little coal had been brought, and she wanted to know "how come." I told her I had ordered only a "jag" and explained that a "jag" is but a small part of a load. And that seemed to satisfy her.

The rug comes on apace. She has enough material to finish it—all but the final row or two, for which she wants some brown material. However, when she runs out of the material on hand, the rug will be considered finished for use until a row or two of the proper material shows up in a year or two or three maybe. When so almost finished, the rug will be about 9′11″ x 11′10″—in other words, about an inch to go, less than two rows all the way round.

There is little news. Jimmie was with us Saturday night, and your mother and he played games and read and built with the blocks, etc., etc., practically all the time and so strenuously that your mother was rather tired, though not at all tired of Jimmie. Dirk is reported well and making manful strides in growth and mental development, as he was when you left. Jimmie cannot seem to get rid of his cold. I think his rapid growth makes him an easy victim. Well, it's getting late.

January 24, 1940

Your mother told me yesterday that she had a couple of newspaper clippings to send you when she or I should write. The clippings are at home and I at the office. Think I shall hold this letter till afternoon and try to remember the clippings at noon. She has been cleaning house the last two days getting ready to entertain her card club today, and of course today is given over to final preparations and getting something to eat ready for them.

There is little news. Alice phoned day before yesterday that Harold has flu with fever. The fever was lower yesterday but still above a hundred. The rest of the Tolle members were well, as are we here. Since you left, one cold snap has followed right after another, there being no time in between sufficient to melt the snow on the ground when you left. A little melted from time to time in the middle of the day and changed to ice by night, and a little more snow has fallen now and then. Use of the car has been at a minimum. We had it in Mattoon Sunday for dinner at Buckler's and a call on the Tolles after dinner. I saw by the papers that a strike was threatening the coal supply of New York but suppose it was not serious enough or so long-continued as to cause any real inconvenience. It seems that you also have had cold weather there and even southern Florida has been shivering.

It's really pitiful—the dearth of interesting things to tell you. I cannot think of a thing. The office routine is deadly dull, the home runs along as usual except that the furnace requires more attention, one day runs along at a dead level with the others. Mrs. Taylor called your mother last night and invited her to go along to a sale in Paris, an administrator's sale of the household goods of an old lady who died at 94, who had married 72 years ago and had a wealth of fine old furniture. Luckily perhaps for me, the club meeting was on today. It would not have been a bad day for the drive. The thermometer is a few degrees above zero and there is a brisk northwest wind, but the sun is bright and it's not too cold.

We saw a picture show here Sunday evening—"He Married His Wife,"—inane, tiring, and so far as I could see, without point or interest. At any rate both of us were left with the feeling we so often get after going to a show—that we probably won't want to see another for some time. "Gone With the Wind" has not been in this neighborhood and I suppose will not be for quite a while. After all the build-up and whatnot, as someone said, "It had better be good."

Well, I will close this.

January 30, 1940

I am very glad that you have met both Mercer Mooreman and John Gaines. Regretted that on neither of my visits in New York I had an opportunity to look them up. They were both good students and well-liked by their fellows. John was perhaps faster in learning than Mercer or I. At any rate I will not try to spoil his story. My rule or principle rather with reference to storytelling is, as you well know, that if the exact story is not quite good enough, the teller should give it such embellishment as it needs to make it good.

However, if you see John again, tell him it was unkind, even though he also believes in embellishment to make a story good, to pick a story which might undo all that I have no doubt succeeded in doing toward building up in my offspring an abiding belief in my intense application to college work and consequent high standing in the Georgetown College world. Ask him if he ought not to have chosen some other incident to recall in detail, especially as he too knows the difficulty a parent has in appearing in a good light to his children—and the effort a parent makes to stand well with them.

By the way, John is the other hero of that French class story that you have heard me tell. I propose to put that story in writing *without embellishment* (if my memory is correct). And if you see him, ask him what embellishments he wishes to add to it. The facts were these (well, approximately so): The senior French class had struggled painfully through almost the full two years allotted to that study. The professor had been patient and long-suffering at times and sharp and caustic, as he knew well how to be. In all that distressing period not a single correct translation from English to French had been turned in—a remarkable thing when it is considered that John and I were members of the class. Upon assigning us the final such translation of the course, the professor somewhat caustically commented on the failure of the class, of a single member of the class, to make a single correct translation, and as a parting crack said that if the final one was turned in without a single error by a single student, he would not require anyone to take a final examination. The whole class, not excepting John and me, no doubt were afraid of that particular examination, perhaps dreaded it a little more than most examinations, and so there was a frantic conference of the class. We had a week—maybe two weeks—to produce the translation.

Of course John and I each considered that he was far the best in the class and perhaps was rather aggressive in his belief. There was probably considerable dissent amongst others, still we, as I say, were aggressive, and by hook or crook it became necessary to decide as between us to whom should be delegated the task of making the translation. It must have been that there could be no compromise of our pretensions, and as the matter had to rest, John and I were instructed to each make a translation and use the one as a check against the other. So this we did. There were of course irreconcilable differences in the two translations, and, John and I being as we were, it was very difficult for us to decide which was right and which was wrong—that is, to reach a unanimous decision, there being two involved and two necessary to a decision. Perhaps we tossed a coin. I wouldn't remember as to that, or, for that matter, if it was ever decided.

In the meantime, perhaps growing out of a class feeling about our qualification for the task we had thrust upon ourselves, a "Jack" or "Pony" had been sent for and the help of a Harvard professor, teacher of French, had been invoked. And the Pony having come, we felt pretty safe; then the Harvard translation showed and there was a slight difference or so between the two. What a quandary to put our Georgetown class in, for the Pony must be right and Harvard must be right. How we solved the problem I do not remember (maybe John does) but solve it we did, at any rate to the satisfaction of our teacher, for the entire class turned in perfect papers—all but one. Co-ed Billie had miscopied one word. We were lost. The professor, in his inimitable way, made it very plain that he was wise, that the perfect papers did not in any sense measure our lore. Still he was game and a good sport and wound up announcing that there would be no examination.

Perhaps it is upon incidents of this sort John bases his belief (no doubt he thoroughly believes it after so long a lapse of time) that he carried me through college. I may be wrong, but as I now remember, John and I were both good enough at what it takes or took at that time to make teachers think we were good students and deserved good marks.

Well, this letter would not have been written today except that your letter came in, was at home at noon, and the idea occurred to me that the story might be useful if you see John again. I haven't seen him for so many years that I don't know what manner of man he is, and it may be well not to use this story. Really, I don't vouch for the absolute truth of all of it. The basic facts are that the class did try to get a perfect translation and did use a Pony and the Harvard professor, and that one girl made a slight mistake in copying; still the professor excused the examination. . . .

Your mother is feeding and watering some birds (including a mockingbird) on the bedroom window ledge, which is quite interesting for her and Jimmie. Alice E. discovered last night that Dirk has a tooth. He also has some cold but keeps in good humor. There is practically no other news. . . .

February 7, 1940

A few days ago your mother opened a letter addressed to you thinking it was an advertisement because the stamp was printed on the envelope as so frequently is the case with second-class mail and so seldom with first-class. The letter contained the enclosed bill and your mother is sorry she opened it. I saw it again on the table last night and decided that, as she had not had the chance to write you, the bill would furnish me a good excuse for writing.

I keep up with her writing to you, and when she lets too long a time go by without writing, I write. This is one of those times. She keeps so busy with one thing or another that she never seems to have time to spare. Last week she had Jimmie here. He was sick, as you know. As Harold was also sick, your mother took charge of Jimmie. Harold is well. Jimmie was much better at the end of the week and is in school now. Dirk caught the cold and has been pretty uncomfortable. At last reports he had two teeth and was keeping in excellent humor, improving from the cold, and Alice E. had not taken the cold so far.

This week your mother has been fighting a cold and darning the cold and the winter's accumulation of socks. Yesterday afternoon she played cards at the faculty club as a substitute and today plans to play at her own club.

Practically all of the snow—not all—which was first on the ground when you were here melted by Monday night, and yesterday morning another three inches fell as the result of which the streets and walks are again slippery and treacherous. The weatherman thinks it will be warmer tomorrow and if so, this snow will melt, for it is just below freezing today and if the temperature goes up at all, the snow will melt.

There is no news of any importance. Mrs. Wyeth is back from Chicago. It is said that the association with Bobbie's baby has done wonderful things for her, and I wouldn't be surprised if that is true. Have not seen her since her return, however. I am also wondering how long it will be before she decides that it is absolutely necessary for her to go back to Chicago on the excuse that the baby is sick or that Bobbie needs a rest or something of that kind.

Of course, you may not find it possible to come home at Eastertime but your mother and I are not letting that possibility interfere with our firm belief that you will be able to come. Easter is said to be early this year. Maybe some of the upstairs redecorating will be done by then. Your mother does herself more harm by borrowing in advance from some job that is ahead, and right now the redecorating job is concerning her so much that she has trouble sleeping at night. I think her borrowed troubles are with her asleep or awake. It's the same sort of thing which bothers her when she has a dinner or party planned. Such things always go off fine, but by the time they are set, your mother's nerves are loaded with static.

I am well. Get very tired of the monotony and responsibility of office. Would like just to get in the car with your mother and not stop until a Gulf surf stopped us, then to head around east to Florida or West Texas and loaf around down there until spring in Illinois is ready to ripen into summer, then loaf around here until the summer holds full sway, then head north to some lake until the spirit or weather moved us south. There isn't very much of the nomad in me; still at times what little there is seems to have a rather strong influence.

Well, I must close.

February 13, 1940

I got the easel down from the top of the garage yesterday and tried to figure a way to wrap it so it would carry safely. Eventually decided I didn't know how. I think anyway you probably will always want it here in the summer, and it doesn't look very costly. Wouldn't it be a good idea to get another one out there? Second-hand ones ought to be in every shop. What do you think?

Your mother got into her closets yesterday—in my room and the hall—and they are cleaned, ready for the plasterer to plaster the cracks and then they will be ready for painting. It was a long, hard, dirty day for her, and her man to plaster disappointed her this morning; but she got in touch with Mr. Butler, and he will take over. She would rather have him anyway than anyone who ever worked for her.

There is no news. I will try to write a longer letter later in the week.

P.S. No one quite knows what constitutes legal residence. So much of it is a matter of intention and having a home which you do not intend to abandon, and not living elsewhere with an intention of making it your permanent home. You always have had a home—permanent home—here and my view has been that this has never ceased to be your permanent place of residence. Your voting elsewhere has a tendency to show that you abandoned Charleston, but is not conclusive. I have always thought that your voting should have been here—that you have been sojourning elsewhere in rooming houses and whatnot. You certainly never had any intention to live anywhere else than here permanently. No papers are necessary. If you want to come back to your old home in intention, during your temporary sojourn elsewhere, there is nothing to stop you, and that being your intention now, this is really your permanent home. You may have had the intention to live somewhere after awhile, but I don't think you ever lost your residence here. At any rate no action is necessary. If you wish I will have ballots sent you at voting time. *When did you last vote elsewhere?*

February 24, 1940

Well, we have done a poor job of writing you this week. Have thought of it every night, but at the office it's income tax return time and about all my spare time has been taken up with helping people report to their financially embarrassed Government just how much they have to pay in direct taxes. Your mother has been, and for that matter will be for some time, a very busy woman. . . . Yesterday she cleaned the bathroom (I started this letter at 8:30 this morning and it's now close to noon). My bedroom has been cleaned, papered, and painted, and it is nice. The hall closet, my closet, and Mother's closet have been cleaned and painted. This morning the paperhanger was to come and finish papering Mother's room. It had been freshly painted. Mother is driving to Mattoon this afternoon. She is a very busy woman, and if she holds out will start on the big living room next week—probably with painting. I am well, and I suppose the Mattoon end of the family has no sickness in it, though we haven't heard for several days.

Your last letter was exceptionally interesting. Heywood Broun must have been an interesting character. I saw him in New York, I think, taking part in an inane and uninteresting play which I think he wrote. His part was just as uninteresting as the rest. Have read little, if any, of his writings but know of him because he often has been a matter of news. I have the impression that he was merely one of those brilliant men who were not very solidly balanced, who have been and are interesting writers with little to say that has back of it the wisdom that should have come to the people of the world by reason of the experiences of history, or of the solid reasoning that is so often lacking in the especially brilliant man, and most always present in the man who does accomplish much for men. My impression is that the class of writers to whom Broun belonged have had no small part in the breaking down of true culture and sane living that has been going on for some years now. The world has been changing, and the brilliant writers of his class have had a real part in the change. My views may be far from the truth as to Broun, still they are true of the class to which I have assigned him. I may have him in the wrong class.

I bid on a farm last week, but didn't get it. A well-improved 160-acre tract, level, black, very well drained and diagonally across the road from the corner of a 60 of your mother's. It would have been a good buy at $135 an acre. My last bid was $17,000 all of which I would have had to borrow (had the credit arranged, however), but I quit there because I didn't want to stretch my credit too far. If I had got it I would have, at my leisure, sold 100 acres; that is, the 64 in Sangamon and a 40 here, and my debt would not have been too large. The land sold for $17,735, but had I kept on, it probably would have gone higher. Sure wanted that 160. At $17,735 it was a mighty good buy.

If you had a bunch of money laid by, there would come after awhile a good chance to get your "mitts" on some black land. In this case there is a Federal Land Bank mortgage of eight thousand dollars on the land, and a fellow only had to have cash or bank credit for enough to pay the difference between the mortgage and the purchase price. The mortgage bears only about 4% interest, and the principal is payable in full or in part at any interest-paying date. It was an ideal "set-up", as you would say, and as I would also say.

There is little news. Between the painting and paperhanging and the income tax returns we have little leisure, but your mother did go to a luncheon bridge at Mrs. Andrew's this week.

February 28, 1940

Your letter for Mother's birthday came in on the dot and she appreciates it much. I also enjoyed it thoroughly. Am anxious to see the picture painted for her birthday remembrance and to hang it somewhere on the newly decorated wall. The decoration comes along slowly and still persistently. The two bedrooms upstairs are done, painted, papered, and "wax-floored." The north bedroom is cleaned, including wall paper and wax on floor. The painting is now on its way downstairs, your mother leading by washing the woodwork. The second coat will start tomorrow, and it will be ready for paper Monday. After that the big living room comes on, which may take a matter of ten days. The house ought to be well out of the way by the time you get here except perhaps for the kitchen and dining room. Maybe it will all be done. Mother faithfully promises not to get pushed and overdo herself, yet almost regularly every other day, she does get in a push and overdoes herself—and nothing can be done about that.

Tonight we go to Mattoon for Mother's birthday dinner with the Tolles. I have not seen Dirk since his teeth began to come in. He is reported to be 28 inches long and to weigh 24 pounds—if your mother's memory of the figures is right. He seems to be a baby of even temper somewhat disturbed, of course, by the business of cutting teeth—still, putting up with that without much complaint. We will be counting the days until March 22. And, of course, barring snows and one thing and another which are possible in March, even late in March, in Illinois weather, *we will be on hand at Terre Haute* the evening of the 22nd to bring you home from there. You get in at 7:40, you say. If you are to have your evening meal along the way, let us know and we will also have ours before you reach Terre Haute. If you are not to eat on the way, we will wait also and we will all eat together in Terre Haute. Let us know as to this and we will act accordingly.

There is no news of any importance that I know of. Imagine there will be little in the society line during your visit. I am rather selfish about the evenings you are to be here anyway, and if there are no parties to disturb our evenings together I will be very much delighted.

March 7, 1940

Well, the homework still continues. The hall woodwork has been painted—two coats—and the paperhanger is at work there. We decided not to paint the big livingroom woodwork, and the paper man will go from the hall to that room, and then, when he has finished there, the house can be set in order, and such cleaning in dining room, kitchen and library as is usually done in spring can be attended to at any convenient time. The hall paper is certainly well chosen—in fact, the choice of paper in both living rooms was excellent also.

I had a cold which is about gone now. Your mother hasn't been as careful about association with me as she should and complained of a tickling in her throat this morning, but she is so full of vitality that she firmly believes a cold cannot catch her. She has been in remarkably good health following the medical treatment given by Dr. Iknayan. Alice E. called just before I left home this morning. The family there is on the up and up also. There has been little sunshine here this year, but today the sun is breaking through a hazy sky. It was clear early, but the prediction is for rain or snow and the symptoms are showing up. . . .

A week from Saturday I plan to drive to Sangamon farm dropping your mother off in Springfield. We may take Miss Johnson and another girl with us to Springfield. Further than this the days as planned have nothing unusual in them. No one knows what a day may bring forth, however, and that, I reckon, is one of the joys of living—always the unexpected thing is coming along to vary the monotony and add a bit of spice.

April 16, 1940

I doubt whether we wrote you a letter last week, nor have we yet received your letter following your trip down into Pennsylvania. It may come today. We had quite a bit of weather last week, the thermometer registering down in the twenties at one time. With it was rain followed by quite a driving snow which left perhaps three inches on the ground. Eloise Barrick chose that day to drive to Mattoon and Mother went with her. The drive home was difficult and almost dangerous as quite a number of cars were in the ditch on their way back to Charleston. However, the Barrick car got home safely and not too long delayed, though driving was slow. The windshield wiper did not work, and stops had to be made to wipe the snow off by hand.

Last week we also saw "Gone With the Wind." It was good, worth the time and money. Your mother has also got the curtains up in the front half of the big living room and they are fine, give the correct finish to the room, a much lighter room, but the light is soft.

However, at the close of the week Mother had a splitting headache which persisted through Sunday and yesterday. . . . She hasn't got over her flu attack or whatever it was—a day perhaps feeling tolerably good, and a day feeling all shot and weak. She is mad about it and probably by the end of the week will be well. She is not in bed. Yesterday was very warm and bright. Today is bright and a bit cooler and the better weather ought to help.

There is little news. I am well. Raked the trash off the asparagus bed—which was about a nickel's worth of work—yesterday afternoon. Before I did that I had taken your mother for about fifteen miles of slow driving on country roads, and our supper was a fresh supply of soup made yesterday. We had dinner in Mattoon Sunday at Buckler's and after that were at the Tolles' for a couple of hours. Jimmie had dinner with us. None of these things are exciting but they are the little things which are the joys of life. I drove across the river bridge Sunday also. There were a number of persons fishing from the banks—one with a crooked stick as a pole. Whether there was any luck or not I don't know. The water was clear and high enough to promise some luck, but some of us doubt whether any fish are left in the river. In raking the asparagus bed I turned up a nice fat worm. He ought to have been put on a hook and dangled in the river. You know how I feel about that.

Well, I will hold this letter until afternoon. Maybe your mother will write you also and if so we can save 3¢, the tax on a dollar purchase, by putting both letters in the same envelope.

June 15, 1940

The week of the 23rd will soon be here and soon after the 23rd you will be here—and that makes a fine sequence, for we think it has been plenty long enough since we have had you with us. No one knows whether the taking of a new job would have made for your happiness or not, so there is nothing to regret in the loss of the Pennsylvania prospect. I have no doubt you feel the same way about it.

News here is not to be found. Painting is all done inside and out at home, and the back porch floor is being waxed today for the summer. It's been a long, tedious time and I for one am extremely glad that it is over—especially because of the uncontrollable tendency of your mother to so tire herself out as to be practically sick and exhausted all the time.

Jimmie has been with us about all this week, and that is pleasant, but still your mother manages to put all she has into entertaining him. He seems to demand and certainly expects that of her—probably training. Yesterday, a load of sand was secured for his sandpile, and that is of great interest to him. He goes home this afternoon. Your mother has definitely abandoned any thought of driving out to New York after you. And there are no definite plans for the summer. I think I will stay here, no matter what the rest of you do.

Sentiment has been changing as to America's proper place in the war. A good many feel that we should have started at least six months ago preparing and also giving what aid was possible short of sending men. If Government was informed of the immense superiority of the Germans, it certainly was careless in not informing Congress and the public and permitting this country to prepare. We could have, ere this, been in mass production of machines for protection, and, for that matter, indirect protection, by furnishing the allies what they needed in the way of material. If Gov't was not informed, we should have spoken softly and prepared for any eventuality—to the end that when time to speak should come we could speak with authority. As it is, we spoke brashly before and after the war began, and at the critical time when we are forced out in the open, our stick is so small as to carry no authority in the rush of events in Europe. England, France and now the United States have shown a failure to appraise correctly the situation that was in preparation. Lindbergh should have been heeded and not discredited. The work that the Dies Committee has been doing will prove invaluable. He should not have been discredited. We should not have a debt of 45 billion as a nest egg on which to build safety from outside interference, for to build a much greater debt on top of that will bring internal disintegration. So do republics destroy themselves. Bryce in his great work saw very well the weaknesses in our system.

It seems to me now that the only possibility left to us to retain our liberties is to have a great political and social revival, cease looking to Gov't for the correction of all our ills, depend on our own health and strength and energy, stop looking for personal advantage at the expense of our neighbors and quit making demands upon Gov't to do this, that, and the other thing for us—in other words, let the old constitutional restraints resume their sway and go to work at something except the pockets of the public. We are not a democracy—no nation can be. We should stop trying to be and should let our representatives in legislative, executive and judicial office put into their official actions the expression of their judgment and not of our clamor for this or that. If we have representatives of poor judgment or dishonest character, kick them out next election.

Well, the prospect of war is no reason for a political harangue, I reckon, but I still can give vent to my dissatisfaction with the guidance of our ship of state in many of the years of this century—from a purely internal view. As to the war, so far as I know, the people of this section received no word of the immense superiority of the Nazi equipment, except from Lindbergh, and that was discredited.

September 13, 1940

We received your letter about the unsatisfactory condition of your room last night and are sorry, and particularly sorry that you had an emotional upset about it. I had an idea that Mr. Heller's sentence or two about the condition he found—removal of partition and that he feared you would find your things in bad condition from dust, etc.—had something very wrong at the base. I do hope that the landlord will make good and that there will be no more trouble about it, and especially that you will not worry about whatever the outcome may be, or however slow the process of making good. One cannot afford emotional upsets for the reaction is injurious to a Kelly, especially in the region of the stomach.

Your mother and I drove to Springfield and the farm yesterday leaving here at 8:30 and returning at about 5:30. It was a beautiful day and the drive did us no harm. In Springfield I attended to some business, your mother looked at cloaks, and we had lunch at Maldaners.* Then drove to the farm where I made some inspection of the crops. The beans are good—the corn very good considering the drouth—better than I thought possible, though not a big crop of course.

I have never sent for the picture of those six fish we caught and must do that to bolster my credit at church.

The war grows closer, and the people around here seem at last—as in the earlier war—to be getting the war spirit, the expression being to this effect: that we have already got our feet wet by sending the destroyers, that if England whips Hitler we will never have to do it, and that the most practical thing to do under the circumstances is to remove all restrictions and give England every help possible in the line of furnishing material and credit. Of course, Churchill's assurance to Roosevelt that the fleet would never surrender would mean nothing if England has to surrender, but the longer he fights the weaker will Hitler be and the better chance for the United States to thoroughly prepare.

There is no news. The fall beauty of weather has set in. Have had a fire in the furnace for a couple of days, the thermometer having hit in the fifties and below that, one night. Last night it was 50 at the lowest.

Dirk is very proud of himself in that he can balance himself on his feet a moment or two and while doing so look up with his smile of good friendship and good will and of triumph as well. You know the smile I mean. When his balance becomes unstable, however, he loses no time in trying to recover but drops at once upon that part of his anatomy which seems to take the unkind blows of life with least discomfort to him.

*A well-known restaurant in Springfield, Ill.

Write when you can. Compose your soul to take the discomfort of rearrangement of your room without disquiet, and it will work out all right, no doubt.

Lots of love from both of us. We still feel lost without you. . . .

October 8, 1940

Somehow time has seemed to be so taken up with the office affairs during the days that I have not written you at all hardly. Writing to you is one of the pleasures of life that there is no reason for me to put aside very long for any matter which might at the moment seem pressing.

We are well. Your mother has given two of her luncheons and another will come tomorrow—the three making a total of 48 guests. I think there is a fourth in the offing and whether any more are to follow, I know not.

Today is Dirk's first birthday following his first steps in walking. I ate lunch alone today in the kitchen while Dirk traveled back and forth in sitting room and kitchen, most of the time on the floor, much of the time weaving from one handhold to another, on his feet, dropping solidly or, if time permitted, carefully to the floor, into this and that and frequently into or after something forbidden—happy and smiling. Mother, Alice E., Hilda Heller and Helen Colvin sat eating their lunch at a card table set in front of the French door, talking—content, it seemed, that I should have the responsibility of seeing to it that Dirk did not harm himself or anything else. I wonder if that's the reason I am at my desk early enough to feel I have time to write you a letter.

Mother wants me to tell you the pearls which were lost have been found and *PM** still continues to come daily. We don't want it cluttering up the house. My guess is that it will not last long—not have a long life and its policy is very far removed from my idea of what a paper should follow in this year of our Lord 1940. I guess your subscription has expired. At any rate, if you wish to renew it, you should do so, or at least order it discontinued.

The weather has been beautiful and the water supply has been threateningly low, but we had a rain night before last which gives us a respite from disaster.

There is little news. We are planning to drive to Kentucky for the weekend of the 19th unless we go sooner. If we go the 19th, it will be in the nature of a belated wedding anniversary trip. I wonder whether the 14th will be clear

---

**PM*, a short-lived newspaper.

and bright. It has been so for 37 years, wherever we were. We go to Springfield the 10th to the Memorial exercises in the Supreme Court in respect to Judge Dunn. Helen Colvin said she might ask you to Washington for Thanksgiving. There is little news.

October 29, 1940

Mother wanted to write you yesterday but didn't find time and threatens to write you today but probably won't find time, so I will *take* time to let you know we are well, that we sold the Sangamon farm for cash, that I mailed you yesterday the two pictures of Dirk and you are to choose the one you want for yourself and save the other for us, that the trip to Kentucky was without accident to us, though we saw the results of two accidents—to cars, and to car and wagon, though occupants and horses were gone—one accident where the instrumentalities were still in motion as we came over the brow of a hill with brakes set hard having been warned by a sudden cloud of dust ahead. In this one the elderly, heavy woman was just settling to a prone position on the slab where she had been thrown—the mark on her forehead gave some indication that her head had struck first—a clothes hamper was still wobbling on its base in the middle of the road. The woman was still breathing slowly and in great gasps when we left, and we do not know whether she lived or died. Your mother had a close call between Mt. Sterling and Winchester by a wild-driving youth, where only her instantaneous action saved her.

Lillian is no better, but *do not* write in such a way that you have the slightest fear that she will not recover. The folks are building up her faith, and she does not know how serious is her condition. I told her you and Tom had something in the way of faith that I was going to try to get for myself, and had several talks with her which I think were helpful in building up her will and faith to believe that she will recover.

We saw Tom in Cincinnati and enjoyed our visit with him and Cora a great deal. He is recovering. We were with them about an hour and got home at 6 o'clock in the afternoon. Had an engagement to eat lunch with James Hugh and his wife in Louisville on the way down to Kentucky but had to be in Court here the morning we left and didn't get started until after 10, so wired him cancellation.

Got the deed from Tom Thursday morning at a little after nine together with assignment of lease and other necessary papers, went to Springfield at once, into conference with the buyer's attorney about noon. All papers were in order and we went to lunch, a leisurely affair—leisurely and interesting—two attorneys, a loan company head, the real estate agent—then to the bank where papers were delivered and the money paid—$46,000 and some odd dollars—concluding about 4 o'clock.

Then I drove to the farm, told the tenant what had occurred, told him how much I had appreciated my business relations with him and that I had taken the opportunity to tell the purchaser of my high regard for the tenant's integrity and industry and ability as a farmer. The tenant's lease expires March 1, 1942, and I hope the purchaser—the Springfield Marine Bank and Trustee under a certain trust—will keep the tenant on under a new lease when the present lease expires. . . .

The weather and colors have been marvelous. Last night a rain. Today still beautiful and warm.

I put on the package I sent you some new stamps and they are carefully cancelled. Please return them to us.

November 16, 1940

Of course, we are trying to get the Sangamon County farm money back in land. Have made an offer to buy 100 acres here at $100 an acre which, if accepted, will require us to borrow $4,000. Now if you had $4,000 and if the offer should be accepted, you could put in your four and take 40 acres. Wouldn't that be nice? I had $7,500 from the Sangamon land but paid $1,700 debt at the bank and have only $6,000 left that I can spare from living expenses.

In answer to your question, there isn't much to tell—that is, I don't know much to tell about the move of the Browns and Smiths from Kentucky, which occurred some time in the 1830's. The Browns and Smiths were related and the sister of James U. Brown was your great grandmother, Mrs. James D. Smith. William Brown was a congressman living in Cynthiana, Kentucky. The old house is standing there yet on a hill at the edge of town. It was a fine old place but is in bad condition—much neglected. Out back of the house in the field are two graves—small ones, badly neglected. I asked my mother about them. She said that the tradition in the family was that two of the Brown children were poisoned by the Negro cook, and the tragedy led the tribe to move out of slave territory.

I was in Illinois visiting at the Grove when I was between ten and fifteen years of age, I think. I remember that the train on the Wabash on which we were (that is, Tom, Will and myself) did not stop, and we went on to Jacksonville where Dr. Lloyd Brown, a very handsome man—old man as it seemed to me—met us and brought us back to the Grove on a local train. He was tall and stately, white, silky-whiskered, wearing a silk hat and Prince Albert, and on the way back his hat blew out of the window. The trainmen were notified and the train backed up and the hat recovered. I am not sure but think that he was the father of Ed Brown, who married your great uncle John Smith's daughter, Ruth, and as far back as you can remember, lived in Jacksonville; and his son (I don't know how many children he had) I think was William Brown the lawyer, who was general attorney for the Chicago and Alton Railway, with office in Chicago and home in Jacksonville, who was alive when I came to Illinois. However, William Brown, the congressman, may have been the father of all the old-timers, but I think they were brothers and not children of his.

James N. Brown and James D. Smith, brothers-in-law, settled in the Grove (Island Grove) near each other. The groves scattered around through the prairie were quite like Kentucky in appearance, wooded and rolling, with not good soil. The prairies were not habitable, wet and swampy in spots, a resort of ducks and geese, full of mosquitoes, loaded with malaria. Whiskey and quinine were the approved remedy, and mayhap the Browns and Smiths found them necessary, as others did. The families built their homes in the Grove and took up much prairie land from the Government. I think the stock price was $1.25 an acre. A part of the prairie patented by the Government to James D. Smith, in 1837 I think, was the larger part of the farm which we have just sold. It was deeded by your great grandfather to your grandmother before she married. She in turn deeded it to three of her brothers—as trustees—for her use during her life, and at her death to her children or their children if any of them died before she did. So it came to us by virtue of the deed which she made sometime before her marriage in 1874.

Sometime, I think in the last quarter of the last century, some theorist conceived the idea that the prairie could be drained, for the soil was porous. His idea was tried out and proving successful, was used generally until the entire prairie became underlaid with a system of tile drainage. Tile drainage is porous tile laid below the surface. Water seeps into it through the pores and at the joints and is carried to some natural outlet which may be miles away. The state facilitated the draining by adopting laws permitting the formation of drainage districts with power of eminent domain to condemn rights-of-way and power to levy special taxes—measured by benefit to each particular tract of land in the district—to construct main ditches and lay main tiles, etc.; and the lands in the district could be connected with the main tile and ditches. When a prairie was drained, it became magnificent corn land. The first drainage district law was passed in 1879, I think.

I have managed the farm we just sold beginning in 1901. At that time it was and, for some time before that (how long I don't know), had been in cultivation with corn-oats-wheat rotation. I don't think before 1901 it had ever had clover in the rotation or any other variance in rotation of crops tending to keep its fertility up. I know that since 1901 there has been continuous outgo of fertility with nothing added. In other words, it has been farmed hard. The tile drains are stopped at their outlets into the draw.

Washing has been going on for some years. Much needs to be done to bring the farm back, at much cost. Still, I hope to replace my acreage there with soil here as good as the best on that farm at a less price than I got there. The 100 acres on which I have made an offer are as good as the best of that farm. In the farm sold were 387.57 acres of which I owned one-sixth, or a 64-acre interest. It brought $120 an acre. Sale commission was 3%. Revenue stamps of $51.70 were required on the deed and I have yet to pay for abstract of title-extension to date. The net amount to each sixth owner was $7,510.17. We retained crops—corn and beans—and buyer pays the taxes levied this year and payable next. Cost of abstract and other incidental expenses will be paid out of crops. Usually when seller retains crops, he pays the taxes.

The Browns and the Smiths were not pioneers in the sense that Lincoln was, for they apparently were rich for those days. James U. Brown, brother-in-law of James D. Smith, settled in the Grove where Billy and Ben (his sons) lived. You visited Ben and May, his wife, there. Neither Bily nor Ben had a child. I think another son died without children. A daughter married a Hitt and had three daughters, Mary, Hal, and Priscilla, and one son, Brown Hitt. The Browns and Smiths lived high. James U. introduced the shorthorn beef cattle into America, and his picture is in the Agricultural Hall of Fame at Urbana because of that. The sons of James D. went in for fine horses and cattle. One of them imported a French artist to paint a picture of one of his horses—cost $1,000. Came the depression of 1893 and all were in debt. The Smiths lost their lands, Billy and Ben Brown owed $25,000 and didn't know where to turn. But some insurance agent in the past had sold them large policies and eventually they learned that the policies had large loan value. From that source they got the $25,000 needed and saved their three thousand acres. There were many of the Smith children, each deeply indebted and nowhere to go for money. They owed your grand aunt Patty Prewitt for almost the entire value of her farm which they had bought from her. They owed your grandmother many thousands for rent, and as is often the case, the creditors on the ground got better settlement than did your grandmother and grand aunt. They got two hundred acres of the timberland in the Grove with a mortgage against it of $6,000, which they sold to William Brown, the lawyer, for $12,000—netting them $6,000. William Brown was a brother of Uncle Jim's wife (James D. 2nd), and when the Smiths broke, William began to buy land that they had owned. Before he died he had several hundred acres of it, but he too had to die. Jim Smith 3rd had, all the time following, a job with McCormick and saved enough to buy 200 acres over about Pleasant Plains (not Smith land) by the time he took the notion to farm. When prairie was worth $300 to $400 an acre, during the war, he sold his 200 acres and bought, with Ed Brown, 400 acres of the Smith land for $120,000. That broke Jim. And so it goes.

Well, I have spent the morning writing this disconnected letter. We are well, except your mother has a touch of something which I think is a cold. We jumped from almost warm to cold weather in one jump, and your mother got chilled at a sale of some household furniture Ruth had at the Dunn home. There is no news.

1941

January 27, 1941

The pipe and tobacco came in a couple of days ago. Have tried the tobacco and like it a lot. Have not tried the pipe as yet but am curious to know something about it. It seems lighter than wood and I think wood walls are thicker. The finish also seems to me to be somewhat different from what would be possible with any type of wood that I know of. It is stamped "Shellmoor." I wonder if that means that its shell is made from some product of a moor, or if it is of a shell composition. Someday tell me something about the pipe. Thank you a lot for pipe and tobacco.

There is little news. The sun rarely shows his face in this section this winter. Much fog and mist, very little cold weather, altogether not a very attractive climate. But Illinois is not weather-consistent ordinarily—winter or summer. The best way to prepare for life here is to adopt the rule to expect the unexpected.

Yesterday was the wedding anniversary of the Charley Colemans. They were entertained last night by two of the college teachers—the Colemans inviting the guests. So your mother and I were there. Except for us it was a college crowd, no one on his or her dignity, and therefore very vivacious, sometimes very noisy, but very enjoyable as well. It was Smorgesbrot—really almost as varied and quite as good and tempting as the one at Ephraim. An old-time fiddler and a man with his guitar were on hand, both quite good at the old-time tunes. After a time, Heller started at the piano and eventually took the music program over, and towards the last your mother's memory was sufficiently revived—as well as her spirits—to prompt her to take over the piano for some of the old rags and other tunes of yesterday. Somewhere during the evening Guinaugh became an Italian, looking, acting and speaking the part, excited, voluble, introducing the great Italian singer, Seymour, who earnestly and seriously, with flourish and gesture, sang in Italian some great opera music, not at all flustered or disturbed by the great volume of mock applause and catcalls. We had a good time and got home, I think, by 12:30.

Your mother talked of going to Mattoon this morning. She simply can't keep away too long. I have to close before I have finished as something has come up here at the office that needs attention. We are well.

P.S. I believe a good many words are not spelled correctly. Somehow or other several words didn't look right as I tried to spell them and I couldn't make up my mind what was right.

February 10, 1941

I was a bit pleased to find the $50 money order in the letter. Am not going to say that I was surprised, for I know I talked with you about the value of having a stake for emergencies and this $50 will be a fair beginning for the accumulation of a stake. As I told you when you were here, the building and loan company is the best aid to saving money that I know anything about. One of their plans calls for the monthly investment of a dollar a share and after a while the accumulation of payments and interest will amount to $100. Twenty shares will eventually accumulate into $2,000—at a cost of $20 a month. I don't know just how long it takes to pay out a share. When the B & L was able to lend money at 7%, the interest addition was more than it is now. Still I think it earns a fair percent. I think I will go downstairs and ask now. . . . I have asked. The earning now is 4%, and under present conditions it takes 87 months to bring a share to maturity. I think there is a penalty if your dollar is not paid on time. Of course, if you want to draw out after having paid for a specific time, perhaps a year, you can do so without loss of interest earned before the last prior interest-crediting date. I am going into detail, for it may be that you have now got your budget so arranged that you will have, say $20 a month to spare. If so, it should go in the Federal B & L here (guaranteed by Government up to $5,000). In the hope that it may be included in your budget from now on, I have placed the $50 in a very safe place, your mother's savings account, and it can be used next summer to pay B & L for two of the summer months. If you would get something like this started, considering the monthly payments as necessary, say, as your food or room, your mother and I would feel very happy and a great deal relieved that you had seen the wisdom, if not the necessity, of trying to take care of yourself, or us for that matter, should real misadventure come. Misadventures do come. For instance, Dr. and Mrs. Hite are hard hit in two ways, the lesser of course financial, by Bob's long illness. In the same family almost, Ernest Freeman and Mrs. F. are hard hit in two ways, and they are up against surgical operation cost and long expensive hospitalization for Mrs. Freeman. Without a money cushion—money or credit—the situations would be more poignant in that the needed care could not be had. True, what one saves may itself meet with misadventure. Still one can be found trying to look after the future.

Leaving out the question as to whether sickness will come and looking purely to the financial, in buying the 100 acres your mother and I went in debt $4,000. That is enough to ruin one under certain financial conditions. While I do not anticipate it, a depression following our spending spree is conceivable of such degree as to permit $4,000 of debt to wipe out a lifetime's saving effort. If that should happen—that sort of a depression—where would I turn for $4,000? First, to an insurance policy I have which has a loan value of approximately $2,000. When that is got, I am still $2,000 short. If you in the meantime had been accumulating $20 a month, it might well operate to save the whole works. This is a situation I do not at all expect; still, it can happen here. There may also come a time, even if I get the $4,000 paid (and I expect fully to do that eventually) when my income would not pay taxes. This could happen with ten-cent corn which has occurred in my lifetime. And in that case also, a reserve stake would be important. In my whole life I have never had a reserve and have not yet. So I have lived dangerously too, and so far have not been hurt. If I cannot secure a reserve, still I have hopes you can do it for me. It is all purely selfishness on my part. That is, you get some money and I will do my best to spend it.

Well, I had an hour's interruption here and my writing time is gone. We did not send your letter to Lillian because it made a pessimistic reference to her condition—your talk with Captain Prewitt. We are well. Mother was out to luncheon today—I guess bridge in the afternoon. The sun is shining brightly, as it did yesterday also. No really cold winter yet, and time is getting short until spring is due. I assure you your $50 is safely placed for the present.

March 17, 1941

Your mother opened this letter thinking it was of no importance and afterwards decided that, whether important or not, you should see it. I deposited the $50 in the bank to your mother's savings account. Don't know just the process or the devices needed to be resorted to to get it out again. That account is beginning to have an importance in my eyes leading to the thought that I might be led to an effort to talk her out of it.

There is no news. The first fifteen days of March were somewhat of a nightmare—income tax returns by people who had never made returns—no records—in most cases no tax, still with enough gross income to require returns. It was quite a relief when the last of those who came to me signed his and got out about 5 o'clock the afternoon of the 15th. Today I have been trying to find out how much of the regular law business on hand is how far behind.

The Tolles were over yesterday afternoon. It was a windy cold afternoon. At Sunday school time it was fine and bright and fairly warm. When church let out, a raw cold wind which got stronger and colder as the day wore on—the advance of the storm which took so many lives in the Dakotas and on Lake Superior. Someday I will write you a real letter but not today as it's 5:30 now and time to go home.

April 25, 1941

Your mother has got into the cleaning of the big living room. The paper has been cleaned and woodwork washed. The curtains have been put through their bath and will probably be ready for hanging by night, and the floors should be polished and perhaps the rugs and furniture back in place. At any rate I am hoping that the place will look much more orderly than it did last night. When that is done, nothing is left but the cleaning and papering of the library, the washing and waxing of kitchen floor, the making of curtains for the library, the dressing up of the back porch, and the exchanging of storm windows for screens. In other words, there will be little left to do. The wall paper in the library will be a dark red, I would call it, closely matching or shading into the color of the furniture. I think it will make the room what it should be—of course, with the help of the "tasselated" curtains.

Linder Rosebraugh died yesterday—42 years old—a hard-working, reliable, substantial man. He was secretary of the Building and Loan below me here. I do not think he ever had the capacity to play, even as a boy—an earnest, serious, hard-working type of man whom the town respected and whose loss will be generally regretted.

We have been running the furnace ever since you left and always hate to do that after the housecleaning has started, but always do. It's an old established custom and cannot be broken in this part of the world. There is little other news. The Langford case is still untried, set for tomorrow afternoon, but I doubt it that the prosecuting witness will ever be able to attend a trial.

The Tolles are well. We were there one evening this week for the evening meal. Dirk was in good spirits, but one side of his face was pretty well bruised up by a fall on a concrete pavement sometime during the day. At times he is in such a hurry that his feet just cannot keep up, I think. At any rate he falls rather easily.

September 10, 1941

Life has not been quite the same since you left and we have missed you considerably. Still we go on enjoying the days as they come. Today mother is canning apples. At noon she had fifteen pint jars full of the nicest canned apples. They looked good and I know they will taste as good as they look, for there were some left over for lunch.

I drove out to the Sears 60 this morning to look at the beans there and to sell some if the prospect of their maturing before frost looked good enough. The price has been going up by leaps and bounds and is now so high that I would really like to sell the whole crop if I were not afraid they would not mature. The Sears field is the earliest of our plantings and I found that it will take ten days or two weeks yet to mature. Still if it matures it will produce 30 bushels an acre (15 for us) and the 20 acres will make 300 bushels for us. So I took a chance (the first time I have sold what was not ready for market) and sold 150 bushels at $1.68 a bushel, which is almost a dollar more than the crop brought last year by the bushel. This is the best field of beans we have. The 48 acres at Ashmore will do well to make 20 bushels an acre, which by the way would make a good enough income if the price continues at $1.50 or better.

I have a story which will be hard for you to believe. You know that I don't think I had ever won the solitaire game prior to last Friday, but that night after several tries, the thing worked out. I was extremely suspicious for your mother had helped, as we are all inclined to help one another in that game. In fact, on this particular game, the help was continuous and so fast I had a hard time to keep up. Then Saturday night came and the thing worked fine—just went right along—and every card fell into place by the end. Then your mother tried two or three times, and the game worked at last for her. So it *will* work, and I even believe that the Friday game was on the up-and-up.

We called on the Tolles last night after supper. Found them well and in good spirits. Dirk has not abated one jot in his physical culture training, self-imposed apparently, after every successful meal. There is no news really. Our broomcorn is all in the shed. The last crop was badly cut by chinch bugs. A neighbor had raised rye and wheat adjoining the field, and the bugs had found my broomcorn and corn the best feeding grounds in the neighborhood. I have raised no wheat or oats since the chinch bugs did so much damage some years ago, but neighbors, in some cases, have not been so thoughtful. This was one of the cases.

Well, this was not intended for a letter, just a chat. There are probably some things I might tell you if I could think of them, but just now nothing in the way of news occurs to me. Your mother sends love, as do I.

November 15, 1941

Your mother was going to write you yesterday, but she was a bit tired—had her bridge club Wednesday, was at Alice's caring for Dirk Thursday and then had an accumulation of work in the house and yard which went rather slowly yesterday. And so the letter didn't get itself written.

You will be glad to know that today will probably finish my bean harvest, though I am not sure as to that. There is several cents dockage on each bushel of beans that I have sent in—the result of their long being subject to wet, rainy weather. Also, a lot of beans were beaten down and lost. Still, I don't think my loss is over three or four hundred dollars and we felt pretty good about that. The corn is also getting sent to market. The price is not as good as I would like. Still it makes good revenue on the money invested. Except for one forty-acre tract the land will yield a gross of $10 an acre, which gives a good net. Even with the 40, the gross will almost reach $10 an acre. It will reach that counting what the Government will probably pay under its agricultural program. One 20-acre patch of corn, planted in blackest of black land where clover had been for two years and using "160 Pfister" and "13 US" hybrid corn for seed, made 100 bushels an acre. It is the new land that brought the gross down. Another prairie patch of 20 acres is making about 70 bushels an acre. I don't know the hybrid used there. Another patch of 14 acres should have made 65 or 70 but is badly down—stalk and roots not strong enough to support the ears—and there will be some loss there. The 34 acres of new land in corn will average about 40 bushels. I will have to doctor that land considerably.

There is little news. Christmas is getting fairly close and we are "honing" to see you. Mother's house is at its best in interior decoration, furnishings and arrangement. We like it a lot but don't get as much time in the evenings there as we would like at this season of the year. Too many outside things. Tonight a dinner given by the Weirs. Tomorrow night at the Colemans'. A church dinner last Tuesday night. A bar dinner the Friday before. Chamber of Commerce dinner Wednesday night, etc., etc.

Mother just phoned that Dirk was taking care of her today and would meet me as I walk home at noon. She still thinks he's wonderful. Maybe she is right. Charley Miller, Byron, Harold and a fourth were hunting Monday and Tuesday. They did very well. Harold, Byron and Charley spent Sunday and Monday night in a cottage at Oak Grove, and Byron and the other man joined them Monday. It's lunch time and I have to meet Dirk and Mother.

November 24, 1941

I don't know when I have written you a letter from home here on 6th Street, but it's 5:15 and your mother and I have not taken the clothes to be washed and she has started to get our supper. It will be Hungarian goulash, with cornbread and potatoes. And—will it be good! We had the goulash last night and it was better than the Hungarians ever could make.

I want to tell you about our Thanksgiving day on the 20th. We had talked of hunting for several days and I had made inquiries as to where we could go without trespassing. Finally decided on a place suggested by Charley

Miller who said that if I should tell the owner, Fields, that Charley suggested that I hunt there, Fields would not object. (I just asked Mother the man's name, and she said she had told you of our interesting day. She also said that she ordered a turkey from his daughter, Mrs. Merritt, and she turned out to be a schoolmate of yours and with a distinct memory of you.)

Well, Friday I went to the office and worked awhile. Then Mother called and said Harold wanted to take Jimmie and me and his two new dogs hunting, to leave Mattoon at 1:30. Harold has two young dogs whose mother he formerly owned, and he thinks they are the best prospects he has ever had. They are industrious, seem to know what it is all about, and obedient. He is quite excited over them. There had been an all-night rain Wednesday night and, of course, the country, wet as it was, is soaked, and on Friday water was standing in the fields in places six inches deep, but we all had rubber boots and splashed through the water and mud, up and down the broomcorn fields, up and down the hedge rows, but no trace of the birds was found. The dogs covered lots of ground too and I think did it well. So we consulted together and decided to go to another place several miles away. I hated to give up and suggested one more trip into the broomcorn. Remember this suggestion, for it was followed; but for it, this story would have ended normally.

The suggestion resulted in no birds, and a bit before 4 o'clock we loaded into the car, Harold's car, Harold driving, Jim and I on the front seat and the dogs in the luggage compartment, and were on our way, driving on the blacktop Lincoln Trail a mile or two or three beyond Lincoln Park—a big broad trail, lots of room, little traffic. Harold seemed to me to be driving rather slowly, considering that the day was about done and little time was left for hunting. After a bit a car approached from the east. The car was on its proper side, we on ours, it going west, we going east, then without warning, the car turned left across our lane not more than 20 or 30 feet in front of us—no place to go, no time to go anywhere if there was anywhere to go. Harold slammed the brakes on, and then crash, a split second after the car turned. Result: the whole front end of Harold's car wrecked, the gear shift on the wheel bent down three or four inches—the result of the blow Jimmie gave it with his nose—Jimmie out for a few moments—the shatter-proof windshield dished out, the glass coatings so criss-crossed with cracks that it could no longer be fairly called transparent—the result of the forward dash of my hat-covered head—and I guess I was just about out for a few moments.

Harold was not used as an instrument to help break up the car and therefore was not hurt. He was intensely alert, every sense working at top speed—out of the car looking me over, giving me time to come alive, waiting till I said the word to go into the farmhouse, helping me in, then giving his attention to Jim, then getting a written statement from the driver of the other car, witnessed by a witness of the accident, taking pictures of the dogs, tinkering with the car, getting it in such shape that it would at least start to go back to Mattoon, and by that time Jim and I were ready to go. The car took us to the farmhouse (where you and Alice E. had a drink of milk on your walk to Mattoon that time), and someone pushed us in from there.

Jim was a sight. The blow had been on the bridge of his nose and a cheekbone. We thought, of course, that his nose was broken, but the doctor said that it was not. We drove over there yesterday afternoon to see how he looked. He was at the picture show but got back before we left. He has a peach of a black eye and the bruise on his nose and cheek, but the skin was not cut and there will be no scar. The doctor looked me over and approved a glass of Scotch and drank one with me. Had a bit of fever that night—excitement and all—and your mother called Herb Iknayan who looked me over and gave me some pills to take and a capsule to put me to sleep. Saturday morning I did a good half-day's work at the office and had my office at home in the afternoon. Today I did a good half-day's work at the office, and this afternoon stayed at home leaving word that I could be seen here. The blow left a slight mark on my forehead and a bruise across the bridge of my nose and a small lump under my chin. I took some of the force on my knees, and my legs were a bit stiff and sore Saturday. An accident is quite an exciting event, I find, but when there is only a split second of anticipation, one has not the time to really measure the value or lack of value of anticipation. We were a very lucky bunch.

Harold and Alice postponed their hunting trip to Kentucky, for they now have no car. We are to have a real Thanksgiving turkey Thursday evening entertaining twelve, counting me and omitting Mother who will serve. Then there will be cards until midnight, I reckon. Alice and Harold won't be at the party. Mother says she will read this and maybe add a few sentences.

1942

January 19, 1942

Your letter came in and your mother and I, as well as Harold and Alice E., were relieved and pleased that the health threat was a false alarm. It made the picture much brighter for the entire family. We were, however, a bit worried about the chance of your being so fed up with teaching that you would step out of that without any especial consideration of the future. As a matter of fact, I think that at times everyone gets thoroughly tired of what he is doing. I know that sometimes it is all I can do to force myself to the grind of the office, but I also know that we have not enough to live on without what I get here in the office—that is, to live as we have been accustomed to living. During this war period the future of everything is so uncertain (including land ownership), and taxes are to be so high that it is very certain that all outside activities, except those connected with war, and all absolutely unnecessary expenses are taboo. While my earnings here at the office do not equal your earnings in teaching, still I have to earn what I can. As a matter of fact, I am going to charge a more nearly sufficient fee this year for what I do and thus increase my earnings, and I do not expect a vacation at all. I am looked upon as a rather old man, and am an old man in the business view—on the downside and getting well toward the bottom of business life. I am in a different position from you who are at the high point for the next ten years, though in one respect we are alike, for neither of us knows more than one thing which is of financial value. You know teaching. I know a bit more about law than the average man—just that and nothing more.

My aversion, or rather dislike which at times becomes aversion, to my work, I think grows out of the fact that I dislike controversy and in addition I dislike to ask my clients to pay for my work. Sometimes I think that lawyer's work should be free in every case; that one of the qualifications of a lawyer should be that he have sufficient income to support himself from that and work for the pleasure of working.

It was quite gratifying to read your article in print. You write well. Miss Ragan and Miss Thereau (the teacher from Mississippi who lives in her house) were quite excited over the article and its publication. It may be that you have the imagination, which is necessary in this generation to please the public, to write successfully. There was a time when words flowed easily and in ordered array from my pen, but I lacked the time and the imagination. Now, writing is hard both in substance and proper sequence. As you have discovered, the secret of a happy life is to have something to do and an interest in doing it well.

To me the most unhappy people about town must be those with nothing to do (either from choice or necessity) who loaf or walk aimlessly about the streets. It has been said that work is the salvation of the soul. One of the best examples in my experience was your great grandmother Reed. Others, your grandfather and grandmother Kelly. Therefore, for all these reasons, it was a relief to your mother and me to get the report of the phone call. I think and hope that you will not find your schoolwork so distressing when you get a bit of your pep back. You used it too fast and it is depleted but will return.

We are well. Went to the faculty comedy last night. It is good to have a good laugh now and then. We had one last night. The faculty riot was a thing long to be remembered—good for the soul. The Ballet Russe was a bore to me. . . .

January 28, 1942

In the reorganization of United Aircraft a subscription right was sent to you—right to subscribe for four-tenths of a preferred share of new stock. I sent it to N.Y. for sale at a market, hoping to get you a dollar or two for it. Had the returns from the sale yesterday. The price was 8 cents. Of that amount you owe me 3¢ for stamps, 3¢ for letterhead and envelope, and 2¢ for your share of the steno's wages. So that account balances. It had to be used by January 13, else it was void. . . .

Contentment is largely an inner matter—self-controlled or rather self-centered—also a condition which makes for efficiency. A contented man is a valuable man to the extent of his capacity. A discontented man is unsatisfactory to himself or his work. And it all lies within him. As a matter of fact, "As a man thinketh in his heart, so is he." (That I feel sure should not be in quotation, for it is probably not exactly quoted.) You are not contented with teaching. Therefore, your work will no doubt be unsatisfactory. A teaching job is one of the highest in the United States—that is, if the teacher has the necessary outlook—because the proper training of the youngsters is entrusted to him. I think the teachers have in many respects fallen down and their product is too often a person who is hardly worthy of citizenship. True, most of the blame goes back to the parents. Most of the fault is there.

I don't know what to suggest about your own frame of mind or what work you can get into with which you would be satisfied. War-needs offer nursing and factory work. Nursing takes long training, and I do not think you are mechanically inclined. Stenography also takes considerable study and training. Painting can only be a sideline, a matter of recreation. Writing is indulged in by many. In most cases their product merely contributes to the mass of useless books. "Oh, that mine enemy would write a book!" Writing or painting as a sideline can be indulged in during those spare hours which are now wasted, anytime day after day, but will not be if the person interested has something worthwhile to put on paper or canvas.

I should not send this letter because I did not intend when I started it to make any comment on your situation, but I am going to send it anyway. It's merely the fulmination of one who does not know your situation well enough to give any advice whatever, and you are not to take it even as a suggestion.

We have not heard from you this week—unless a letter came to the house this morning—and are afraid you are still not very well and have not written for that reason. At any rate we love to get your weekly letter. . . .

April 2, 1942

When it was learned Jim had measles, it was necessary to give Dirk a shot to render him immune or to weaken the attack if he is already infected. There was no vaccine in Mattoon or Charleston, so Harold drove to Decatur and got it, and Dirk had his shot last night. There seems to have been no severe reaction. Jim is still sick but should begin to feel better in a few days. He can't keep anything on his stomach and is red in the face and dark under the eyes. So far, he likes your mother to be in the room and she has a time getting anything done outside the bedroom.* We believe the situation is now under control. Alice feels the "grade" is up now, and I believe it is. The reason Dirk needed the shot was because he had the ear trouble, and measles so frequently attacks the ears. Herb Iknayan lost his boy just that way, and the danger was a very present and pressing thing in his view of such a case.

There is no news. The office work has been keeping me busy. Think I have taken in more fees in the last three months than you earn in three months, and that is unusual for me, but I had to keep working to do it. Think there will be a slowdown for awhile and I don't care if there is. Would like to get out on the bank of the Ambraw with you, Alice E., Harold, Jim, Dirk and your mother to help Jim fish and keep an eye on Dirk while something was cooking on an open fire. The weather has not been right for that yet, but it won't be long now, and it would be nice.

Have got all my taxes paid for the year, have paid the interest on the farm loan until December, have all current accounts paid except the usual run of insurance to Charles Miller. (I only catch up with that bill once a year.) The next thing to meet is the $300 premium on life insurance, including $72

---

*In order to prevent Dirk from catching measles, Jimmie was staying with his grandparents in Charleston.

interest on a loan on one of the policies. This I expect to have on time. The first six months of the year have usually been the hardest because of taxes, insurance, etc. coming in that period.

The farmers have not yet been able to do spring work as the ground is soaked. Water is back in the subsoil again. It went out a few years ago in the drouth and had not again filled the subsoil until this winter. In times of dry weather a wet subsoil is to be desired, and there is always a dry spell in summer as you know.

Your mother is in good health and I don't think will be worn out when spring-cleaning season opens. That's not far off now. We will not attempt a vacation unless your mother or Alice E. or you or one of the children needs it, but we can have a happy time at home and won't miss a vacation much.

April 24, 1942

There was a nice letter from you at home at noontime. It was the one with the commendation of the publishing house in it. No doubt you have a fine storehouse in your mind upon which to draw for the stories you are writing, and the publisher's letter should be of much value. It may well be that you have found a congenial employment in which you will excel. You have our hope and our belief as well.

Little news here. Mother is having Mr. Butler give the back porch its first cleaning of the year, remove the storm windows from the French doors, put in bedroom and front door screens, saw some dead limbs from trees, and do other things around the place, getting ready for summer. There have been several pretty days this week, and now that Dirk has got his fishing worms and has planned to take us all to the river Sunday to cook our dinner and fish and whatnot, it begins to look and feel like a rain is getting close.

The war effort continues to dislocate business—auto merchants, builders, plumbers, hardware men, concrete men, and through a long list including farmers, who are to feel the pinch of a short labor supply. Soon—May 4th to 7th—the bond drive is coming, asking now a subscription for the duration of the war of 10% of earnings or income. You probably know the program. $23 billion from taxes, $12 billion from popular bond sales and $20 billion from banks, insurance companies and the like. It's magnificent in size and after-possibilities. Young men from all over are already scattered around the world. More are being called for. This World War is a magnificent display, thrilling, terrifying, calling into play the physical and mental efforts of about all of humanity in its presentation. One can but contemplate the results of such efforts being given to the good rather than the harm of man.

Mother's pet squirrel bit her finger the other day. Still she was feeding him again today—a bit more carefully, for she did not want another trip to the doctor to have a wound cauterized. . . . The squirrel bit after she had fed him two nuts and he had gone away, satisfied she had no more. Then she called him back and he smelt her fingers, and finding nothing but the odor of a pecan, he nipped a finger to see what it was like. Mother felt like a nut herself.

Dirk was here with Alice E. yesterday. He looks and feels fine. Still wears a bandanna around his head to protect his ears. . . .

May 14, 1942

I think this is your "birthday." May life be very good to you and each successive birth anniversary find you happier as the many years of life, which I hope will be your portion, complete their circles from May 14 to May 14.

There is little news. Your mother and I tried fishing for a couple of hours this spring and had a mess large enough for two. We tried again with Dirk, but that was a failure. He is not interested. He has been with us the last two nights but is going home this afternoon. His mother has been cleaning house. Last night he had a bad dream (I think). At any rate he cried long and quite lustily, not as one in pain, but apparently from fright mixed possibly with some anger. He says he dreamed of a bear, but that may have been a suggested explanation.

Your letter to your mother came in today. We, of course, do not know what the war may have in store for us. Whatever it may be, it still is not of the class as what may be dealt to one in the military service. Our thought is that if we are guilty of any fault, of omission or commission, which results in anything undesirable happening to anyone in the armed forces, we will have seriously failed in our responsibility. These civic duties, in my case acting as government appeal agent, in yours the various registrations and whatnot, are mere incidents growing out of the war, changing our lives somewhat but really not hardships. Bond subscriptions and taxes merely require that we either make more money or quit doing some of the things we have been doing, but the man in military service chances his whole life. The lives of young men are of course thrown completely out of gear. At first in drafting men they had a real physical examination here at home and were examined, I think, sixty days prior to induction. If they went in 4F, they thought they had some real reason to feel that the army would not accept them, and could govern their affairs accordingly. There was then little uncertainty and they did not have to dispose of their businesses and property in a hurry. Under the rules since the first of the year the local doctors have to answer two questions. If both answers are "no," the registration is Class 1A, though he had been 4F before, and is subject to induction having no idea whether the Army will accept him or not. It is true that the Army will grant him a ten day's furlough after induction if the local board requests it, but in a number of cases that have come to my attention ten days are not enough, and if a going business has to be disposed of, it will undoubtedly be at a sacrifice. These situations arise with men who have got their starts. Young men, in good health, have only the choice of volunteering for a specific service or of waiting for the draft. Many, of course, do not wish to wait. Married men who are not in essential work, by next year—by fall some think—may be in line to be drafted, and men of that type are wondering what they had better do now in the way of changing employment so that their families at least will not be put on too close rations.

Harold, I think, would like to be in military service, and may try to get into officer's training camp. If he does do this (and this information is not to be mentioned to anyone), there is a period of nine months in which the trainees will have opportunity to demonstrate that they will or will not make good officers. If Harold should do something of that type or go into essential industry, the Kelly family would probably again have need of the whole house. If it should happen, and it would be mighty fine to have you, Alice E. and the two children as part of the family, with Harold coming home as permitted, you would need Mrs. Marshall's room as a studio, for painting would not go well with Jim and Dirk both around. Alice E. might be able to do some substitute teaching, and you could preempt some spot in the house where silence could be enforced for your writing. I think it would be a desk in my room.

Spring is here. It has been a wet fall, winter, and spring, and farmers are somewhat behind with their work. They are catching up fast though. They let no time slip when farming is possible. They are getting shorthanded but in most cases will make out. There was little plowing done last fall. Usually it is about all plowed in the fall, but now the farms have been plowed for the most part and some crops are in. The yard is pretty. Mother's housecleaning is well in hand and will be done when time and inclination meet.

I, too, think air-raid alarms are important in New York City. Back here we are not particularly concerned about that yet. Eventually, I reckon they will find some way to stop the submarines off the east coast. The Army and Navy seem slow in meeting that destruction of ships. The Navy is, of course, engaged elsewhere, but destruction is so close to shore that Army flyers should suffice. The *Tribune* thinks civil flyers could be used for observation planes and should be tried out.

Well, I have to close this. Glad you are well and happy. You are in the frame of mind and have the ability to succeed in your plan of writing.

June 5, 1942

Your mother is getting better—still has to be very careful not to over-exercise and tires easily, but having had one back-set and having been soundly lectured by Dr. Iknayan, she is behaving herself fairly well. We were at Harold and Alice's for dinner a couple of days ago. They are all well there. Dirk has a good, brown healthy color on his body as he has been going around without much clothes on. Harold has given up the idea of trying for officer's training, and that is just as well. Would hate to see him actually in the Army in any capacity though we did not discourage the idea in any way. So the house will not be so full as we once thought it might be and you can choose your place for typewriting.* The weather has been extremely hot and stormy the last few days, so much so that one has the feeling of being in a Turkish bath all day, and that is too enervating to take for long. The thunderstorms have not cooled the atmosphere at all.

There is little news. . . . There is a rabbit nest in Mrs. Thomas's flower garden—several young rabbits. Mrs. Thomas discovered it almost at once. It is located and hidden in a densely-growing foliage plant, covered with cut leaves and lined and stopped thoroughly with rabbit hair. When Dirk was over a few days ago, the eyes were not thoroughly open yet, but the babies were conscious of a touch on the nest and responded with movement and sound, evidently hopeful that it was dinner time. Perhaps you could use that incident as a basis for a story. The plants are of low growth, and some of the nest must be underground, though I will not know certainly till the young are out.

The other evening the jaybirds set up a clatter on the north side of the back yard which moved slowly toward the center of the yard, and a moment later a cat moved across an open space and went through the shrubbery to the Thomas yard, more birds and jays taking up the alarm. I thought of the rabbits and went through the Thomas flower garden down to the pool where a thrush was in a high state of noisy excitement in the top of the shrubbery there, evidently wildly concerned about her nest or young and extremely vocal in her alarm. Her eyes pointed exactly to a spot almost below her, and a clap of my hands sent the cat in great leaps down the back of the yard toward 4th Street. The thrush actually seemed to look me over as if in thanks. Then all was peace among the birds and their evening calls were resumed.

There seem to be more and more birds each year which like our neighborhood—the shrubs are high and there are plenty of trees and always water to be had at the bird bath. The robins find good worms in the early morning and bugs are plentiful. In the winter, red birds congregate under

*Emma C. had resigned from Madison High School.

the hackberry tree to eat the seeds that are always there. I think several times last winter as many as twenty were there at once, giving a red tone to the ground itself.

Well, this nature story must close. We are getting pretty anxious to see you and hope you will not stay in the East too long.

September 22, 1942

I wrote you several days ago, but you had not received it when you wrote on the 18th. My impression is that New York should obey the air raid warning's rules, for I think that city is open to a token bombing at any unexpected time. It has always been considered true that Americans are prone to lose their heads in the presence of an out-of-place fire in their homes, and no doubt we will carry that trait with us in the matter of air raids.

There is little news here. I had the Tolle family to Buckler's for dinner Sunday, and Alice and Dirk came over to see me yesterday. She was a bit restless, of course. No one could know for sure what was best for Harold and the family. His best judgment was that he should make a try for a commission. No one had any basis for concluding he was wrong. I am sure I might very well have reached the same decision if I were situated as he is. His examination was set for yesterday and today in Rockford. I told him when I left him Sunday that I would not be disappointed in either event, that is, if he made the grade or didn't make it; that nevertheless I thought or rather hoped he would make the grade, for if he became an officer he wouldn't have to start as a buck private. Alice is standing up very well and I think has eliminated any fear that he has not taken the right path.

I am quite anxious to know when your final test comes on your Waves application. I do not know what investigation the Navy makes of prospective officers in the Waves, but have the impression that its investigation of the personal history of prospective male officers is intensive and sometimes protracted—that is, it uses the FBI in such matters. On that score, in your case the investigation might be somewhat protracted because of the numerous places where you have taught, but the answer should be favorable. I don't know what questions you will be required to answer on your mental test, but you are liable to be asked more questions than you or anyone else can answer in the allotted time, and I suspect that some of them will be trick questions.

The wreck a mile east of Ashmore was a serious one—three dead, I believe I wrote you. There was no sabotage, though 300 or more soldiers were aboard. I think the automatic signal to show the open switch did not work, or the switch opened without human intervention. It seems there has been something wrong with the switch and its tower control, and men were working to get it in place at the exact time the passenger showed up, but hadn't had time to get a man out far enough to flag the fast-moving passenger. The coroner's jury gave the verdict as "cause unknown."

I enclose a newspaper picture. It will be of little interest to you. Send it back as it may have some interest for your mother. Roy Seeley sent it to me. He is the little fellow in the front row. The last time I saw him he was pretty fat. The picnic was on Twin Lakes, a very pretty place indeed and about eight miles from Springfield. As I remember it, a good many other lawyers were there besides those in the picture, and it was a full afternoon of relaxation. Those were the "horse and buggy" days, and Twin Lakes had the characteristics of a park, though privately owned as I remember.

Let me know the Waves situation and prospects. I have the same concern in your case if you become a member of that branch of the service as I have if and when Harold becomes a part of the military force. Still, I don't think I will worry, and I have an idea that your mother will also be able to look at the situation, whatever develops, without too much worry. I don't know yet when she will come home. Think she will get a better start for the winter by reason of having had the trip.

September 25, 1942

There is no news. Harold has not heard from his Rockford examination. Byron and his father are going on a fishing trip soon, as he does not expect to be called before October 8. His call will come on only 24-hour notice. . . . It has been cold and have had the furnace going since Monday night. No frost as yet, but it has been close and will be close tonight. Your mother expects to come home next Wednesday or Thursday.

The Army is certainly taking the boys. Forty-three are called for the 1st and forty-two for the 8th. The American Legion is erecting a board at the corner of the square for the names of those from the east side of Coles County in the military service. It is large enough for 1,040 names. With these two October calls there will be over 800—and that, my dear, is a goodly number for east Coles County. The Board is ready, as soon as the authorities give the word, to start sending married men, though none could go in October unless as volunteers. Should think they would be reached rather soon after election, however—that is, married men without children.

October 14, 1942

I don't know whether you have had a recent letter from us or not. There is little news. Jim has been with us since Sunday and is attending the Model School at E. I. Alice E. and Dirk are still in Mattoon trying to get the house ready for the tenant who moves in Saturday. There are floors to varnish, furniture to have fixed, a room to paper, the house to clean—and above all, the furnace to fix and the repair part not immediately available. All the rest ought to have waited for the furnace repair, but Alice has got to go ahead with the varnishing, cleaning, etc. and maybe have it all pretty well marred when the furnace is being repaired. She and Dirk are eating and sleeping at the Tolles. The woman she had engaged neglected to come help. The dogs—two fine hunting dogs—are still unsold and unprovided for. The piano, Dirk's bed, Jim's dresser and desk are at our house along with the silver, bedding, towels, food, canned fruit and a host of other things. Harold has been at Camp Grant since Monday unless he has been moved. Our square piano did not sell and if we can get it in tune (to stay) with the other one, we should have some duets this winter. Your mother, Jim, Dirk and I are all well. Alice E. is tired and very thin and is having a hard time to keep from feeling depressed and worried. Tom (their dog) is still in Mattoon and will come over when Alice E. does.

I am quite interested to know how you like your new work* and if you can keep the wolf from the door out of your earnings. Not suggesting that you can't do so; I do suggest that if the going gets too tough and you see financial obligations begin to pile up, or rather about to be incurred, which you see no way to meet, that you come home rather than incur them. We simply can't rock our boat purposely "for the duration." This suggestion does not arise from fear but from a sane desire to take what reasonable precaution may be taken to prevent undesirable happenings. We would be glad to have you here—and that statement has no strings to it and is meant without reservation of any kind. It would also help to keep Alice E.'s chin up, I think, and she will need that help as long as Harold is in the Army.

It's been harder than you might think to see him go, and it's hard to always feel that it was right to let him go. Alice E. will bear the brunt of that thought. Your mother and I will stand by and never a suggestion of a doubt as to the wisdom and propriety of the move will emanate from either of us. The contrary will be true, and she will be treasured and cared for and protected from her own thoughts in our house as far as that is humanly possible. . . .

*Free lance advertising research for Daniel Starch & Staff, Young & Rubicam, *et al.*

November 14, 1942

Perhaps it seems to you as if we had been remiss in not writing you shortly after our return from Louisville, but we got back Monday evening. Jim went to school Tuesday and has been in bed ever since. Sore throat with fever. The two Alices have been busy with the kids and housekeeping, though your mother was at her luncheon bridge Wednesday afternoon and we went to a picture show that night, and Alice E. has been to an evening picture show. . . .

I have had my time more or less occupied with one thing or another as usual. The draft board meeting last night didn't adjourn until after midnight. This letter may be the last you get until after Thursday. Alice E. said at noon she had a good letter from you, but with Dirk requiring me to read funnies to him, I didn't get a chance to read it. This is not an answer to that letter. . . .

We* left here last Saturday at 7 o'clock. Had appointment with Harold and Jim Kelly** to meet at Jim's office in the afternoon. We got there about 1:30, and one of the office force phoned to Jim. Harold*** got there 15 or so minutes later and Jim about 15 minutes after that. I didn't know it, but Jim lives out toward Cincinnati almost in the woods—open country behind him and timbered tract between him and river. There are a number of widely spaced residences there—a high-class residence group opened within recent years, not a part of the city of Louisville but only ten miles from Jim's office. The residences are on "Indian Hill." There are several of the hills, however. . . . The home is new and beautifully furnished and modernly equipped—three bedrooms upstairs, big living room, dining room, breakfast nook, kitchen and garage downstairs, and bedroom and Ping-Pong set in the basement. The furniture is a collection of various old family pieces, most of which Will had accumulated before his divorce, though there are other Anderson pieces and one Kelly piece which I recognized. Jim and Billie are perfect Kentucky hosts.

Harold was suffering from the aftereffects of the third typhoid shot. He had quite a bit of fever and a cough—almost continuous—which probably resulted from the severe physical exertion of his training schedule combined with typhoid shot, to produce excessive fatigue and the cough. It was entirely from the throat. He is a pretty determined fellow, yet he promised to see the doctor on his return to Camp Sunday afternoon and did so. The doctor took his temperature and sent him to the infirmary where he got a

---

*Mrs. J.Y., Alice E., Jimmie and Dirk.

**Nephew James Hugh Kelly of Louisville, Ky.

***Undergoing basic training at Fort Knox.

much needed rest. He was not allowed to leave the hospital for forty-eight hours after the fever left him, but he was without fever more than forty-eight hours ago and I suppose is back with his battalion.

Ruth, Kirtley and Helen* came down to Jim's for Sunday dinner and we almost had a family reunion. It was a most satisfactory trip except for Harold's condition. Alice has had three letters from him since we left about the contents of which I got no chance to ask her at noon.

The foregoing constitutes about the full history of this end of the Kelly-Tolle families since I wrote you. We got the dog (Tom) back from Mattoon day before yesterday. Mrs. Tolle reported that while in Mattoon he stayed out front and looked over every car that came along and gave other evidence of chagrin and sorrow at having lost his folks. I don't think he quite understood how the separation occurred. He had jumped into Mrs. Tolle's car here when Alice E. got in. Then Alice E. got out downtown, and the car went to Mattoon without her. He didn't see her again until Thursday, and of course the car couldn't have got away without him. I was really glad to get him back as he seems a part of the family.

*From Georgetown.

1943

January 11, 1943

We had your interesting letter and were glad to know that your train ride had not been uninteresting and for that reason, probably not tiring; also glad that you fell into the work harness.* Hope you had more success getting a typewriter than I did. Owing to a change in the stenographer situation, I thought I needed a typewriter and sent your mother out to buy the one you looked at. However, that had been sold more than two months ago and I am reconciled to the thought that I do not need a typewriter. We are not pleased that the Red Cross Overseas Service may still be open to you. Neither your mother nor I would want you in any overseas service at this time. We are decidedly of the opinion that one of the family is enough to have in an uncertain situation at this time. You, perhaps, can appreciate some of the reasons which we have for our view, for you were here long enough to observe the situation and draw your own conclusions. . . .

Have had considerable cold weather with snow which has not yet begun to melt. However, I have my second cellar full of coal and we are set for the winter, probably, in respect to heat. This is Eastern Kentucky coal and far better than my first supply of Indiana coal which I put in last summer. . . .

Jim is getting back in harness, and Harold was well a few days ago and I suppose still is. He should have a furlough the latter part of this month.

Let us hear as often as you can.

P.S. I enclose your bank dividend.

June 24, 1943

If you judge from the paper you will probably conclude that it is night and I am at home trying out Alice E.'s machine,** and if you so judge, you will be right. Mother said that she had indirect news from you through Mr. Freeman. We always enjoy your letters. We enjoy also hearing from you indirectly.

There is little news here. It has been hot and sticky for the most part with frequent showers and thunderstorms. Last Sunday we had a great afternoon planned, fried chicken lunch at the Ashmore gravel-pit pond and fishing thereafter until sundown. As it turned out we had a completely satisfactory lunch, but as we got up from the ground to put the remains away and get

*Writing advertising copy for the American Book Company.
**Alice E. takes a course in typing, requiring a second-hand typewriter.

our fishing tackle, we noticed a heavy, black, windy cloud coming. So we threw the remains in the car and beat it for home. It rained practically all afternoon.

The duck* is having a lot of varied experiences in life. Some time ago Dirk tried to teach him to stay under water for a length of time far beyond anything that the duck would have ever experienced if left to his own devices. As a natural result the duck is very much afraid of water, except small mud puddles. As a natural result, also, the duck became dirty, so dirty that his skin became rather itchy, or so we judged from his apparent efforts to scratch himself with his bill. Dirk and Susan** apparently noticed his unkempt condition and when no one was near to interfere today, they got the soap, took Donald to the dishpan full of water—left for him to swim in if he ever takes the notion—wet him good, rubbed him with ashes, covered him with soap and proceeded, in their own way, to try to clean him. Mother said that when she noticed the condition, it looked almost hopeless to expect Donald to come clean, but with much care picking the ashes out and washing and rinsing him he did come clean, shivering and shaking from the cold. So she wrapped him up and put him in the sunshine. When I saw him at noon he was clean and fluffy and apparently didn't itch any more; at least he was not scratching himself.

Your mother has been sewing for many days. I think she has made one dress for herself. I think she also sent you one. She now has the odd-looking material about made into a very attractive dress. I think she has made a dress or two for Alice E. She has promised to sew a button on one of my shirts. This promise was made some time ago. Eventually she will do it. But I noticed today that the shirt collar was getting frayed. Alice E. also is getting a yen to learn to sew. I think, after much planning and many backsets, she has made two or three sunsuits for Dirk. He is very proud of one of them, I know. It has red stripes in it. I call it a dress and he thinks that is funny.

Jim*** is at the swimming pool every afternoon. To a boy there is nothing like the water in summertime; however, he lost his bathing suit yesterday and is pretty much worried about the possible consequences, for it will take a considerable time for his allowance to buy a new one. He borrowed one today, and of course a new one will be bought soon after he has learned a lesson in care.

I read with a great deal of interest the copy you wrote in advertising the series of readers. It struck me as being very good indeed—so good that I almost felt that I would like to look the readers over. I have noticed in the

---

*Dirk's pet.

**Susan Cavins, neighbor and playmate.

***Jimmie—now age nine—insists on *"Jim"*.

Reader's Digest recently from month to month a few advertisements quoted as being "advertising that sings," I believe the expression or the heading is. Since you have been in the game these items have been of more interest to me than formerly.

As I said in the beginning, there is little news. We are well. It is a quarter till eleven. Last night we were up until midnight. In fact, we are becoming night owls. Still it is time to go to bed and I will close. Mother and Alice E. send love, as do I.

July 14, 1943

Letter-writing is one of the pleasures which seem to be much interfered with by war conditions. Mother told me last night that no letter had gone out recently to you and that she could not get to write it today. Therefore, this letter is to tell you that we are all well.

Memory does not go back to bring in review the details of the ordinary events of living, and so a letter can merely recount the things which have happened which are a bit out of the ordinary. One thing I recall as far back as the 10th, perhaps because it happened to me. Mother and I have an oil lease up in escrow at the bank to be delivered to the lessee if a commercial oil well were produced within one mile of our land by July 10. So, late on the 10th I drove Jack Claar and Bob Jeffries out to look at the well. It certainly does not seem to be a commercial well. At any rate, it was not producing apparently. Then we got in the car to start home but could get no sound from the battery. Investigation disclosed that the cable connecting the battery with the works was corroded in two, and no connection could be made. So I set out down the road to find a house with a phone, and having found one, phoned to Edman, Charleston, to come fix us up. In the meantime Jack and Bob had found a bit of baling wire and made a rough uncertain connection. They met me on my way back from the phone, and I got in. The thing held and we were able to flag Edman down at the river bridge. He followed us in, took Jack and Bob home from his garage, and my car was fixed in about fifteen minutes, and I went home.

Sunday, after church, the family—Kelly-Tolle—went to the dam with fried chicken and all the trimmings and the fishing equipment and worms. Eddie Tolle was spending the weekend with Jim. We ate. Then Jim and I seined and got a bunch of minnows for bait. Jim and Ed got on their bathing trunks and played around in the river all afternoon. Mother and I, helped occasionally by Alice E., fished and fished, standing in rushing water well above our knees—but no fish. The fish were taking neither the worms nor the minnows. Got home about 6 o'clock having enjoyed the trip greatly.

Monday night Mother and I went to a picnic at Lincoln Cabin Park. There were 28 there—mostly people of our age. . . . The dinner was of that kind which results in the ruin of a night so far as sleep is concerned. Everyone brought his own meat and buns for hamburgers. Then each family brought a covered dish, and there was ice cream and cake. Charleston has good cooks in that bunch of people and the results so far as I was concerned were uncomfortable. That was also the night that Alice E. left on the 12:51 a.m. train to go to Fort Knox for a week in the hope that Harold would have one day off this week. He had had no day off for more than two weeks and so engaged a room in the officers' quarters for Alice for the week. After I put Alice E. on the train I tried to sleep and did sleep some, but very uncomfortably.

Last night we drove out into the country. Left Alice E. and the boys at Frank Craig's and then inspected the crops on the Hudson and Sears farms. The crops are late but in perfect condition and looking fine. They will make crops if the season from now on is favorable and frost does not come too early.

Tonight I will be at the meeting of the draft board and tomorrow night Mother says I must see a show at the Lincoln. She has seen it and it is pure entertainment—the music especially good; the title: "For Me and My Gal." Mother has quit sewing for the summer, she says. It became a bit trying on her eyes and weather too hot. It is hot. Mother is standing it well, as am I. The office work is boring—more so in hot weather than in winter. Still I like the summer. Chiggers are plentiful and industrious. They are all over town—that is, wherever I have gone on the grass. I harbor them now not with venom and malice in my heart but as just one of those things which are to be expected.

July 17, 1943

This is the birthday anniversary and I did appreciate your good letter. There is nothing I want this year. Have plenty of ties and am not taking on any book-reading at present. My eyes are tired when I reach home at night.

I have not seen a contract such as publishers offer and don't know just what you should look out for. However, you are well enough trained in language to look out for unfair conditions. You should read the entire contract and if there is something in it which *seems* unfair, no doubt it *is* unfair and should be corrected before signing. A verbal promise, unwritten, will not change the written contract. When the written contract is signed, it supersedes all that has gone before and is the whole contract. So, read it carefully—fine print as well as the outstanding provisions. I would be glad to look it over if you have the time to send it to me, but my advice might not be of much value. . . .

We are thrilled that your book has been accepted. Mother said that Mrs. Marshall at Mrs. Shafer's yesterday announced to several people that she had heard from you—also she told about the acceptance of the book. By the way, it seems to me that the 50-50 split of royalty seems fair.

August 13, 1943

As hot as it is, I am going to write you a line—not to tell you any news—just to let you know that I am still able to write at least a short letter. Jim was over in Mattoon for a night and a day, then went to the country to a farm home and spent the night there last night. I think the farmer took him fishing yesterday afternoon. Alice E. went after him this afternoon. . . . I came home from the draft board meeting Wednesday night and found a bunch of Alice's friends on the back porch. . . . I merely stopped a moment and said good night. Your mother was enjoying them immensely. . . . The rest of the pears—the few that are left—are to be gathered this afternoon. Suppose I will do that as Jim is off his feed. The weather has really been trying. A number of the older people have dropped off, probably hurried along by the weather which has been hot and sultry. However, August is about half gone and there should be relief soon.

We are anxious to hear anything new about your stories, and, of course, anxious to see them in print. By the way, I don't believe we have heard from you very recently but have seen no disturbing news from New York since the race riots. Suppose Harlem is under control and somewhat chastened by the experience.

August 20, 1943

We had your letter and enjoyed it very much. However much your own feelings may have led you to magnify such minor praiseworthy elements of character as your mother and I, particularly I, may have, it is indeed agreeable to know that you do think so well of us, and to read the glowing words—glowing, as we feel, from the warmth of your own feelings toward us—you have used to portray us. Thanks a lot.

We were also just as much pleased—really more pleased—to know that your first work has been accepted for publication, and we are very much of the belief that the text will not be so altered that one cannot recognize anything but the subject. That just can't be true to the extent you forecast. Your type of writing is such that it seems to me the material alteration of the form of expression would harm rather than benefit. However, I am not acquainted with publishers or their methods, and I suppose in the publishing game the authority to whom a manuscript is submitted has his own type of expression and seeks to conform publications to the same or like type. It would probably be an instinctive reaction. Nevertheless, we will be glad to receive a copy. You may enter my subscription right now for one. Just let me know the price and I will send it along. The split fifty-fifty between author and illustrator seems fair enough. I suppose there are many drawings to be made of the birds, etc., and of course drawings should be fairly close to nature; therefore, the illustrator must make his own study of his subjects. Congratulations from all of us.*

There is little news. The Alices are canning some most every day. A few jars today, a few more tomorrow, and after a time the basement is pretty well supplied. Just now pears are being canned a few pints a day. Also, every day or so there are three or four quarts of tomatoes to can, and so it goes.

Yesterday afternoon the Alices were busy and suggested that I go fishing in the afternoon by myself. Well, I couldn't resist. So about 2:30 I went home from the office, got myself dressed for an outing, my equipment together in the car, bought me some good minnows, drove to the river at the bridge above the "Rocks" park, walked down the stream along the bank, through tall trees, shrubs, poison ivy and possible snakes to a well-shaded, high-banked fishing hole, as it appeared to be, though there was no evidence that others had thought enough of it to fish there. It was shady and comfortable, and I fished until 7 o'clock. Was well repaid by the quiet and solitude in really wild-appearing country. There were no noises save an occasional animal voice from the top of one of the large trees towering over me, the occasional splash of a bull frog changing from bank to river, the occasional creak of a tree branch or trunk, and one sharp noise as if a large rotten limb had broken cleanly. No branch fell to the ground, however, and I was unable to decide what caused the noise. The minnows were large and very active. It was a pleasure to watch the corks as the minnows sought to get out of the neighborhood of a bass or turtle or some other fish. Twice the minnows failed in their efforts. The first time, the cork disappeared suddenly and the line started down stream fast, stopping after about thirty feet of running. The cork stayed under, and the bass sat down to kill and eat the minnow. After a little, the bass and line started on downstream again. The impatient fisherman, thinking that the feast was over and the minnow swallowed, tried to set the hook, but his judgment was wrong. The bass had

---

*A children's book to join Holt & Co.'s *Twenty Little* series. However, war shortages of paper, etc., stopped publication of Emma C.'s volume, *Twenty Little Houses*.

merely had time to kill the minnow when some predatory water denizen had come along and a safer place had to be sought. So that one got away. The second was exciting only momentarily. The cork disappeared, the line moved fast out diagonally to the center of the stream, made a sharp turn, came close to the bank and stopped there—and the cork came up and stayed up. The minnow showed signs of ill treatment but was still alive. I suppose a bigger fish had come along and driven the first off.

Jim is in Mattoon. Dirk had four or five playmates yesterday noon when I got home, and he undoubtedly had a fine time all day. He declined to go fishing with me, but when I drove in he came running out to the garage—dressed in his blouse but minus his pants—wanting to know if I had caught any fish. Supper was over for the rest of the family but Dirk sat enthralled while I told of the trip and ate my supper. He was also angelic until bedtime at 8:30 and went to bed in that mood. Your mother said he was angelic all day.

Alice E. and your mother are well, but your mother is tired. This letter must close whether it is finished or not.

October 1, 1943

I am as yet unable to give a fair estimate of crop income, though I had to make an estimate for income tax purposes shortly before September 15—estimate of both crop and office income. Your mother doesn't have to make an estimate until December 15 because her income is all from farm land.

The planting season was late. The absence of killing frost to this date has permitted all of our crops to mature. There was a dry spell with very hot wind while many of the bean pods were forming and while much corn was in the pollen stage. We haven't harvested anything yet but bean harvest is from 16 to 25 bushels an acre. Before any beans were harvested, for the September 15 estimate, I considered my beans would average 25 which I thought was too high, but I didn't want to take a chance of being too low. Our share is half of production. It costs $4 an acre to harvest. Beans with as low as 14% moisture sell at $1.80 a bushel. Have not heard how moisture content is running. The more moisture, the less the price.

I estimated corn yield at 60 bushels an acre—my share is half with no expense of harvesting. I think my estimate of the corn is fairly accurate. I have 40 acres of corn and 38 acres of beans. You may make your own estimate of income. I have to pay for half the bean and corn seed.

Your mother has 80 acres of corn and 98 acres of beans. Her income is also still a matter of guess. You may use the same production figures as with mine.

Since the war started we have bought $1,100 of tax bonds, all of which have gone back for income taxes except $400 which will go back in December in all likelihood, along with some cash. We have also paid some on income tax by check. There will be additional income tax in March.

In the meantime we have bought and now own $1,300 in war bonds, all of which are E bonds except $100 which cost par. Our real estate tax—city, school district, township, county and state—is approximately $400 and we have paid that, and my insurance premiums are paid together with such interest as is due. There is a loan against one policy. We wish to save from the crops this year enough money to pay income taxes due March 15, June 15, and September 15 next year, the real estate taxes, the insurance policy premiums and interest, my bimonthly quota of $100 E war bond—one every two months—and the remaining $1,000 mortgage loan debt with interest. All of these things are payable before crops next year. The insurance premiums and interest amount to $320. We are going on the theory that the roof and furnace will outlast the war, though they may not. I hope to get living expenses out of my work, though I have not done that this year.

From this you will be able to get a fairly accurate picture of our present financial situation. I also spent better than a hundred dollars on crop insurance against hail and a hundred or so for lime and clover seed and a few odds and ends. Mother has depleted her reserve somewhat to help do these things.

Alice E. planned to go to Fort Knox today but Harold phoned that he was coming today. He got into Mattoon about 6:30 and Alice E. went over and got him. He ate breakfast at their new home.* I have not seen him yet. He leaves Saturday sometime for Fort Knox. Your letter with the bond came in today. I will put it in my bank box with the other one you sent. We are glad your plans for a homecoming are taking a definite shape, for we are anxious for a visit from you.

October 8, 1943

Either the figures I gave you on beans were wrong or you figured incorrectly. Eighty of Mother's bean acres have been combined. Fifty of the eighty produced 24½ bushels an acre. Mother's share was one-half. She kept 50 bushels for seed and sold the balance at $1.84 a bushel. She paid $100 for combining. Thirty acres produced 19½ bushels an acre. Her share was one-half. She kept 25 bushels for seed and sold the remainder at $1.80 a bushel. She still has 19 acres on the Ashmore farm. It will not produce more than 20 bushels an acre—her share is one-half. She will keep 33 bushels and sell the balance. She will pay $38 for combining.

I really don't know what corn sold direct from the field will bring. Here-

---

*A furnished house down the street, rented by Alice E. for the duration.

tofore, I have got from 62¢ to 66¢ a bushel. I think this year it will not be less than 80¢. I used the price 80¢ in preparing my September Income Tax Return for the Government. Have since heard that based on present taxes, corn direct from the field is in part, though I think not much, to blame.

There is a 12-inch tile under the low ground and that is not large enough to carry all the water which comes down when the rains are heavy. A rather extensive area is drained over the 40 and the 60. The outlet of the tile is usually below soil accumulated in the stream below, which makes the outlet slow and insufficient. I had the outlet cleaned last year at a cost of $100. It helped this year, but is probably filled up again. A neighbor who was benefitted by the cleaning paid $10 of the cost. Others should pay but have not.

The other problems affecting the 60 acres grow out of a lack of smaller-tile branch drains going to various parts of the 60 and the insufficiency of the 12-inch tile and its outlet. I have learned from examining the land when full to overflowing with water and know fairly well where the small tile should go, but it will take a survey to know accurately. The other 40 also lacks smaller tiles at several places. The land has been a problem but a very interesting one. Have spent as much gas and tire substance on it as on all the other tracts in the same length of time.

I must close this, as I can spare no more time. Glad to know you are taking an interest in the land. You might preserve this letter as your mother is not inclined to learn anything about any of it except by absorption, and that is a slow process.

1944

January 3, 1944

As a relaxation from what I have been doing Saturday afternoon and evening, Sunday afternoon, and all the morning of today, I will start this letter. Have been studying a complicated and difficult abstract of title to real estate and preparing an opinion as to validity of the title. Your letter came today and in it you ask what sort of an isolationist I am. I think in the discussions that are now being put before the public the term "isolationist" has a very nebulous meaning. The term as formerly understood has been corrupted to include a much wider sphere than it used to include.

I believe a republican form of government is the best devised so far. Some people believe that kingdoms are best. Apparently some believe that dictators whose word is law can operate best. I believe that we should have the privilege of choosing our own form of government. Having that belief, I necessarily believe that all other peoples should have that same privilege. Therefore, I have no wish to impose a republic on any other government. (Germany, Italy, and Japan are eliminated from this discussion by the war, of course.)

I have no wish, nor do I think it would be proper for me, to impose my will upon nations which now hold other nations subject in any effort to secure for such subject nations what I consider to be a better form of government. I may be wrong from the point of view of the subject nations. They may like their present forms of government. Even if they don't, I am not a god to dispose of peoples by the application of force to make their situation conform to my idea of what is good for them—no more than I would make them conform to moral code by the application of force.

We have a good moral code in the Bible. I think it is the best code that could be devised. It emanates from God, but is not to be imposed by force but by education and belief—that is, by the conscience of the individual. Where the individual has no conscience imposing the code in various of its more serious aspects upon him, he must be restrained for the safety of the people with whom he associates. So with nations.

As long as a nation does not follow a course which threatens us in our association with it, I am an isolationist with reference to the control of that nation. It is going about its own business. If it threatens us, I am still an isolationist with reference to that nation and will have no dealings with it save such as will remove the threat presented by it.

I live among people and deal with them. . . . They are restrained by force. If I trust the efficacy of the code they follow, my business dealings are those of an isolationist who relies solely on a moral code.

If I do not trust a man, my dealings are hedged about with the greatest of care and the most meticulous safeguards that I can devise under the circumstances so that he may not enforce an unfair settlement from me—a settlement by law. I try to take no advantage of him and permit him to take no advantage of me. I deal with him also as an isolationist, though I may live within a block or less of him and associate with him from day to day. I would like to win him over to my way of thinking through the Bible, church, etc., but I do not fight him if I can't.

Every man is an isolationist in his private affairs—almost. We do have associates, a few of them, whom we think more of than we do of ourselves. You know how it is with a mother, and your mother in particular. With these people we are not isolationists.

As with individuals, so with nations. One nation can deal with another. Its people can fly back and forth to nations the world over. Not all its people can fly at one time, but if planes ever become plentiful enough, every person could hope to visit some other country—hope to save enough money to buy a plane ticket. People of one country could trade with people of other nations, if they have confidence in the integrity of one another, knowing that, whether confidence existed or not, contracts would be difficult to enforce. Likewise, a nation could make contracts or treaties with other nations, knowing full well that if either violated the contract, enforcement would not exist unless the wronged nation thought it worth while to enforce it by arms.

I am not an isolationist in the sense that I want to cut off all contact with other nations. I want their sugar, coffee, tin, rubber, and many other things. Your mother at least would like to visit some of them, and that means I would like to do so too. I want our nation to be friendly with other nations—to live up to its contracts entered into in a constitutional way—to harm no other nation—to remain a republic and not become a democracy or empire. I see no reason why an international court could not be erected by agreement of nations with a code of laws dealing with international trade contracts, contracts which involve nothing in the nature of sovereignty—a court to which the member nations bind their people to submit their disputes with peoples of member nations—a court to which they may bind themselves to submit their disputes arising out of treaty or otherwise, provided sovereignty be not involved—a court which would depend for its power upon reason and not force.

Such a court, as it seems to me, is possibly the first organization which could be safely set up as a step toward a better understanding among nations.

An international police force to which any nation would be subject would be abhorrent to me. It would eventually destroy us, of course. An international police force whereby my nation would try to enforce its will upon other nations is abhorrent to me. We would be but a part of an empire so long as the police force was not itself destroyed by a greater power. "He who lives by the sword, dies by the sword." That last statement contains a thought expressed by One who is above all men, as you know. I believe it to be true.

Yet, I believe that man must defend himself against aggression. So with nations. We live in a world which occasionally becomes aggressive. So long as nations and their people want to pick a fight, we must be armed, we must be friends with powerful nations whether we like them or not, and we must do our best to be ready to defend ourselves whatever nation or set of nations may threaten us. I thought for a time after the last war that the nations of the world could be led to peace by a slow process involving a gradual disarmament and a properly constituted court. The world was not ready for that—is probably not ready now. Just another combination of nations to control the world seems to me to have not the slightest merit. It has been tried for centuries—and failed.

These thoughts expressed in this letter are not well-ordered—in fact hardly connected. I have written hurriedly and made no effort to create an ordered presentation. If you have time, you may correct the grammar, put the sentences in their proper order and paragraphs, and see what they amount to. Maybe nothing.

Mother is better—was down to breakfast and lunch and expects to be down to supper. Alice E. cooked the dinner yesterday and washed the dishes. I was at church and Sunday school and spent the afternoon in the office working. Your mother has been gracious enough to say that I have been a good nurse, cook, and housekeeper, but maybe she is afraid I will quit if she doesn't brag on me. We couldn't get a trained nurse. I am dead tired of my own cooking. I know no news. . . .

February 12, 1944

I don't remember whether the last letter from you came this week or last, but in it you gave the impression that you were cheerfully tracking a job of the kind you want and had no doubt you would find it—and I have had the same freedom from doubt. However, when you get the job let us know. In the meantime, it may be that you are running short of money. Your mother, as you know, still has some of your money in her bank account, and you should feel free to call on her for your needs. I have only one suggestion. Don't let bills accumulate. Life is too short to be worried by bills and they do worry one when they become overdue.

In my religious thought, I try to combine common sense with faith. Faith is wonderful in its strengthening power. It has strength to bring out of a man what good there is in him—to make him worthwhile to his associates and incidentially to himself. Religion, in my common sense (I think "common sense") view, is to find practical application in a man in the conduct and feeling of the man to others. The good which comes to the man is purely incidental and not the motive. In my view faith does not protect a man from his follies. If he seeks to oppose a natural law, that is, a law of God, he takes the punishment. If he jumps off a high place he is hurt. If he seeks to oppose another kind of natural law, that is, a law of God, he is hurt, regardless of his faith. Among the natural laws are those which require the exemplification of the human moralities in the life of the believer, that is, industry, integrity, kindness, and so on, and the disregard of the consequences in so far as the consequences will affect the believer himself. If he exemplifies the human virtues as the result of his belief, the consequences will find expression in the salvation of the soul. If he disregards these natural or God-given laws, his disregard will result in the staining of his soul. I have never been able to take the view that faith was the only element essential to the development of the soul. In other words, my thought is that a believer is not at all self-centered. Of any other view, what I think is common sense, says it is purely a selfish idea. Therefore, faith which results in a concentration on self is not a true faith. In expressing these views, I do so with the reservation that what I think is common sense may in truth be something else. I do not believe that faith is an end to itself. Therefore, church work is valuable for the purpose of furnishing a period of rest from the very powerful influence of the physical things of life and an opportunity for a close contemplation of the Divine—communion with God as it were. Church work has other values in itself, but to me it is not an end but a renewal, as it were. However, I haven't the time to go any farther with this. What it really gets down to, I think, is that a true faith brings its own rewards in conduct and the resulting growth and development of the individual—this as the result of the obedience to the law of God.

We are very well. Dirk won't blow his nose or have help from a doctor. His nose is always choked, and he sticks around in the house. He is with us until Monday night. Jim is in Mattoon until Sunday afternoon. Alice E. went to Fort Knox . . . and plans to return Monday afternoon. The dog (Butch) is with us for the weekend. I know no other news. . . . Am still hoping you come home for a while.

July 3, 1944

I suppose the letters from your mother and Alice E. have told you all the news of any importance that has happened since you left—the beautiful cool weather when a rain is badly needed—that mother spent quite a busy day Saturday in her flower garden, mostly there by the lawn chairs, and as a result it has a well-kept appearance. This morning we got up a bit early, shortened the porch table, and moved most of the furnishings into the dining room. She expects to scrub and varnish three-fourths of the floor this morning.

I suppose you know that Jim and I took Saturday afternoon off for fishing. We had a good but hurried lunch at home. Jim got the worms out of the box while I attended to the equipment—two rods and reels and two cane poles, the former for cork and minnows for bass, and the latter for worms and catfish. Then, shortly after one o'clock, with all the necessary equipment including net and minnow bucket, we set out to try to find minnows. At the first hopeful stop there was a "Keep Out" sign. At the second, a hog wallow just below the road and the water still tainted from a hog wallow about a quarter of a mile above the road. However, we tried hard and with much energy above the road—result four minnows, some exposure to poison oak, and *we* pretty well discouraged and somewhat tired. At the third stop there was too much water and great growth of weeds and brush along the edges. So we gave up and bought 50¢ worth of small croppie minnows in the hope that a bass might be too hungry to care whether his dinner was big or little. Then on to the Rocks. The river was not too high, but from some unknown cause is still murky, perhaps from hog wallows along the creeks. You know we drink the river water after it has been more or less purified and plan to dam the river for a permanent sufficient supply. The mental association of hog wallows with our drinking water is still a bit disquieting, even after the process of purification is given full weight by the contemplative mind.

At the Rocks, loaded down with fishing equipment, including a heavy minnow bucket, we proceeded—slipping and sliding down the steep, baked-clay path or trail through the poison ivy—the bank baked and steep almost to the river's edge, past various women and one old man fishing, getting reports of failure everywhere, no fish—just minnows eating the bait and so on down the river until we passed all the fishermen and came to a rock—a big one longfallen from the cliff above where it looked as if fish could be caught, if fish there were; and there we baited our hooks—two with minnows and two with worms. After losing various worms to the little fishes and various minnows by their untimely deaths, I caught an eight-inch bass on a worm but had to throw him back. He was not ten inches long. After that, nothing—except to feed the little fishes until Jim said it was time for our supper. I didn't have my watch but his stomach kept good time and we lugged our stuff back to the car and got the lunch—all put up by Alice E. . . . It was a good one: tomatoes grown at 820 6th for Jim; cookies for Jim and me; milk and four kinds of sandwiches—bacon, jam, peanut butter, and cheese. Then being much refreshed we took our equipment along the faint trail up the river. There we fished in a likely spot, and fished and fished. Small fishes were there also, keeping our bait more or less stripped, till at length Jim yelled he had a fish, and as he yelled and as I looked, and perhaps as he turned to look at me, the fish which I saw—about 12 inches long and of the tribe of bass—gave a mighty flop, dangled there in the air, broke loose from the restraining hook and plunged into the welcoming bosom of the river. After that we merely fed the little fishes until it was time to go home a little before eight o'clock—Jim not tired at all, and I completely worn out.

Yesterday, Sunday, was a quiet day. Sunday school and church for me, church for Mommie, dinner downtown and good long naps after dinner. . . . Later in the evening we ate a meagre supper and Mommie called on Alice E. while I listened to the radio. For a short time I played and lost solitaire, and as I started to go to bed at 9 o'clock, the *Hour of Charm* came on and for half an hour the music was of the best. As it finished, Mommie came home and so the day ended.

Your cards have been interesting and your mother expects to number them as they come. We have not yet heard from you after you reached Fort Oglethorpe.

July 8, 1944

Your address came in today and the break in letters from home will probably stop. In the meantime your interesting letters, written either by moonlight or while you sat on the floor near that infernal made-up bed, came in regularly and were enjoyed by the three of us. They sure show that you have the proper spirit to make a good soldier, and that is very important. I felt sure you would. . . .

We are all well. Your mother has kept herself busy this week and about has everything in shape so that she may have some leisure to enjoy—if perchance she can enjoy leisure at all. She wrote you of her treatment of the back porch. Well, the second coat of varnish was dry last night so I spent a couple of hours on it and got it waxed in good shape. The furniture will go back tonight. It was a nuisance to be off the porch, but we were off only from Monday breakfast until this morning, and you ought to see it shine!

Jim came down about dark yesterday and got himself a pole and some worms. He planned to go to the college lake about 4:30 this morning and catch himself some fish. He hadn't reported when I left home after breakfast, but when I got home at noon, I found he had reported to Mommie shortly after I left. He had caught several fish which he thought it unlawful to keep because of their size, and one good-sized perch or blue gill or croppie which he had cleaned nicely and brought down for me. Mommie, of course, told him to take it home for Dirk and himself. Dirk came in while I was eating canned salmon and wanted to stay for lunch. He asked me if I was eating the fish Jim caught. I told him his mother was cooking that for Jim and him, and he went out like a shot, not stopping for the courtesies due the occasion.

There is little news here. Have had no real use for an office girl since you left. Law business is not pressing at all, and little has had to be done about appeals in draft cases. Have shifted half of them to Wayne Shuey and have contented myself with a very short formal statement for the Government Appeal Agents' statement to the Appeal Board. . . .

July 15, 1944

I have nothing newsy to write about—just feel like having a chat with you to let you know that we appreciate and enjoy your letters. They contain a good picture of your present activities and life in all details, and by reason of the complete change from your ordinary course of living and habits and customs, we are inclined to think that it will keep you on your toes constantly to get through five weeks of preliminary training without 20 gigs. Nevertheless, we think you will make it.

When I was young a gig meant a fork (I have forgotten whether it had two or three prongs), and the Kentucky use was to take one out at night when the suckers were running the riffles in the creek and gig as many as possible by impaling them on the tines of the gig. I never had the opportunity to try the sport. Have forgotten whether it was forbidden by law or that we were not permitted to go out at night to the creek during the years when the urge to gig was upon us. The, gig of course, had a long wooden handle—almost as long as a hoe handle, and a lantern had to be carried so that the fish could be seen. It was said to be great sport—for the men and not for the poor fish. You apparently, with all beginning soldiers, are the poor sucker at the wrong end of the gig. But such is Army life, and you went in prepared to take it and like it and we do not doubt that you will do so.

The office has been dead—more so than is usual even for July and August. They were always the poor months. Our fishing vacations, as you know, came in July and I never felt that the office was missing me much, but there is no incentive to plan a trip. Train travel is inconvenient and unpleasant, and to be at place of vacation without a car is not to be contemplated with any pleasant anticipations. The Ozark play country is about 500 miles away and I have no doubt it is filled up by vacationists from the more or less immediate neighborhood—people who ordinarily would go elsewhere for vacations.

Your mother and I are doing fine here at home. Except for the excessive heat of the days—not the nights—we have a real pleasant spot at 820 Sixth and it would be hard to find a better within auto striking distance. "Starved Rock" is of course not too far away, but it may be overflowed or in the Army now. If we, at any time, conclude that a vacation is called for, we will probably learn what the conditions are at Starved Rock.

Harold has come and gone. His visit was satisfactory in every way and he is well, as are Alice E. and the children. When they were out of town, Butch adopted us and our home, as is usual with him. Last night he went with us to the Frazier Cafe (near the fire hall) and waited at the door for us. Mrs. Frazier gave us a big knuckle bone for him. It was so big that it rather discouraged Butch and he was not much interested in it and left it in our back yard. No other dog seemed to have disturbed it during the night. Of course there was very little meat on it. Mr. Holmes, who was eating at the cafe, went out while Butch was at the door. Jim Holmes is fond of dogs and understands them—and they him—so he stopped and made friends with Butch—did it quite easily. Butch enjoyed it even though Holmes was a stranger. . . .

As I said, I have no news to tell you and this letter has therefore been uninteresting. Still, I have had the pleasure of a chat with you. Lots of love.

July 18, 1944

I suppose you really haven't the time to decipher a letter in my handwriting, and so I resort to the typewriter, hoping that I will not make so many mistakes that this, too, will be difficult. There is little news—just the ordinary run of home and town life. I have been out to the farms lately. Mommie went with me Saturday after supper to the Ashmore farm. We found no one at home at Mr. Woodyard's place except the dog. He was keeping guard, I suppose, but very lonesome and very anxious for company. He welcomed me in the best dog manner, invited me to stick around awhile, and distinctly and attractively expressed his disappointment at my going. The drouth there is severe, as it is at all the places. The crops there were of necessity planted late. They are taking the drouth in good part as yet and have not become discouraged, nor do they seem to be hurrying too much to produce their seeds. Perhaps they are still sending their roots down trying to find the moisture. I am hopeful that they will not be too much hurt.

I went out on the prairie Sunday afternoon after a nap of an hour. It was hot and I did not even invite your mother to go along. However, she was still sleeping when I left home and I would not have wakened her anyway. At the Hudson place I walked out into the field. The crops there are the earliest we have. Some of the corn is just beginning to send out its tassels. Some of the beans are just beginning to form their blossoms. All will be doing so very soon. As I understand, when those things happen the plants have decided that in view of the circumstances and after due reflection it is necessary that they get busy on seed production. I reckon they take into consideration the date of planting, the probable frost-due date, and all other things which plants of their nature find important, and then act upon their best judgment. Therefore, the crops at Hudson's are probably through growing, and the beans at least are not tall enough to produce the ordinary heavy crop which that farm usually delivers.

From the Hudson place I drove to the Sears 60, and walked out into the field. The oats had been combined. That was merely a cover crop for the ten acres of sweet clover planted for fertilization. This was the first cover crop of small grain I had planted since the heavy infestation of chinch bugs some years back, and as it turned out, chinch bugs are plentiful this year. However, only a thin planting of oats was sowed and the corn which we had on both sides of the oats seems not to have suffered any important damage from the bugs from our oats. However, the ten acres on the west side of the oats has, to about half of its width, been rather seriously damaged by bugs from the oats field of the neighbor just over the line. The corn on that place was later planted than Hudson's because at planting season there was more heavy rain, but still it is making preparation to put out tassels. I do not think there will be any tall corn in this neighborhood, nor is anyone yet able to estimate or guess with any particular reason back of his guess as to whether the shortness of the stalk will lower production of corn. As to the beans, it seems a fair guess that when the blossoms come, the crop is limited by the height of the plant. The Sears beans are not as tall as Hudson's, still they are beginning to blossom. They are way back in the field and cannot be seen from the road. Haven't heard what the oats crop produced, but it was merely a cover crop, planted thin, and nothing was expected. Yet it was harvested and there will be some return—maybe enough to pay the taxes on the 60 acres.

From the Sears place, after a visit with the Sears family, I drove to the Lowry 40, got out at the edge of the beans and looked it over from the roadside, and—at the edge of the corn—looked that over also. These crops are late also and small. They look good, are clean and have a good color, as do the crops on all the places. As the Lowry 40 was late planted there is no formation of blossoms on the beans or tassels on the corn. The Lowry family had had a reunion that day. The boy was home on furlough—probably the one allowed just before shipment abroad—and his grandmother and grandfather had been brought up from a considerable distance (I have forgotten the name of the town), some other relatives had come, and all of Lowry's considerable family had been there. When I was there, they had all gone to take the grandfather and grandmother home except the soldier, whom I met as he went to the pasture to bring the cows in and milk them, and one of the girls who was at the home. This is the family in which the nine-year-old boy drove the tractor pulling the disc some this year and in which all of the girls and the mother help when the need is pressing.

Mother and I went to the picture show last night. It was a comedy and we enjoyed it. The comedian was new to me and I have forgotten his name, and

I do not believe I ever heard the name of the play. Tonight we have the birthday dinner at the Country Club. This is the third, I believe, that we have had. There are three couples concerned: the Greers, the Hites, and the Kellys. Each family invites two guests thus making a party of 12. One dinner was in February; I think that was the one for the Greers; then one in the spring for the Hites (or vice versa). Each of the three families pays one-third of the cost. Tonight, however, we are varying the program somewhat, for the Hites will have their daughter-in-law, and we will have Alice E. to the dinner. They will not return to our house for the card game, but will be on their own when they get back to town.

Well, this letter ran on for a considerable length without telling anything of particular interest. I do know that your suitcase came in and Mommie has unpacked it. I do know that I seem to be planning a fishing trip in the Lake of the Woods neighborhood, perhaps on the Canadian side—as I estimate the distance about a thousand miles from here—with Ed Taylor and his son, late in August and early in September. There seemed to be a conspiracy to get me away from home for a while and the power of the conspiracy, together with the lure of the bait offered, was more than I could resist. I don't believe I have ever taken a vacation without your mother and think this will be a new experience. There seems always something new happening to a fellow as he passes along the road of life. It will be lots of fun thinking about in advance and getting fishing equipment in order. That surely will take about a month as my equipment has been deteriorating since our last trip north, and inquiries will have to be made as to the proper outfit of clothes and fishing equipment for fishing at Lake of the Woods. Charley Miller has been there two or three times and can put me wise.

July 22, 1944

The enclosed letter, envelope, and receipt or notice of premium due Travelers Accident Ins. came addressed to you and was opened by me through mistake. Just didn't look at the address. If it is a receipt, return it to me and I will put it away. If it is merely notice to pay, I wonder if you should keep up the insurance in view of the fact that you now have your government insurance. I don't believe I would now use $5 on accident insurance if I were you. If you want me to send the $5, I will do so.

I have the receipt for your bond buy and will put it away the next time I am at the bank. There is little news. It is still dry and beautiful weather. The last two days there has been a breeze from the north and the nights have been quite cool. In fact, it was 62 on the porch yesterday morning and we ate in the kitchen at breakfast. Have had a blanket over us for several nights.

It was so nice and cool yesterday that before noon the idea hit me that Jim and I should go fishing at the hole near the bridge on the South Ashmore road, and while we were at lunch the idea hit Jim that he and I should go fishing. So he called me and we arranged to go at three o'clock. He told me not to let Dirk know anything about it. However, I let mother know and, in view of the weather condition and because I knew she would enjoy it, I invited her to go. As it turned out, we went to the dam. Alice E. went along. Dirk went along. Butch went along. I knew there would be no fishing of the slightest importance at the dam. It's too easy to reach and too much used. But a fine lunch went along also: hot coffee, bacon and eggs to fry, cheese, ginger cake, bananas, tomatoes—all eaten out on the sandbar and with few flies to bother. So as a picnic, the trip was fine (except for Butch), but as a fishing trip it was a failure. Mother thinks she slept through the night without moving and could hardly get her eyes open at breakfast time. That was the result of climbing up and down the steep bank to get from river to bridge a number of times and the use of all the muscles used in garden work and all other muscles as well. (I don't know what is the matter with the ribbon on this machine nor how to make it behave, but have pulled out that plug or button on the right side of the machine.)

I really have no news this morning and don't seem to be wide awake yet myself, so will bring this letter to a close. Your letters are the most interesting things in our lives at present, but don't write when it is really hard for you to do so.

P.S. I put the $8.00 and $13.10 checks to my credit and when you have $100, I will start your bank account.

July 27, 1944

Will try to write so that reading will not be too difficult. Your mother is canning applesauce this morning and won't have time to write today. She still finds something to do each day causing her to be well-worn by night. Alice E. and I lectured her last night.

The drouth has been broken and the farmers are much encouraged, though much damage has been done to both corn and beans. The second crop of chinch bugs is very large and scattered through the corn fields. It is dangerous. The farmer's life (financial) is uncertain—perhaps as uncertain as that of any business that makes any claim to be non-speculative.

Plans are slowly developing for the fishing trip. If we go, and Mr. Taylor and I think we will, there is much planning and preparation in the prospect—clothes—tackle—place to go, etc. Last night we had a session. The choice of place lies now between the Bemidji neighborhood and the

International Falls neighborhood. Both are in Minnesota. One bunch of Charleston people have been to one place and one to the other—both bunches enthusiastic. Bemidji is at the head of the Mississippi, and International Falls, as its name indicates, is on the Canadian border on the chain of lakes leading to Lake Superior. There are a thousand lakes near Bemidji—some large, some small. There are many lakes at the border—some large, some small. The lake we are considering near Bemidji is comparatively small. The one at International Falls is quite large. Both sections are in wild territory. The Paul Bunyan statue is at Bemidji. Where shall we go? What clothes shall we take—both winter and summer? What is the best official bait? The cottages at both places are modern—heat, water, gas, well-furnished. Their care is excellent, the fishing grand, as Charley Miller would probably put it.

At International Falls there are such large fish that you are liable to lose some of the equipment when one of that type strikes. The boats are wide, flat bottomed, 18 feet long—seaworthy when a squall comes up—with motor available to push them along. They are too heavy for successful use of the oars. The lake there is large and waves at times are high and would swamp lesser boats. I imagine that on the lake we are considering at Bemidji, the boats are smaller because the lake is smaller.

Well, fishing is not your job at present and you wish to know that we are all well—as we are. Mother had one quite satisfactory experience. She has been throwing stones and things all summer at squirrels and rabbits. Yesterday she had the experience of knocking a squirrel out of a tree with an apple. It didn't hurt the squirrel but was a very satisfactory experience for Mother. Her aim has been gradually improving, and the arm has more strength in the muscles necessary for the throwing than early in the summer. Perhaps with the skill acquired this year she can wage a successful war next.

But waging war against animal enemies of pears and garden truck is not your job at present. We had a dandy letter from you yesterday—all of your letters are interesting, exceedingly so. Yet we do not wish you to feel that you have to write when and if you are worn to a frazzle by your work there. So your line buckled during inspection. A long line sure buckles easily as it turns the corners. I don't know that in my so-called military training at college, where I rose to the rank of corporal, we ever had a line that didn't buckle in turning corners. It requires team work of a class which the ordinary college student of the late nineties was not disposed to give—in our college, and under the captain sent there to train us.

This letter has run on far too long without telling you any of the little details of family life. I have the feeling that mother and Alice E. tell you all that news. We had supper last night at the restaurant near the fire hall. It was very good.

August 1, 1944

Well, here it is Tuesday and nothing done yet this week. However, it is Fair Week and this is a Fair-minded community. The town gets more or less on the dead side along about 1 o'clock all the week. Yesterday afternoon I kept office in the heat with the only visitor being Butch. He came down with me, for Jim was under the weather from too much swimming or too careless eating or something else. Alice E. was also a bit under the weather and no one was available for Butch, as yesterday was Children's Day at the Fair and Dirk and your mother took in the show in the afternoon, going out in the Cavins' car along with Mr. Cavins, Jane and Susan. No doubt they had a great afternoon—saw the circus, the clowns, the elephants, the lions—including a six-weeks old baby lion—the horses, the acrobats, and all that goes to make a circus a circus. After that they saw a man milking a cow and witnessed a display of show farm animals and Dirk and Mommie had a fine ride on the merry-go-round, I think with Jane and Susan—that is, the four children rode.

In the meantime Butch slept and paced the afternoon away, occasionally urging me to go home, but sticking around faithfully until time to close. He didn't want to be at the office very much but knew of no other place where he would be able to find congenial company. He is said to have acquired a mess of fleas and I have been itching a good deal ever since, but really don't think I have fleas. I think it's just the chigger bites which I manage to keep in good store over summer—just seem to be more troublesome than they usually are when no thought of fleas intervenes.

Well, Dirk had supper with us last night and after a while Mommie took him home. He wanted her to stay, but she needed a rest and left him at his home comforting him with the suggeston that he get up this morning and come down in his pajamas to breakfast without waking his mother or Jim. He must have had the invitation on his mind—he usually sleeps until near nine—for as I shaved and just as your mother got up, he was at the door in his pajamas and with his bit of clothes in his hand, bright and cheery. But it was a little too early for his breakfast. He ate only an egg and went off to chat with Mr. Thomas whom he saw come out of the back door. (Dirk may have remembered, as he went to bed last night, the lions in the cage with their trainer—grudgingly and with growls and threats going through their show-paces.)

I spent an hour or two going over my fishing equipment last night. The fish are said to be big and plentiful, so it requires strong lines. I have bought two and got them on the reels last night. The pike have teeth so metal leaders are necessary, as the fishing is pike—not bass. Some of the northern pike there are so big that ordinary fishermen, such as Taylor and I are, cannot be expected to handle them, and some equipment will go to the big ones. The fish there like the artifical jointed pike-minnow, which seems to be a war casualty. We still hope to get a few, though hopes are not strong. I have bought a medium-deep-running wobbler but don't know whether the pike will care for that or not. I will have to look up some winter clothes and borrow Harold's leather jacket. It is some job to get ready for a fishing jaunt to the wilds of northern Minnesota. We don't know yet whether we can secure a cottage at this very wonderful place but Mr. Taylor has written trying to engage one. . . .

Mother has been busy. As you know, hers is a busy life—almost comparable, though not quite, to the life of a WAC in basic training. She will, nor can, take no rest here. Her Kentucky-Tennessee trip has simmered down to a train trip alone—I think first to the Fort (Fort Oglethorpe) and then back to Lexington and its surrounding relatives. She is so constituted that a visit among relatives is a vacation and restful, though it may consist largely of continuous activity.

There is really no news. Butch and I were the only ones who had time to write you yesterday, and I perhaps was too lazy, and Butch didn't know how. The burden of your failure to get a letter, therefore, falls squarely on my shoulders. You are in your fourth week of training. I hope your legs no longer complain or look upon you as a brute—that the worst of the training is over and especially that you have kitchen police not more than once more. We don't expect frequent letters from you, however much we enjoy your letters. Mommie has a good many tomatoes to can today and may have to take an appointment which Alice E. has at the beauty shop—this among her other tasks. So she has no hope of writing, and I rather suspect that Alice E. will find her duties plenty in her under-the-weather condition.

August 14, 1944

Just a line. I enclose application for ballot. This the only official form on which to make application. It is under state law, and the federal application is invalid in the state. You are registered in the name of Emma Chenault Kelly, and the application should be signed in that way. I do not know what your address will be by September 20, but you will probably know soon. The address to which you wish the ballot sent should, of course, be written-in on the application. At any rate, you may execute the application and have the ballot sent to your present address if you are sure your mail is to be forwarded when you are moved. You will mail the application to Elmer F. Elston, Clerk of the County of Coles, Charleston, Illinois.

I had Mother's two cards and letters this morning. In the meantime, I was concerned that she may have had to be in a crowded, hot coach all the way to Cincinnati, and possibly to Chattanooga. The mail was wonderful in the word it brought, both as to the trip, her condition, and your appearance of health and well-being.

There is no news here, except, of course, what Mommie told you. The fishing plans move on. I have plenty of artificial bait. It may not be just what the fish ordered or want, but in the absence of something more to their liking, they may find some of it attractive. I haven't the time to write you a letter just now. We expect to leave Mattoon at 4:15 Wednesday morning, leave Chicago at 10:40, leave St. Paul at 9:40 that night and reach International Falls—our train destination—at 9:20 the next morning. From the Falls we go to the lake, about 35 miles away. Either by bus to Ray where Mrs. Jap Carlyle, wife of the man from whom we buy gas here, will meet the bus; or it may be that she will meet the train at International Falls. My address will be in care of Rocky Reef Resort, and I would like hearing from you as you find time to drop me a line now and then. We are buying our train tickets and checking our heavy baggage today. Charley Miller and Sam Harper plan to take the train trip with us. They go on some farther from International Falls, west and north, to Lake of the Woods and into Canada. The lake we will be on is, I think, named Kabetogema (Kab-e-tog-e-ma, "a" as in cabin, "o" as in hope, with primary accent on "tog" and secondary on "Kab").

August 23, 1944

I haven't written a letter to anyone so far—just a few postals. There seems to be no time. Will have a lot to tell about the lake and our trip when I see you, but most of the details will have to keep. The lake and the surrounding country are beautiful. The many islands are wooded, and after I get on the far side of one of them, I am lost—don't know the way to go home. Many of the islands come down to the water in spots as sloping water-worn stones—a few cliffs also, some bogs along the lake shore but mostly sloping tree-and-bush-covered hillsides. This morning the three of us went straight across the lake—six miles at the point—and fished around an island on the far side. Mr. Taylor caught four nice walleyes and I caught one. Sonny didn't catch any. I let a nice one go, by trying to bring it over the boatside just by lifting with the rod. It fell off just before it got over the boat. That was plain laziness on my part. We had a sandwich in the boat and came back about 2 o'clock. Gave the fish to Mr. and Mrs. Wolf, who ran the northside drugstore and restaurant when you were in Charleston. He sold it because of his health—and his wife's—and they have been here for a couple of months. Found him on his dock (the next dock to the one belonging to the resort) with a string of northern pike two yards long. There must have been a dozen fish, the largest about forty inches long. They were glad to get the walleye as they are good eating. We have eight or ten on ice and have to get rid of fish. Think we will fish for big northern tomorrow—just for the fun.

Yesterday we took the long trip down or up the island with the proprietor—went about 30 miles up the lake behind a powerful motor at 30 miles an hour and fished there. A little after noon we stopped fishing because we had the limit (32 fish) and had to stop. Went to a wooded island and had our lunch—sandwiches and coffee from a thermos bottle—and came on home. Mr. Lynch (the proprietor) packed about 20 pounds of the fish on ice and they went out to Ray last night on the midnight train addressed to me at Charleston in care of Alice E. (I can send only 20 pounds and that has gone.) However, some were for Mrs. Taylor, and as he can send out 20 pounds, we hope to send a box when we start home.

Mr. Taylor and I had dinner today about 3:30—each had one side (fillet) of a pound-and-a-quarter fish, coffee, potatoes, and shredded wheat for dessert. I took a nap and Mr. Taylor went fishing by himself. He goes twice a day. . . . I am well; we all eat a lot. Haven't had any meat except bacon now and then. (Our red points will just about carry us through on butter.)

I lost my two best spinners this morning. Had only three, and the one I have left is not particularly attractive to fish in their present mood. By the way, our trip back for the 30 miles was rough. The waves had caps on them and came toward us. We met them at 30 miles an hour. The first half-hour was not so bad, but it got to be painful in spots. However, there were no ill results. The pains all vanished as soon as the boat got into the still water of the bay. We are out of touch with everything. Don't know even how the war is going. Alice E. wrote a letter last week. She was hoping Harold would get home for good Sunday. She enclosed mother's card written between Chattanooga and Lexington. Otherwise have not heard from her. Haven't been to town since we got into International Falls last Thursday.

Rochester, Minnesota
September 10, 1944

I have neglected you in writing, but have not written much to anyone. However, have written two or three letters to Mommie which I asked that she send to you, and so I suppose you know that we reached the lake without having sleeper accommodations and that I was pretty well worn-out. The lake was beautiful and full of islands. The water was high—said to be several feet higher than usual—and it was apparently so, for trees near the edges of islands and the lake borders were submerged several feet, and islands of bog held together by roots of grass, cattails and whatnot were floating around when winds were up—islands of considerable size in some cases. It was not possible to see much of the main shore on the northside of the lake across from our dock—just two or three short patches—the rest was all island shore. When the lights were right—shadows moving across the lake—they would pick out one by one the various islands they hit, clothing it in dark green while the island back of it in part was still in sunlight. Sometimes the far shore was bathed in sunlight while the islands near were in sunlight and shadows darkened the farthest islands. It was interesting to see islands separate themselves from others and assume an identity of their own.

Fishing in August is said never to be good and to pick up as September moves along; however, we had to give fish away—a good many—and wasted two or three after they had been steaked and put in the icebox. Could have caught many more but what was the use? True, the cottagers had to help make up our second 20 pounds to send home, but we had helped others in the same circumstance, and nobody had to do without fish as often as they wanted to eat it.

Also, we would have caught many more fish and probably wasted many more as well except that Mr. Taylor and his son were intent on catching big northern pike by casting. They worked at it faithfully by casting—said here to be the wrong way—day after day, and on the last Monday, all day. They brought in the three largest they had caught, and we ate the smallest of the three and sent the others home in the box. They were only about 26 inches long. I had caught several that size and had not even brought them back. I gave them the last Monday and reserved the right to do the directing on Tuesday so that we might catch enough walleyes for our box. Monday was perfect for fishing. Tuesday was windy and fishing was hard. Nevertheless, I found where the fish were biting three times, but they insisted that we go elsewhere and elsewhere we went. So it went through the vacation. I fished with them in the morning except for three days when we took our lunch. They fished in the afternoons as well day after day. Still I caught about as many as either of them. On the trip up the lake with the proprietor, I watched his method of fishing and tried to copy it. He caught 15 to Mr. Taylor's three, Sonny's six and my eight. I also copied it in my fishing after that, and it brought results. It also served to prevent the hook getting stuck on the bottom. The Taylors were stuck four or five times to my once. However, this is just for your perfect understanding of the trip and you are to destroy this letter and not repeat the information. Your mother does not yet know.

After the first all-day trip I took, I decided not to do it again. It was too hard. Still I "fell" twice more, and each time was not home till 7 or after in the evening. The last day—Saturday before leaving—was the worst, as was Sunday. I ate a big meal cooked by the proprietress which included raw vegetables, a rich cake, meat, etc., and thereafter was no good. So I decided to run down here (Mayo's) and take the examinaton which I would probably do later anyway.

Came down to St. Paul Wednesday night, and after coffee and toast hurriedly eaten, just caught the train for this town and got here at noon. Immediately registered and had my date fixed for next Thursday with the possibility of having date moved up and orders to call the next day to find out. It was moved up to Tuesday, but I have orders to come back Monday afternoon at 3:30 in the hope of starting then. In the meantime I am loafing, sleeping, eating, and walking. Saw the picture "Mark Twain" yesterday and went to the Christian Church today for Sunday school and morning service.

It is a small church—small attendance also—about one-quarter of the attending were out-of-town people whose names were read and each asked to stand as the name was called. The town is full of hotels and hospitals and out-of-town people, with the clinic and its building dominating the whole.

The building is beautiful, quite tall, and above is a dome with light serving as a beacon for the transport of airplanes that pass over—many of them; and high up is a set of carillon bells played mechanically at certain hours and after hours operated by a musician. The building is perfectly adapted to its purpose and the big crowds are handled with precision and dispatch, the papers of a patient preceding him from one appointment to another, not by messenger but by conduits set inside the walls. Most of the force met at the counters and on the elevators are girls, each knowing her own job and each seeming to have had voice culture, so that if she must make herself heard in a room, she need not raise her voice but merely deepen it to carry as far as needed—somewhat the voice of an actor. The clinic is a big business. The building was erected in 1912.

I was pleased with your letters and the spirit they showed. Never lose that spirit. Take what comes with chin up and a sense of humor. Don't take much chance with drinking, especially while in the Army. Wait until you are your own man again. It's too dangerous any time to monkey with, and especially in the Army. Alice E. was good enough to slip a bottle of whiskey in my grip for emergencies, and I certainly appreciated her doing so. Still, I could not drink it, nor could Ed. I did take three drinks and he one. The aftereffect was bad each time, so I got a cottager to help me out. He was the best-humored fisherman I ever saw and was called Pete. He was 51 years of age and had only five years to go to retirement. He loves to hunt and fish. We flagged him down once when the waves were pretty high and against us as we rowed about a mile from home after our motor had died; he towed us in. So I had an excuse for asking him to the cottage and one of my drinks was taken with him then, and I called him in again before he left. He took a hearty drink and one only was left in the bottle. I took that the Saturday I got back to the cottage after my last all-day trip.

Well, this letter has run on at great length and told little but perhaps too much. I am sleeping well, eating well and feel much refreshed. Will gain by the rest if nothing else. Also hope to find out what my diet should be. . . . You will make good in your public relations assignment.* I have no fear about that.

September, 1944
(Exact date unknown)

I got to Mattoon at 1:30 yesterday afternon, and having wired your mother from Chicago, found Harold, Alice E., Jim, Dirk and your mother at the station waiting for the train. Harold had business to attend to, and the others went with me to Buckler's where I had my lunch and they had their dessert. I felt very much honored that they all came, and the reception would have been perfect had you been along. I am going to really answer some of your letters some day—not as a duty but as a pleasure. Don't plan to do much of anything for a while as a duty. Your mother also says that she is going to do very little from a sense of duty so long at least as *I* work on that plan.

You want, of course, to know what the result of the clinical examination was. It turned out practically as I had hoped and suspected it would. My organs are in somewhat better shape than is usual in men of my age. I *must*, and this is important, put on some flesh. I must also cut down considerably on my office work, at least until I can assume and carry on work without taking it to bed with me and sleeping with it. I should resign as Government Appeal Agent and as chairman of Military Affairs Committee of Illinois State Bar Association for Cole County. I need no operation at the present time but should have an examination every year or two. My pains very probably come from adhesions left from peritonitis which followed the bursting of the appendix. That occurred almost fifty years ago when I was strong, of course, and I lived through it, but adhesions were left, etc., etc. The pains are, therefore, of no particular importance or significance.

We plan that my office hours will be from 9 to 12 and 2 to 4, and I will drop all income tax work which I can get out of. Also for a time will take on no heavy responsibility, at least until I pick up weight and strength. Your mother and I may go picnicing or fishing when we feel like it, do what we

*Emma C. now at air force training camp, Bainbridge, Ga.

please and when we please. This morning about 10, we drove out on the prairie, looked at crops, ate our lunch at the roadside and came home and took naps.

7:40 p.m. We have now had supper—baked chicken with all the trimmings—chicken the best cooked and tenderest I ever ate. Mr. and Mrs. Thomas came over and brought their dessert and ours, a wonderful blueberry pie with ice cream. We sat around the table and talked until now, and it's almost time to go to bed, so I will not make this a letter but only a note. Mommie is sitting here and starting to read the *Tribune*.

September 22, 1944

Your special of the 21st just came in. Surely you have heard by this time that nothing of real importance is the matter with me. The substance of the thing is this. I am 66 years old with vital organs in better shape than most men of that age, not needing an operation or medicine. Am badly run down—below par. . . . All I need is to cut my office hours down, take no work carrying much responsibility for the affairs of others (that is, nothing I could find an excuse for thinking and worrying about after I leave the office or at night when I should be sleeping), eat a lot, pick up about ten pounds, and I will find myself in trim for complete occupation of business hours.

In following the advice I received, I have cut my office hours to five, tendered my resignation as Government Appeal Agent and as chairman of the east side of the county of the Military Affairs Committee of the State Bar Association, declined employment by the City to bring and conduct condemnation suits to condemn land for the river lake the City proposes to build, am eating three fairly large meals a day and waking up hungry in the mornings. Think I have already gained a pound or two. Also, I was advised to cut out much of the cigarette smoking and take up the pipe, so I have cut my cigarette allowance to three to five a day, and smoke a pipe some but not very much. We are going to bed early and I am sleeping better. That is a good thing for your mother also, and I think the three good meals will help her as well. She promises, and is doing her best to keep the promise, to slow down her own activities.

Your work for the paper has been really good. You write well, in a light vein, and what you have to say is of the type to interest people generally, and I have no doubt, to be of interest to Army people especially. I don't think I exaggerate to say you are good. I imagine you are following the best course by proceeding as you are, doing what you find worthwhile to do, helping with the morale building work as a volunteer, going into officers training if it seems to come your way without too much effort, doing the private's job wherever you are put, etc. Mother and I both would regret if you are completely removed from your newspaper work. We think you shine there and that experience there will be of great importance to you after the war. Still, we don't know what you had best do and your own judgment is good and worth relying on. Office work without stenography is, in most offices, more or less part-time employment, but it may not be so in the Army. We have enjoyed what you have written. Haven't got around to sending your painting equipment but reckon we will soon.

Mother and Alice E. are in Mattoon today. Had my lunch downtown, went home, and slept an hour. Butch has come to the office with me and is sleeping on the floor. When I went home, found that Mommie had put up five pints of canned apples this morning. Apples have taken on dignity in my estimation. Poor ones cost a nickel each at the store near the lake and in the restaurants at International Falls, and in Rochester a tablespoon of applesauce or canned apples cost 20¢. They are also $3.25 a bushel here, and so they have become of high standing in my view.

Mommie and I went to Fox Ridge Lake to fish Wednesday afternoon but did not have a bite. Several boats were cruising around trying one bait or lure after another—but no fish, no bites. Am to take Jim out tomorrow afternoon and am extremely anxious that he catch a bass. He has been a faithful fisherman at the college and for small fish all summer and deserves to catch a real fish—for encouragement if nothing else.

To write an editorial is something else yet. Politics is out in the Army; most public questions are political in their nature now. Business and its management are much concerned in politics. Farming has its close touch with politics. Religion is a matter with which Government is not empowered to interfere. Any Army matters and the method to be followed to win the war the quickest and easiest way with less cost in men, etc., are beyond my ken. About what may I write an editorial? I suppose one could write a very good editorial concerning the advisability of the general public taking a humorous view of the serious vein in which most editorials are written, but one of my two afternoon office hours is now gone, and there is a little I should do here before I go home. Therefore, while there is no "must" in my scheme of life, I am closing.

September 26, 1944

Having cut my office hours to five and taking more exercise after hours, I find that I have little time at the office to write letters and am pretty sleepy shortly after supper. So though I have been intending to write to you for a couple of days, just haven't got to it before. You would be surprised at the peace of mind attained by divesting myself of considerable responsibility and changing my habits slightly—resulting in large appetite satisfied three or four times a day. Yesterday afternoon when I closed the office at 4, I took a chocolate milkshake and at midnight a shredded wheat with cream. Was hungry both times.

Two things have contributed—less responsibility, or rather sense of responsibility, and fewer cigarettes. I smoke four or five cigarettes a day—sometimes three. What other times I want to smoke I try to keep a pipe going. Result of pipe efforts: yesterday one pipe and half a folder of matches finished in the three office hours before noon and almost a pipe and the rest of the matches in the two hours after noon. I plainly see why the pipe is best for health. I think I have put on a pound or two since getting home. Mommie too is profiting by the well-ordered meals and her own determination to take things easier. But enough of this. Your mind may be at rest about us.

Harold is in Massachusetts for the week. Jim and Mommie and I hope to go fishing at Fox Lake tomorrow. It's the last day fishing will be open there.

Your mother and I think you have found your proper activity. What you choose to write about is well chosen. The language you use is well chosen—both topic and form tending to arouse and keep the interest of the reader. Homely topics and homely language are nearer the hearts of people than any others and homely language—not the language of pedants, or scholars for that matter—is the best garment in which to clothe the topic. You, we think, will be—indeed are—excellent in choice of both topic and language. Even if the Army puts you to doing something else, keep this in mind and maybe from time to time you will find opportunity to express your thought as you have been doing.

I still have no editorial to write. Indeed I have no topic in mind. Perhaps if you could suggest a topic I could try my hand at it, but I know of no reason why anything I might do as a writer of an editorial would be of value as a sample to follow.

October 8, 1944

I have been thinking about this "editorializing" and am not much in favor of it. Somehow, I have got the impression that the specific subject mentioned is taboo in Army circles. While I may have a vague impression for which there may be not the slightest basis, still the impression exists that in the Army there is more or less an indoctrination course which permeates the Army atmosphere or the atmosphere of Army life relative to the subject mentioned. In the practice of law, once in a while, in jury trials, I have got the impression that an entire courtroom and its occupants have been permeated or inoculated with the thought that there should be a conviction, or that there should be an acquittal. I have the same kind of impression about the Army, and if the impresion is well-founded in fact, one who might seek to overturn habit or custom or unanimity of thought would probably find himself in difficulty of one kind or another.

There is no news. We are all well. The weather is beautiful today after quite an extended period of gloomy weather.

October 11, 1944

I suspect that some of the slowness in mail delivery to you (if not all) has been caused by my jumping to the conclusion that you were to be addressed at the Public Relations office. The express package was so sent as well as the German book, the letter which I forwarded from New York which I thought was from Dr. Lordi,* and other letters. I understand now that your address was unchanged and your mail should reach you in apt time. . . .

There is no news with us. . . . I am doing fine. Have weighed once since getting home and showed a five-pound gain.

Hudson is harvesting the bean crop on time. It is a good crop. In spite of the unfavorable weather for planting and the drouth, his crop will run close to par. It is on our best land and has the best bean crop on it that we have this year. Nothing else of ours is yet being harvested, but I have seen all the crops. All corn crops are badly spotted both by planting and growing conditions and by bugs. I can't make an estimate of any of the fields but all will be well below par. The remaining beans are all short and production will be short. Still, they will probably support us for a year. I went out to the Ashmore farm Sunday afternoon during Dirk's birthday party and after my nap. Walked over some of the fields and then went to the Ashmore pond and, using a plug (artificial bait) and casting from the bank, spent an hour trying to catch a fish but had no luck. Some men fishing there with cane poles and minnows had caught a few croppies.

Mrs. Kenyon drove into town yesterday afternoon on her way to California and we called on her last night at Taylor's. There were a good many people there and I didn't get to talk to her or hear her talk, for the men sat and talked together at one end of the room while the women had their assembly at the other. Your mother, however, should know the news. I was

*Emma C.'s landlord in New York City.

through breakfast when she got down today and haven't heard anything. Mrs. Kenyon looks fine and young and seems in good spirits. She has run into some hitch about gas and will be around until she gets the gas situation straightened out. If she doesn't get it fixed, she may have to abandon the car and proceed on the train, but I suppose she can get gas. It seems that she had the coupons issued in the East for the trip, but the trip was delayed and time for using the coupons expired. Also, my guess is based on something that was said by her—that the coupons were issued for moving to California. I suppose they are moving, but Ross is not with her. There is a little girl, her granddaughter maybe or some relative, but no Ross Kenyon.

Well, this letter has little news in it and I have no doubt there are many little items about the Tolles and Kellys which would be of interest to you. These little things that happen from day to day in family life in America are really the big things of life—and that's as it should be—what Dirk and Jim say and do, or do not do, how Butch behaves under varying circumstances, and so on. Each member of the family is a character with individuality. You remember the interesting characteristics of the duck, Donald. Squirrels are either a nuisance or interesting depending on what they are doing. The nuts have about all been stripped from the hickory tree and buried in the ground. Therefore, the squirrels have been a nuisance lately. A stray dog seems to have adopted our neighborhood and Butch cannot handle him as he handles some other strays which seem to encroach on our place, and so on.

October 18, 1944

Your letter of October 15 (Sunday) came in today and we enjoyed it a lot. Travel conditions are bad and will be worse around Christmastime, of course. I don't know what advice to give as to time of taking your furlough. We want you any time you can come and I don't know whether we would enjoy you more during the Christmas excitement, when there is always more or less turmoil, or some other time—nor which sort of vacation you would enjoy most. Haven't talked to your mother about that.

When I left home a bit before 2 o'clock this afternoon, Dirk was out on the concrete pump-stand painting the wooden flower-stand blue. Susan sat beside him—watching. Your mother was on the back porch painting one of the iron chairs blue. She sandpapered them all and the stool this morning. The harvest gnats are pretty thick at this time and committing suicide by resting on the wet paint. Your mother doesn't like that very much. . . . Yesterday afternoon the front yard was full of children raking leaves. They had to have some outlet for their exuberant spirits, I reckon, and knew of nothing else to do for the moment.

Harold bought a second-hand car yesterday—at the ceiling price. I hope there are not too many headaches in it. The car looks all right. It's a Model 37 Pontiac. Mother has had 60 acres of beans harvested. The crop was very good for the season: 31 bushels for one 20 acres, 26 for another and 24 for the third. Her share is half, and combining is (her share) $2.50 an acre. Other than this I don't know much news except that Butch got in a fight with a much larger dog and is lamed in one foot for the present. He should use more discretion. . . .

The notice of $73.44 due Massachusetts Mutual November 3 came in today. I will pay this. You have sent me, in all, $36.10, and I will apply that on the premium and sue for the balance some day, if I ever get around to it. If I don't sue you, remind me to do so.

Well, I will close this. Am supposed to be studying a real estate contract which a client wants to know about—whether he would be safe in relying on it in the purchase of a $38,000 farm, and I better get busy. By the way, he told me he was using the corn picker from midnight to noon—before the shucks get so dry that the picker won't take them all off. That is something new in farming even to me. . . .

October 31, 1944

Your letters and your newspaper work both continue to be very interesting. Since your last letter I have been mulling a bit about this officers training business. An officer does, I think, have an easier time in some respects, though his responsibilities are heavier. The question, therefore, for a private to consider is whether he prefers an easier life and one of heavy responsibilities to the drudgery of a private's life as exemplified by K.P. work. The officer receives better pay, of course, but that is incidental to the main question. You went in to make a good private—and you are doing that. I think that, if you followed the suggestion made to you, you would go from officers training to officer's rank and that you would make as good an officer as you are a private. I have the feeling also that as an officer you would be put to the same sort of work you are doing now. And, of course, the war will not have been finished by the time you have finished the training. However, you are on the job and know the situation much better than I, and your decision, whatever it may be, will be the right one. Your own work, and no influence other than that, has brought you to the attention of those in authority, and that's the way it should be.

We are well. Your mother cannot seem to find time to do some things in the house she wanted to do before winter sets in. The weather has been grand and she finds herself doing outdoor work in spite of herself—raking leaves, re-potting plants, etc., etc. This morning she made a resolution to start a couple of lampshades. I will believe that she started when I get home and she shows me the start. The weather today was as beautiful as ever. There was perhaps a little rain in the first two or three days of the month, but none since and no threat of rain. Bean harvest went on so fast that elevators were loaded to the bursting point almost, and wagons and trucks level-full of beans lined up at the elevators early in the morning hoping that sometime during the day a railroad car (or cars) would be left to receive their beans.

The bean harvest is almost done now. We have all ours either delivered to the elevators or stored on the farm of the Ashmore tenant. He couldn't get all his beans delivered as he combined them and has about six loads (half ours) stored in bin and chicken brooder house at his place. . . . Our tenant will probably finish harvesting his other beans today or tomorrow and after that is done can deliver the beans we have stored. Mrs. Woodyard, the tenant's wife, is worried for fear the beans in her brooder house will break its sides out before they are moved. There are nearly 300 bushels in that house and that is 18,000 pounds. The side pressure exerted by flowing grain is severe.

We are all well. Jim and Dirk have been going through the usual Hallowe'en motions. Dirk came in last night all dressed up in up-and-down stripes of red and white and with a marvelous false face on—a fully matured Turk of the bandit aspect with long black mustachios. He was quite thrilled by his appearance, as were we.

November 4, 1944

You may not have run into it, but there is "office politics" in most business establishments of any size. I think you did run into that sort of thing in a school operation. It would be exceptional if there were not some of the same sort of thing in an institution as large as our army now is. I read with interest the "poem" you called my attention to and thought at once of the old exclamation of Mr. Lord, "Oh! that mine enemy might write a book."

I believe I am glad you are thinking of taking further training looking to advancement in Army rank. Your letter reminded me of an income tax experience with an agent of the income tax force. He was the same nationality as the architect of the "poem" and came from the streets of New York attached to the Collector of Internal Revenue office at Springfield. He was an excellent accountant but knew absolutely nothing about farms and farm operations and expense. His ignorance did not lessen his self-satisfaction nor raise an ambition to learn—and as long as he was in this section reviewing farmers' tax returns he was an unmitigated nuisance. We civilians are getting pretty well fed up with being required to come in contact for various needs of life with little men dressed in a little authority—which we hope will be brief authority.

There is no news with us. The Tolles, having sold their Mattoon house, are busy today collecting the "remains" of their furniture which had been rented along with the house to a tenant. From what your mother reports, the "remains" is properly used here. Since lunch your mother and Alice E. have started to Mattoon to inquire about a chair which doesn't seem to be in evidence at all, either as a chair or as "remains."

I started this letter long before lunch and will have to make it short. Keep a stiff upper lip and don't get mad or appear in bad humor. If a situation exists in the Army and nothing can be done about it, then nothing can be done about it—just one of those things. A superior in the Army is a superior, in fact as in name whether in merit or not. However, a superior who uses his grade to effect a personal objective will some day be himself put in his proper place. . . .

November 11, 1944

It has been more than a week since we had a letter from you and as today is Armistice anniversary we will probably not have mail delivery until Monday. Suppose you are very busy and possibly the sergeant has been throwing his weight around. I have no particular news to tell—am merely writing because I want to.

Today is also the opening day of the hunting season in these parts and I reckon by now all the hunters and their dogs are in the fields. Harold finished his preparation for hunting last night. He has a gun, shells, a dog, and probably his hunting license. Have not heard whether the birds are plentiful or not and have not heard of anyone seeing a pheasant recently. I saw one covey of quail along the roadside about two weeks ago but have seen fewer quail than usual this summer. The rabbits and squirrels are plentiful in Charleston, but I do not know whether there are many out in the country or not. . . .

It has been a pleasant fall. There has been no hard freeze yet. Ice formed two or three nights, and the trees, except for a few oaks which bear their leaves almost through the winter, are bare. Some hardy flowers are still full of bloom. This is especially true of the hardy chrysanthemums. Mother has had little more success with hardy chrysanthemums than with turnips. She has tried many times to raise turnips but with the negligible success. Likewise with the flowers. She has had many starts and has a good many plants around the place, but they never have done very well. When your mother undertakes to do something she expects to succeed and usually does. Therefore, her failure with turnips and hardy chrysanthemums is rather griping to her.

Well, the election is over. It is up to the Democratic party to furnish the leadership for all of us, Democrats and Republicans, in the most difficult period of United States history—difficult in social, economic, political, and international affairs. I have no doubt that all will be united in every soundly based effort of the administration to overcome the difficulties.

Your mother has just phoned that she has a fine letter from you. I was mistaken about the mail. Traveling is bad now at Christmas time, but it is bad at all times, and we are especially pleased that you will be here Christmas. You will no doubt need money for your trip. Let me know how much.

Your mother also phoned that Mr. Hudson had brought in a nice fat hen for our dinner tomorrow. So we won't do so badly—nor diminish our red ration points.

Well, I must close. Lots of love. See you Christmas.

November 29, 1944

Mother's hands have not recently found an idle moment. Having about finished her Christmas sewing, she has been getting the house and clothing arrangement battened down for the winter. In the process, she has hunted up all my socks—twenty-two very good pairs—and got them into my top bureau drawer. Socks in the drawer had been a scarce article for some time. She has relined all the drawers. In the top one are my socks, ties, belts, and all new handkerchiefs, of which it seems I have a goodly supply. In the middle drawer are all my shirts, and in the bottom one are my winter pajamas, underclothes, etc. I am set for the winter. She has rearranged the closets in the two front rooms, put away all summer goods, cleaned and arranged and classified the contents of the back hall closet. In general, she is getting set both for the winter and for your coming.

There is no particular news. Harold picked me up on the way to town this morning. He was starting out for a hunt. Has had very little success this year. Alice E. finds her household duties almost all-absorbing. However, with mother's help she is entertaining her club, I believe it is tomorrow. . . .

Your letters continue most interesting. At this distance it is hard for one to get a complete picture of what goes on in an army training center—especially one who has had no experience. It does seem as though the camp is to be abandoned for the present, and if that is so, you will probably be somewhere else soon. Perhaps you will know something definite by the 16th. I hope you succeed in getting a sleeper, at least to Louisville. We can't meet you there because of gas shortage, if for no other reason. By the way, though it is probable we will not use the car much while you are here—we use it comparatively little in winter—it might be well for you to apply at Bainbridge A.A. Field for a gas allotment. I understand that is the way for a soldier to get gas for use on furlough. The car is a Chevy, 1939, two-door sedan with Illinois license no. 32559, owned by me. We have considerable of our allotment of "A" gas yet and if you secure a supply and the weather is good, it might be possible to use the car to put you a good distance on your way to your station, wherever it may be by that time, whether in the frozen North or the orange groves of Texas.

Helen sent us a copy of the picture of you and (Logan) Campbell* as it appeared in the Lexington *Herald* and I suppose she sent you a copy also. The article accompanying the picture referred to your Kentucky scholastic work and your family origin and was very good.

Mother would have written you today but she still has her hands deep in other things, important though more or less routine—cooking, keeping house, helping Alice E., taking care of Dirk from time to time, and what not. I sometimes wonder how your mother got along in a strange community with you and Alice E. to bring up and care for, and no help from anyone except a little from "Mother Hubbard" for a time, from Mrs. Feltham now and then, and what help I could give.

Well, I must close this as the morning is going by fast. We can hardly wait for your coming on the 16th. That has a much larger place in our thoughts than the Christmas routine.

*A cadet at Bainbridge and former second grade pupil of Emma C.'s in 1928 at Charleston, Illinois.

1945

January 16, 1945

Glad you are at the Gulf coast and hope that you are in the newspaper business. At any rate, weekends can be used for fishing and swimming and both of those sports are attractive. A big city has nothing to offer to compare with either of them in my view of the pleasures which may be enjoyed as we pass through this life.

There is little news here. Dirk is getting out some now and is doing much better. Jim was in Mattoon a day and succeeded in upsetting his stomach to such an extent that he had to go to bed yesterday afternoon and had much pain and a bit of fever. Have not heard from him this morning. The fifteen days of constant income tax work were finished last night—with me yesterday afternoon. I have not worked nights, but Harold* has and after he had worked with them all of Sunday, he worked that night until 1 o'clock. Have not heard how late he worked last night. If he worked at all, it must have been in Mattoon, because it was the last day and he couldn't bring his work home as he had been doing at night. He has got a kick out of being constantly busy—the difference between ages forty-two and sixty-six. I have no undue lot of the work to do, for I have tried to discourage its coming to me. Still, I had all I could do without straining myself more than I wanted to do.

Your mother is well except that she is again having trouble with her fingernails—may have to give them X-ray treatment again—is losing one of them. She has helped her condition of like kind heretofore twice by using calcium tablets, and while this was developing neither of us thought of calcium until this morning when she thought of them while we were eating breakfast. So I have a box in my pocket and she will start on them at noon today. Why we didn't think of them sooner is inexplicable.

Most of the snow that was here while you were with us melted last Saturday and Sunday but it snowed Sunday night and even though this snow is still nice and white, still we are very tired of having snow around.

We are quite anxious to get your first impression of your new surroundings. I just called Mother to ask whether the field is Tyndall or Lyndall (couldn't decide from my own copy of the address). She said to ask you if you got the two Kodak pictures she sent.

January 23, 1945

Sorry you have not heard from us. The letters sent you so far have had one error in the address. It may be an error of minor or major importance. I

*Harold, now released from the service and employed in Mattoon as an accountant.

wouldn't have any way of knowing which. The capital letters heretofore used in the address were as follows: A.A.F.B.U., A.A.F.G.S. The error was in the last bunch of capitals which should have been A.A.F.F.G.S., according to your last letter. I hope the error is minor.

Your tax withholding receipt from Daniel Starch and Staff came in yesterday. It shows that your wages in 1944 were $67.61, and tax withheld was $8.74. I think you also worked for someone else—perhaps more than one—during the year. All tax withholding receipts should be mailed to you by January 31. If you did not earn above $500 before becoming a WAC, you do not have to file a tax return. But I suspect you have money coming back from the Government whether you earned more or less than $500; therefore, you should make a return before March 15 and ask for refund. If you do not hear from your other employer, or employers, by the first of February, write to them and ask that they send the withholding receipt (Form W2) to me, and say to them that if they have already mailed the receipts to an address which will not reach you, to send duplicates to me.

I know what your income from the bank was. It was $16. I do not know what you received in 1944 from the aircraft concern or whether you had any other or not.

Starch withheld $8.74 out of $67.61, and if you had any real income in addition to that and tax was withheld from it, you probably have a considerable sum coming from the Government—and no doubt you can use it. So take care of the situation by getting the information to me from your employers.

February 14, 1945

Alice E. said she had a letter saying you had a head injury of minor importance suffered while attempting to board an army truck gracefully, but that it had been thoroughly bandaged by a doctor and no serious consequences were anticipated. Glad it was no worse. We have not seen the letter but supposed you fell.

There is no news of any importance. Harold and Jim went to the Country Club last night for dinner with the Kiwanis Club. They reported a rather poor dinner. Some of the boy scouts and cubs were asked to be present for some sort of program and Jim went as a cub, Harold as the mentor or leader of one of the cub organizations. Alice E. and Dirk had supper with us, and Dirk and I played dominos without knowing the rules very well. He beat me most of the time, and I did my best.

Mommie still keeps busy. She is starting to clean house little by little and expects to have it done sometime in March—that is, except for the dining room papering and painting. Percy Hampton is booked solid till August in papering and painting on the inside of houses, so it will be August before that part of the renovation of the house is done.

We had three nice, sunshiny days, and all began to feel better. The snow is just about gone—a little patch of dirty ice here and there but it's practically gone—and it is still above the freezing point though today is a gloomy damp day—not raw but damp and dark, the air surcharged with moisture. The wind, however, is from the north, and there may be a cold rain or snow.

Was afraid the suitcase would disappear enroute and was glad to learn through Alice E. that it had finally reached you. Perhaps it is better to send packages by mail. At any rate, the last package was mailed.

Suppose fishing will soon start at Panama City. If I remember correctly, some of the red snappers grow to be a pretty good size. Let me know how you make out and the correct weight of the largest fish you catch. Also let me know when fishing promises to call for more money than will be available to you.

I don't work as fast as I once did and consequently have found myself fairly busy so far this year, as busy as I want to be. As long as chances for a Florida vacation seem to make the vacation impossible, I am better off to be busy than not. So things in that respect are as they should be.

I am planning a birthday party for Mother and have ventured to buy some underthings for her—a slip, nightgown, panties, and stockings, I think. Miss Grant made the suggestions of what would be pleasing to Mother and ordered them for me and I have them in the office. I also have some stationery with her name and address on it. Alice E. wants to cook the meal and I will try to have Mother out of town on some business trip with me on that afternoon. By the way, I enclose a check for $5 and would like for you to cash it and send Mother a remembrance. I don't know what she would like best to have, but the cigarette supply may be growing slim as she asked me if I had got any lately and I had to confess that I had not been able to do so. Send the present *in your name*. It does not have to be cigarettes. Send what you think best.

February 20, 1945

I judge from the last *Target* which came in that you are extremely busy and at the work you wanted most to do, that your surroundings are exceptionally good as to personnel, and they must be good as to climate. You seem to have come to the fore there as your personality justifies—that is, fast. Congratulations. I saw an airman getting out of an auto on the north side of the Square the other day and as he was apparently the man whose picture was taken with you at Bainbridge, I introduced myself. His wife was there also and said that they had enjoyed you a lot. She was very complimentary in her references to you. I judge Campbell is not very talkative, or maybe he is not talkative when his wife is with him. He is a handsome man and looks as if his nerves were steady. Was glad to see them and sorry that Mother did not.

There is little news here. Mother is busy as usual. Is having her club tomorrow afternoon and, as is usual when she plans something in advance, has it much on her mind and is doing a good many things about the house which she would not do if she had no advance engagement, but merely put on the party on the spur of the moment as it were; consequently, I will be glad when the party is over.

I suppose fishing is on the schedule now and enclose check for $5 for a trip. Hope you enjoy it. You might make a good story for the *Target* out of the trip.

Alice E. is to prepare the dinner at our house. Phone 1062 the evening of February 28. We hope the dinner will be a surprise—not expecting to have anyone there except the Tolles. It occurs to me that it would add greatly to the pleasure as well as the surprise if you could get through on the telephone. You can either have the call charged to our phone or pay it out of the fishing money and put off the fishing trip. Don't know whether there would be a chance for you to get through on the phone. In a field the size of Tyndall, the phone must be very busy after the evening meal.

We are all well. There have been a good many things to do at the office since the New Year—some of them will have work coming along until it will be too late for a trip to Panama City. If one accepts business, one has to take care of it. Believe me, it was a mistake not to send you to a law school. . . . Mrs. Henry, who was seeking the job when you were here, was employed by Jeffries and in her spare time is doing my work. As you know, that is a great help. Still it does not do away with the necessity of the lawyer being on the job to carry on at the proper time.

It's noon and I should close.

March 10, 1945

I received your letter with the money order for $30 in it and deposited it to my credit. Also gave your account in my office book credit for the $30. The monthly bond for $10 came in, and that is still in my safe along with the bond last month. Will put them in the bank box the next time I have occasion to go to the box. The pin adorns my coat. Thanks a lot for it, though with your small income you should not be spending money for the gratification of my pride.

Jim went to Mattoon yesterday. He has had an ingrowing toenail which got pretty bad, and it is being cared for there. Alice E. went to Mattoon with Harold this morning for some reason, and Dirk—in a cheery mood—came in about the time I had finished my breakfast. About the first thing he did was to knock on the back bedroom door and waken Mommie. They were both on the stir as I left. Butch was in the house also with Dirk, and when I left Butch came along with me to the office. Later I had occasion to go to the Courthouse and he went with me and stayed with me in the County Clerk's office. Came back to my office door but didn't enter, and I suppose he is home by this time.

Today is a beautiful day. Yesterday was fair but rather cold. The farmers would like to be in the fields to sow clover and oats—and I suppose conditions will be right in a couple of days if it doesn't rain heavily again. There have been two heavy rains, each more than an inch and a half, the second one on the day mother and I went to Tuscola.

I reckon it is well for you to be busy. Time will not hang heavy on your hands, but I hope you will not be too busy to fish a few times for red snapper—and perhaps a more sporty fish will take you on for a round or two. There is no news here. We are all well. Mother is still spending a large part of each day gradually getting the spring housecleaning done.

March 13, 1945

Your letter of the 10th came this morning. I will first have to learn how to go about the job suggested. . . . I do not know how a civilian can be of service, however. Would not one have to proceed through officers of the Women's Army Corps in order to secure an opportunity for a WAC to take officers training? I don't see how an effort made through Army channels—male—could be very effective, but it might be. I don't know much about the Army.

When you had an opportunity, afterwards repeated, to secure officers training, my guess as to the source from which the opportunity came, or probably came, was that it may have been suggested by the recruiting officer who secured your enlistment. If so, and if you know his name and address, it might be well for you to write him and suggest to him that you should have a chance at officers training if you are to do a worthwhile job in the Army—that you are not now doing a worthwhile job, or one for which you are fitted, and your enlistment was solely on the theory that your services were needed—that up to the present job you were engaged in work for which you were especially fitted and in that sort of work you were content as a private, etc. . . .

As I have said, I will have to learn how. As soon as I see the method I will, of course, use every effort to get you an opportunity to take officers training. You are thoroughly qualified in every respect and the Women's Army Corps would profit by having you in a position where your attainments would find full expression. To be an officer is of no particular importance in itself. Importance comes through the giving of your best to that for which you are best qualified which, as a private, you cannot now do in your present job. . . .

March 17, 1945

I enclose Tom Marshall's letter. He takes the same view I take or practically the same view. Nothing that seems practical for me or any civilian to undertake has occurred to your mother or to me. Tom's suggestion that I go to Tyndall Field might have a bit of value in it, but even if I were there and got from you and your surroundings and associates a clean picture, it is not clear to me how I could give any help. Perhaps, if you find time to write a bit more fully, I could get the picture without taking the trip. From an earlier letter of yours, I got the impression that you had no application in for officers training but had applied to be admitted to some sort of special training in a school or camp in Virginia or in that section of the country. Have you applied for officer's training? Let us know, if you have time to write, if your duties now include nothing more than those of an office boy. Do you write for the paper anymore? It's hard to conceive of you doing nothing more worthwhile than the duties you mentioned in your last letter. Would the immediately superior officer be inclined to speak well of you for officers training? He may be glad to do so as a provision for the safety of his own position.

Received a letter from Fles today in which he said of *Little Houses*: "This is a charming juvenile, and I have all confidence in its salability." Sent them a check for $10 of your money to pay for the retyping he had done at your request.

Mother was out in the yard after I went home yesterday watching while I spaded some ground as Dirk and Bobby Bruce gathered the worms. The accumulation of worms suggested that it was time to put the worm box in the ground and so I took it off the back porch, and Bobby and Dirk rolled it down to the neighborhood of the garage and your mother watched as I dug a hole for it and Dirk and Bobby looked for worms. She watched also as the three of us filled around it with dirt. Then Dirk and Bobby abandoned us to watch Fred Cottingham rake along his parkway on 6th Street and burn the trash, while Mother removed the covering of leaves from some annuals—flowers—which she had covered hoping they would live through the winter. They lived, and I hauled the leaves and trash away in Bobby's wagon.

While we were all yet in the yard, a rabbit streaked from the back of the yard toward the front between Thomas and us—with Butch on the Thomas side yelping his head off, quite a bit behind the rabbit which had come through the fence while Butch lost time trying to get through; however, he went between the houses yelping and going like a shot, but the rabbit went around Thomas's house and back through their yard, while Butch came out on the north side of our house completely off the trail. He just made a poor guess as to the strategy of the rabbit.

By the way, Mother said at noon that Jim and a gang of kids were all over the back yard this morning collecting worms from the top of the ground. They came up during the rain which had been quite heavy during the night and the robins hadn't got them all. So Jim and a friend went fishing at the college lake or pond.

There is little news with us. Mother is about well. She was talking this noon of going to the picture show this afternoon but I tried to talk her out of it—just recovering from a cold and to go into a crowd might not be good for her.

Perhaps the officer in charge of public relations would be glad to put you up for officers training in order to secure you for his office? Could that be possible?

March 21, 1945

Tom has written again and I send his letter. It seems to me that his suggestion is worth consideration—that it may have merit. I don't know enough about the Army to be able to judge. I don't think, however, that resignation from the Army is among the possibilities.

There is no news with us. Mother is practically well. The weather was wet off and on all day yesterday—a rather cold north wind, and very dark, gloomy weather this morning. Took a business trip yesterday in the car to Albion and Bone Gap down in Edwards County, about 85 miles due south. Total driving was 220 miles. So left here at 7:15, drove east through Ashmore almost to Kansas to pick up a client, then south on 49 to Route 33, went to 130 and on south to Albion. Got home at 4 o'clock. Didn't drive fast at all, but the roads were not as much cluttered up with traffic as they used to be.

Haven't heard from you since your disquieting letter but suppose conditions haven't changed. It's important that at this stage you keep your chin and spirits up—that you take what is dished out and like it—important from your personal point of view. You will come through in good shape if you do and if you do not keep your spirit up, there will be an almost permanent and more or less important changing of your outlook on life.

Am going to a judicial convention at Paris this evening. Will not drive but will be in the Sheriff's car as a guest and not a prisoner. Guess I will have to eat a fairly early supper here as we leave at 6 o'clock, the convention is at 7:30 and, while there may be dinner after the convention for the delegates, it might be a bit late. The proceedings of the convention are cut and dried in the absence of something very unexpected. Republicans and Democrats are in coalition. There are three judges to elect in the district. The Democrats will nominate one—the sitting judge who lives in Danville. The Republicans will nominate two, both sitting judges—Ben Anderson from here and George Bristow from Paris. Speeches and all, the convention shouldn't last more than an hour: a little time for organization and election of a permanent chairman; appointment of a committee or two to eventually bring in pre-prepared resolutions; two nominating speeches—perhaps two seconding speeches also—all short and very flattering; report of committee and adoption of resolution providing for the choosing of a new candidate in event of death of one. Then adjournment, everything having gone according to schedule. As a matter of fact, our three judges are excellent and should be retained and not at this time be subjected to the stress and strain of an election. As a matter of fact, the coalition came on petition of practically all the lawyers in the district. Judges have practically no appointments to make—no patronage. Each does appoint a well-paid stenographer as court reporter. She, of course, has to be good to be able to take testimony as it comes, in a fast trial, and such stenographers are scarce—no competition. Each judge also appoints a Master in Chancery who is paid by set fees which he earns when a chancery case is referred to him by the Court to take testimony. But that is the entire extent of the judges's patronage. Therefore, professional politicians are not much interested. Well, you are not interested in this sort of thing, and I have nothing else to report.

March 24, 1945

We have your two letters and are happy that you have got yourself so thoroughly under control. Events will be better now. Am not entirely in agreement with the wisdom of your deduction drawn from Tom's letter. The German war may be over soon. The time of the end of the Japanese war cannot be estimated with any degree of accuracy by a civilian, or a soldier for that matter, from any of the facts which have been made public. There may, even in Europe, be belated additions to the number of warring nations. Turkey and Russia may have a bone of contention still to be gnawed, and there is a danger spot in Spain. Furthermore, your enlistment is for a period ending six months after the war. So I think it would be the better course to take officers training.

There is little news. Jim went fishing this morning and caught three nice perch at the school pond. Mother and Alice E. and I suppose Dirk and perhaps Jim are going to Mattoon this afternoon. Your mother wants one more X-ray treatment on one of her fingernails. We are all well. Your mother worked all day yesterday out of doors and is a bit sore in muscle today, but otherwise in fine fettle. I worked an hour after office hours in the yard and was glad to call it a day. Reckon I am lazier than Mother. . . .

We haven't decided whether to approach Miss McKinney or not. Will think that one out and if we decide to do so, will call on her tomorrow. Am considerably impressed with the view that civilian interference may do more harm than good, unless the influence is from such a source that it commands respect—either through personal knowledge of the high merit a mere suggestion or a recommendation is entitled to receive because of the integrity and good faith of the civilian, or unless the civilian occupies a commanding position for some other reason than merit. If the WAC knows Miss McKinney's good faith as well as you and I know it, her suggestion would command respect even though she is a mere civilian and has no other means to support her.

Mother joins me in the belief that officers training should not be abandoned as a goal.

April 5, 1945

The enclosed letter is from Dirk. He apparently intended that it should have been sent by air mail, but I am sending it this way for the reason that I doubt that what he has written is of sufficient consequence to justify the additional postage especially as air mail to you would be very little if any faster than regular mail. Mommie and I ate soup and gingerbread and coffee at the Tolles' last night and Dirk's mother handed me the letter to mail. I understood her to say that she had not read it. Yesterday was a raw, windy day—a cloudy day—and Dirk was much indoors; consequently, he had a good chance to write a good letter. No doubt you will enjoy it.

Today is brilliant with sunshine but near freezing at 7:30 this morning—near enough to indicate that it may have fallen to 32 during the night; and the wind is still from the north though the weatherman thinks it will be warmer. Mommie has all the big living room furniture stacked in the dining room and hall and the curtains down—expects to wash the woodwork and floor this morning and have the cleaning woman wax the floor and help with the woodwork—washing that she doesn't get done by noon. The wallpaper there and in the library was cleaned yesterday. I expect to take the afternoon off and go to the picture show, "A Tree Grows in Brooklyn."

Jim went fishing after school Tuesday at the school lake and caught three or four nice perch. I think he will find that his childhood experiences will make him enjoy fishing as a recreation all his life. Dirk would still rather more enjoy messing with fishing worms than do most anything else. He finds many during the rainy weather but most of them are pretty well worn-out by the time he gets through holding them and admiring them, pouring them and the dirt out of his tin can on some one of our stepping stones quite frequently, taking each one in his hands, looking it over to see how it's getting along, and eventually abandoning the tin can with the worms in it at the place he happens to be when something more interesting at the moment is to be done. Sometimes I run into the can in time to save a few live worms for the worm box. It's a great life.

There is little news. We are all well. Your picture—the one where your group was marching with "eyes-right" past the Field Commander—came in. It is an excellent picture. The Army has excellent equipment and operators, and this war will find permanent records in pictures of all its phases and activities. You do have a serious expression on your face but it becomes you and is appropriate to the occasion. The WAC at your left and the captain, I think, could give good account of themselves in any physical combat which might be forced on them in Army life. You look too thin and puny to be much account in fighting, but that appearance may be only because of the setting.

Well, it's after 9 o'clock and I should be doing other things.

April 11, 1945

Sure hope your forlough comes through soon. It seems a long time to all of us since you were here. Glad you are thoroughly yourself again. The Army system is in a class by itself. There is nothing else similar to it. Have heard the thought expressed this way: "There is a right way and an Army way."

There is little news here. Jim and I went fishing day before yesterday down on the Kickapoo near its mouth. The creek was still too high and cloudy, so we had a good time and got home before dark. We left town shortly after 4 o'clock.

Yesterday noon I found your mother deep in the job of cleaning the library—furniture in various places, rug ready to be carried out of doors, curtains washed and drying outside, and the house in general turmoil. Tried to stop her for the day but no soap. So I got out as quickly as possible. Went home about 4 and found her still going, not nearly finished, and lectured her a few times. Eventually, about an hour later, she quit and began to prepare supper. In the meantime, I washed the three windows on the outside—windows in my room—and put the screens in them and carried in the rug and a few things she left outside, and we had supper. She was in good shape this morning and set out to finish the job as I set out for the office. The house is fine to live in, but when no help is available, it's a big job for your mother. She has not had time to do any painting. Alice E. is kept busy, too, by her house and children—though your mother has Dirk much of the day time, as the place here is more attractive as a playground.

Jim wishes to get a set of miniature war machines like the jeep you sent Dirk—says they cost $10. I have arranged with him that he shall help me this summer at 25¢ an hour (with rest periods in the hour, of course). Jim says he is to earn the $10, and if he does, his mother will let hm buy the set. It seems to me he should not have the replicas until he has earned them. I think to give them to him in advance would harm him and I don't want that done. However, I am willing to go this far: buy $5 worth now, don't let him know I have them, know the cost of each, and as he earns money enough to buy one, give it to him in settlement. So I enclose five dollars. If you can carry five dollars' worth when you come home, buy what that money will buy and bring it along with a price list. Money has come to Jim too easily, and I have never contributed—because it *has* come easily. Do not intend to begin now. It's not good for him.

April 23, 1945

It was good to hear your voice yesterday. Mother especially enjoyed your laugh. Glad you passed the test. Knew you would. Hope that your furlough will not be longer delayed than three weeks. Mother has the house ready for the summer and until August 4th, when Hampton has promised he will paper and paint the dining room and paint the kitchen.

I paid, from your funds, your Massachusetts Mutual Life Insurance premium the other day. Jim decided that he preferred to work for cash rather than the Army truck, tank, etc. So if you can get a fishing trip on that check, I will be particularly well pleased. By the way, if you think you will need money for your trip home, let me know in time so I can send a check.

We are, of course, quite curious to know what your job is. My guess is that it has to do with the hospital. The number of men who are wounded is so large that a great many WACs will be needed in the rehabilitation program, and I suspect that branch of the service is being much enlarged. If I remember correctly, it was your original choice and that fact is a part of your Army record, and you almost had the high qualifications which were first set. The standards have probably been lowered somewhat and your very slight deficiency may no longer be important. You say your work is interesting. The hospital work will be interesting, though quite a strict master of time and thought. You will do well at it, if it falls to your lot.

Well, as there is no news, I will close.

May 1, 1945

I have not written you for some days but there has been little to write about. The weather is still cool—48 this morning. The furnace still has fire in it. The high winds died down last night, and it is bright and still this morning. We have had much east wind—good for neither man or beast—much north wind, many clouds and chilly weather regularly. The back porch still is not dressed up. We have not had a meal out there yet. The grass has been cut twice. Mother has many of her flowers in the ground. Some of the garden is planted. We have set six more trees—two apples, two red plums and two of the big sweet purple plums, and two cherries which latter we bought for $8.25. That makes eight instead of six—quite a lot of trees considering that the back of the house is almost a dense woods already.

Sunday the Tolles ate chicken with us. Then we all drove out on business to the Ashmore farm, and on the way to see a setter of Harold's which has six nice new pups, and as Harold hadn't seen the Ashmore lake, we stopped there and fortunately found in the trunk of the car three fishing rods and a can of worms. So there was some fishing, interesting but unsuccessful, while Mother gathered a fine mess of wild greens. Then on to the farm where the main purpose of the trip was properly attended to, two dozen eggs were gathered and bought, and Mother made an important addition to her mess of greens by adding wild mustard—altogether a pleasant and successful trip except for the lack of fish.

We are certainly anxious for your furlough to begin and are counting the days until June 6. Hope nothing occurs in the meantime to delay it further. We will certainly have the porch dressed up by that time and the furnace abandoned for the summer. The crops should mostly be in and up. And fishing should be comfortable if not successful. . . .

We saw—"Keep Your Powder Dry" last night and enjoyed it thoroughly—primarily because you are a WAC, I think. Mother enjoyed it especially because she had seen you in the same setting.

The enclosed letter is from Elaine Bousha Brown whom you will remember as the stenographer up here for a considerable time. I think you will enjoy it.

The Helen Hunt Jackson mentioned in the letter was a writer and, as I remember the conversation in my father's home, much admired by my mother and father, and on the question of naming their seventh child—having run out of other names, I guess—the name Helen Jackson Kelly fell to Helen's lot. I should read something of Helen Hunt Jackson's writings.

Well, there is little news, as I said once in this letter, I think. The Tolles and Kellys are all well and enjoying life. June will come pretty fast. Farmers will think that it comes with the speed of a P-38. Out on the prairie there will not be a moment of wasted time when farming conditions are right. I suspect that considerable has been done in the last three days as the soil must have been getting in fair condition.

Write as you can. Your letters are always looked for anxiously and enjoyed thoroughly.

May 8, 1945

I went to the bank box this morning with your March and April bonds. They had been in the safe here at the office since their receipt. You have war bonds, $10 of the issues of August, September, October, November, and December, 1944, and January, February, March and April, 1945. This includes, I think, all you are entitled to until the May bond comes in early in June.

We heard the President's announcement of the surrender of Germany at breakfast time this morning and hung out our big flag. It's been a long time since that flag was out. Charleston is very quiet. The stores are open as usual. Few people are in the street. I suppose no one feels much like working. I know I don't—nor do I think many people feel like celebrating much. The war experience has been too costly in lives and health. I feel that we could not have come thus far without God's help, and I pray that He will find this nation worthy to survive that which is yet to come and that so much to human advantage and Christian advancement may come out of this tragedy, that those who have lost someone dear to them and those whose health and bodies have been broken will find a great measure of comfort and solace because of the result. For this, I pray that all thought inspired by personal and national self-interest to be served at the cost of injustice to others may be removed from the minds of those men who are now serving at the peace conference. This, too, I think needs the help of God. Therefore, my prayer is to Him.

Your birthday is less than a week away. It would be nice if we could have you here for that day. Can't you pick up a bomber ride long enough to give you a few hours before the bomber returned to Tyndall? Of course you can't, but it would be nice for us. Mother practically finished the back porch yesterday—worked all day at it. The weather is still too cold to eat outside or to be without a furnace fire, but on the 14th it will be warm and bright. The yard is pretty with foliage and flowers and it will still be pretty in June, though it may also be pretty hot.

You will not be too disappointed, I know, if you do not become an officer or get the chance to take the training. The training—Ah! there's the rub. Also, the aftermath, when you have to think for others and always be on your toes to keep your brass hat from becoming offensive. You can and will be happy as a private. Last night I looked through the pictures we have had of you as a WAC. The thing that impressed me most as I looked at the pictures, one after the other, was that there was not as happy or charming a face among the lot of WACs as yours. True, you had a very serious, soldierly perhaps, face in the picture of the squad marching past the reviewing stand, but that was an event which did not call for the smile and your face in its earnestness was still charming. So I am not going to worry if you do not even get the chance to try out as an officer candidate. What's the difference except a little money and some extra responsibility supposed to be commensurate with the money advancement? No matter how high you go in the Army, you still are not your own boss.

Mother and Mrs. Thomas are taking lunch in Mattoon today. Mother asked for what money I had in my pocket, but I had little and I don't think she could spend much anyway, for the Mattoon stores are closed and many people are on the street. I had enough for her to buy lunch for the two and a few flower plants if she so desires—and I think that is as much as she could spend in any event.

There is little news. We are all well. Had a taste of pheasant for lunch yesterday. In fact, I had a fair-sized piece. Alice E. had had some folks for supper the night before, and the guests furnished the pheasant. There was enough left for the five, I think. Dirk, Jim and I had enough, but Alice ate after we had finished. I asked your mother if she had a fair-sized piece and she said she did, but I doubt it, though I didn't see what was available. It was brought to our house and served in our kitchen to the five of us. At supper time, as mother had worked all day, we came down to Wickham's. Mother was apparently pretty hungry and enjoyed the meal—good roast beef, fried potatoes, salad, vegetable, asparagus, peach pie and coffee—all good.

Well, I reckon I will close this. Dirk was vaccinated a few days ago. Took it without flinching and is proud of his sore arm. He was in on a snake-catching expedition a few days ago in Mattoon, wherein the squad took twelve or fifteen snakes, capturing two of them alive. Dirk brought the dead ones home and the live ones were brought along by Jim, I suppose, and *all* in the car with Alice E. I think they are pretty well-treated prisoners around the Tolle mansion. Well, goodbye for now.

May 23, 1945

Your letter to Alice E. and the one to Mother and me came in today. I reckon it's getting pretty hot down there now. Florida is probably not an ideal place to spend a summer, but you may be booked for that little experience. Maybe you can get transferred to some Michigan, Wisconsin, or Minnesota lake—or would it even be worth trying under the circumstances? Around here we have had very little pleasant weather. Have eaten on the porch three times—the third time this noon. I let the furnace fire go out Saturday and changed to summer underwear. The time was well-chosen, though it has since been quite cool—still today it's more comfortable outside than in the house. That house is cool even in the summer, and the thermometer registered 60 degrees. The house felt at noon that it might still be 60 degrees. It was comfortable in the sunshine and not bad on the porch. Farmers are probably planting corn today. They have had no chance until now. A little was planted early in the month, but it didn't have a chance to get out of the cold, cold ground.

We sure hope that nothing delays your furlough. The 7th is only a bit over two weeks off. I am not sure of the rules of OPA about gas, but think that if you are to be allotted gas, you are to have the allotment made before you leave Tyndall Field. If you are required to have information about the car to use the gas in, my car is a 1939-model Chevrolet, 2-door sedan, Factory #3JB07-31873, Engine #2282706, with Illinois license plate 32559. In spite of the end of Germany, gas is still hard to get and there cannot be replacement of tires easily made for cars used as mine is. A Kentucky trip would be very hard to arrange under present allotment of gas. I don't know when present "A" tickets expire. If it's June 21, we could save enough gas to go to Kentucky just before the 21st and come back here after the 21st on the tickets coming into validity. If it's July 21, it seems to me there is no hope for the trip. As tickets are good for only the three or four months, if all are used for a single trip, the car becomes of little value for quite a spell. We could negotiate the trip to Scott Field or Terre Haute all right—but Kentucky is almost out.

There is little news. We are well. The sand in the sandbox has been replenished for the use of Dirk and Susan. Jim will keep my grass cut. He is a strong boy and does a good job. No doubt the weather will be fine by the 7th. Had you come up to now, there would have been no outdoor pleasures, but from now on I think it will be fine. About half of the garden is not yet planted—not even spaded. It will be all in by or before the 7th, and Mother expects to have everything done and out of the way by then so that her hands will be free. You will have to get such ration stamps as you are entitled to. Meats are about off the market. Mother made two trips to the Piggly yesterday and two today trying to be on hand when the fish came in. I made two trips there today for the same purpose, and Mother will make another. Getting food is becoming a problem—that is, food one would prefer to have.

Well, I have read this letter over. I must be in rather a gloomy frame of mind—a condition I did not suspect until I read this letter. The sun is shining bright. The air is bracing and everything in business line and at home are fine. Therefore, this should have been a good letter. Nevertheless, it is not. Perhaps the thought that I could not really expect to pick you up and see the folks in Kentucky is responsible, for I would so like to do that very thing.

May 29, 1945

Well it won't be long now—just a bit over a week. Hope you get to fly up. The long train ride would be tiresome. I suppose we could get into the flying field to meet you, but I don't even know about that, nor do I know whether there would be gas enough. Mother is *set* in her hopes and plans to drive to Kentucky to Emily's wedding. By the way, the date of the wedding is uncertain. It was thought that the furlough would come early in June, but now it is thought that it will come late in June, and if it does she feels that, by using all gas for both the tickets which expire June 21 and all the tickets which expire three months later, she could make the trip taking you part way back to your present Army home. (That is all "A" gas tickets.) Frequently things work out as Mother hopes—almost always when she has control of events. But in this case circumstances beyond her control will dictate the event.

The weather has been delightful for the past three days and no doubt the farmers are working late into the nights, and in some cases all through the nights getting the corn and beans planted. If the weather holds a few days longer, I have confidence they will get the work done. There is some compensation in late planting of corn, for the late-planted corn has a better chance to miss the ravages wrought at times by the worm called the "corn-borer."

The river must be right at this time for fishing. I took the two families out about 4 o'clock Saturday afternoon. It was still too high and too muddy. Jim gave up quickly, but I had the pleasure of sitting for a couple of hours on the bank and in the sunshine and holding a rod. Would be going out this afternoon again except that the garden is still not all spaded and the ground is right for spading. This is the last year we will have a garden. There is too much spring work of other types to be done about our home to permit us at our ages to have a garden of our own cultivating. Jim cuts most of the grass as it needs cutting. In fact, he takes care of the grass-cutting in several yards. He is big and strong and old enough to have some sense of responsibility.

Sunday Harold took the Tolle family out to the country more on a snake-hunting venture than anything else. The kids came back thoroughly delighted. Jim had a beautiful green tree snake in a glass jar. It was quite long. I never saw it stretched out, but it must have been 15 inches—almost as slender as a pencil, and the most delicate green—so delicate that it seemed transparent almost. The kids were proud. Harold always scoffed at our stories about green tree snakes along the river. Said there was no such reptile. I asked him if he was finally convinced; he said that he still doesn't believe it. Jim told me last night that he had turned the snake loose, for he thought it would die if he didn't—that it was losing its green coloring, etc.

Dirk brought home a land terrapin and loved it like a brother—kept it in his hands all during the waking hours and tied it up or covered it when he was called away, showed it to all the neighbors, covered it with sand, treated it with loving care. Last night he forgot its wayward tendencies at supper time and failed to fence it in, and so the turtle, having patiently bided its time, made its slow escape from too close confinement and effectually passed out of Dirk's life. Dirk couldn't be comforted.

Well, as usual I have been interrupted several times in writing this letter. The flower garden women visited the flower gardens yesterday and Mother spent the day dressing hers up. She is also on the trail of a fourth glass plate of the "Ivy and Snow" pattern—knows where it is, has seen it, has won the sympathy and good will of its owner. How will you bet? Will she get the plate or won't she?

Will have to close this letter. Sure will be glad to see you. We all hope to have everything done—nothing to do but to do what you want to do and be with you in the enjoyment of doing it with you.

July 14, 1945

Yesterday was Friday the 13th. So after lunch, Jim with the able assistance of a youth of his own age, went to a creek out on the wide prairie and caught some minnows. Mommie acted as chauffeur and sat in the car by the roadside. Along about 3 o'clock, Jim and Mommie in the car honked me out of the office, and the three of us with minnows and without Butch went to the lake at Fox Ridge and went through all the formalities of securing a boat, including the surrender of fishing license temporarily and the inspection of the minnows to see that no objectionable one was present.

After the formalities were over, we loaded our equipment into a boat and set out slowly, Jim and Mommie fishing and me rowing along the middle of the glorified pond toward the shallow end and the weeds. As we approached the weeds but were still in the clear water, Jim had a strike—his first by a good fish. At the proper moment I told him to jerk, and I suppose because he feared to injure or hurt the fish, he pulled his line tight, but gently so, and as Jim pulled—with excitement heavy on him and in his voice—and as the fish pulled hard and harder and finally leapt into the air and shook the hook loose, excitement rose to a peak—excitement and hope—hope blasted in the very moment it was highest.

Jim was disheartened, downcast—the picture not of hope deferred but of hope blasted forever. But after I had put him on a new minnow and he had fished in gloom for a minute or two while I made the boat move slowly around in and out of the moss, gloom was just as quickly removed as hope had been blasted, for Jim had another strike—and this time he cruelly struck back, embedding the hook firmly and brought his catch to boat with the skill of an old master at the art, and I hauled it in for him. This experience was repeated not once not twice nor three times but four times, until Jim had five nice bass—11 to 12 inches long on the stringer, and Friday the 13th had turned into a blessed day of luck replete with memories that will persist through life. In the meantime, Mommie had had two strikes one of which resulted in a catch, but the other got into the weeds and pulled loose. You should have been along. You would have enjoyed it as much as we did, and we would have enjoyed it the more. When I left the office I was quite tired and nervous; when we got home I was lazily tired and not nervous. . . .

We are all well—except for Dirk. Mommie is much improved and is taking life easier. She has seen a doctor. There is little other news. Have not yet read the camp papers you sent. Suppose you are writing nothing for publication at present. Take it as easy as you can down there in the heat, and enjoy the Gulf as often as you can. Lots of love.

(Exact date unknown)

You ask my opinion generally about present conditions—and the future. As to the conduct of the war, I am not well enough informed as to present situations to form an opinion, even if I were enough of a military man to justify an attempt. As you know, I have no military training or inclination.

As to the world future: I am still of the opinion which I held after the last war. The present war or world situation has not offered anything new, which seems to me to justify a change. We are still a world of different peoples each having its own ideas about society and government and indeed about life itself. Each people is pretty well wedded to its ideas, just as we are. It has never been possible for a single nation to police the world—nor a coalition of peoples. If a coalition is formed, another and stronger coalition comes along and upsets the first. I believe firmly that a police power based on the sword will perish by the sword. Therefore, you will say I am pessimistic.

I am far from pessimistic. There will have to be temporary governments set up after the war. Whether the temporary governments are to be permanent or not, it is not entirely for us to say. Even if we *could* say, they would be temporary until the peoples involved could set up their own governments—England, Russia, China—all must have their say. We are but one of four. You can see the result. England will hold what she desires to hold. Russia will take what she wants. We should want nothing perhaps but a few protecting islands. I would like to see China left to her own devices and I think she will be. A considerable part of her leadership is shot with Communism and I think if she is left to decide for herself, there will possibly be a long conflict between *republicanism*—as we *have* known it up to Roosevelt—and Communism. We cannot forestall that conflict—nor should we try to do so.

As it was after the last war, so it is now. I hope for an age of reason—not war. As it was then, so it is now in my judgment. An advanced step toward coming to an age of reason would be the establishment of a world court with jurisdiction to try international cases or disputes, provided such cases in no way involve sovereignty. Nations could be forced into the court—that is, the judicial process could be gone through to bring them constructively into court, whether they might choose to appear and contest or not. Having thus secured jurisdiction, the court would decide—but never a question of sovereignty. The power of the court would not rest in arms—merely international opinion. If the opinion of the court meets with the approval of the peoples of the world—that is, if the judgment of the world is with the reasoning on which the opinion of the court is based, no nation would lightly disregard the judgment of the court, unless willfully misled as Germany and Italy were, and Japan as well when she entered Manchuria. Such a court would, I think, be a first step toward an age of reason. Many years of course would elapse before an age of reason would be established, for nations have different viewpoints and international controversies will long cloud world thinking.

As to the United States now and after the war, you well know I have very firmly fixed ideas. I haven't the time this morning to present them. The financial end looks destructive. Debt is so large already that it seems hopeless almost. If waste could be avoided, it would not be too bad yet, *if* Congress would impose and the people would back-up the imposition of greatly increased taxes during the war and thereafter long enough to get the debt down to a reasonable amount. I fear Congress will not dare impose the high taxes necessary, or the people submit if imposed, though the people, if left to honor, will go much further with the Government than under the directives of Bureaus backed up by threats of fine and imprisonment.

As to our republican form of government, it is in serious danger. I wouldn't be surprised if the Federal Courts—that is the majority of the judges, District, Circuit and Supreme—have been replaced since 1933. The people themselves began to break down the element of republicanism—that is representation in goverment—many years ago. The early encroachments were unnoted, such as the influencing of Congress and legislatures by power, place and money; the taking back to the people of the power to nominate at primary elections, their officers; the taking from the Legislatures the power to name United States Senators; the building up of blocks or classes, such as farmers, labor organizations, organizations of capital and hundreds of minor blocks, each going to legislative bodies through block representation—who perhaps by the way—did not really represent that block—and asking and in some cases demanding special privilege; the taking back to the people of much of the power and discretion entrusted to the officers sent to represent all the people.

It goes without saying that there can be no true Democracy where 130 million people are involved. Government must be either dictatorial or representative. What the people take from their elected representatives a dictator will seize. It cannot be otherwise. When a man or set of men asks and receives from representatives a special privilege, he is making the people's representative serve him and not the people. Under present conditions, a representative tends to give expression to the wishes of what he thinks the majority of the people in his district want, not exercising the judgment which he was elected to exercise. Thus, in many ways in addition to those mentioned, we have taken back power which we cannot exercise and live as a Republic. The pace toward the destruction of the Republic has grown faster and faster during this century, and since 1933 has become terrific.

Can inflation be avoided? The citizens can only hope and try. War and Victory bonds in the hands of citizens which may be surrendered to the Government for money amounts to millions and millions of dollars. The needs and wants of the people are enormous and supplies are few. Economists are in agreement that this condition, unless controlled, will result in wild inflation. The condition was caused by the war. Even while the war was still being fought and while the citizens generally were moved to the highest degree of patriotism and sought by word and act to avoid everything which would weaken the war effort or disturb the domestic economy, there was still a considerable measure of inflation and a considerable black market which developed because a comparatively small number of people were moved only by their own selfish desires—were ready to sacrifice their future and the future of their country provided their wishes of the moment were gratified. Since the war ended, there are many more people who are not impressed with the thought that inflation is either destructive or in prospect. Consequently the pressure against the controls set up by the Government is enormous, the safety valve is almost insufficient and the boiler is about to "burst."

There are outstanding examples of the extent to which people are misunderstanding the situation and minimizing the danger. Some labor unions have insisted on and have secured substantial increases in wages for their members. This has necessitated the raising of prices of the goods made by the workers, for it would be unfair and unlawful to require a manufacturer to continue in business at a loss to his capital and unfair to require him to produce without a reasonable return on his invested fund. This is one example of things now being done the result of which is a dangerous bulge in the line established to hold inflation back.

Another example is in this: owners of grain have so held from the market corn and wheat that the Government has, as a last resort, been compelled to raise the price in order to secure food to actually save from starvation millions of people in various parts of the world. This, too, will result in a considerable inflation in food costs to the citizens of this country. For the increase in grain costs necessitates increase cost of meat and eggs, and of milk and milk products, if we are to have meat, eggs, milk and milk products. This is another example of a dangerous bulge in the line.

There are other examples of smaller import, each in its small way adding to the effect of the larger bulges and of the constant attacks of the black market.

It is obvious that where a bulge in the line has been produced from whatever cause, except the minor bulges of an unlawful black market, the line must be advanced as a whole to the extent of the bulge, for the bulge cannot be continued in existence to the destruction of the mass of people affected by it. The black market, if it be approved by a great part of the people—ceases to be a minor and becomes a major factor—can destroy the line entirely and inflation will be upon us in all its destructive fury.

The Office of Price Administration is the Bureau set up by the Government in its effort to avoid the destructive inflation which will result in the absence of control. This Bureau known familiarly but not affectionately as the OPA with various more or less profane qualifying nouns and adjectives before and after the letters, has the odious duty to fix prices at such figures that no class of citizens will be benefited at the expense of another class. This duty cannot be performed with exact accuracy by any set of men, and mistakes have occurred and will occur. People who are adversely affected by the mistakes are inclined to become enemies of the OPA and many do become enemies, vocal in their enmity to such extent that there is a possibility that the Government's effort to control the inflated condition will fail. If this effort fails, what other instrumentality can the Government use? No one has yet suggested another preventative measure which would have any tendency to prevent inflation destructive of our economy and perhaps to our form of government itself.

Is it not apparent that the OPA must be permitted to live so long as there is a possibility that we, the people, may understand that our only hope is in its success—permitted of course to grumble and growl at it because of its mistakes, but backing it up as a hated but necessary instrumentality to impose restrictions upon us, that we may not be permitted to destroy ourselves as we would probably do if left to ourselves.

August 10, 1945

I suppose that the offer of the Japs to surrender—report of which has just been made over the radio—will be accepted and that you will be out of the Army soon. It would be far better for the Emperor to be retained as ruler of Japan under the direction of the allies; otherwise we could find ourselves in the necessity of taking over an entirely disorganized nation and retaining control until, if ever, a new government could be built up out of material that was probably only carrying out the supposed will of an emperor, who was in turn only carrying out the will of the navy and army. At any rate we can act on the assumption that the Emperor was merely a figurehead who, because the people worshiped him, could give orders which the people would obey fanatically. The experience with the atomic bomb seems to have had immediate results with the leaders of the navy and army of Japan—and possibly with Mr. Stalin. At any rate both acted quickly. What men will do with the tremendous power that has been developed remains to be seen. Heretofore they have used power to destroy. This is so tremendous that we should be afraid to use it hereafter to destroy. Will any man in the future come along with ambition so great that he will be able and have the desire to lead his people in a contest wherein such power will be unleashed? What do you think?

But, to get back to the personal element, every time a big airplane goes over I will be wondering if—and hoping that—you are on it. You have been in the Army long enough and could do with a long rest here at home. To keep you in trim we could *let* you do *some* of the lawn mowing, some of the tomato and apple canning, some of the potato digging. We could even *let* you do a stint of K.P. now and then so that you would not find the break between the Army and civilian life too severe. However, we cannot furnish the beach, and the trees are too thick in the yard to let much moonlight through. You can have some fun standing in line for soap, meat or some other thing which most of us feel we need—especially after it becomes a bit hard to get. We do want you home as soon as possible. You have been a good soldier and have learned something of life and people generally, and incidentally you have learned a bit of army politics which will stand you in good stead if and when we get into another fight.

You know, or you will know when you get to reading the other side of this sheet, that I am not expecting any business at the office today, that I have just thought that I should celebrate the prospective peace, that the Ashmore farm might need inspecting, that Jim might have nothing to do today, that the Ashmore farm is near the Ashmore lake, that we might—Jim and I—go out to the Kickapoo and find some fairly good minnows, that we might wet a line apiece either on the way to the farm or on the way back, and that if the thought develops into action, this letter might be brought to a quick conclusion. However, before the thought is translated into action, I want to tell you a story about your mother.

A few days ago when Mother got up and down, she found the ground under the pear trees literally littered with the residue of pears left by squirrels after they had extracted the seeds. I had seen the litter from the back porch at breakfast but had done nothing about it, and Mother's day was ruined. Since then she has got up as I did and with the gun in hand has made a quick trip to the pear trees with no success. This morning she beat my time by about five minutes, and while I was shaving I heard the crack of her rifle and then a thud as something hit the ground. The rifle with the grains of shot does not kill when the distance is from the ground to the top of the tree as it was this morning, and so the squirrel made his escape as Butch was not on the job; but when I got down, breakfast was ready, Mother was happy, and the day was bright in every respect—except the war. Then a few minutes later the radio announced the Jap broadcast which seems to betoken peace. So I must see the Ashmore farm—if Jim can go along.

Your July bond came in a day or two ago. All your bonds are now in my bank box. Mother told you, I reckon, that we got the cigarettes and the Gov't check. There is no special news. The pears have been gathered from the big tree and some of them have been canned. The medium-sized tree is the one that your mother—and the squirrels—are interested in.

Lots of love.
Come home soon.

IN A LETTER TO HER SISTER, MRS. J.Y. NARRATES A NEW YORK CITY VISIT

January 6, 1941

My dear Sister,

. . . Now for my trip to New York City.

I decided very suddenly to go, and then went earlier than first planned. I left Mattoon on Saturday, December 6th; arrived in New York City at Grand Central Station at ten o'clock Sunday morning. I enjoyed being on the train all night, lovely air-conditioned one, enjoyed eating on the diner. Chenault met me at train, and we walked around that part of town as it was at 42nd, and was where I would have to go alone to some shows, and she wanted me to get on to the run of the streets and playhouses. Then we took a bus and went downtown to her apartment. (Old New York *is down* town.) She has a lovely one-large room, kitchen, hall, bath and big closet apartment and in splendid location just off 6th Avenue and 5th Avenue, three blocks from John Wanamaker's, one block and a half from Washington Square; New York University is on Washington Square. All this neighborhood is old and interesting; it is Greenwich Village.

The day was beautiful—sunshiny and warm, so after lunch, we walked all around that part of town, and saw many interesting places, and passed *the* Whitney home which is now an art museum, so we took that in. I was more interested in the lovely old home than the pictures. That night we went to Tony's for an Italian dinner—a noted place on 5th Avenue.

Monday E.C. off to school by seven. After I had breakfast and put place in order, I struck out, and shopped *all* day on 14th Street (E.C. is on 9th) and I shopped at Wanamaker's, buying books and toys for Jimmie and Dirk, etc., enjoying looking in funny little shops, some antique. I was in our neighborhood so went back for lunch at apartment, rested and out again in afternoon, almost walked my legs off. I bought some things for supper and had it ready when E.C. came home at five o'clock. She wanted to know if I was too tired to go see the Ice Follies at Madison Square Garden, and as I wanted to go to something there, I said *indeed* I was not too tired, and again that was the only night we could go, as it was ending on Wednesday.

Well, of *all* the spectacular and wonderful things, that was that. We laughed until our sides hurt at the comic parts, and ah'd and oh'd at the other. We got out at eleven o'clock and, of course, exhausted, so we went to an unusual place near there that was packed, for oyster stew. My eyes were as big as moons all the time, E.C. said, and she said *I* did not miss a thing, that things just fell into my lap. I see I will have to shorten this.

So Tuesday, took a bus and went *up* town and shopped, had lunch with Mrs. Kenyon. That evening E.C. and I went to a swanky night club just so I could see what it was like. It cost me $6.00 for our dinners and a *small* bottle of wine, but it was worth the price. I had my taste of night life.

Wednesday afternoon I went alone to see *Life With Father* at the Empire Theater. Back home and E.C. and I had dinner and then went to John Wanamaker's to see the big Christmas tree in center of the store and we sang

Christmas Carols with hundreds of other people. A man standing by us stood with tears streaming down his face; the Xmas bell ringing and the singing and silence in between was very impressive; I felt like crying myself.

Thursday morning I rested, had lunch and off for 42nd to the beautiful and wonderful Metropolitan Opera House to have my first taste of "Grand Opera," *Tristan and Isolde.* I had a $3.00 seat in dress circle. I was alone, so after the second act, I had to get up with hundreds of others and go out into the lounge and I followed the main crowd down a beautiful wide stairway, carpeted in deep velvet, and found myself in a beautiful Buffet and Lounge on the Grand Tier floor where all the beautifully dressed men and women were having cocktails, smoking, and being very gay and all the chatter and thrill going on and believe me, little Alice, all alone was the most thrilled person in that big crowd, so she walks herself to a table and ordered a bottle of Coca-Cola, price $.25. Even that was a thrill for an ordinary $.05 bottle of Coca-Cola.

After the third and last act, I followed the crowd and found myself on the street, just jammed with people. I stood for a while and looked and listened, carriages being called for the rich, and just drinking in all of it, the noise, bright lights, and being alone was part of it. I finally had to go along with the crowd, could not do otherwise. I had come out on a different street, so had to try to find myself without asking and ended up by getting on a Broadway bus instead of 5th Avenue, but did ask the driver before getting on if *it* was a *down*town bus and would stop at 9th and he said "yes," so on I got and off at Wanamaker's and only had three blocks to walk. You see, it was after six when Opera was out and I was pleased I could find my way around.

Friday, I was invited to *luncheon* at the Astor Hotel by Mrs. Kenyon, a friend of mine who lived here (Charleston) twenty years ago. Her other guest was a Mrs. Crawley. Her husband, Mr. Crawley, had a good part in the play with Ethel Barrymore. The luncheon was perfect, Hotel beautiful, and company very interesting. Mrs. Crawley was a Kentucky girl born in Maysville and we each knew people that the other knew, she having been in Mt. Sterling, etc. I left them about three and went to Cousin Eva Hollaway Deppe's hotel as invited. Cousin Eva and Billie then took me on a beautiful drive north along the Hudson river and up to Tarrytown on Hudson and saw so many wonderful homes and places of interest. Cousin Eva chatting all the time about Aunt Alice, Aunt Nannie and the past. We got back to hotel at six. E.C. came in a little while; they then served us a glass of wine and we then went down to the dining room and had a perfect full course dinner, lovely orchestra. Back to their rooms and played bridge.

Friday morning at eleven o'clock before lunch at the Astor, I met Mrs. Kenyon (my friend) and Mrs. Crawley and we went to the Astor Hotel Auditorium to hear Emmet Fox preach and a wonderful sermon it was; the place was packed, which made an impression on me to be so on a week day during Xmas rush shopping. Lunch at Astor's. (This was on the first Tuesday.)

Mrs. Kenyon took me to lunch at Mayards, a very swanky place; from there we went to Radio City Music Hall and saw a beautiful floor show, and afterwards we went through part of the building and lovely shops in building, then on to her home on Grammercy Park for dinner, E.C. meeting us there. After dinner she and Mr. Kenyon took us to see an art exhibit.

Saturday E.C. and I did some shopping in the lovely stores on 5th Avenue, mostly looking, and met two of E.C.'s teacher friends at The Cortile, we being their guests for lunch. Then E.C. and I went to Saturday matinee to see Ethel Barrymore in *The Corn Is Green*. She and her cast were wonderful and a fine play. I had never seen her, and the play is rated the best in City. After the play E.C. had an appointment at beauty parlor, so we went there so I could locate the place; and she went in and I then walked up 5th Avenue to 57th, just window shopping and seeing the people and lights, passed by Rockefeller Center, looked at the beautiful tree, and listened to the Christmas carols. At 57th, I took a bus back to 34th, met Chenault, and we started down 5th Avenue. I was a little cold and tired by that time, and in passing Longchamp's, the most wonderful and very swanky and very *expensive* cocktail bar in New York, we (being sports) stopped in for a cocktail, it being cocktail hour. Well, it was a thrill, one cocktail each, and my bill $1.55; but you see, I was out for the high spots and fun and that place was one of them, and I saw more beautifully dressed women and men. From there we went to the famous Paddy's Clam House for a seafood dinner. That's on 34th Street.

Sunday we went to church to hear Emmet Fox again and there were 8,000 people there. We met by appointment there Mr. and Mrs. Kenyon (my friends and E.C.'s). They took us to Park Avenue for Sunday noon lunch. Then Mr. Kenyon took his wife and E.C. to their home, and he and I started out to see New York City. We drove from 1:45 to 4:30, using sixty miles on trip. Mr. Kenyon was born on Park Avenue, lived there all his life, a very prominent lawyer on Wall Street and very interesting and brilliant person. We saw all the lovely bridges, the fairgrounds, the airports, Brooklyn, Long Island Sound, etc., etc. When we arrived at his home, he and Mrs. Kenyon were giving a tea for me. I freshened up a bit and the company began to arrive. She has two splendid and well-trained servants, a maid and man, who served tea, etc. (no cocktails). I think she had about twenty-five guests and by seven o'clock half of them had left, and about twelve of the most interesting people younger than I and older than E.C. stayed on. Then the servants came in and gave each of us a dinner napkin and fork and plate. We were in the big living room, small tables here and there, then they passed a real Sunday night supper. We left at midnight, Mr. Kenyon taking us home; well, by that time I was really tired and did not sleep much. It had been a real week for me and E.C. made me promise to stay in bed next day until noon.

Monday was the only day it rained, and I decided I wanted to go up town to Macy's big store and finish my toy shopping for E.C.'s gifts for Dirk and Jimmie, and I took the bus, was there when the store opened and one of the first of about a hundred people to get in. I rushed to toy department, bought three toys, then down to book department and bought four books. By then it was eleven o'clock, the store was jammed. (E.C. had said I should never even attempt to shop there, but I had and got just what I wanted and things were much cheaper than any other place.) I then went to their tea room and had lunch, listening to beautiful music and watching the people for an hour. When

I left the tea room, could hardly get through the crowds to the street but did, took a bus home and rested *all* afternoon, cooked a supper for the two of us, then we were off again on subway up to 42nd Street to see Helen Hayes and Maurice Evans in *Twelfth Night*. Both were marvelous.

Tuesday I was to rest in the A.M. but so far I had not had time to call Fan Rogers. She had entertained us when we were there before, and I wanted her to know my other friend and meet E.C. again so I called to ask her to meet the three of us for luncheon on Thursday. She was so glad to hear my voice and accepted the invitation, but said, "Why do I have to wait until Thursday to see you? Can't you meet *me* for lunch today?" And having nothing to do I said yes so I met her at "Theodores" on 57th Street just off 5th Avenue, place I would not have gone to otherwise because of price, etc., ritzy, swank, etc. She was just the same dear Fan and we had a grand visit. After lunch, she took me through some of the most wonderful shops and places on 5th Avenue in that neighborhood that I would not have had the nerve to go in because I could not even have priced things. We went through the Steuben glass salon, also in Tiffany's, and every place we went it was "Mrs. Jeffries this and Mrs. Jeffries that" (she is Mrs. H. Jeffries). At Tiffany's she asked one of the men to show me a bracelet. I was allowed to hold it in my hand, price $31,500.00, all diamonds. He also showed me the famous Canary diamond; then he showed us all through the building. She took me in to see a beautiful bank building and many lovely shops.

That same morning after I had called her, I called Mrs. Kenyon to ask her to have lunch with me on Thursday and she accepted and said "What are you doing today?" I told her I was to meet Fan Rogers Jeffries for lunch and she said, "Well, after you leave her, come on down to the house and have dinner with us; leave a note for Chenault to join us here." Then I told her E.C. was going to spend the night in Madison, N.J. to attend a school party; then she said, "All right, you come on anyway and we will take you home later." So down I went. When Mr. Kenyon came home, he said, "How would you girls like to go to Chinatown for some Chinese food?" and, of course, *I* was delighted as I had always wanted to do that. Well, we drove down and saw the sights of Chinatown and had an unusual dinner; then he drove us all through the slums, the ghetto, Eastside, and Westside, all around the town, then over the beautiful Triborough Bridge. It was a beautiful, clear night and we had a glorious and wonderful view of the City; drove on up to the new Washington Bridge and crossed and back through the City on to my home; the doorman of our apartment opening the car door for me; after saying good night, our doorman then opened the door to let me in (great style for me), and I slept well and was not a bit afraid.

Wednesday morning I really did stay in the apartment and rested and wrote some Xmas cards. After lunch I dressed in my best and took the subway to go under the Hudson to Hoboken; then took a train at three o'clock for Madison, N.J. Chenault met my train and marveled at all I had done all on my own on the day before and to see me looking fresh as a daisy. We called on an elderly couple, friends of hers; then we went to the home of Mr. and Mrs. Park (E.C.'s second home as she calls it) and from there we all went to the annual Christmas turkey dinner given by all the teachers and heads of her high school. It was a gay dinner, and I was so glad to meet all her friends and they were very attentive to me. We took the ten o'clock train back to Hoboken and E.C. said to me would I like to take the Ferry back across the Hudson, so, of course, I said yes. We took the longest way over so rode up the Hudson and had another view of New York City.

Thursday she took the day off from school and we went up town and did some of the stores; then at noon met Fan Rogers Jeffries and Mrs. Kenyon and I took them to lunch at Stouffer's on 57th off 5th Avenue. Mrs. Kenyon and Fan liked each other and we all had a nice time, much talk of Georgetown and the old crowd and talk of Charleston, etc. Fan and Chenault made plans to meet soon after January 1st.

Fan had to leave after lunch, and then I took Mrs. Kenyon and Chenault to Radio City Music Hall to see the Christmas show, which was lovely. After supper in our apartment, E.C. and I did some shopping in her part of the City and to bed rather early for a change.

Friday she went to school for her last day, and, as she said, to get her pay check. I packed hers and my bag, and all our packages, then went to the famous little candy shop on 8th Street and sent Aunt Nannie a small box and got one for Jim and ran into Mrs. Kenyon; she said most people, friends of hers, I mean, came to this little shop for candy.

E.C. came home about 3:30 and we finished packing and took a cab for Grand Central Station and had our dinner in the station. It is noted for its oysters and fish dinners. Then we got on our train at eight o'clock and on our way, arriving in Mattoon at 2:30 Saturday, just two weeks to the hour after I had left.

The weather was beautiful *all* the time I was in New York. Had my coat open at neck most of the time. I walked *miles* and felt like a million. I said it was the air, water, and freedom that did it. Really it was a *real* vacation just being on *my own* and *no* responsibility of *any* one or responsible to any one. One grand time all along.

Alice.

Mrs. J. Y. Kelly, 3rd.